THE 17 ESSENTIAL QUALITIES OF A TEAM PLAYER

Becoming the Kind of Person Every Team Wants

John C. Maxwell

The 17 Essential Qualities of a Team Player

Becoming the Kind of Person Every Team Wants

Nelson Books
A Division of Thomas Nelson Publishers
Since 1798
www.thomasnelson.com

Published in Nashville, Tennessee, by Thomas Nelson, Inc.

Nelson Book titles may be purchased in bulk for educational, business, fund-raising, or sales promotional use. For information, please e-mail SpecialMarkets@ThomasNelson.com.

Library of Congress Cataloging-in-Publication Data

Maxwell, John C., 1947–
The 17 essential qualities of a team player : becoming the kind of person every team wants / John C. Maxwell.
p. cm.
Includes bibliographical references.
ISBN 0-7852-7435-9 (hc)
ISBN 0-7852-6313-6 (ie)
ISBN 0-7852-8881-3 (se)
1. Teams in the workplace—Psychological aspects. I. Title: Seventeen essential qualities of a team player. II. Title.

HD66 .M374 2002
658.4'036—dc21 2001054676

Printed in the United States of America

06 07 08 09 10 QW 9 8 7 6 5 4 3 2 1

This book is dedicated to the people on every team of which I've had the privilege of being a part.

Contents

Acknowledgments

I'd like to say thank you to the people who helped me with this book. Every one of them is a true team player:

Linda Eggers, my administrative assistant
Kathie Wheat, my research assistant
Stephanie Wetzel, my proofreader
Charlie Wetzel, my writer

Introduction

You cannot build a great team without great players. That is a fact. As the saying goes, "You can lose with good players, but you cannot win without them." So how are you going to get good players? For that matter, how are you going to become a better player? When it comes to having good people on a team, you really have only two choices: train them or trade for them. You grow the players you already have into champions, or you go out and recruit championship-caliber people and bring them onto the team. This book can help you do either.

Developing a better team always begins with you. To improve the team, improve the individuals on the team. You can become a better team member by embracing the qualities outlined in the following pages. My recommendation is that you work your way through this book slowly. Read a chapter. Digest it. Use the "Bringing It Home" section to help you improve your grasp of each quality. By embracing the process, you can become the kind of person every team wants.

Improving yourself will add value to your team. But if you have a leadership role on your team, it's especially vital. Why? Because you can effectively teach only what you consistently model. It takes one to know one, show one, and grow one.

Once you model the behavior you expect from your teammates, begin using *The 17 Essential Qualities of a Team Player* as a training manual. You can use it to help your players become better team contributors—regardless of their level of talent. And if you desire to recruit new players from outside the team, turn to the book as a guide for finding the kinds of players who will put the team first. You can be sure that anyone who displays all seventeen qualities will be a team player.

God-given ability may be out of our control, but the ability to work as a team isn't. All people can choose to become better teammates. All they need to do is to embody the qualities of a team player. Do that yourself, help your teammates do the same, and the whole team will excel.

1

Adaptable

If You Won't Change for the Team, the Team May Change You

Inflexibility is one of the worst human failings.
You can learn to check impetuosity, overcome fear with confidence, and laziness with discipline.
But for rigidity of mind there is no antidote.
It carries the seeds of its own destruction.

—Anonymous

Blessed are the flexible,
for they shall not be bent out of shape.

—Michael McGriff

A Bebop Mind

His friends call him Q. He has become a legend in the entertainment industry. He has worked with the best in the business, starting in the bebop era: Duke Ellington, Count Basie, Lionel Hampton, Frank Sinatra, Ella Fitzgerald, Sarah Vaughan, Ray Charles, Miles Davis, and the list goes on. He produced the best-selling music single of all time: "We Are the World." He produced the best-selling album of all time: Michael Jackson's *Thriller*. He has been nominated for more Grammy Awards than any other person, and as of today, he has won a total of twenty-seven. The person I'm talking about is Quincy Jones.

Quincy Jones was born in 1933 in Chicago and spent his first decade in one of the city's roughest neighborhoods. By his own admission, Jones says that he and his brother got into a lot of trouble in those early days. Then his family moved to Bremerton, Washington.

Soon afterward Jones discovered his love for music. At age eleven, he decided that he wanted to play an instrument. So he started with percussion. Even back then he showed signs of a quality that would mark him as a professional—his adaptability. He began staying after school and trying out a variety of other instruments. He tried the clarinet and violin, but ultimately he was attracted to brass. So he tried out all the brass instruments: baritone, French horn, sousaphone, and trombone. Finally he landed on the trumpet, and he excelled.

By age fourteen, he had his first paying job as a musician. As a teenager, he became friends with Ray Charles, who is just a few years older than he. Jones began to compose music and to learn how to do arrangements. And when the best bands and singers came through Seattle, he either went to hear them play or played with them. At age eighteen, he was on the road touring with Lionel Hampton.

Jones has always displayed a strong hunger to learn—which he calls an "obsessive curiosity"—and an amazing adaptability. Through the years, he has easily transitioned from musician to arranger to band leader. In the 1950s, he worked with many of the greatest jazz performers. In 1957, when he thought he could use more education, he moved to Paris and studied under Nadia Boulanger, who had tutored Aaron Copland and Leonard Bernstein.

At that time, Jones took a position with Mercury Records to make ends meet. That's where he learned the business side of the music industry. He was so good at it that in 1964 the company made him a vice president. (He was the first African-American to hold an executive position at a major record company.) It was also in the sixties that Jones decided to tackle a new challenge: scoring movies. He has gone on to write music for more than thirty movies and numerous television programs.

Throughout his career, Jones has worked with the best singers and musicians in the world. Because he spent so much time in the jazz community, when he worked with Michael Jackson in 1982, some of his colleagues accused him of selling out. Jones thought that was ridiculous, as he explained:

> When I was twelve to thirteen years old, we played everything—strip music, rhythm and blues. We played pop music, schottisches [similar to polkas], and Sousa . . . We played every club in town—black, white, tennis clubs. So, I've always had a range of styles to draw from. Working with Michael Jackson or Frank Sinatra has never been a stretch. Bebop was one thing I was deeply involved with musically, and bebop does affect your thinking. It takes you away from being rigid and helps you always keep your mind wide open.[1]

His flexibility and creativity have served Jones well. They have not only enabled him to work with all kinds of musicians—from Latin to pop and from jazz to rap—but they have also made it possible for him to bring the best out of any person he works with. He adapts to the person and the situation to create a win for everyone. "Everyone has a different way of relating to people," observed Jones. "I take everybody one-on-one, and I'm happy I do because I've had some great relationships that transcend show business."[2]

Jones himself has transcended professionally. He has used his adaptability to branch out into other industries. He broke into filmmaking when he coproduced *The Color Purple*. Then he took on television, producing several hit shows including *The Fresh Prince of Bel-Air.* Jones and several partners launched Qwest Broadcasting, and he is also the founder and chairman of *Vibe* magazine.

To Jones, being able to adjust or stretch himself is not a big thing; it's just who he is. Currently he's working on writing a Broadway show based on the life of Sammy Davis Jr. He says it makes him feel like he's fifteen years old. Jones has never been afraid of a new idea, a new team, a new industry. Challenges have been no problem to him because he is so incredibly adaptable.

FLESHING IT OUT

Teamwork and personal rigidity just don't mix. If you want to work well with others and be a good team player, you have to be willing to adapt yourself to your team. Harvard Business School professor Rosabeth Moss Kanter observed, "The individuals who will succeed and flourish will also be masters of change: adept at reorienting their own and others' activities in untried directions to bring about higher levels of achievement."

Teamwork and personal rigidity just don't mix.

Team players who exhibit adaptability have certain characteristics. Adaptable people are . . .

1. Teachable

Diana Nyad said, "I am willing to put myself through anything; temporary pain or discomfort means nothing to me as long as I can see that the experience will take me to a new level. I am interested in the unknown, and the only path to the unknown is through breaking barriers." Adaptable people always place a high priority on breaking new ground. They are highly teachable.

Look at Quincy Jones and you see someone who is always learning. His belief is that if a person works hard and becomes highly skilled in one area, he can transfer that ability to new endeavors. That approach can work for anyone who's teachable. On the other hand, unteachable people have a difficult time with change, and as a result they never adapt well.

2. Emotionally Secure

Another characteristic of adaptable people is security. People who are not emotionally secure see almost everything as a challenge or a threat. They meet with rigidity or suspicion the addition of another talented person to the team, an alteration in their position or title, or a change in the way things are done. But secure people aren't made nervous by change itself. They evaluate a new situation or a change in their responsibilities based on its merit.

> **A person's age can be determined by the degree of pain he experiences when he comes in contact with a new idea.**
>
> **—QUINCY JONES**

3. Creative

Creativity is another quality you find in adaptable people. When difficult times come, they find a way. Quincy Jones remarked,

> There's an expression that says a person's age can be determined by the degree of pain he experiences when he comes

in contact with a new idea. Somebody might say, "Let's try it this new way." You can actually see the pain. These people will grab their heads. It physically hurts to think of doing something different. The ones who don't react with fear are the really creative people. "Let's try it," they'll say. "Let's go there even if we blow it."[3]

Creativity fosters adaptability.

4. Service Minded

People who are focused on themselves are less likely to make changes for the team than people focused on serving others. Educator and college president Horace Mann stated, "Doing nothing for others is the undoing of one's self." If your goal is to serve the team, adapting to accomplish that goal isn't difficult.

Reflecting on It

How are you when it comes to adaptability? If improving the team requires you to change the way you do things, how do you react? Are you supportive, or would you rather do things the way they've "always been done before"? If someone with greater talent in your current area joins the team, would you be willing to take on a different role? Or if a key player in another area is having a problem, are you willing to change positions to help out? The first key to being a team player is being willing to adapt yourself to the team—not an expectation that the team will adapt to you!

BRINGING IT HOME

To become more adaptable . . .

- ***Get into the habit of learning.*** For many years I carried a three-by-five card in my pocket. Every day when I learned something new, I'd write it down on the card. By the end of the day, I'd try to share the idea with a friend or colleague and then file the idea for future use. It got me in the habit of *looking* for things to learn. Try it for a week and see what happens.

- ***Reevaluate your role.*** Spend some time looking at your current role on your team. Then try to discover whether there is another role you could fulfill as well or better than you do your current one. That process may prompt you to make a transition, but even if it doesn't, the mental exercise will increase your flexibility.

- ***Think outside the lines.*** Let's face it: many people aren't adaptable because they get into negative ruts. If you tend to be prone to ruts, then write down this phrase and keep it where you can see it every day: "Not why it *can't* be done but how it *can* be done." Look for unconventional solutions every time you meet a challenge. You'll be surprised by how creative you can become if you continually strive to do so.

Daily Take-Away

One of the greatest generals in military history was Napoleon Bonaparte. Made a full general at age twenty-six, he utilized shrewd strategy, bold cunning, and lightning speed to his advantage to win many victories. The Duke of Wellington, one of the general's most formidable enemies, said, "I consider Napoleon's presence in the field to equal forty thousand men in the balance."

"I will tell you the mistake you are always making," Napoleon said, addressing an opponent he had defeated. "You draw up your plans the day before battle, when you do not yet know your adversary's movements." Napoleon recognized in his losing opponent a weakness that he himself did not have: lack of adaptability. If you are willing to change and adapt for the sake of your team, you always have a chance to win.

2

Collaborative

Working Together Precedes Winning Together

All your strength is in union,
all your danger is in discord.

—Henry Wadsworth Longfellow

Collaboration is multiplication.

—John C. Maxwell

Underground Movement

They called it the Great Escape. It wasn't great because it had never been done before. Prisoners of war had previously escaped from enemy camps. It wasn't called great because of the outcome: the results were terrible for most of the escapees. It was great because the scale of it made the task seem impossible!

Stalag Luft III, a Nazi prisoner-of-war camp one hundred miles southeast of Berlin, was a huge compound that once held as many as 10,000 Allied POWs. Within that camp in 1944 was a core group of prisoners determined to escape. In fact, their goal was to facilitate the escape of no fewer than 250 men in one night, something that would require the utmost cooperation among the prisoners. An escape so daunting had never been tried before.

Getting men out of a German prison camp was a very complex task. Of course there was the challenge of digging and hiding the tunnels that would provide the means of escape. Together, prisoners engineered the tunnels, dug them, shored them up with wooden slats taken from prisoners' beds, and disposed of the dirt in amazingly creative ways. They pumped air into the tunnels with homemade bellows. They created tracks and trolleys used by men to move through the tunnels. They even wired the narrow passages with electric lights. The list of supplies needed for the job was unbelievable: 4,000 bed slats, 1,370 battens, 1,699 blankets, 52 long tables, 1,219 knives, 30 shovels, 600 feet of rope, 1,000 feet of electric wire, and more.[1] It took an army of prisoners just to find and steal all the materials for the tunnels.

However difficult building the tunnels was, creating the means of escape was only part of the whole project. Every man who would attempt escape needed a host of supplies and equipment: civilian clothes, German papers and identity cards, maps, homemade compasses, emergency rations, and other items. Several prisoners continually scrounged for anything that might aid the team. Others worked systematically and relentlessly at bribing and then blackmailing the guards.

Each person had a job. There were tailors, blacksmiths, pickpockets, and forgers who worked secretly month after month. The prisoners even developed teams of men who specialized in distraction and camouflage, keeping the German soldiers off guard.

Perhaps the most challenging job was that of "security." Since the Germans employed many guards who specialized in escape detection—called ferrets by the prisoners—the security team kept a log of every movement of every guard who came through the compound. And they used an elaborate, yet inconspicuous, set of signals to warn other security men, lookouts, and working team members when a guard posed a threat to their efforts.

On the night of March 24, 1944, after more than a year of work, 220 men prepared to creep through the tunnel and into the woods outside the prison camp. The plan was to send out one man per minute until all had made their escape. German-speaking prisoners would board trains and pose as foreign workers. The rest would lie low during the day and travel at night, hoping to avoid German patrols.

When the first prisoner popped up out of the tunnel, though, he discovered that its exit was short of the woods. Rather than get out a man per minute, they were barely able to get out a dozen per hour. In all, eighty-six men escaped before the tunnel was discovered. It created chaos for the Nazis, who ordered a national alert to deal with it. Eighty-three of the prisoners were captured, and forty-one of them were executed by order of Adolf Hitler. Only three made it to freedom.

John Sturges, the man who directed the 1963 movie *The Great Escape* based on the real event, said of the prisoners' effort, "It demanded the concentrated devotion and vigilance of more than 600 men—every single one of them, every minute, every hour, every day and every night for more than a year. Never has the human capacity been stretched to such incredible lengths or shown with as much determination and courage."[2]

Fleshing It Out

Great challenges require great teamwork, and the quality most needed among teammates amid the pressure of a difficult challenge is collaboration. Notice that I didn't say "cooperation" because collaboration is more than that. Cooperation is working together agreeably. Collaboration is working together aggressively. Collaborative teammates do more than just work with one another. Each person brings something to the table that adds value to the relationship and synergy to the team. The sum of truly collaborative teamwork is always greater than its parts.

Becoming a collaborative team player requires a change in focus in four areas:

1. Perception: See Teammates as Collaborators, Not Competitors

Look at any team, and you can see the potential for competition. Siblings fight for their parents' attention. Coworkers compete for raises and promotions. Ballplayers go head-to-head to see who will be the starter and who will sit on the bench. Because all people have hopes, goals, and dreams, they want to achieve. But to collaborative team members, completing one another is more important than competing with one another. They perceive themselves as a unit working together, and they never allow competition between teammates to get to the point where it hurts the team.

To collaborative team members, completing one another is more important than competing with one another.

2. Attitude: Be Supportive, Not Suspicious, of Teammates

Some people are so preoccupied with looking out for their own interests that they are naturally suspicious of just about everyone, including their teammates. But adopting the mind-set where you complete rather than compete with teammates is possible only if you suspend your suspicions and become a supportive team player.

It's a matter of attitude. That means assuming that other people's motives are good unless proven otherwise. If you trust people, you will treat them better. And if you treat them better, you and they will be more likely to create collaborative relationships.

3. Focus: Concentrate on the Team, Not on Yourself

As a person on a team, you will usually ask one of two questions when anything happens: "What's in it for me?" or "What does this do for the team?" Where you focus your attention says a lot about whether you compete with others or complete them. Author Cavett Roberts points out, "True progress in any field is a relay race and not a single event." If you focus on the team and not just yourself, you will be able to pass the baton when necessary instead of trying to complete the race by yourself.

> **True progress in any field is a relay race and not a single event.**
>
> **—CAVETT ROBERTS**

4. Results: Create Victories Through Multiplication

When you work together with your teammates, you can do remarkable things. If you work alone, you leave a lot of victories on the table. Collaboration has a multiplying effect on everything you do because it releases and harnesses not only your skills but also those of everyone on the team.

Reflecting on It

Are you a collaborative person? You may not be working *against* the team, but that doesn't necessarily mean you're working *for* it. Do you bring cooperation and added value to your teammates—even to the people you don't enjoy being with? Do you help to multiply the efforts of others? Or does the team become slower and less effective when you're involved? If you're not sure, talk to your teammates.

Bringing It Home

To become a collaborative team player . . .

- ***Think win-win-win.*** King Solomon of ancient Israel observed, "Iron sharpens iron, so one man sharpens another."[3] Usually when you collaborate with others, you win, they win, and the team wins. Find someone on the team with a similar role whom you have previously seen as a competitor. Figure out ways you can share information and work together to benefit both you and the team.

- ***Complement others.*** Another way to collaborate is to get together with someone who has strengths in your area of weakness and vice versa. Seek out others on the team with complementary gifts and work together.

- ***Take yourself out of the picture.*** Get in the habit of asking what's best for the team. For example, the next time you are at a problem-solving meeting and everyone is contributing ideas, instead of promoting yourself, ask yourself how the team would do if you were not involved in the solution. If it would do better, then propose ideas that promote and involve people other than yourself.

Usually when you collaborate with others, you win, they win, and the team wins.

Daily Take-Away

Some boys were hiking in the woods one day when they came across part of an old abandoned railroad track stretching off through the trees. One of the boys jumped up onto a rail and tried walking on it. After a few steps, he lost his balance. Another boy soon tried the same thing, and he also fell. The others laughed.

"I bet you can't do it either," he barked at the others. One by one, the boys tried it, but they all failed. Even the best athlete of the bunch couldn't go more than a dozen steps without stumbling.

Then two of the boys began whispering to each other, and one of them challenged the others: "I can walk on the rail all the way to the end, and so can he." He pointed to his buddy.

"No, you can't," said one of the other boys who had tried and failed.

"Bet you a candy bar each we can!" he answered, and the other boys accepted.

Then each of the two boys who had issued the challenge hopped up onto a rail, reached out an arm, locked hands with the other, and carefully walked the whole distance.

As individuals, they could not meet the challenge. But working together, they easily won. The power of collaboration is multiplication.

3

Committed

There Are No Halfhearted Champions

The moment one definitely commits oneself,
then Providence moves too. All sorts of things occur
to help one that would never otherwise have occurred.
A whole stream of events issue from the decision,
raising in one's favor all manner of unforeseen incidents
and meetings and material assistance which no man
could have dreamed would come his way.

—*William H. Murray*

Ordinary people with commitment
can make an extraordinary impact on their world.

—*John C. Maxwell*

Taking One for the Team

In 1939, a twenty-five-year-old man from New York City named Jonas Salk completed his training at NYU Medical School. As a boy, he had dreamed of becoming a lawyer, but somewhere between his graduation from high school and his entrance into college, his interest shifted from the laws of the land to the laws of nature. He decided that he wanted to be a doctor. Perhaps he made the switch because his mother had discouraged his pursuit of law. "My mother didn't think I would make a very good lawyer," he remarked years later, "probably because I could never win an argument with her."[1] His working-class immigrant parents were proud when he graduated with his medical degree because he was the first person in his family to have received an education.

Though he chose to become a doctor, Salk's real passion was research. He was intrigued by contradictory scientific claims by two professors, which prompted him to begin studying immunology, including influenza research. And during his second year of medical school, when he got the chance to spend a year doing research and teaching, he took it. "At the end of that year," he recalled, "I was told I could, if I wished, switch and get a Ph.D. in biochemistry but my preference was to stay with medicine. I believe that this is all linked to my original ambition, or desire, which was to be of some help to humankind, so to speak, in a larger sense than just on a one-to-one basis."[2]

In 1947, Salk became the head of the Virus Research Lab at

the University of Pittsburgh. It was there that he began investigating the polio virus. In those days, polio was a horrible, disabling disease that claimed the lives of thousands of people every year, with children being the most frequent victims. The New York polio epidemic of the summer of 1916 left 27,000 people paralyzed and another 9,000 people dead. After that year, epidemics became common, and every summer hordes of people escaped large cities to try to protect their children.

In the first half of the twentieth century, viral research was still in its infancy. But in 1948, a team of scientists at Harvard University discovered how to produce large quantities of viruses in laboratories, and that made more extensive research possible. Salk capitalized on those scientists' findings and others' groundbreaking work and began developing a polio vaccine.

After more than four years of continuous work, Salk and his team at the University of Pittsburgh developed a vaccine in 1952. They did some safe preliminary testing with it on people who had previously contracted polio and survived. But the true test would be injecting the vaccine, which contained inactive polio cells, into people who had never had polio.

Salk had shown his dedication to helping people through years of study, preparation, and research. However, it's one thing to believe in something you're doing, and another to be totally committed to it. In the summer of 1952, Jonas Salk inoculated healthy volunteers with his vaccine. Included in that group were himself, his wife, and their three sons. He was committed!

Salk's commitment paid off. The trials of the vaccine were

successful, and in 1955, he and his former mentor, Dr. Thomas Francis, arranged to inoculate 4 million children. In 1955, there were 28,985 cases of polio reported in the United States. In 1956, that number was cut in half. In 1957, there were only 5,894. Today, thanks to the work of Jonas Salk and subsequent efforts by other scientists such as Albert Sabin, cases of polio in the U.S. are virtually nonexistent.

Jonas Salk dedicated eight years of his life to defeating polio. But his real desire was to help people, which he further demonstrated by never patenting the vaccine he created. In that way, it could be used to help people around the globe. You could say that the team he was most committed to was mankind.

Fleshing It Out

Many people tend to associate commitment with their emotions. If they feel the right way, then they can follow through on their commitments. But true commitment doesn't work that way. It's not an emotion; it's a character quality that enables us to reach our goals. Human emotions go up and down all the time, but commitment has to be rock solid. If you want a solid team—whether it's a business, ball club, marriage, or volunteer organization—you must have team players who are solidly committed to the team.

There are some things every team player needs to know about being committed:

1. Commitment Usually Is Discovered in the Midst of Adversity

People don't really know whether they are committed to something until they face adversity. Struggles strengthen a person's resolve. Adversity fosters commitment, and commitment fosters hard work. And the more you work at something, the less likely you are to give up on it. As NFL Hall of Fame coach Vince Lombardi said, "The harder you work, the harder it is to surrender." Committed people don't surrender easily.

> **The harder you work, the harder it is to surrender.**
>
> **—VINCE LOMBARDI**

2. Commitment Does Not Depend on Gifts or Abilities

Sometimes when we know of talented people who are highly successful, we may be tempted to think that commitment is easier for them because of their talent. It seems as if it might be easier for first-rate athletes to practice or skilled artists to refine their craft or natural businesspeople to work at their businesses. But that isn't true. Commitment and talent are unconnected—unless you connect them.

Haven't you known highly talented people who have squandered their potential because they wouldn't *do* anything? And don't you know people less talented than you who are more successful? That is often due, in part, to commitment. Author Basil Walsh said, "We don't need more strength or more ability or greater opportunity. What we need to use is what we have." If we will commit ourselves to using what talent we have, then we will find that we have more talent—and more to offer our team—as the result of our commitment.

3. Commitment Comes as the Result of Choice, Not Conditions

When it comes right down to it, commitment is always a matter of choice. In *Choices,* Frederic F. Flach writes,

> Most people look back over the years and identify a time and place at which their lives changed significantly. Whether by accident or design, these are the moments when, because of a readiness within us and a collaboration with events occurring around us, we are forced to seriously reappraise ourselves and the conditions under which we live and to make certain choices that will affect the rest of our lives.[3]

Far too many people think that conditions determine choices. More often, choices determine conditions. When you choose commitment, you give yourself a chance for success.

4. Commitment Lasts When It's Based on Values

It's one thing to make a commitment in a moment. It's another to stick with it. How do you remain committed? The answer lies in what you base your commitments on. Anytime you make choices based on solid life values, then you are in a better position to sustain your level of commitment because you don't have to continually reevaluate its importance. It's like settling the issue before it is tested. A commitment to something you believe in is a commitment that is easier to keep.

Anytime you make choices based on solid life values, then you are in a better position to sustain your level of commitment.

Reflecting on It

How important is commitment to you? Are you someone who values loyalty and follow-through? When things get tough, are you in the habit of standing firm? Or do you have a tendency to compromise or even quit? More specifically, how committed are you to your team? Is your support solid? Is your dedication undeniable? Or are you tentative in your level of commitment? If you find yourself reevaluating your intention to stay with the team whenever you and your teammates face adversity, then you may need to become more committed.

Bringing It Home

To improve your level of commitment . . .

- ***Tie your commitments to your values.*** Because your values and your ability to fulfill your commitments are closely related, take some time to reflect on them. First, make a list of your personal and professional commitments. Then try to articulate your core values. (This will take some time, especially if you've never done it before, so don't rush it.) Once you have both lists, compare them. You will probably find that you have commitments unrelated to your values. Reevaluate them. You will also find that you have values that you are not living out. Commit yourself to them.

- ***Take a risk.*** Being committed involves risk. You may fail. Your teammates may let you down. You may discover that fulfilling your goals doesn't give you the results you desire. But take the risk of committing anyway. George Halas, former owner of the NFL Chicago Bears, asserted, "Nobody who ever gave his best regretted it."

- ***Evaluate your teammates' commitment.*** If you find it difficult to commit in particular relationships and you cannot find a reason for it in yourself, consider this: you cannot make a commitment to uncommitted people and expect to receive a commitment from them. Examine the relationship to see whether you are reluctant because the potential recipient is untrustworthy.

> **Nobody who ever gave his best regretted it.**
> **—GEORGE HALAS**

DAILY TAKE-AWAY

How do you define true commitment? Let me tell you how Hernán Cortés defined it. In 1519, under the sponsorship of Cuba's

Governor Velásquez, Cortés sailed from Cuba to the Mexican mainland with the goal of gaining riches for Spain and fame for himself. Though only thirty-four years old, the young Spanish captain had prepared his whole life for such a chance.

But the soldiers under his command were not as dedicated as he. After he landed, there was talk that the men might mutiny and return to Cuba with his ships. What was his solution? He burned the ships. How dedicated are you to your team? Are you totally committed, or do you have an "out," just in case things don't work out? If so, maybe you need to burn a ship or two. Remember, there is no such thing as a halfhearted champion.

4

COMMUNICATIVE

A TEAM IS MANY VOICES WITH A SINGLE HEART

If you have not a good degree of eloquence in speaking and writing you will be nobody; but will have the daily mortification of seeing people with not one-tenth part of your merit or knowledge get the start of you.

—Lord Chesterford

Think like a wise man
but communicate in the language of the people.

—William Butler Yeats

THE TEAM THAT SAVED A TOWN

A few years ago, screenwriter Gregory Allen Howard moved from Los Angeles to Alexandria, Virginia. He was no stranger to the state, having spent some of his growing-up years in Norfolk, but he found that he especially liked Alexandria. It had the historical interest of having been George Washington's hometown, but the thing that really impressed Howard, an African-American, was that black and white people lived and worked closely together, unlike in many other parts of the South.

One day after he had settled in, Howard was at a barbershop and heard men talking about a local high school football team and how great it was. They went on and on about the players and their accomplishments. Finally Howard asked where the team would be playing their next game so that he could watch them. That's when he found out that the team the men loved was from 1971!

Howard couldn't believe it. After nearly three decades, that particular team was just as important to the people of the town as a team that was still playing. Howard got to thinking. Then he started researching. The more he found out, the more intrigued he became. He decided to write a screenplay about the true events surrounding that team, and that script was made into a movie called *Remember the Titans*.

If you've seen the movie, you probably remember that it was set at a time when many communities in the United States were in the process of dismantling segregation. In 1971, the town of Alexandria took tangible steps toward racial equality when it combined the populations of three high schools—two white and one black—into a new integrated school call T. C. Williams High School.

It was a difficult time, and people from both racial communities were tense over the forced interaction. The first groups to come together were the black and white high school football players who were on a team together for the first time. Adding to the tension was the fact that Herman Boone, a black coach, was selected to be the head coach of the Williams football team rather than Bill Yoast, a local white coach who was very popular in the community.

Boone did everything in his power to bring the players of that team together. He forced black and white players to ride on the buses together up to training camp. He also made them room together, but he was having a hard time getting them to come together as a team. The players kept separating themselves by race—all but one white player. In a pivotal moment in the movie, Coach Boone asks that white team member for some facts about some of his African-American teammates. The player easily answers the questions. That's when the coach tells all of the young men that until they all learn about every other player on the team, they can expect to endure grueling practices three times a day. It didn't occur easily, nor did it happen overnight, but the team started to come together.

Years later when asked in an interview what the keys were to getting the team to bond, Herman Boone said, "Winning did it. Winning solves everything . . . It's also about communication.

Talking to each other. We forced the kids to spend time with each other, [to] find out things about each other. Every player was required to spend time with teammates [who] were a different race."[1]

That action turned the Titans around. And the team did win. They won every game of their regular season, the play-offs, and the state championship. By the time they were finished, the Titans of 1971 were ranked the second best high school team in the nation. But more important than their wins on the field was their impact off it. In response to the Titans, the president of the United States, who lived less than ten miles away across the Potomac River, stated simply, "The team saved the city of Alexandria."[2]

Boone agreed. He remarked,

> The town decided to follow the team rather than those who wanted to tear the team and the town down. I believe the team did play a great role in keeping the city calm, focused, positive towards these young men who'd shown the city that you can get along if you just talk to each other. It was a powerful message that they passed on for generations, and it will be passed on for generations . . . At a time when the city was ready to burn itself to the ground, these kids stepped out and changed attitudes among themselves and their community.[3]

And that is why to this day the people of Alexandria still remember—and talk about—the Titans.

Fleshing It Out

To state it bluntly, you cannot have teamwork unless you have communicative players. Without communication, you don't have a team; you have a collection of individuals.

If you evaluate a good team, you will find that its players have some common characteristics. Communicative players . . .

1. Do Not Isolate Themselves from Others

The key problem Herman Boone had to overcome on his newly formed team was isolation. The players of one race isolated themselves from the players of the other. Anytime a player becomes isolated, it is a problem for the team. If entire sections of the team become isolated, that problem grows. The more teammates know about each other and about the team's goals and methods, the more they'll understand. The more they understand, the more they'll care. A player with passion as well as information and connection is a powerful asset to the team.

2. Make It Easy for Teammates to Communicate with Them

Most communication problems can be solved with proximity. That's why Herman Boone used it to get his team to gel. Putting players of different races on the same buses and forcing them to room with one another made communication more likely to happen. If you look at good

Most communication problems can be solved with proximity.

leaders and impact players on a team, you will find that they not only stay connected with their teammates; they also make sure their teammates are able to make contact with them easily.

3. Follow the Twenty-Four-Hour Rule

When some people are faced with conflict or interpersonal difficulties, they avoid the person with whom they are having the problem. But time alone doesn't usually fix such situations. Without knowing both sides of the story, people tend to give the benefit of the doubt to themselves and to assign negative motives and actions to others. Without communication, the situation just festers.

That's why team members need to follow the twenty-four-hour rule. If you have any kind of difficulty or conflict with a teammate, don't let more than twenty-four hours go by without addressing it. In fact, the sooner you communicate, usually the better off you and your teammates will be.

4. Give Attention to Potentially Difficult Relationships

Relationships need attention to thrive. That is especially true of relationships between people who have potential for conflict. One of the most volatile relationships on the Titans' team was that between white linebacker Gerry Bertier and black defensive end Julius Campbell. The two started out hating each other, and they butted heads constantly. But through the course of the season, they became fast friends. When Bertier was paralyzed in an auto accident and lying in his hospital bed, the first person he asked for was Julius. Their relationship may have developed slowly, but it grew strong. What Aristotle said is true: "Friendship is a slow-ripening fruit."

5. Follow Up Important Communication in Writing

The more difficult communication becomes, the more important it is to work to keep it clear and simple. That often means putting communication in writing. It's not accidental that most marriages have vows, football teams have playbooks, and partnerships have contracts. When communication with your teammates is important, you'll find it's easier to keep everyone on the same page if you've written it down for everyone's benefit.

REFLECTING ON IT

How are you doing when it comes to communication? Are you well connected to all of your teammates? Have you neglected some people or excluded them from your circle of communication? Or have you isolated yourself from others for the sake of being more productive? (Recognize that you may accomplish more individual goals that way, but you may be hurting the team's productivity.) How about accessibility? Can members of your team get to you, or do you make it hard for them to follow the twenty-four-hour rule? Anytime you're on a team but not communicating with team members, the team suffers.

Open communication fosters trust.

Bringing It Home

To improve your communication . . .

- ***Be candid.*** Open communication fosters trust. Having hidden agendas, communicating to people via a third party, and sugarcoating bad news hurt team relationships. Think about a poor relationship you have with someone on your team. If you haven't been candid with that person, then determine to change your ways. Your goal should be to speak truthfully but kindly to your teammates.

- ***Be quick.*** If you tend to sit on things instead of saying them, force yourself to follow the twenty-four-hour rule. When you discover an issue with teammates, find the first reasonable opportunity to address it with them. And invite others to do the same with you.

- ***Be inclusive.*** Some people hoard information unless forced to divulge it. Don't take that approach. If you *can* include others, do. Certainly you need to be discreet with sensitive information, but remember this: people are *up* on things they're *in* on. Open communication increases trust, trust increases ownership, and ownership increases participation.

> **People are *up* on things they're *in* on.**

Daily Take-Away

A story called "The Lion and the Three Bulls," written by the Greek fable writer Aesop, gives insight into how important it is for teammates to be communicative. Three bulls lived together for a long time in a pasture. Though they ate and lived side by side, they never spoke with one another. One day a lion came along and saw the bulls. The lion was very hungry, but he knew that he could never attack three bulls at once because together they would overpower him and kill him. So the lion approached the bulls one at a time. Since one bull never knew what the others were doing, they didn't realize that the lion was working to separate them. The lion, who was crafty, succeeded in dividing them, and with them successfully isolated, he attacked them individually. Thus he overcame all three of them and satisfied his hunger.

Aesop concluded the story by stating, "Union is strength." But there can be no union without good communication.

5

Competent

If You Can't, Your Team Won't

The quality of a person's life is in direct proportion to their commitment to excellence, regardless of their chosen field of endeavor.

—Vince Lombardi

People forget how fast you did a job—but they remember how well you did it.

—Howard W. Newton

Wizard of the Wood Shop

When I was the senior pastor at Skyline Church in California, I became friends with a wonderful man in my congregation named Bob Taylor, who eventually became the vice chairman of my church board. Bob has always liked to build and tinker. When he was a kid and got something on Christmas morning, chances were that before the sun went down that night, he had taken apart his gift to see how it worked. And most of the time, he put it back together, and it still worked. He had a special knack for it.

Once as a kid, when his mom was on the telephone, he and his friends were jumping on the couch when they heard a loud crack. They had broken the frame of the couch, and it was resting on the floor! Before his mom completed her phone conversation, he had found the problem and then glued, clamped, and screwed together the broken wood to repair it. Good as new.

It was natural that when he got to junior high and then high school, he took every industrial arts class he could. "I had some great teachers," Bob recalls. "I had one who would open up the shop even on holiday weekends so that I could keep working on my projects."

One of Bob's other interests is music. When Bob was in high school, he decided he wanted a good twelve-string guitar. He had started playing when he was in third grade after a neighbor had given him an inexpensive guitar (which he subsequently sawed open to see how it was built). The only problem was that Bob didn't really have the money to go out and buy the instrument he wanted. *No problem*, he figured, *I'll just make one myself.* And he did—as an eleventh-grade wood shop project! In fact, while in high school, he made not one but three guitars and a banjo.

Lots of people pick up interesting hobbies in high school. Some individuals continue to pursue those hobbies. Others drop them as they grow older. But Bob did something really special with his. You see, if you play guitar, you've probably walked into a music store and seen a Taylor guitar. Yes, he's *that* Bob Taylor. He went from building guitars in his spare time as a teenager to cofounding his own company.

Bob's business partner of twenty-seven years, Kurt Listug, has the passion for marketing and building a business while Bob provides the passion and technical expertise for building guitars. Today Taylor Guitars constructs some of the finest acoustic guitars in the world, and the manufacturing plant does it at the pace of two hundred instruments a day.

What has enabled Bob to go from solitary luthier to employer of more than 450 people who occupy a 124,000-square-foot complex? The answer lies in his incredible competence and tireless dedication to excellence.

"I'm a 'tweak head,'" says Bob. "I'm continually trying to refine the process." That desire is focused on more than just the guitars themselves. True, Bob Taylor has introduced numerous innovations to guitar building. But Bob's real focus is on the manufacturing process and on the people who build the guitars.

> **Building the team is as important as producing the product.**
>
> —BOB TAYLOR

"Good guitars are really the by-product of good tools and a good facility," explains Bob. "And of course the people part is so important. Building the team is as important as producing the product. You have to let the people be a team. That means fostering an environment where people say what they really think. You can't be too dogmatic." That attitude has allowed the best ideas to rise to the top and get implemented.

"One of the things I've found with people is that they don't want to let the next person onto the team," observes Bob. "Once they get on the team, they want to keep it the way it is. They say they're doing it to protect the quality. But I tell them, 'Don't you think I have the same concern? If I were like you, *you* wouldn't be on the team.' To keep getting better, you have to let people come onto the team and let the quality of the product suffer for a while. It's a constant struggle to achieve."

It's easy to talk about letting the quality suffer in the short term when your competence is so high and your product is so good that even at its worst, it is better than most in your industry. But that willingness to risk and innovate keeps paying off with better guitars. Right now Bob and his team are working on their newest innovation in the area of acoustic guitar amplification. "We're about one year into the process of designing pick-ups [electronic devices that 'pick up' a guitar's sound]," says Bob, "and we've got about another year to go. It's the closest to pure invention we've ever come. We started from scratch with a blank sheet of paper and asked, 'What do we want?' Now we're creating it."

> **. . . inspiration is easy. Implementation is the hard part.**
>
> —BOB TAYLOR

Bob continues, "You know, inspiration is easy. Implementation is the hard part." Implementation may not be easy, but Bob continues to succeed because of his competence and dedication to following through.

Bob's daughter, Minét, sums up his ability by saying, "He has this amazing desire to always make things better. If there is a way to improve, he has an ability to envision it . . . He was just saying the other day that he is still working out ideas that he's had since he was 19 . . . that he would probably die before he could ever use them all."[1] When you bring that kind of ability to the team, how can it lose?

Fleshing It Out

Bob Taylor isn't a flashy guy. He's soft-spoken, and if you met him on the street, you probably wouldn't guess he owns a company that grossed $30 million in 1999.[2] But if you spent any time with him, you would almost instantly recognize his incredible competence.

The word *competent* sometimes is used to mean "barely adequate." When I talk about the quality of competence that is desirable in teammates, I mean it in the sense of its most basic definition, which means "to be well qualified, fit." Competent team members are very capable and highly qualified to do the job and do it well.

Highly competent people have some things in common:

1. They Are Committed to Excellence

John Johnson in *Christian Excellence* writes, "Success bases our worth on a comparison with others. Excellence gauges our value by measuring us against our own potential. Success grants its rewards to the few but is the dream of the multitudes. Excellence is available to all living beings but is accepted by the . . . few." The reason Bob Taylor says that you can let quality slip while accepting new people on the team is that his standards are already so high that a small slip doesn't hurt him much. He and his people are thoroughly committed to excellence.

> **Success bases our worth on a comparison with others. Excellence gauges our value by measuring us against our own potential. Success grants its rewards to the few but is the dream of the multitudes. Excellence is available to all living beings but is accepted by the . . . few.**
>
> —DALE CARNEGIE

2. They Never Settle for Average

The word *mediocre* literally means "halfway up a stony mountain." To be mediocre is to do a job halfway, to leave yourself far short of the summit. Competent people never settle for average. They focus their energy and efforts on what they do well, giving all they've got.

3. They Pay Attention to Detail

Dale Carnegie said, "Don't be afraid to give your best to what seemingly are small jobs. Every time you conquer one it makes you that much stronger. If you do little jobs well, the big ones tend to take care of themselves." When Bob started out making guitars, he did all the little jobs himself. Now he functions more as a team leader and designer of processes and manufacturing equipment. But he and his people still pay attention to the details. That has earned them the place they have achieved in the industry: Taylor is the largest producer of acoustic guitars in the world.

4. They Perform with Consistency

Highly competent people perform with great consistency. They give their best all the time, and that's important. If 99.9 percent were good enough, then 811,000 faulty rolls of 35 millimeter film would be loaded this year, 22,000 checks would be deducted from the wrong bank accounts in the next 60 minutes, and 12 babies would be given to the wrong parents today alone.[3]

I'm not a musician, but I'm told that if you try out a dozen identical instruments from most guitar manufacturers, you find some good ones, many average ones, and a few real stinkers. But a producer/songwriter friend says that if you pick up a Taylor guitar, there's never a bad one in the bunch. That's consistency.

Reflecting on It

One of the things Bob Taylor says about himself is that he's good at "editing" himself. He does what he does well, continually persevering and distilling what's best—and he stops doing what he doesn't do well. Does that describe you? Do you focus your energy on what you can do well so that you become highly competent at it? Can your teammates depend on you to deliver in such a way that it brings the entire team success? If not, you may need to get better focused and develop the skills you need so that you can do your job and do it well.

Bringing It Home

To improve your competence . . .

- *Focus yourself professionally.* It's hard to develop competence if you're trying to do everything. Pick an area in which to specialize. Bob believes he wouldn't be successful at anything but running Taylor Guitars. What is the one thing that brings together your skills, interests, and opportunities? Whatever it is, seize it.

- *Sweat the small stuff.* Too many people don't take their work as far as they can. To do that, you need to develop an ability to get all the details right. That doesn't mean becoming a micromanager or control freak. It means doing the last 10 percent of whatever job you're doing. Try doing that on the next project or big task that is your responsibility.

- ***Give more attention to implementation.*** Since implementation is often the most difficult part of any job, give it greater attention. How can you improve the gap between coming up with ideas and putting them into practice? Get your teammates together and discuss how you can improve the process.

Daily Take-Away

A sea captain and a crusty chief engineer were talking one day, and they began to argue about whose expertise was most needed for the running of the ship. The debate got more and more heated, and finally the captain decided that they should trade jobs for a day. The chief engineer would be on the bridge, and the captain would go down to the engine room.

Only a few hours into their shift, the captain emerged from belowdecks sweating, his face and uniform covered with dirt and oil.

"Chief," he bellowed, "you need to get down to the engine room. I can't get her to go."

"Of course you can't," barked the chief. "She's aground!"

6

Dependable

Teams Go to Go-To Players

Fear not those who argue but those who dodge.

—Wolfram Von Eschenbach

Dependability is more than ability alone.

—John C. Maxwell

But Whom Does Superman Depend On?

In 1995, Christopher Reeve had it all. He was married to his best friend, Dana. He had three wonderful children. And his family enjoyed a house and estate in beautiful Westchester County, New York.

It seemed that he could do anything he put his mind to. He was an accomplished pianist who had composed classical music. He was an avid outdoorsman and a superb athlete: an expert sailor, a licensed pilot, an excellent skier, a scuba diver, and a horseman.

And of course he experienced great success in his acting career. As a teenager, he had decided to pursue a career in show business, and by age sixteen, he had an agent. He attended Cornell University and the Juilliard School, learned his craft, and began getting work as a professional actor.

At the 1979 Academy Awards, John Wayne turned to Cary Grant and said of Reeve, "This is our new man. He's taking over [for us]."[1] Aided not only by his acting skills but also by his good looks and imposing physique at six feet four inches tall, he became a star. In 1995, at age forty-two, Reeve had performed in seventeen feature films (including the blockbuster *Superman*), a dozen movies for television, and about 150 plays. He was financially secure and had achieved critical acclaim. But then his life was turned upside down.

On May 27, 1995, during the cross-country portion of a riding competition, Christopher Reeve was thrown from his horse,

Buck. He crashed headfirst into the fence his horse refused to jump and then fell to the ground. He sustained an injury to his spine at the first and second vertebrae, and his breathing stopped. He was paralyzed from the neck down. If the paramedics hadn't arrived in minutes, he would not have lived.

Reeve has no memory of the fall. He remembers the time he spent in the stables a few minutes before his ride. The next thing he remembers is waking up a few days later in the intensive care unit of the University of Virginia. During those few intense days, doctors kept him alive with a respirator, stabilized him, and literally reattached his head to his spine surgically. The damage Reeve had sustained is sometimes called the hangman's injury. Reeve later quipped, "It was as if I'd been hanged, cut down and sent to rehab.[2]" He was given a 50 percent chance of surviving.

A serious spinal cord injury is difficult for any person to survive, emotionally as well as physically. An injury that leaves you helpless must be unfathomably devastating. But in the hours after he first woke up, he began to understand the real importance of a team.

"When they told me what my condition was, I felt that I was no longer a human being," he recalls. "Then Dana came into my room and knelt down to the level of my bed. We made eye contact. I said, 'Maybe this isn't worth it. Maybe I should just check out.' And she was crying, and she said, 'But you're still you, and I love you.' And that saved my life."[3]

Before the accident, Christopher and Dana Reeve had a good

marriage. But in the years since then, they have developed an even stronger partnership. Chris, Dana, and their son, Will, function as the core of that team, but they have also developed a wonderful larger team around them, consisting of an army of medical professionals. Some assist Chris with rigorous physical therapy, exercise, and respiratory therapy. Others feed, clothe, and bathe him, as well as help with other personal needs. Someone has to turn him over hourly each night as he sleeps. And he sees numerous specialists on a regular basis.

At first, the people around him simply kept him alive. But now they work to keep him healthy. "What you begin to say to yourself, instead of 'What life do I have?' is 'What life can I build?' And the answer, surprisingly, is, 'More than you think.'"[4]

Reeve hopes someday to walk again. Meanwhile, he understands his need for dependable people on his team. "If all the people who are around to help me were mad at me or in a lousy mood or whatever, and they went away," he observes, "there'd be nothing I could do about it. Absolutely nothing . . . It all comes down to goodwill. Nobody has to do any of those things; I'm completely dependent on them."[5] That's the way it is on every team, whether we can see it as clearly as Reeve does. Teammates must be able to depend on one another.

Fleshing It Out

Dependability may not always be a matter of life and death, as it is for Christopher Reeve, but it is certainly important to every team's success. You know it when you have people on your team upon whom you cannot depend. Everyone on the team knows it. Likewise, you know the ones you *can* depend on.

Allow me to note what I consider to be the essence of dependability:

1. Pure Motives

Aristotle believed that "all we do is done with an eye to something else." Evidently he believed that you can't trust anyone's motives. I don't agree with that. Most of the time I give people the benefit of the doubt. I try to keep my motives right, and I encourage my teammates to do likewise. However, if someone on the team continually puts himself and his agenda ahead of what's best for the team, he has proven himself to be undependable. When it comes to teamwork, motives matter.

2. Responsibility

Another quality of a dependable team player is a strong sense of responsibility. *New York Times* best-selling author and former editor Michael Korda emphasized, "In the final analysis, the one quality that all successful people have . . . is the ability to take on responsibility." While motivation addresses *why* people are dependable, responsibility indicates that they *want* to

> **In the final analysis, the one quality that all successful people have . . . is the ability to take on responsibility.**
>
> —MICHAEL KORDA

be dependable. That desire is described effectively by poet Edward Everett Hale, who wrote,

> I am only one,
> But still I am one.
> I cannot do everything
> But still I can do something;
> And because I cannot do everything
> I will not refuse to do the something that I can do.

Dependable team members possess the desire to do the things that they are capable of doing.

3. Sound Thinking

Gene Marine, the editor of the *Bellefontaine Examiner,* once sent a new sports reporter to cover an important game, but when the young man returned, he didn't have a story. Marine asked why, and the reporter replied simply, "No game."

"No game? What happened?" asked Marine.

"The stadium collapsed," responded the reporter.

"Then where is the story on the stadium collapse?" asked the editor.

"That wasn't my assignment, sir," answered the reporter. The potential for a news scoop went right down the tubes because of the young man's inability to think well.

Dependability means more than just wanting to take responsibility. That desire must also be coupled with good judgment to be of real value to the team.

4. Consistent Contribution

The final quality of a dependable team player is consistency. If you can't depend on teammates all the time, then you can't really depend on them any of the time. Consistency takes more than talent. It takes a depth of character that enables people to follow through—no matter how tired, distracted, or overwhelmed they are. As Britain's eloquent and steadfast prime minister of the last century, Winston Churchill, said, "It is not enough that we do our best; sometimes we have to do what's required."

> **It is not enough that we do our best; sometimes we have to do what's required.**
>
> —WINSTON CHURCHILL

REFLECTING ON IT

Are your teammates able to depend on you? Can they trust your motives? Do you make good decisions that others can rely on? And do you perform consistently, even when you don't feel like it? Are you a go-to player, or do your teammates work around you when crunch time comes?

BRINGING IT HOME

To improve your dependability . . .

- ***Check your motives.*** If you haven't committed goals to paper before, stop and do it before reading any farther. Now, look at those goals. How many of them benefit the teams you're part of—your family, the organization you work for, your fellow volunteers, the other players on your ball team? How many benefit only you personally? Spend some time working to align your personal priorities with those of your team.

- ***Discover what your word is worth.*** Approach five teammates with this question: "When I say that I intend to do something, how reliable am I? Rate me on a scale of one to ten." Include a superior and a subordinate in your survey, if possible. If the answers you get don't match your expectations, don't defend yourself. Simply ask for examples in a nonthreatening way. If the average answer is lower than a nine or ten, then start writing down your commitments as you make them from that day forward, and track your follow-through for one month.

- ***Find someone to hold you accountable.*** You are more likely to follow through and develop dependability if you have a partner to help you. Find someone you respect to help you keep your commitments.

Daily Take-Away

In the mid-1800s during an economic depression, many state governments in the United States began to panic and started looking for solutions to their financial hardships. Pennsylvania, for example, simply declined to pay its debts in order to remain solvent, despite what many considered to be a relatively strong financial position.

When the legislature of the state of Ohio considered following Pennsylvania's example, Stephen Douglas, who eventually became a U.S. senator and ran unsuccessfully for president, resolved to try to prevent it. Unfortunately at the time he was deathly ill and restricted to his bed. But Douglas was determined. He had himself carried into the state legislature on a stretcher, and lying on his back, the "Little Giant," as he was known, spoke out against the policy. Due to his efforts, the legislature decided not to default on its obligations; instead, it met them. After the difficult economic times were over, the state prospered. It has been speculated that one of the reasons was that the government's dependability helped to set the stage for economic prosperity.

Never underestimate the long-reaching benefits that being dependable can bring.

7

Disciplined

Where There's a Will, There's a Win

What we do on some great occasion will probably depend on what we already are; and what we are will be the result of previous years of self-discipline.

—H. P. Liddon

Discipline is the refining fire by which talent becomes ability.

—Roy L. Smith

THE MAKING OF A WINNER

In his book *The Life God Blesses,* my friend Gordon MacDonald tells a story about his experiences on the track team at the University of Colorado in the late fifties. In particular, he remembers the difficult workouts he did with a teammate named Bill. "To this day I have anguished memories of our workouts each Monday afternoon," says Gordon. "The memories are onerous because the workouts were. When those Monday workouts ended, I would stagger in exhaustion to the locker room."

But Bill was different. Undoubtedly those workouts were demanding to him too. When he was finished, he would rest on the grass near the track. But after about twenty minutes, while Gordon showered, Bill would repeat the entire workout!

Bill didn't consider himself to be an exceptional athlete in college. During his years at the University of Colorado, he never earned a medal in national collegiate championship competition, nor was he named an All-American. "I was not a great athlete," observed Bill, "but I had the 'bag of tricks' theory . . . that is, there is no big move you can make in your training or in competition, but there are thousands of little things you can do."[1]

Bill might not have made a great impact during his college years, but his discipline and desire paid off over time. His best events were the long jump and the 400. He kept working on those and added other skills so that he could compete in the decathlon. Through disciplined effort and continual improvement, the un-spectacular college athlete who had worked out next to (and ahead of) Gordon MacDonald became a world-famous athlete. Bill was none other than Bill Toomey, the decathlete in-ducted into the Olympic Hall of Fame in 1984. He set a world record in the decathlon in 1966, won a gold medal in the Tokyo Olympics in 1968, and won five national decathlon champion-ships in a row—an accomplishment that has yet to be matched in his sport.

What elevated Toomey to such high accomplishment was his discipline. Gordon MacDonald's insight says it all: "The difference between the two of us began on Monday afternoons during workouts. He was unafraid of discipline and did the maximum; I was afraid of discipline and did the minimum."[2]

Fleshing It Out

Discipline is doing what you really don't want to do so that you can do what you really want to do. It's paying the price in the little things so that you can buy the bigger thing. And just as no individual succeeds without discipline, neither does any team. That's why it needs disciplined players. To become the kinds of players that teams want, people must develop discipline in three areas. They must possess . . .

> **Discipline is doing what you really don't want to do so that you can do what you really want to do.**

1. Disciplined Thinking

You can't get far in life if you don't use your head. To do that, you don't have to be a genius; you just need to use the mind God has given you. Playwright George Bernard Shaw remarked, "Few people think more than two or three times a year; I have made an international reputation for myself by thinking once or twice a week." If you keep your mind active, regularly take on mental challenges, and continually think about the right things, you will develop the disciplined thinking that will help you with whatever you endeavor to do.

2. Disciplined Emotions

People have just two choices when it comes to their emotions: they can master their emotions or be mastered by them.

People have just two choices when it comes to their emotions: they can master their emotions or be mastered by them. That doesn't mean that to be a good team player, you have to turn off your feelings. But it does mean that you shouldn't let your feelings prevent you from doing what you should or drive you to do things you shouldn't.

A classic example of what can happen when a person doesn't discipline his emotions can be seen in the life of golf legend Bobby Jones. Like today's Tiger Woods, Jones was a golf prodigy. He began playing in 1907 at age five. By age twelve, he was scoring below par, an accomplishment most golfers don't achieve in a lifetime of playing the game. At age fourteen, he qualified for the U.S. Amateur Championship. But Jones didn't win that event. His problem can be best described by the nickname he acquired: "club thrower." Jones often lost his temper—and his ability to play well.

An older golfer that Jones called Grandpa Bart advised the young man, "You'll never win until you can control that temper of yours." Jones took his advice and began working to discipline his emotions. At age twenty-one, Jones blossomed and went on to be one of the greatest golfers in history, retiring at age twenty-eight after winning the grand slam of golf. Grandpa Bart's comment sums up the situation: "Bobby was fourteen when he mastered the game of golf, but he was twenty-one when he mastered himself."

3. Disciplined Actions

Albert Hubert said, "Parties who want milk should not seat themselves on a stool in the middle of the field and hope that the cow will back up to them." Sharpening your mind and controlling your emotions are important, but they can take you only so far. Action separates the winners from the losers. The running back who does wind sprints, the attorney who reads up on cases, the doctor who keeps focused in the emergency room, the parent who comes home when promised instead

> **Parties who want milk should not seat themselves on a stool in the middle of the field and hope that the cow will back up to them.**
>
> —ALBERT HUBERT

of working later are all people practicing disciplined action. And when they do, the other people who are depending on them benefit.

Reflecting on It

How are you doing when it comes to discipline? Do you take on mental and physical challenges just for the practice? Or are you constantly seeking a way to stay in your comfort zone? Do you sometimes regret that you've been unable to get yourself to do what you know to be right? Or most of the time do you believe that you do the best that you can? And how do you react under pressure? Do the people on your team expect extra effort or a sudden explosion from you when things go wrong? Your answers to those questions will give insight into whether you are winning the battle for discipline.

Bringing It Home

To become a more disciplined team player . . .

- ***Strengthen your work habits.*** Biologist and educator Thomas Huxley remarked, "Perhaps the most valuable result of all education is the ability to make yourself do the thing you have to do, when it ought to be done, whether you like it or not; it is the first lesson that ought to be learned, and however early a man's training begins, it is probably the last lesson that he learns thoroughly." Discipline means doing the right things at the right time for the right reason. Review your priorities and follow-through to see if you're on track. And do something necessary but unpleasant every day to keep yourself disciplined.

Discipline means doing the right things at the right time for the right reason.

- ***Take on a challenge.*** To strengthen your mind and resolve, pick a task or project that will put you in over your head. Doing that will require you to think sharply and act with discipline. Keep doing that and you will find yourself capable of more than you imagined.

- ***Tame your tongue.*** If you sometimes overreact emotionally, a first step to improvement is to stop yourself from saying things you shouldn't. The next time you want to lash out, hold your tongue for five minutes, and give yourself a chance to cool down and look at things more rationally. Use this strategy repeatedly and you will find yourself in better command of your emotions.

Daily Take-Away

During the fourteenth century in what is now Belgium, there lived a man named Reynald III. Reynald was a nobleman, the rightful duke over his ancestral lands, but his younger brother revolted against him and usurped him. Reynald's brother needed the duke out of the way, but he didn't want to kill him. So he came up with an ingenious plan. Because Reynald was a very large man, his brother had him put into a room with a smaller-than-average door. If Reynald would simply lose some weight, he would be allowed to leave. In fact, the usurping brother promised that if Reynald left the room, his freedom and his title would be restored.

But Reynald was not a man of discipline, and his brother knew that. Every day, the brother had trays of delicious foods delivered to his older brother's room. And Reynald ate. In fact, instead of growing thinner, he grew fatter and fatter.

A person lacking discipline is in a prison without bars. Are your habits making a prisoner of you?

8

Enlarging

Adding Value to Teammates Is Invaluable

The purpose of life is not to win. The purpose of life is to grow and to share. When you come to look back on all that you have done in life, you will get more satisfaction from the pleasure you have brought to other people's lives than you will from the times that you outdid and defeated them.

—Rabbi Harold Kushner

Most of us plateau when we lose the tension between where we are and where we ought to be.

—John Gardiner

BRAVE HEART

In 1296, King Edward I of England assembled a large army and crossed the border of his own nation into Scotland. Edward was a skilled leader and fierce warrior. A tall, strong man, he had gained his first real combat experience beginning at age twenty-five. In the following years, he became a seasoned veteran while fighting in the Crusades in the Holy Lands.

At age fifty-seven, he was fresh from victories in Wales, whose people he'd crushed and whose land he'd annexed. In that conflict, his purpose had been clear: "to check the impetuous rashness of the Welsh, to punish their presumption and to wage war against them to their extermination."[1]

For a time, Edward had attempted to manipulate Scotland's fate. He managed to make himself overlord of the territory and then placed a weak king over it, a man the people of Scotland called Toom Tabard, meaning "empty coat." Then Edward bullied the straw king until he rebelled, thus giving the English monarch a reason to invade the country. The Scottish people crumpled.

Edward sacked the castle of Berwick and massacred its inhabitants. Other castles surrendered in quick succession. The Scottish king was stripped of power, and many believed that the fate of the Scots would be the same as that of the Welsh. But they didn't take into account the efforts of one man: Sir William Wallace, who is still revered as a national hero in Scotland even though he has been dead for nearly seven hundred years.

If you saw the movie *Braveheart,* then you have an image of William Wallace as a fierce and determined fighter who valued freedom above all else. His older brother, Malcolm, as the firstborn son, was expected to follow in the footsteps of their father as a warrior. William, as many second sons of the day, was being groomed for the clergy and was taught to value ideas, including freedom. But he grew to resent the oppressive English after his father was killed in an ambush and his mother was forced to live in exile. At age nineteen, he became a fighter when a group of Englishmen tried to bully him. By his early twenties, William was a highly skilled warrior.

During the time of William Wallace and Edward I, warfare was usually conducted by trained knights, professional soldiers, and sometimes hired mercenaries. The larger and more seasoned the army, the greater their power. When Edward faced the smaller Welsh army, they didn't stand a chance. And the same was expected of the Scots. But Wallace had an unusual ability. He drew the common people of Scotland to him, he made them believe in the cause of freedom, and he inspired and equipped them to fight against the professional war machine of England.

William Wallace was ultimately unable to defeat the English and gain Scotland's independence. At age thirty-three, he was brutally executed. (His treatment was actually worse than that portrayed in the movie *Braveheart.*) But his legacy of enlargement carried on. The next year, inspired by Wallace's example, nobleman Robert Bruce claimed the throne of Scotland and rallied not only the peasants but also the nobility. And in 1314, Scotland finally gained its hard-fought independence.

Fleshing It Out

Team members always love and admire a player who is able to help them go to another level, someone who enlarges them and empowers them to be successful. Those kinds of people are like the Boston Celtics Hall of Fame center Bill Russell, who said, "The most important measure of how good a game I played was how much better I'd made my teammates play."

> **The most important measure of how good a game I played was how much better I'd made my teammates play.**
>
> **—BILL RUSSELL**

Players who enlarge their teammates have several things in common:

1. Enlargers Value Their Teammates

Industrialist Charles Schwab observed, "I have yet to find the man, however exalted his station, who did not do better work and put forth greater effort under a spirit of approval than under a spirit of criticism." Your teammates can tell whether you believe in them. People's performances usually reflect the expectations of those they respect.

2. Enlargers Value What Their Teammates Value

Players who enlarge others do more than value their fellow team members; they understand what their teammates value. They listen to discover what their teammates talk about and watch to see what they spend their money on. That kind of knowledge, along with a desire to relate to their fellow players, creates a strong connection between teammates. And it makes possible an enlarger's next characteristic.

3. Enlargers Add Value to Their Teammates

Adding value is really the essence of enlarging others. It's finding ways to help others improve their abilities and attitudes. An enlarger looks for the gifts, talents, and uniqueness in other people, and then helps them to increase those abilities for their benefit and for that of the entire team. An enlarger is able to take others to a whole new level.

4. Enlargers Make Themselves More Valuable

Enlargers work to make themselves better, not only because it benefits them personally, but also because it helps them to help others. You cannot give what you do not have. For example, in basketball a great player like Karl Malone is aided by a great passer like all-time assist leader John Stockton. If you want to increase the ability of a teammate, make yourself better.

Reflecting on It

How do your teammates see you? Are you an enlarger? Do you make them better than they are alone through your inspiration and contribution? Do you know what your teammates value?

Do you capitalize on those things by adding value to them in those areas?

Becoming an enlarger of others isn't always easy. First, it takes a secure person to add value to others. If you believe deep down that helping others somehow hurts you or your opportunities for success, then you'll have a hard time enlarging others. But as Henry Ward Beecher insisted, "No man is more cheated than the selfish man." When a team member unselfishly enlarges others, he also enlarges himself.

> **No man is more cheated than the selfish man.**
>
> **—HENRY WARD BEECHER**

Bringing It Home

If you want to be an enlarging team player, then do the following:

- ***Believe in others before they believe in you.*** If you want to help people become better, you need to become an initiator. You can't hold back. Ask yourself, *What is special, unique, and wonderful about that teammate?* Then share your observations with the person and with others. If you believe in others and give them a positive reputation to uphold, you can help them to become better than they think they are.

- ***Serve others before they serve you.*** One of the most beneficial services you can perform is helping other human beings to reach their potential. In your family, serve your spouse.

Free up time and resources for enriching experiences. On the ball field, find a way to get your teammate the ball. In business, help your colleagues to shine. And whenever possible, give credit to others for the team's success.

- ***Add value to others before they add value to you.*** A basic truth of life is that people will always move toward anyone who increases them and away from others who devalue them. You can enlarge others by pointing out their strengths and helping them to focus on improvement. But remember this: encourage and motivate people out of their comfort zone, but never out of their gift zone. If you try to push people to work in areas where they have no talent, you will only frustrate them.

People will always move toward anyone who increases them and away from others who devalue them.

Daily Take-Away

For as long as he could remember, a boy named Chris Greicius dreamed of someday becoming a police officer. But there was a major obstacle standing in his way. He had leukemia, and he was not expected to make it to adulthood. When he was seven years old, Chris's battle with the disease took a turn for the worse, and that's when a family friend, who was a U.S. customs officer, arranged for Chris to come as close as he could to living his dream.

He made a call to Officer Ron Cox in Phoenix and arranged for Chris to spend the day with officers from the Arizona Department of Public Safety.

When the day arrived, Chris was welcomed by three squad cars and a police motorcycle ridden by Frank Shankwitz. Then he was treated to a ride in a police helicopter. They finished the day by swearing Chris in as the first—and only—honorary state trooper. The next day, Cox enlisted the assistance of the company that manufactured the uniforms for the Arizona Highway Patrol, and within twenty-four hours, their people presented Chris with an official patrolman's uniform. He was ecstatic.

Two days later, Chris died in the hospital, his uniform close at hand. Officer Shankwitz was saddened by his little friend's death, but he was grateful that he had experienced the opportunity to help Chris. And he also realized that there were many children in circumstances similar to Chris's. That prompted Shankwitz to cofound the Make-A-Wish Foundation. In twenty years since then, he and his organization have enlarged the experiences of more than eighty thousand children.

There is nothing as valuable—or rewarding—as adding value to the lives of others.

9

Enthusiastic

Your Heart Is the Source of Energy for the Team

I feel sorry for the person who can't get genuinely excited about his work. Not only will he never be satisfied, but he will never achieve anything worthwhile.

—*Walter Chrysler*

Nothing great was ever achieved without enthusiasm.

—*Ralph Waldo Emerson*

HOG LOVERS

Their passion is legendary, just as the object of their passion is. Many of them are members of an organization called HOG. And in June of 1998, more than 140,000 of them rode through the streets of Milwaukee, Wisconsin, to celebrate their love. They are owners of Harley-Davidson motorcycles.

June of 1998 marked the ninety-fifth anniversary of the Harley-Davidson Motor Company, an organization that began when twenty-one-year-old William S. Harley and his twenty-year-old friend Arthur Davidson decided to motorize bicycles in a small wooden shed in 1903. That first year they hand-built and sold three motorcycles. It didn't take them long to find success and to expand their enterprise. Each year they produced more vehicles.

As motorcycle racing came into existence and gained popularity, Harley-Davidson dominated. When World War I broke out, the Allies quickly discovered the value of motorcycles in the war effort. Harley-Davidson estimates that the company provided most of the twenty thousand motorcycles used by the U.S. Army in the war. And after the armistice was signed, the first American to enter Germany did so on a Harley-Davidson motorcycle.[1]

For more than half a century, the company thrived. One of its strengths was that it was a family-owned business whose employees and customers felt connected by their love for Harley-Davidson motorcycles. And the company continued to grow, to update and improve their motorcycles, and to gain fans. By the early 1970s, Harley-Davidson owned nearly 80 percent of the large-motorcycle (850+ cc) market in the United States.[2]

But even before Harley-Davidson reached their peak in the seventies, they began to have major problems. In the early 1960s, the company went public to raise funds so that it could modernize, diversify, and better compete against Japanese manufacturers. In the late 1960s, AMF acquired the firm. After a proud sixty-five-year history in Milwaukee, the company's headquarters was abruptly moved to New York, and vehicle final assembly was moved to Pennsylvania. The people on Harley-Davidson's staff were demoralized.

Over the next decade, Harley-Davidson's reputation slid. The motorcycles became notoriously unreliable. Police officers in departments around the country who were once proud to ride the company's American-made vehicles began to buy Japanese products, which were cheaper and more dependable. By 1980, Harley-Davidson possessed slightly more than 30 percent of a market that it had once dominated. And for the first time in its history, the company lost money. Harley-Davidson's future looked grim.

The thing that saved Harley-Davidson was one of the things it always had going for it: the passion of employees and customers for the motorcycle that bore the company's name. In 1981, thirteen senior executives of the company bought the company, including Vaughn Beals, a Harley enthusiast since World War II who ran the motorcycle division for AMF. They quickly began to turn Harley-Davidson around. They streamlined operations, improved manufacturing methods, and introduced new products. They also harnessed the enthusiasm of Harley owners by creating HOG, the Harley Owners Group (which has more than six hundred thousand members today). In 1985, Harley-Davidson earned a profit for the first time in five years.

A lot of people left the company during those years, but the employees who stayed were dedicated. In the years to follow, Harley-Davidson decided to harness their commitment, knowledge, and enthusiasm in a unique partnership that began between labor and management and then expanded to include all of what the company identifies as its various stakeholders: customers, employees, suppliers, shareholders, government, and society. Today the enthusiasm and partnership are paying off. Harley-Davidson manufactures and sells more than two hundred thousand vehicles in countries around the world every year with net sales of more than $2.9 billion.[3]

Fleshing It Out

What saved Harley-Davidson? I believe it was enthusiasm. It was the enthusiasm of Beals and the other twelve executives who bought the company and kept it from going under in 1981. It was the enthusiasm of the employees who stayed with the company under difficult circumstances in order to produce better motorcycles as 40 percent of the organization's workforce was

> **People can succeed at almost anything for which they have enthusiasm.**
>
> —CHARLES SCHWAB

cut. And of course it was the enthusiasm of the customers—who have long considered a Harley-Davidson to be the pinnacle of motorcycles—that has made the company the financial success it is today.

There is no substitute for enthusiasm. When the members of a team are enthusiastic, the whole team becomes highly energized. And that energy produces power. Industrialist Charles Schwab observed, "People can succeed at almost anything for which they have enthusiasm."

Think about people who bring an enthusiastic attitude to teamwork and you will realize that they . . .

1. *Take Responsibility for Their Own Enthusiasm*

Successful people understand that attitude is a choice—and that includes enthusiasm. People who wait for external forces to help them spark their enthusiasm are at other people's mercy all the time. They are likely to run hot or cold based on what's going on around them at any given moment. However, positive people are positive because they choose to be. If you want to be positive, upbeat, and passionate, you need to take responsibility for being that way.

> **Positive people are positive because they choose to be.**

2. *Act Their Way into Feeling*

You cannot win if you do not begin. That's one of the reasons why you need to act your way into feeling. You can't break a cycle of apathy by waiting to *feel* like doing it. I addressed an issue similar to this in *Failing Forward:*

> People who want to get out of the fear cycle often . . . believe that they have to eliminate [their fear] to break the cycle. But . . . you can't wait for motivation to get you going. To conquer fear, you have to feel the fear and take action anyway . . . You've got to get yourself moving. The only way to break the cycle is to face your fear and take action—no matter how small or seemingly insignificant that action might seem. To get over fear, you've got to get started.[4]

Likewise, if you want to be enthusiastic, you need to start acting that way. If you wait for the feeling before acting, you may never become enthusiastic.

3. *Believe in What They Do*

So how do people who don't *feel* enthusiastic engender enthusiasm? One of the best ways is to think about all the positive aspects of your work. Believing in what you do and focusing on those positive beliefs will help you to act and to speak positively about what you're doing. That helps to spark the fire of enthusiasm inside you, and once that starts, all you need to do is to keep feeding the flames.

4. *Spend Time with Other Enthusiastic People*

If you want to augment your enthusiasm, hang around enthusiastic people. The author of books on the psychology of winning, Denis Waitley, says, "Enthusiasm is contagious. It's difficult to remain neutral or indifferent in the presence of a positive thinker." And when you put together a whole team of enthusiastic people, the possibilities for that team are endless.

> **Enthusiasm is contagious. It's difficult to remain neutral or indifferent in the presence of a positive thinker.**
>
> —DENIS WAITLEY

Reflecting on It

Microsoft chairman Bill Gates remarked, "What I do best is share my enthusiasm." Obviously that ability has brought the people in his organization immense success. If asked, would your teammates say that you have a similar effect on them? Enthusiasm increases a person's accomplishments while apathy increases his alibis. Which are people more likely to discover in you?

Bringing It Home

To improve your enthusiasm . . .

- ***Show a sense of urgency.*** A good way to fire up your own furnace is to do things with greater urgency. Identify a project that you are currently less enthusiastic about than you should be. Give yourself deadlines for completing its steps that are a little more ambitious than you feel comfortable with. Doing that should help you be more focused and energized.

- ***Be willing to do more.*** One way to demonstrate enthusiasm with your teammates is to go the extra mile with others. This week when someone asks you to do something, do what's required and then some. Then quietly observe its impact on the team's atmosphere.

- ***Strive for excellence.*** Elbert Hubbard said, "The best preparation for good work tomorrow is to do good work today." Nothing breeds enthusiasm like a job well done. If you've allowed yourself to ease off when it comes to your work standards, redouble efforts to do things according to your highest levels of excellence.

> **The best preparation for good work tomorrow is to do good work today.**
>
> —ELBERT HUBBARD

DAILY TAKE-AWAY

They donate time every month to something that will ultimately last only a few hours. They work every New Year's Eve and New Year's Day, volunteering their time instead of going to parties or staying home with their families. They are the men and women who build and decorate the floats for the annual Tournament of Roses Parade in Pasadena, California.

Each year, more than 1 million people line the parade route, and more than 400 million people tune in via television to watch the colorful flower-covered floats of the parade that has been held every year since 1890. Though many of the floats are now created and produced by professional float-building companies, some are still designed and built by volunteers. Float construction goes on from spring to December. And then the entire float has to be decorated with flowers, seeds, and other natural objects in the days just before the parade.

"It's a lot of work, a lot of volunteers," a float coordinator explains. "[It takes] about 4,000 man hours to actually build a float, and probably equally as many hours to decorate a float."

What keeps people coming back to volunteer as members of a float team year after year? Their enthusiasm. Volunteer Pam Kontra explains, "It is a lot of fun. It's a lot of work, and it's a lot of time, but to see [a float] rolling down the road and saying, 'I worked right there on that part!', is like so exciting to see."[5] That kind of enthusiasm gives an individual—and a team—the energy required to accomplish even the most difficult tasks.

10

Intentional
Make Every Action Count

It is easy in the world to live after the world's opinions;
it is easy in solitude to live after your own;
but the great man is he who in the midst of the crowd
keeps with perfect sweetness the independence of solitude.

—Ralph Waldo Emerson

You've got to think about "big things" while you're doing small things, so that all the small things go in the right direction.

—Alvin Toffler

What a Doll!

In 2000, my wife, Margaret, and I became grandparents. Our daughter, Elizabeth, and her husband, Steve, brought a girl named Madeline into the world, and then a few months later our son, Joel Porter, and his wife, Elisabeth (yes, it does confuse us too!), brought us a girl named Hannah. For years, friends with grandchildren had told us how great it is being a grandparent. It's all that they claimed and more.

Margaret and I now have a new pastime: searching for books, toys, and gifts for those two children. One day Margaret came home and said, "John, I just found the most wonderful things for the girls. They're not old enough yet, but it's a series of books that teaches about American history from the point of view of a girl."

She showed me a catalog. "It's called the American Girls Collection," she continued. "Each group of books is set in a different time period in American history. There are dolls for each book series, period clothes, accessories, and other things. There's even a magazine the girls will be able to get."

The whole series sounded like a wonderful thing for our granddaughters. I became intrigued, too, not just because of my grandchildren, but because I was impressed with the company. So I started to do some research.

What I discovered was an organization called Pleasant Company that was founded in 1986 by Pleasant T. Rowland, a former teacher. In the classroom, Rowland had been frustrated by the uncreative textbooks she was given, so she began developing her own materials. Later, she worked in educational research and publishing. Eventually she began her own company when she and friend Valerie Tripp came up with a creative idea for girls. Rowland says, "As an educator, I wanted to give girls an understanding of America's past and a sense of pride in the traditions they share with girls of yesterday. Out of this desire, The American Girls Collection was born."[1]

At the heart of the collection are the books. The process of bringing the books together is complicated, and it requires a high degree of intentionality every step of the way. First, Pleasant Company editors create a proposal for a character to be set in a particular time period and location. It includes information on the period's significance to American history and how girls today will relate to it. It examines the culture, including housing, clothing, food, and more. It also identifies possible experts, authors, and illustrators who could work on the project. Once every department has reviewed the potential project, the editors choose an author, and the project development department begins researching products that could be created to enrich the learning process for children.

Obviously the strategy has worked. The company has been highly successful, both educationally and financially. So far, the company has sold 61 million books and 5 million dolls, and its magazine has 700,000 subscribers.[2] And Pleasant Rowland has received numerous awards and honors, such as recognition by the Institute of American Entrepreneurs (on whose board she now serves).

Since Rowland is an entrepreneur, perhaps her greatest recognition came when her company was acquired by Mattel in 1998 and she became Mattel's vice chairman. Undoubtedly Mattel's decision makers were impressed by her business skill, sense of mission, and ability to turn her vision into reality by making every move count through intentional leadership.

Fleshing It Out

What does it mean to be intentional? It means working with purpose—making every action count. In Chapter 11, we're going to talk about being mission conscious, which relates to keeping the big picture in mind. But being intentional is different. It's about focusing on doing the right things, moment to moment, day to day, and then following through with them in a consistent way.

Successful individuals are intentional. They aren't scattered or haphazard. They know what they're doing and why they're doing it. For a team to be successful, it needs intentional people who are able to remain focused and productive, people who make every action count.

Anyone who desires to live with intentionality will have to do the following:

1. Have a Purpose Worth Living For

Being intentional begins with a sense of purpose. Willis R. Whitney, the first director of General Electric's research laboratory,

> **Some men have thousands of reasons why they cannot do what they want to, when all they need is one reason why they can.**
>
> —WILLIS R. WHITNEY

offered this thought: "Some men have thousands of reasons why they cannot do what they want to, when all they need is one reason why they can." You can see that one strong reason at work in the life and work of Pleasant Rowland. Her goal was to educate children and particularly to help girls. That desire became a guide to her actions and helped her to build a $300 million company. You can't be intentional if you don't have a strong sense of purpose.

2. Know Your Strengths and Weaknesses

Filmmaker Woody Allen remarked, "No matter what I'm working on, I like to do what I'm not doing." While he may not love *every* aspect of his profession, he has made so many movies that he must enjoy most parts of it. And he's good at it too. The truth is that people like to do what they're good at. Playing to your strengths rekindles your passions and renews your energy. If you know yourself and what you do well, then you can direct your time and energy in an intentional way.

3. Prioritize Your Responsibilities

Once you know the *why* of your life, it becomes much easier to figure out the *what* and *when*. *Walden* author Henry David

Thoreau observed, "One is not born into the world to do everything, but to do something." That means knowing your priorities and working according to them continually.

> **One is not born into the world to do everything, but to do something.**
> **—HENRY DAVID THOREAU**

4. Learn to Say No

Another thing an intentional person has to learn is how to say no. For me, that has been really difficult. I never met an opportunity I didn't like, so my natural desire is to say yes to everything. But you can't accomplish much without focus.

Chemist John A. Widtsoe said, "Let every man sing his own song in life." If you try to do every good thing that comes your way, you won't excel at what you were made to do.

5. Commit Yourself to Long-Term Achievement

A short-term, all-or-nothing approach to life works against many people. They have a kind of lottery mind-set: either they want to win big, or they don't want to make any effort at all. However, most victories in life are achieved through small, incremental wins sustained over time. Being willing to dedicate yourself long term to the process of achievement, instead of to its immediate rewards, will enable you to be more intentional. That's true when it comes to personal growth, relationship building, financial investment, or professional success.

Reflecting on It

How intentional are you? As you proceed through your day, do you have a plan and a purpose for everything you do? Do you know where you're going and why you're doing what you're doing? Or are you simply drifting down the stream of life? If your teammates don't detect a sense of intentionality in you, they won't know what to expect from you, and they will be unlikely to count on you when it really counts.

Bringing It Home

To improve your intentionality . . .

- ***Explore your strengths and weaknesses.*** You can't be intentional and effectively focused if you don't know yourself. If you've not done much self-examination, take an inventory of your strengths and weaknesses. Then survey family members, friends, and colleagues for additional insight. The more information and honest feedback you can get, the better.

- ***Specialize in your specialty.*** When you have a solid understanding of your strengths, you will be able to focus. Your goal should be to spend 80 percent of your time and effort on what brings high return to you and your team. Adjust your daily schedule and to-do list as much as possible to conform to that standard.

- ***Plan your calendar with purpose.*** The longer the time period you can plan with intentionality, the more you can get done. If you think in terms of a few hours or a single day, there's only so much you can do. You're better off thinking in terms of what you want to get done in a week or a month. (It's also a good idea to give yourself annual goals.) Set aside time this week to plan your activities in a longer block of time than you're accustomed to doing. If you're used to thinking daily, then plan for a week. If you usually plan weekly, then work out your goals for a month. It will help you to be more intentional throughout your days.

Daily Take-Away

My friend Dwight Bain sent me a story of a ham radio operator who one day overheard an older gentleman giving advice to a younger man on the air.

"It's a shame you have to be away from home and your family so much," he said. "Let me tell you something that has helped me keep a good perspective on my own priorities. You see, one day I sat down and did a little arithmetic. The average person lives about seventy-five years. Now then, I multiplied 75 times 52 and came up with 3,900, which is the number of Saturdays that the average person has in his lifetime.

"It took me until I was fifty-five years old to think about all this in any detail," he continued, "and by that time I had lived through over 2,800 Saturdays. I got to thinking that if I lived to be seventy-five, I only had about a thousand of them left to enjoy."

He went on to explain that he bought 1,000 marbles and put them in a clear plastic container in his favorite work area at home. "Every Saturday since then," he said, "I have taken one marble out and thrown it away. I found that by watching the marbles diminish, I focused more on the really important things in life. There's nothing like watching your time here on this earth run out to help get your priorities straight."

Then the older gentleman finished, "Now let me tell you one last thought before I sign off and take my lovely wife out to breakfast. This morning, I took the very last marble out of the container. I figure if I make it until next Saturday, then I have been given a little extra time."

We can't choose whether we will get any more time, but we can choose what we do with it. If you are intentional with what you have, then you will make the most of the time and talent that God gives you.

11

Mission Conscious

The (Big) Picture Is Coming in Loud and Clear

The secret of success is constancy to purpose.

—Benjamin Disraeli

He who has a "why" to live for
can bear almost any "how."

—Friedrich Nietzsche

STICKING TO HER GUNS

It was particularly hot and humid on June 28, 1778, near the Monmouth Courthouse in the town of Freehold, New Jersey. That was the day during the American Revolutionary War that General George Washington, who had spent most of the war waging a battle of strategy and movement against the British, finally determined to fight the enemy in a full engagement.

After a tentative attack and withdrawal by American general Charles Lee, the revolutionary forces rallied under General Washington and engaged in a fierce artillery battle against the British. It turned out to be the largest and longest battle of that type staged during the Revolutionary War. For hours, in heat that approached nearly 100 degrees, the two opposing artillery groups hurled tons of shells and iron shot at one another. Each side fought using ten guns, and for a long time neither side gained the advantage.

As the men fought on, exhaustion threatened to overcome them, and many of them called for water. Mary Hays, the wife of artilleryman William Hays, rushed to the front lines with water to help the soldiers keep fighting. It was the kind of thing she had done before. She had traveled with her husband throughout the war, as many spouses did in those days. She cooked, helped to look after the men, and even tended to the wounded during battles. She was as dedicated to the cause of freedom and the defeat of the British as any soldier in the Continental army. She had even suffered through the horrible winter at Valley Forge with the army.

On this day, because of the heat, fetching water was a full-time job, although she did help with the wounded as well. After she returned to the battle line from one of her trips to a stream, she noticed that her husband, William, who had been relieved from his gun so that he could rest, was back in the fight because the man who had replaced him had been wounded. The battle was so even that the Americans couldn't afford to have a single cannon out of commission for fear of losing the battle.

As Mary watched, her husband was also struck down by enemy fire. He was dead. She didn't hesitate. Mary had been with the army long enough to know what must be done. With the battery short of gunners, she stepped forward and took her husband's place as the cannon's gunner.

A Connecticut soldier described Mary's actions during the battle in his autobiography:

> While in the act of reaching a cartridge and having one of her feet as far before the other as she could step, a cannon shot from the enemy passed directly between her legs without doing any other damage than carrying away all the lower part of her petticoat. Looking at it with apparent unconcern, she . . . continued her occupation.[1]

After hours of fighting, the British artillery was forced to withdraw. The Continental army had won the battle.

Though it was not considered a major military victory, the Battle of Monmouth was a political triumph and a tremendous morale booster for the revolutionaries. The Continental army had faced the British in the open field and forced them to retreat. And in this longest of battles of the American Revolution, the British had suffered two to three times more casualties than their American counterparts. For her actions in the battle, Mary Hays was issued a warrant as a noncommissioned officer by General George Washington.

Fleshing It Out

Mary Hays, who has come to be known as "Molly Pitcher" in history books, is symbolic of the attitude of many of the people who fought in the American Revolution. They were highly mission conscious, and that sense of purpose and mission continually drove them to do what was best for their cause, their fellow fighters, and their nation.

Not many of us can relate to the battlefield heroics of someone like Mary Hays, but we can certainly embrace the mission-conscious attitude she brought to her team. She exhibited the four qualities of all mission-conscious players:

1. They Know Where the Team Is Going

As Americans, we admire the people who founded our nation. We respect their courage, commitment, and sacrifice. We also admire their sense of vision and mission. They knew they were fighting for freedom and the future of a country that had the potential to give its people great opportunities. There is immense power in a sense of mission. Author W. Clement Stone stated, "When you discover your mission, you will feel its demand. It will fill you with enthusiasm and a burning desire to get to work on it." That sense of desire—and direction—is as indispensable for a team to be successful as it is for any individual.

2. They Let the Leader of the Team Lead

Mission-conscious team players who have committed themselves to a team allow the leader of the team to do the leading. Ironically the American army almost lost the Battle of Monmouth because of the actions of one of its own generals: Charles Lee. Commander in Chief George Washington, ordered Lee to attack the British and to harass them until the full force of the American army could engage them. Lee, who opposed Washington's plan, advanced tentatively and then suddenly retreated without cause. Lee nearly lost the Americans the opportunity to engage and defeat the enemy. Fortunately Washington was able to take over his subordinate's command, but Lee was ultimately relieved of his command following a court-martial.

Leadership is the capacity to translate vision into reality.

—WARREN G. BENNIS

Any time a team member hinders the leader, it increases the possibility that the team will be hindered in its goals. However, mission-conscious players understand what leadership expert Warren G. Bennis articulated: "Leadership is the capacity to translate vision into reality." For a team to win, the leader must be allowed to lead.

3. They Place Team Accomplishment Ahead of Their Own

Teamwork always requires sacrifice. Good team players put team accomplishment ahead of what they can accomplish personally because that's what it takes to achieve the team's mission of the team. Often that means sacrificing personal goals or even personal safety, as was the case for Mary Hays. In the heat of battle, she didn't even allow herself to grieve for her lost husband. The stakes were too high for her to do anything but serve the team.

4. They Do Whatever Is Necessary to Achieve the Mission

It's obvious that Mary Hays was willing to do whatever it took to achieve the mission of her team, whether it was the common duties of a woman who traveled with the army, such as cooking, washing clothes, or serving, or the duties beyond her typical role, such as stepping into the battle lines with the soldiers. Mission-conscious team players today should have the same kind of attitude that Mary had. If success can come to the team only by your compromising, trying something new, or putting your agenda on hold, then that's what you need to do.

Reflecting on It

Do you and your teammates keep the big picture in mind? Are you continually looking for ways to help the team realize its mission? Or do you tend to get so bogged down in the details of your responsibilities that you lose sight of the big picture? If you in any way hinder the bigger team—your organization—because of your desire to achieve personal success or even the success of your department, then you may need to take steps to improve your ability to keep the team's mission in mind.

BRINGING IT HOME

To improve your mission consciousness . . .

> **A team isn't really a team if it isn't going anywhere!**

- ***Check to see if your team focuses on its mission.*** It's difficult to maintain a mission-conscious mind-set on a team that lacks a mission. Truthfully a team isn't really a team if it isn't going anywhere! So start by measuring the clarity of the mission. Does your team or organization have a mission statement? If not, work to get the team to create one. If it does, then examine whether the goals of the team match its mission. If the values, mission, goals, and practices of a team don't match up, you're going to have a tough time as a team player.

- ***Find ways to keep the mission in mind.*** If you're a strong achiever, the type of person who is used to working alone, or you tend to focus on the immediate rather than the big picture, you may need extra help being reminded of the mission of the team. Write down the mission and place it somewhere you can see it. Put it on an index card on your bathroom mirror, make it a message on your computer's screen saver, or have it made into a plaque for your desk. Keep it in front of you so that you are always conscious of the team's mission.

- ***Contribute your best as a team member.*** Once you're sure of the team's mission and direction, determine to contribute your best in the context of the team, not as an individual. That may mean taking a behind-the-scenes role for a while. Or it may mean focusing your inner circle in a way that contributes more to the organization, even if it gives you and your people less recognition.

Daily Take-Away

For twenty years, one of the most productive players in baseball was Reggie Jackson. Now a member of the Major League Baseball Hall of Fame in Cooperstown, New York, Jackson was called "Mr. October" for his legendary prowess as a batter during the play-off and World Series games in which he played.

In *How Life Imitates the World Series,* Thomas Boswell tells how Jackson, who was then with the Baltimore Orioles, once stole a base in a game without having been given the sign to do so. That was something that manager Earl Weaver didn't allow. But Jackson, who has never lacked self-confidence, did it anyway. He was a good runner, and he believed that he knew the pitchers and catchers against whom he was playing so well that he could judge whether or not he should steal.

Later, Weaver took Jackson aside and explained why he hadn't wanted him to steal. The next batter in the order was Lee May, a powerful hitter. With first base open and the chance of May hitting into a double play now gone, the opposing pitcher intentionally walked May. That brought up the next player in the batting order, a man who had a poor record against that particular pitcher. Weaver then had to send in a pinch hitter to try to get Jackson and May around the bases to score. As a result, he didn't have that pinch hitter available later in the game when he really needed him.

Although Jackson was right in his assessment of his skill against the opposing team, he hurt the team. Why? Because he had his own achievement in mind and not the big picture when making a decision that affected the whole team. Good team players see more than the details of the moment. They are always conscious of a team's mission and act to help achieve it.

12

Prepared

Preparation Can Mean the Difference Between Winning and Losing

Spectacular achievements come from unspectacular preparation.

—Roger Staubach

It's better to prepare than to repair.

—John C. Maxwell

Conscientious Hero

Alvin York is called the greatest soldier of World War I. For his actions during the Battle of the Argonne, York, an uneducated mountain boy from rural Tennessee, received the Distinguished Service Cross, the Croix de Guerre and Legion of Honor from France, the Croce di Guerra from Italy, the War Medal of Montenegro, and the Medal of Honor, the United States' highest decoration. At his medal ceremony French commander Marshal Ferdinand Foch said to York, "What you did was the greatest thing ever accomplished by any soldier of any of the armies of Europe."[1]

Before the war, nobody would have anticipated that York would become a hero—not even York himself! The third of eleven children, he grew up in the mountains of Tennessee. Like his father, he farmed, worked as an unskilled laborer, and took some work as a blacksmith. But his first love was hunting. And like his father and most of the men in the rural valley where he grew up, he was a crack shot.

When York was twenty-four years old, his father died, and he became the family's primary provider. However, after a year or two, York started to spend much time drinking, gambling, and fighting. He soon developed a reputation as someone who "would never amount to anything."[2] But on New Year's Day of 1915, when he was twenty-seven years old, York decided to change. He promised his mother he would turn his life around, and later that winter at a revival meeting, York became a man of faith by giving his life to Christ.

During the next two years, Alvin York became a different person. He altogether stopped drinking, using tobacco, swearing, and fighting. He worked hard to support his family. He studied the Bible. And he helped to found a church in his town where he became the second elder and worship leader. He also embraced the small denomination's stance against war. So when he received a draft notice in 1917, he was in a dilemma. He loved his country, and his family had fought for it all the way back to colonial times. But he also loved God and wanted to obey Him. York wrote,

> You see my religion and my experience . . . told me not to go to war, and the memory of my ancestors . . . told me to get my gun and go fight . . . It was a most awful thing when the wishes of your God and your country . . . get mixed up and go against each other . . . I wanted to be a good Christian and a good American too.[3]

At first, York was classified as a conscientious objector. And though he had not yet resolved whether he would fight, York did go off to army basic training at Camp Gordon, Georgia, when he was ordered to. And there he excelled. York was a natural leader, and his early life had prepared him well to be a soldier. He was physically strong, he was disciplined, and he was deadly accurate with a rifle at two hundred yards.

The only area where York was not prepared was in his heart. He still wasn't sure whether he could take another person's life.

So he endeavored to work through the issue. He consulted repeatedly with his pastor. He discussed the dilemma with his captain and his major. He wrestled with it from November 14 when he was inducted into the army until April 30, right before he was shipped overseas. And finally he came to a conclusion. Knowing the Bible said that peacemakers are blessed, York determined, "If a man can make peace by fighting, he is a peacemaker."[4] That completed his preparation—not only physically and mentally but also spiritually.

Although York saw action in France beginning in June, it wasn't until October 8, 1918, that he performed the acts that made him a hero. During the Battle of the Argonne, when a group of American soldiers from his company got pinned down by German machine-gun fire, seventeen men including York were sent across enemy lines to create a distraction. The men soon found themselves overrunning a camp of more than twenty German soldiers who had set their weapons aside to eat. The Americans took the Germans prisoner, but upon a word from a German officer, the machine guns along the front swiveled and suddenly turned on them. In seconds, all but eight of the Americans were dead or wounded, including all the noncommissioned officers. That left York, a corporal, in command.

For more than two decades, York had hunted or competed in weekly shooting contests in his hometown of Pall Mall, Tennessee. That preparation served him well that day against the machine gunners. As they would stand up to fire on the Americans, York would take them out one by one. After shooting several, he tried to get them to give up, but they wouldn't. He killed seventeen men with seventeen shots, eliminating the threat of the machine-gun nest.

When York ran out of rifle ammunition, a group of Germans charged him with bayonets. He defended himself with his pistol, felling eight men with eight shots. Afterward, as York and the others marched their prisoners back, they continued to take captive other German soldiers and officers. By the time they returned to Allied territory, the eight Americans had taken 132 German prisoners. York's preparation and cool head under fire had saved his squad and helped secure a major victory for the Allies.

York came home to a New York City ticker-tape parade, fame, and numerous lucrative endorsement offers. But York's desire was to help school uneducated children in his community. York wrote, "I kind of figured my trials and tribulations in the war had been to prepare me for doing just this work in the mountains. All my sufferings in having to go and kill were to teach me the value of human lives. All the temptations I went through were to strengthen my character."[5] In 1926, he helped to establish the York Agricultural Institute, which is still teaching students today.

Fleshing It Out

Spanish novelist Miguel de Cervantes stated, "The man who is prepared has his battle half-fought." That was true for Alvin

York, and it can be true for you. If you want to prepare yourself so that you can help your team as it faces the challenges ahead, then think about the following:

> **The man who is prepared has his battle half-fought.**
>
> —MIGUEL DE CERVANTES

1. Assessment

Preparation begins with knowing what you're preparing for. Alvin York knew he was headed for war, and as a result he assessed his personal state of preparation. Likewise, you need to determine where you and your team are headed. You need to examine what the conditions will be along the way. And you need to determine what price you will have to pay to get there. If you don't, you will be unable to prepare yourself properly.

2. Alignment

I enjoy playing golf, and it has taught me a valuable lesson. Although you know where you want to go, you'll never get to your desired destination if you're not lined up right. That's true of personal preparation as well as golf. Good alignment makes success possible. Bad alignment makes success impossible—no matter how much you prepare. You can't just work hard. You have to do the right work.

3. Attitude

Lazy people rarely prepare. Diligent people do, but they sometimes overlook an area that can trip them up when they meet a challenge: they neglect their attitude. To succeed in any endeavor,

Courage has no greater ally than preparation, and fear has no greater enemy.

you must do your homework to take care of the mental aspects of your game. You must prepare physically. But you also must have a positive attitude about yourself, your teammates, and your situation. If you believe in yourself and your teammates, then you set yourself up for success.

4. Action

Ultimately you have to take action. Being prepared means being ready to take that first step when the time comes. Remember this: courage has no greater ally than preparation, and fear has no greater enemy.

Reflecting on It

Are you used to winging it? Do you try to fake it till you make it? Or is solid preparation part of your regular routine? If you continually let your teammates down, you're probably playing in the wrong position or not spending enough time and energy preparing to meet challenges.

Bringing It Home

To improve your preparedness . . .

- ***Become a process thinker.*** Henry Ford observed, "Before everything else, getting ready is the secret of success." Getting ready requires thinking ahead so that you recognize now what you will need later. Create a system or list for yourself that will help you mentally walk through any process ahead of time, breaking tasks down into steps. Then determine what preparation will be required to complete each step.

> **Before everything else, getting ready is the secret of success.**
>
> **—HENRY FORD**

- ***Do more research.*** People in just about every profession utilize some kind of research to improve themselves. Become more familiar with the research tools of your trade and make yourself an expert at using them.

- ***Learn from your mistakes.*** The greatest preparation tool can often be a person's own experience. Think about the mistakes you recently made while completing a project or executing a challenge. Write them down, study them, and determine what you can do differently the next time you face a similar situation.

Daily Take-Away

In 1946, entertainer Ray Charles heard that Lucky Millinder's band was coming to town. Charles managed to arrange an audition, and that excited him. If he could get on with Millinder, he would be in the big time.

When his opportunity came, the young musician played the piano and sang his heart out. Being blind, Charles couldn't see Millinder's reaction to his performance, so when he was finished, Charles waited patiently for his response. Finally he heard the band leader say, "Ain't good enough, kid." Charles went back to his room and cried.

"That was the best thing that ever happened to me," Charles later recalled. "After I got over feeling sorry for myself, I went back and started practicing so nobody would ever say that to me again." No one has. As the saying goes, "You can claim to be surprised once; after that, you're unprepared." Charles's preparation has paid him dividends for more than half a century, and he has played with some of the most talented musicians in the world. Preparation may not guarantee a win, but it sure puts you in position for one.

You can claim to be surprised once; after that, you're unprepared.

13

Relational

If You Get Along, Others Will Go Along

Relationships help us to define who we are and what we can become. Most of us can trace our successes to pivotal relationships.

—Donald O. Clifton and Paula Nelson

Anyone who loves his opinions more than his teammates will advance his opinions but set back his team.

—John C. Maxwell

Connecting with People Wherever They Are

In the early 1960s, Michael Deaver was a young man with a political bent looking for a leader he could believe in and follow. The person he found was an actor-turned-politician named Ronald Reagan. In 1966, Reagan was elected governor of California, an office he would hold for two terms, from 1967 to 1975. During that tenure, Deaver became Reagan's deputy chief of staff, an office he also held when Reagan became the nation's fortieth president.

Deaver admired many things about the man he worked with for thirty years. Ronald Reagan had a lot of remarkable qualities: his convictions and love of country, his understanding of himself, his skill as a communicator, and his honesty. Deaver said, "I would go so far as to say that he was actually incapable of dishonesty."[1] But perhaps what was most impressive about Ronald Reagan was his ability to relate to people.

Deaver commented, "Ronald Reagan was one of the shyest men I'd ever met."[2] Yet the president was able to connect with anyone, whether a head of state, a blue-collar worker, or a feisty member of the press. When asked about why Reagan had such rapport with the press corps, Deaver remarked, "Well, Reagan basically liked people, whether they were part of the press corps or whether they were just ordinary people. That comes through. While many of the press wouldn't agree with Reagan's policy, they genuinely liked him as a person."[3]

Part of Reagan's skill came from his natural charisma and glib verbal aptitude developed in Hollywood. But even greater was his ability to relate to people, something he honed while traveling the country for a decade as the spokesman for General Electric.

It's said that Reagan could make anyone feel like his best friend, even someone he'd never met before. But more important, he connected with the people closest to him. He truly cared about the people on his team. "The chief of staff, or the gardener, or a secretary would all be treated the same, as far as he was concerned," remembered Deaver. "They were all important."[4]

Deaver related a story that tells much about the connection the two men experienced. In 1975, Reagan gave a speech to a group of conservation-minded hunters in San Francisco, and the organization gave him a small bronze lion as a gift. At the time, Deaver admired it and told Governor Reagan how beautiful he thought it was.

Ten years later, Deaver prepared to bring his service to President Reagan to an end after having written his letter of resignation. Reagan asked Deaver to come to the Oval Office the next morning. As the deputy chief of staff entered the room, the president stood in front of his desk to greet him.

"Mike," he said, "all night I've been trying to think of something to give you that would be a reminder of all the great times we had together." Then Reagan turned around and picked up something from his desk. "You kinda liked this little thing, as I recall," the president said, his eyes moist. And he handed the bronze lion to Deaver, who was totally overcome. He couldn't believe that Reagan had remembered that about him all those years. That lion has held a place of honor in Deaver's home ever since.

Fleshing It Out

Teams want people who are relational. Everyone liked being around Ronald Reagan because he loved people and connected with them. He understood that relationships are the glue that holds team members together—the more solid the relationships, the more cohesive the team.

Relationships are the glue that holds team members together.

Here is how you know whether you have built solid relationships with other team members. Look for the following five characteristics in your team relationships:

1. Respect

When it comes to relationships, everything begins with respect, with the desire to place value on other people. Human relations author Les Giblin said, "You can't make the other fellow feel important in your presence if you secretly feel that he is a nobody."

The funny thing about respect is that you should show it to others, even before they have done anything to warrant it, simply because they are human beings. But at the same time, you should always expect to have to earn it from others. And the place you earn it the quickest is on difficult ground.

2. Shared Experiences

> **You can't make the other fellow feel important in your presence if you secretly feel that he is a nobody.**
>
> —LES GIBLIN

Respect can lay the foundation for a good relationship, but it alone is not enough. You can't be relational with someone you don't know. It requires shared experiences among teammates over time. And that's not always easy to achieve. For example, when Brian Billick, coach of the 2001 Super Bowl Champion Baltimore Ravens, was asked about a team's chances for repeating a championship season, he commented that it would be very difficult. Why? Because 25 to 30 percent of the team changes every year. Newer players don't have the shared experiences with the team that are needed to succeed.

3. Trust

When you respect people and you spend enough time with them to develop shared experiences, you are in a position to develop trust. As I mentioned in regard to the Law of Solid Ground in *The 21 Irrefutable Laws of Leadership*, trust is the foundation of leadership. It is also essential to all good relationships. Scottish poet George Macdonald observed, "To be trusted is a greater compliment than to be loved." Without trust, you cannot sustain any kind of relationship.

4. Reciprocity

One-sided personal relationships don't last. If one person is always the giver and the other is always the receiver, then the relationship will eventually disintegrate. The same is true of relationships on a team. For a team to build and improve relationally, there has to be give-and-take so that everyone benefits as well as gives.

> **To be trusted is a greater compliment than to be loved.**
>
> —GEORGE MACDONALD

5. Mutual Enjoyment

When relationships grow and start to get solid, the people involved begin to enjoy each other. Just being together can turn even unpleasant tasks into positive experiences. For example, I'm not the kind of person who enjoys running errands or waiting in lines. But sometimes when my wife, Margaret, is planning to run out and tackle her to-do list, I'll go with her simply because I want to be with her. She is my number one teammate, and there's no one in the world I'd rather spend time with. We both benefit. She completes her list, and I'm able to spend time with her.

Reflecting on It

How are you doing when it comes to being relational? Do you spend a lot of time and energy building solid relationships with your teammates, or are you so focused on results that you tend to overlook (or overrun) others as you work to achieve team goals? If the latter is true of you, think about the wise words of George Kienzle and Edward Dare in *Climbing the Executive Ladder:* "Few things will pay you bigger dividends than the time and trouble you take to understand people. Almost nothing will add more to your stature as an executive and a person. Nothing will give you greater satisfaction or bring you more happiness." Becoming a highly relational person brings individual and team success.

Bringing It Home

To better relate to your teammates . . .

- ***Focus on others instead of yourself.*** The first and most important step in becoming good at relationship building is to start focusing on others rather than yourself. Think about your teammates. How can you add value to them? What can you give them without benefiting yourself? Don't forget that the team is not about you.

- ***Ask the right questions.*** If you aren't sure about your teammates' hopes, desires, and goals, then you need to ask them. What makes them smile? What makes them cry? What do they dream about? Get to know who they really are by asking the right questions and listening carefully to their answers.

- *Share common experiences.* You will never develop common ground with your teammates unless you share common experiences. Time together while working as a team is essential, but so is spending time together outside that setting. Work to make connections with teammates. Do things socially. Spend time with the families. Find ways to share your lives.

You will never develop common ground with your teammates unless you share common experiences.

- *Make others feel special.* One of Ronald Reagan's strengths was making everyone on his team feel special. You can do the same thing by giving others your full attention when you're with them, giving them genuine compliments, and recognizing others in front of their peers and family members. People will connect with you when you show them you care about them.

DAILY TAKE-AWAY

Frederick William I, the king of Prussia, was not known for having a pleasant disposition. His passion was his army, and he spent much of his life building it. He had little love for anything or anyone else, including his family. He was often cruel to his son, who eventually succeeded him on the throne as Frederick II, the Great.

The elder Frederick often walked the streets of Berlin alone, and his subjects fled from him. It is said that on one of his walks, a citizen saw him coming and attempted to escape the monarch by ducking into a doorway.

"You," called out the king, "where are you going?"

"Into the house, Your Majesty," replied the nervous man.

"Is it your house?" Frederick pressed.

"No, Your Majesty."

"Then why are you entering it?" the king demanded.

"Well, Your Majesty," the man admitted, worried that he might be thought a burglar, "to avoid you."

"Why?" demanded Frederick.

"Because I fear you, Your Majesty."

Frederick raised his walking stick threateningly at the man and shouted, "You're not supposed to fear me, you scum. You're supposed to love me!"

Teammates seldom go along with someone they can't get along with.

14

Self-Improving

To Improve the Team, Improve Yourself

Perfection is what you're striving for,
but perfection is an impossibility.
However, *striving* for perfection is not an impossibility.
Do the best you can under the conditions that exist.
That is what counts.

—John Wooden

Learn as if you were to live forever;
live as if you were to die tomorrow.

—Anonymous

From Trees to Telephones

If you own or have quick access to a cellular phone, put down this book for a moment and grab the phone. As I am writing this, I've also stopped to get mine. Now look at the manufacturer's name imprinted on the phone. If you're like me—and like nearly one-third of the people in the world who own a cellular phone—then the name on your phone is Nokia.

Knowing that Nokia is the largest producer of cellular phones in the world, you'd probably never guess how the company got its start. It was formed more than a century ago by Fredrik Idestam. In the mid-1860s, as the lumber industry in Finland started to boom, Idestam built a small pulp mill on the Emäkoski River and began making paper. (So I guess you could say that the company has always been in the communication business.)

The first couple of years, the company struggled, especially in Finland. But when Idestam won a bronze medal for his groundwood pulp at the 1867 Paris World's Fair, Nokia's sales took off, and it soon became firmly established. It excelled not only in its native Finland but explored and established markets in Denmark, Russia, Germany, England, and France. Before long the company had added two more paper facilities.

In the late 1890s, Nokia sought to diversify. The company built a water-driven electric power station near its first mill, and it attracted the Finnish Rubber Works as a customer. After a few years, the rubber company moved its operation to be near Nokia's power plant. Eventually the two companies became partners.

The companies did well during and after World War I. In 1922, they bought a controlling share of the Finnish Cable Works and did even better. They continued selling their existing products from the forestry and rubber industries, but the company's growth for the next forty years was driven by the sales that came from the cable works—items such as power cables, telephone lines, and telephone equipment. By the 1960s, the company had four major business segments: forestry, rubber, cable, and electronics.

During the next two decades, Nokia experienced some difficult times. The one-hundred-year-old company had become a huge conglomerate, and it was losing money. Executives at Nokia knew that the company needed to better its situation.

The solution to Nokia's problems came from an unlikely source. In 1990, a young executive who had been with Nokia for five years was asked to take over the unprofitable mobile-phone division of the company and turn it around. His name was Jorma Ollila, and his background was in finance and banking. He was so successful at the task that he was made the president and CEO of Nokia in 1992.

Ollila's next challenge was to turn the rest of the company around. His strategy was twofold. First, he determined to focus the organization's efforts in the area of greatest potential: communications technology. That meant divesting the company of its other interests, including what had initially launched the company: rubber and paper. Second, Ollila wanted to replace trees with people, meaning that the company recognized that its value lay in human resources, not natural resources. That was especially important for a company whose business is technology. "The key challenge of technology companies today is how we renew ourselves," observes Ollila. "The technology cycles are shorter. We must build on our discontinuities and turn them into our favor."[1]

Ollila personally knows the value of renewing himself. He has earned three master's degrees—in political science, economics, and engineering. He has taken the personal goal of self-improvement and made it a corporate one. The "Nokia Way" is grounded in four objectives: customer satisfaction, respect for the individual, achievement, and continuous learning.

"Continuous learning entitles everybody at Nokia to develop themselves and find ways to improve their performance," says Ollila. "And what's true for the individual is just as true for the company as a whole."[2] To improve a team—even a team of more than sixty thousand people like Nokia—improve the individuals on that team.

That strategy has been right on. Ollila has turned a money-losing conglomerate into a $20 billion global telecommunications enterprise. And Nokia continues to be an innovative leader in its field. Since 1992, the company has introduced fifteen significant market firsts. If your cell phone has a faceplate with a special color or team logo, or it allows you to set it to ring using a fun tune, or it possesses a short-message chat function, you can thank Nokia. The company brought all those ideas to market. And it is still breaking new ground. Why? Because the people on the Nokia team are self-improving, and as long as they keep getting better, so does Nokia.

"I don't think there is any other company which is better placed than we are to tackle the next paradigm," asserts Ollila. "This is an organization where, if you want to prove yourself, if you want to develop yourself, and grow yourself, we will give you the platform."[3]

Fleshing It Out

We live in a society with destination disease. Too many people want to do enough to "arrive," and then they want to retire. My friend Kevin Myers says it this way: "Everyone is looking for a quick fix, but what they really need is fitness. People who look for fixes stop doing what's right when pressure is relieved. People who pursue fitness do what they should no matter what the circumstances are." That's what the people at Nokia do. They go after professional fitness, and as a result they are self-improving.

People who are constantly improving themselves make three processes an ongoing cycle in their lives:

> **It's not what you are going to do, but it's what you are doing now that counts.**
>
> —NAPOLEON HILL

1. Preparation

Napoleon Hill remarked, "It's not what you are going to do, but it's what you are doing now that counts." Self-improving team players think about how they can improve today—not some far-off time in the future. When they get up in the morning, they ask themselves, *What are my potential learning moments today?* Then they try to seize those moments. At the end of the day, they ask themselves, *What have I learned today that I need to learn more about tomorrow?* That positions them to continue growing on an ongoing basis. When individuals are intentional about learning something every day, they become better prepared to handle whatever challenges they meet.

2. Contemplation

I recently came across the following statement: "If you study the lives of the truly great individuals who have influenced the world, you will find that in virtually every case, they spent considerable amounts of time alone—contemplating, meditating, listening."[4] Time alone is essential to self-improvement. It allows you to gain perspective on your failures and successes so that you can learn from them. It gives you the time and space to sharpen your personal or organizational vision. And it enables you to plan how you can improve in the future. If you want to keep getting better, carve out some time to get away and slow down.

> **A time comes when you need to stop waiting for the man you want to become and start being the man you want to be.**
>
> —BRUCE SPRINGSTEEN

3. Application

Musician Bruce Springsteen offered this insight: "A time comes when you need to stop waiting for the man you want to become and start being the man you want to be." In other words, you need to apply what you've learned. That is sometimes difficult because it requires change. Most people change only when one of three things happens: they hurt enough that they have to, they learn enough that they want to, or they receive enough that they are able to. Your goal is to keep learning so that you want to change for the better every day.

Reflecting on It

There is nothing noble in being superior to someone else; progress is becoming superior to your previous self. Is that something you strive for? Do you try to become better than you were last year, last month, or last week? Do you look for a way to learn something every day? Or are you hoping to arrive someplace where you no longer have to improve? (Perhaps you believe you've reached that place already.) You can't wait for circumstances or some other person to improve you. You must take responsibility for that yourself. George Knox was right: "When you cease to be better, you cease to be good."

Bringing It Home

To become self-improving . . .

- ***Become highly teachable.*** Pride is a serious enemy of self-improvement. For a month, put yourself in learning roles whenever possible. Instead of talking in meetings when people ask for advice, listen. Tackle a new discipline, even if it makes you feel inadequate. And ask questions anytime you don't understand something. Adopt the attitude of a learner, not an expert.

Pride is a serious enemy of self-improvement.

- ***Plan your progress.*** Determine how you will learn on two levels. First, pick an area where you want to improve. Plan what books you will read, conferences you will attend, and experts you will interview for the next six months. Second, find learning moments wherever you can every day so that not a day passes without your experiencing improvement of some kind.
- ***Value self-improvement above self-promotion.*** King Solomon of ancient Israel said, "Let instruction and knowledge mean more to you than silver or the finest gold. Wisdom is worth much more than precious jewels or anything else you desire."[5] Make your next career move based on how it will improve you personally rather than how it will enhance you financially.

Daily Take-Away

In *The 17 Indisputable Laws of Teamwork,* I wrote about pioneer aviator Charles Lindbergh, mentioning that even his solo flight across the Atlantic Ocean was really a team effort, since he had the backing of nine businessmen from St. Louis and the help of the Ryan Aeronautical Company, which built his plane. But that doesn't take away from his personal effort. For more than thirty-three hours, he flew alone and covered an incredible 3,600 miles.

That's not the kind of task a person just goes out and does. He has to work up to it. How did Lindbergh do that? A story from his friend Frank Samuels gives insight into the process. In the 1920s, Lindbergh used to fly mail out of St. Louis. Occasionally he would go out to San Diego to check on the progress of his plane, the *Spirit of St. Louis*, which was being built there. Samuels sometimes went along with him, and the two men would stay overnight in a small hotel there. One night Samuels woke up shortly after midnight and noticed that Lindbergh was sitting by the window looking at the stars. It had been a long day, so Samuels asked, "Why are you sitting there at this hour?"

"Just practicing," answered Lindbergh.

"Practicing what?" asked Samuels.

"Staying awake all night."

When he could have been enjoying a well-deserved rest, Lindbergh was putting forth the effort to improve himself. It's an investment that paid off for him—and it can do the same thing for you.

15

Selfless

There Is No *I* in Team

Life should not be estimated exclusively by the standard of dollars and cents. I am not disposed to complain that I have planted and others have gathered the fruits. A man has cause for regret only when he sows and no one reaps.

—Charles Goodyear

When you stop giving and offering something to the rest of the world, it's time to turn out the lights.

—George Burns

The Real Man Behind the Bridge

When the situation is life or death, most people worry more about taking care of themselves than anyone else. Not Philip Toosey. As an officer in the British army during World War II, he had plenty of opportunities to preserve himself, but instead, he always looked out for his team.

In 1927, when the twenty-three-year-old Toosey joined the Territorial Army, a kind of army reserve, he did so because he wanted to do more than merely develop in his career in banking and commodities trading. He had other interests. He was a good athlete and enjoyed playing rugby, but many of his friends were applying for service, so he decided to join as well. He was commissioned as a second lieutenant in an artillery unit where he excelled as a leader and battery commander. In time, he moved up in rank to major.

In 1939, he and his unit were called up to active service as war broke out in Europe. He briefly served in France, was evacuated at Dunkirk, and was subsequently shipped overseas to serve in the Pacific. There he was part of the failed attempt to defend the Malay Peninsula and then finally Singapore from Japanese aggression. By that time, Toosey had been promoted to lieutenant colonel and was in command of the 135th regiment of the army's Eighteenth Division. And although he and his men fought well during the campaign, British forces were repeatedly required to retreat until they fell all the way back to Singapore.

It was there that Toosey displayed the first of many characteristically unselfish acts. When the British realized that surrender was inevitable, Toosey was ordered to leave his men and ship out so that his expertise as an artillery officer might be preserved and used elsewhere. He refused. He later recalled,

> I could not really believe my ears but being a Territorial [rather than a regular army officer] I refused. I got a tremendous rocket and was told to do as I was told. However I was able to say that as a Territorial all orders were a subject of discussion. I pointed out that as a Gunner I had read the Manual of Artillery Training, Volume II, which says quite clearly that in any withdrawal the Commanding Officer leaves last.[1]

He knew the negative effect that abandoning his men would have on their morale, so he stayed with them. Accordingly, when the Allied forces in Singapore surrendered to the Japanese in February 1942, Toosey became a prisoner of war along with his men.

Toosey soon found himself in a POW camp at Tamarkan near a major river called the Kwae Yai. As senior officer, he was in command of the Allied prisoners. His assignment from the Japanese was to build first wooden and then steel and concrete bridges across the river. (The novel and movie *The Bridge on the River Kwai* were based on the events that occurred at this camp, but Toosey was nothing like the character Colonel Nicholson in the movie.)

When first confronted by the orders of his Japanese captors, Toosey wanted to refuse. After all, the Hague Convention of 1907, which the Japanese had ratified, prohibited prisoners of war from being forced to do work that would help their enemies in the war effort. But Toosey also knew that refusal would bring reprisals, which he described as "immediate, physical, and severe."[2] Biographer Peter N. Davies observed, "Toosey, in fact, quickly realized that he had no real option in this matter and accepted that the vital question was not whether the troops were to perform the tasks laid down, but how many were to die in the process."[3]

Toosey chose to ask the prisoners to cooperate with their captors, but he risked his life daily by standing up for his men and arguing for increased rations, regular working hours, and a day off each week. His diligence paid off, though as he later said, "If you took responsibility as I did, it increased your suffering very considerably."[4] He suffered regular beatings and was made to stand at attention in the sun for twelve hours, yet his persistent badgering caused the Japanese to improve conditions for the Allied prisoners. And remarkably during the ten months that work was being done on the bridges, only nine prisoners died.

Later, as the commander of a POW camp hospital, Toosey was known to do everything possible to aid the welfare of his men, including hiking to meet in person every single group of prisoners who arrived at the camp, even in the dead of night. He worked with the black market in order to obtain medicine, food, and other supplies, even though detection would have meant certain death. He insisted on taking responsibility for an illegal radio if it were to be found by Japanese guards. And when the war ended, Toosey's first concern was to find the men of his regiment. He traveled three hundred miles to be reunited with them and determine that they were safe.

After he returned to England, Toosey took three weeks of vacation and then went back to his prewar work with the merchant bank Barings. He never sought glory for his endeavors during the war, nor did he complain about the movie *The Bridge on the River Kwai*, though he evidently hated it. The only thing in his later life related to the war was his work for the Far East Prisoners of War Federation to help other former POWs. It was another act characteristic of a man who always put his team ahead of himself.

Fleshing It Out

Poet W. H. Auden quipped, "We're here on earth to do good for others. What the others are here for, I don't know." No team succeeds unless its players put others on the team ahead of themselves. Being selfless isn't easy, but it is necessary.

As a team member, how do you cultivate an attitude of selflessness? Begin by doing the following:

1. Be Generous

St. Francis of Assisi stated, "All getting separates you from others; all giving unites to others." The heart of selflessness is

> **All getting separates you from others; all giving unites to others.**
>
> **—ST. FRANCIS OF ASSISI**

generosity. It not only helps to unite the team, but it also helps to advance the team. If team members are willing to give of themselves generously to the team, then it is being set up to succeed.

2. Avoid Internal Politics

One of the worst forms of selfishness can be seen in people who are playing politics on the team. That usually means posturing or positioning themselves for their own benefit, regardless of how it might damage relationships on the team. But good team players worry about the benefit of their teammates more than themselves. That kind of unselfishness helps teammates and benefits the giver. The remarkable scientist Albert Einstein observed, "A person first starts to live when he can live outside of himself."

3. Display Loyalty

If you show loyalty to the people on your team, they will return loyalty in kind. That was certainly the case for Colonel Toosey. Time and time again, he put himself on the line for his men, and as a result they worked hard, served him well, and completed whatever mission they had been given—even in the most difficult of circumstances. Loyalty fosters unity, and unity breeds team success.

> **Loyalty fosters unity, and unity breeds team success.**

4. Value Interdependence Over Independence

In America, we value independence highly because it is often accompanied by innovation, hard work, and a willingness to stand for what's right. But independence taken too far is a characteristic of selfishness, especially if it begins to harm or hinder others. Seneca asserted, "No man can live happily who regards himself alone, who turns everything to his own advantage. You must live for others if you wish to live for yourself."

Reflecting on It

If you want to be a contributing member of a successful team, you have to put others on the team ahead of yourself. How are you when it comes to taking a backseat to others? If someone else gets credit for work well done, does it bother you? If you get bumped from the "starting lineup" of your team, do you shout, pout, or tough it out? All of these things are characteristics of selfless players.

Bringing It Home

To become more selfless . . .

- ***Promote someone other than yourself.*** If you are in the habit of talking up your achievements and promoting yourself to others, determine to keep silent about yourself and praise others for two weeks. Find positive things to say about people's actions and qualities, especially to their superiors, family, and close friends.

- *Take a subordinate role.* Most people's natural tendency is to take the best place and to let others fend for themselves. All day today, practice the discipline of serving, letting others go first, or taking a subordinate role. Do it for a week and see how it affects your attitude.

- *Give secretly.* Writer John Bunyan maintained, "You have not lived today successfully unless you've done something for someone who can never repay you." If you give to others on your team without their knowing, they cannot repay you. Try it. Get in the habit of doing it and you may not be able to stop.

You have not lived today successfully unless you've done something for someone who can never repay you.

—JOHN BUNYAN

DAILY TAKE-AWAY

Every fall here in Atlanta, local fans start to get excited about Georgia Tech football. The Tech team is good today, but in the teens, it was an absolute powerhouse. Back in 1916, the Tech team played a tiny law school called Cumberland University, and Tech players were crushing them.

It's said that near the end of the game, Cumberland quarterback Ed Edwards fumbled the snap from center, and as the huge Tech players came barreling into the backfield, he screamed to his fellow backs, "Pick it up! Pick it up!"

The fullback, tired of being pulverized by an opponent, hollered back at the quarterback, "Pick it up yourself—you dropped it." Needless to say, Tech won the game. The final score was 222 to 0.

16

Solution Oriented

Make a Resolution to Find the Solution

Always listen to experts. They'll tell you what can't be done and why. Then do it.

—Robert Heinlein

Don't find fault; find a remedy.

—Henry Ford

His Answer to Tragedy

Few things in life are more tragic or disheartening than losing a child. John Walsh, the host of television's *America's Most Wanted,* understands that. In 1981, he and his wife, Reve, lost their six-year-old son, Adam, when the boy was abducted outside a Florida shopping mall and later found murdered. They were devastated.

People react many different ways to such a tragedy. Some parents become defensive and never trust people again. Others sink into depression. Many react in anger and seek revenge. At first, the Walshes were angry. They wanted the murderer found. But they also wanted to sue the department store from which Adam had been abducted. When he first disappeared, no one at the store would help them find their son, and they later discovered that a security guard who worked there had actually ordered six-year-old Adam out of the store. They were outraged.

But the Walshes soon dropped the suit. Instead of focusing on the past, John Walsh possessed a solution-oriented mind-set that looked to the future. He determined that he would try to do something about the problem of child abduction that was becoming increasingly common across the country. He began working to create a national computer system to aid in the search for missing children. He became an advocate for crime victims and lobbied for legislation. And in 1984, Walsh cofounded the National Center for Missing and Exploited Children (NCMEC), an organization that works to prevent child victimization, assists in crime prevention, and acts as a national clearinghouse for information on missing children.

One of the most important child-safety programs NCMEC has developed is called "Code Adam," which has been implemented in more than thirteen thousand stores across the nation. When a customer reports a missing child, a store-wide alert is announced, and a description of the child is given to designated employees, who then search for the child and monitor the exits. If the child isn't found in ten minutes, employees contact the police.[1]

Over the years, the NCMEC team, which now consists of 125 employees, has assisted in more than 73,000 cases involving children, and the group has helped parents to recover more than 48,000 missing children. NCMEC's work has been instrumental in raising the recovery rate of missing children from 60 percent in the 1980s to 91 percent today.[2]

I don't think anyone would have faulted John Walsh if he had withdrawn from people after the death of his son. But because he was solution oriented, he overcame the difficulty of that event, and he has helped tens of thousands of people by bringing together a team to help children.

Fleshing It Out

Most people can see problems. That doesn't require any special ability or talent. As Alfred A. Montapert observed, "The majority see the obstacles; the few see the objectives; history records the successes of the latter, while oblivion is the reward of the former."

Someone who thinks in terms of solutions instead of just problems can be a difference maker. A team filled with people who possess that mind-set can really get things done.

Your personality type, upbringing, and personal history may affect how solution oriented you are naturally. However, *anyone* can become solution oriented. Consider these truths that all solution-seeking people recognize:

1. Problems Are a Matter of Perspective

No matter what anyone may tell you, your problems are not your problem. If you believe that something is a problem, then it is. However, if you believe that something is merely a temporary setback, an interim obstacle, or a solution in the making, then you don't have a problem (because you haven't created it).

Obstacles, setbacks, and failures are simply parts of life. You can't avoid them. But that doesn't mean you have to allow them to become problems. The best thing you can do is to meet them with a solution-oriented mind-set. It's just a matter of attitude.

2. All Problems Are Solvable

Some of the great problem solvers have been inventors. Charles Kettering explained, "When I was research head of General Motors and wanted a problem solved, I'd place a table outside the meeting room with a sign: 'Leave slide rules here.' If I didn't do that, I'd find someone reaching for his slide rule. Then he'd be on his feet saying, 'Boss, you can't do it.'" Kettering's approach paved the way for a career that included his holding more than

140 patents, founding Delco, and being inducted into the National Inventors Hall of Fame. He believed all problems were solvable, and he helped to cultivate that attitude in others. If you want to be solution oriented, then you must be willing to cultivate that attitude in yourself too.

3. Problems Either Stop Us or Stretch Us

Orison Swett Marden, founder of *Success* magazine, held that "obstacles will look large or small to you according to whether you are large or small." Problems either hurt you or help you. Depending on how you approach them, they'll stop you from succeeding or stretch you so that you not only overcome them, but also become a better person in the process. The choice is yours.

> **Obstacles will look large or small to you according to whether you are large or small.**
>
> —ORISON SWETT MARDEN

Reflecting on It

How do you look at life? Do you see a solution in every challenge or a problem in every circumstance? Do your teammates come to you because you have ideas about how to overcome obstacles, or do they avoid telling you about difficulties because you make things *more* difficult? Who you are determines what you see. When it comes to approaching problems, you really have only four choices: flee them, fight them, forget them, or face them. Which do you usually do?

Bringing It Home

To make yourself a more solution-oriented team player . . .

- ***Refuse to give up.*** At the same moment that one person wants to say, "I give up," someone else facing the same situation is saying, "What a great opportunity!" Think about an impossible situation you and your teammates have all but given up overcoming. Now determine not to give up until you find a solution.

- ***Refocus your thinking.*** No problem can withstand the assault of sustained thinking. Set aside dedicated time with key teammates to work on the problem. Make sure it's prime think time, not leftover time when you're tired or distracted.

> **No problem can withstand the assault of sustained thinking.**

- ***Rethink your strategy.*** Nobel Prize–winning physicist Albert Einstein observed, "The significant problems we face cannot be solved at the same level of thinking we were at when we created them." Get out of the box of your typical thinking. Break a few rules. Brain-storm absurd ideas. Redefine the problem. Do whatever it takes to generate fresh ideas and approaches to the problem.

- ***Repeat the process.*** If at first you don't succeed in solving the problem, keep at it. If you *do* solve the problem, then repeat the process with another problem. Remember, your goal is to cultivate a solution-oriented attitude that you bring into play all the time.

DAILY TAKE-AWAY

In 1939, Soviet troops entered and annexed the Baltic states, including Latvia. The American vice-consul in the Latvian capital of Riga observed what was happening and was concerned that the Soviet soldiers would loot the supply station of the American Red Cross. He wired the U.S. State Department to request permission to fly the American flag over the Red Cross flag to protect the supplies, but the response from his superiors said, "No precedent exists for such action."

The vice-consul climbed the flagpole and secured the American flag to it. Then he sent a message back to the State Department: "As of this date, I have established precedent."

Solutions are usually in the eye of the beholder.

17

Tenacious

Never, Never, Never Quit

To see far is one thing; going there is another.

—Constantin Brancusi

To finish first, you must finish.

—Rick Mears

Another Fab Four?

In the summer of 2001, my wife, Margaret, and I went to England for ten days with our friends Dan and Patti Reiland, Tim and Pam Elmore, and Andy Steimer. We've been close to the Reilands and Elmores about twenty years, and we've done a lot of traveling together, so we were really looking forward to the trip. And though we haven't known Andy nearly as long, he's become a good friend—and he's been to England so many times that he was acting almost like our unofficial tour guide.

As we prepared for the trip, several of us had specific interests and historic sites we wanted to include. For instance, I wanted to visit all the places related to John Wesley, the renowned evangelist of the eighteenth century. For more than thirty years, I've studied Wesley, read all his writings, and collected his books. So we went to Epworth where he grew up, to Wesley's Chapel in London, and to many of the places where he preached. For Tim, we visited Cambridge and other sites related to apologist, professor, and author C. S. Lewis. Andy had only one must-see place on his list since he had been to England so many times: Winston Churchill's war rooms.

Three of us wanted to walk in the places where our heroes had walked, to get a glimpse of history and maybe understand the sense of destiny one of these great leaders or thinkers must have experienced. Then there was Dan. Sure, Dan enjoyed sharing our interests. He loves the subject of leadership, he's read C. S. Lewis's works, and he is ordained as a *Wesleyan* pastor. And he had a great time visiting our preferred sites. But the one place he absolutely *had* to see was the crosswalk where the Beatles had been photographed for the *Abbey Road* album. Dan wanted us to get our picture taken walking across the street, just as John, Ringo, Paul, and George had.

Now, I like the Beatles, and I thought it might be fun to visit the site. But to Dan, it was more than a big deal. It was essential. If we didn't make it to Abbey Road, then his trip just wouldn't have been complete. Because of that, every day as we set out from our London hotel on our itinerary, Dan would press us intently: "Now, guys, we're going to make it to Abbey Road, right?"

On the last day, we were scheduled to finally make our Abbey Road trek. Everyone except Margaret got up at six o'clock and piled into two cabs to make the trip across town to the street outside the recording studio where the Beatles recorded their last album. Dan was so excited that I thought he was going to bounce off the walls of the cab.

When we got there, we couldn't believe it. The street was closed! Big construction trucks were everywhere, and orange cones filled the crosswalk. It looked as if we had made the trip for nothing. Because we would be leaving London later that afternoon, we wouldn't get another opportunity for the picture. Dan would have to go home empty-handed.

We decided to get out of the cabs anyway, just to check out the situation. We figured there might be heavy construction occurring on the tiny street. However, we discovered that a huge crane, which was located about a half mile away, was scheduled to come down the street sometime in the afternoon, and that's why the road was closed. That gave me hope that we might succeed after all. None of us wanted Dan to be disappointed, and I always love a challenge. So we went to work.

We struck up a conversation with the workmen who had closed the road. At first, they had no idea what we wanted. Then when they understood why we were there, they folded their arms, stood as solid as the Rock of Gibraltar, and told us it couldn't be done. It was their turf, it was their job, and they were not going to move. However, I did have to laugh when we talked to one worker who was about twenty-five years old. When we said that Dan wanted a photo like the one on the Beatles' album, and that the original had been taken on that very spot, the young man said, "Really? It was here?"

We talked to the guys some more. We joked. We offered to take them all out to lunch. And we told them how far we had come and how much the whole thing meant to Dan. "You can be Dan's heroes," I explained. After a while, I could see they were beginning to soften. Finally a big, burly guy with a thick accent said, "Oh, let's help the Yanks out. What could it hurt?"

The next thing we knew, it was like they were working for us. They began clearing cones and moving trucks. They even let Patti, Dan's wife, climb up onto one of the trucks to take the picture so that it would be from the same angle as the Beatles' original shot. Quickly we lined up: first Tim, then Andy, then me (with my shoes off like Paul McCartney), and finally Dan. It was a moment we won't soon forget, and the photo sits on my desk today to remind me of it.

Fleshing It Out

On that summer day in London, did we succeed because of extraordinary talent? No. Was it because of our timing? Certainly not, since our timing got us into trouble in the first place. Was it power or sheer numbers? No, there were only six of us. We succeeded because we were tenacious. Our desire to get that picture was so strong that success for our little team was almost inevitable.

It's appropriate to finish the discussion of the essential qualities of a team player by talking about tenacity because tenacity is crucial to success. Even people who lack talent and fail to cultivate some of the other vital qualities of a team player have a chance to contribute to the team and help it succeed if they possess a tenacious spirit.

Being tenacious means . . .

1. *Giving All That You Have, Not More Than You Have*

Some people who lack tenacity do so because they mistakenly believe that being tenacious demands from them more than they have to offer. As a result, they don't push themselves. However, being tenacious requires that you give 100 percent—not more, but certainly not less. If you give your all, you afford yourself every opportunity possible for success.

Look at the case of General George Washington. During the entire course of the Revolutionary War, he won only three battles. But he gave all he had, and when he did win, it counted. British general Cornwallis, who surrendered to Washington at Yorktown to end the war, said to the American commander, "Sir, I salute you not only as a great leader of men, but as an indomitable Christian gentleman who wouldn't give up."

2. Working with Determination, Not Waiting on Destiny

Tenacious people don't rely on luck, fate, or destiny for their success. And when conditions become difficult, they keep working. They know that trying times are no time to quit trying. And that's what makes the difference. For the thousands of people who give up, there is always someone like Thomas Edison, who remarked, "I start where the last man left off."

. . . trying times are no time to quit trying.

3. Quitting When the Job Is Done, Not When You're Tired

Robert Strauss stated that "success is a little like wrestling a gorilla. You don't quit when you're tired—you quit when the gorilla is tired." If you want your team to succeed, you have to keep pushing beyond what you *think* you can do and find out what you're really capable of. It's not the first but the last step in the relay race, the last shot in the basketball game, the last yard with the football into the end zone that makes the difference, for that is where the game is won. Motivational author Napoleon Hill summed it up: "Every successful person finds that great success lies just beyond the point when they're convinced their idea is not going to work." Tenacity hangs on until the job is finished.

Reflecting on It

How tenacious are you? When others have given up, do you keep hanging on? If it's the bottom of the ninth inning and there are two outs, have you already lost the game mentally, or are you ready to rally the team to victory? If the team hasn't found a solution to a problem, are you willing to keep plugging away to the very end in order to succeed? If you sometimes give up before the rest of the team does, you may need a strong dose of tenacity.

Bringing It Home

A. L. Williams says, "You beat 50 percent of the people in America by working hard. You beat another 40 percent by being a person of honesty and integrity and standing for something. The last 10 percent is a dogfight in the free enterprise system." To improve your tenacity . . .

> **You beat 50 percent of the people in America by working hard. You beat another 40 percent by being a person of honesty and integrity and standing for something. The last 10 percent is a dogfight in the free enterprise system.**
>
> **—A. L. WILLIAMS**

- ***Work harder and/or smarter.*** If you tend to be a clock-watcher who never works beyond quitting time no matter what, then you need to change your habits. Put in an additional sixty to ninety minutes of work every day by arriving at work thirty to forty-five minutes early and staying an equal amount of time after your normal hours. If you are someone who already puts in an inordinate number of hours, then spend more time planning to make your working hours more efficient.

- ***Stand for something.*** To succeed, you must act with absolute integrity. However, if you can add to that the power of purpose, you will possess an additional edge. Write on an index card how your day-to-day work relates to your overall purpose. Then review that card daily to keep your emotional fires burning.

- ***Make your work a game.*** Nothing feeds tenacity like our natural competitive nature. Try to harness that by making your work a game. Find others in your organization who have similar goals and create a friendly competition with them to motivate you and them.

Daily Take-Away

People said it couldn't be done—building a railroad from sea level on the coast of the Pacific Ocean into the Andes Mountains, the second-highest mountain range on earth after the Himalayans. Yet that is what Ernest Malinowski, a Polish-born engineer, wanted to do. In 1859, he proposed building a rail line from Callao on the coast of Peru into the country's interior—to an elevation of more than fifteen thousand feet. If he was successful, it would be the highest railway in the world.

The Andes are treacherous mountains. The altitude makes work difficult, but add to that frigid conditions, glaciers, and the potential for volcanic activity. And the mountains climb from sea level to tens of thousands of feet in a very short distance. Climbing to high altitude in the jagged mountains would require switchbacks, zigzags, and numerous bridges and tunnels.

But Malinowski and his work crews succeeded. Jans S. Plachta states, "There are approximately 100 tunnels and bridges, some of which are major engineering feats. It is difficult to visualize how this task could have been accomplished with relatively primitive construction equipment, high altitudes, and mountainous terrain as obstacles." The railroad still stands today as a testament to the tenacity of the men who built it. No matter what happened to them during the process, Malinowski and his team never, never, never quit.

CONCLUSION

I hope you have enjoyed *The 17 Essential Qualities of a Team Player* and have benefited from doing the exercises in the "Bringing It Home" section of each chapter. The assignments are designed to help you get a handle on each quality and start the process of continuous personal growth in your life.

I want to encourage you to keep growing as a team member. Review this book periodically to measure how you're developing. For more resources visit www.maximumimpact.com or contact my organization at:

Maximum Impact
P.O. Box 7700
Atlanta, GA 30357-0700
877.225.3311

Keep growing, keep building your team, and never forget, one is too small a number to achieve greatness! Good luck on your journey.

Notes

Chapter 1

1. "Perfect Pitch," *Context*, April-May 2001 <www.contextmag.com>.
2. Ibid.
3. Ibid.

Chapter 2

1. Rob Davis, "The Real Escape—The Tunnels: 'Tom,' 'Dick' and 'Harry,'" 16 July 2001 <www.historyinfilm.com/escape>.
2. "The Great Escape," 2 July 2001 <www.historyinfilm.com/escape>.
3. Proverbs 27:17.

Chapter 3

1. "Jonas Salk, M.D.: Interview, May 16, 1991," 2 July 2001 <www.achievement.org>.
2. Ibid.
3. Frederic Flach, *Choices: Coping Creatively with Personnel Change* (Philadelphia, PA: J. B. Lippincott), 1977.

Chapter 4

1. "An Interview with Legendary Coach Herman Boone," 5 January 2001 <www.blackathlete.com>.
2. "Herman Boone, Coach," 29 May 2001 <www.71originaltitans.com>.

3. "Interview with Herman Boone and Bill Yoast," *Remember the Titans* (DVD), Walt Disney Pictures, 2000.

CHAPTER 5

1. Minét Taylor, "Minétspeak," *Wood & Steel*, summer 2001, 3, 5.
2. "From the Beginning," 18 July 2001 <www.taylorguitars.com/history>.
3. "Heartline," December 1993.

CHAPTER 6

1. "Biography," Christopher Reeve home page, 30 July 2001 <www.fortunecity.com>.
2. "New Hopes, New Dreams," *Time*, 26 August 1996 <www.time.com>.
3. Ibid.
4. Ibid.
5. Ibid.

CHAPTER 7

1. Christopher Hosford, "30 Years of Progress for the Ultimate 10-Event Man," *Life Extension* magazine, September 1998, 11 June 2001 <www.lef.org/magazine>.
2. Gordon MacDonald, *The Life God Blesses* (Nashville: Thomas Nelson, 1994).

CHAPTER 8

1. "Edwardian Conquest," 14 June 2001 <www.britannia.com/wales>.

CHAPTER 9

1. "History," 7 August 2001 <www.harley-davidson.com>.
2. Rich Teerlink and Lee Ozley, *More Than a Motorcycle: The Leadership Journey at Harley-Davidson* (Boston: Harvard Business School Press, 2000), 8.

3. "Motorcycle and Customer Data," 7 August 2001 <www.investor.harley-davidson.com>.
4. John C. Maxwell, *Failing Forward: Turning Mistakes into Stepping Stones for Success* (Nashville: Thomas Nelson, 2000), 40–42.
5. "Smell the Roses: Parade Floats in the Making," 28 December 1997 <www.channel2000.com>.

CHAPTER 10

1. Pleasant T. Rowland, "Welcome to Pleasant Company," 26 June 2001 <www.americangirl.com>.
2. "Company Profile," 26 June 2001 <www.americangirl.com>.

CHAPTER 11

1. "Who Was Molly Pitcher?" Garry Stone, 3 August 2001 <uweb.superlink.net/monmouth/molly>.

CHAPTER 12

1. John Perry, *Sgt. York: His Life, Legend, and Legacy* (Nashville: Broadman and Holman, 1997), 97.
2. "Alvin Cullum York," 2 July 2001 <volweb.utk.edu.schools/york>.
3. Gladys Williams, "Alvin C. York," 2 July 2001 <volweb.utk.edu/schools>.
4. Perry, *Sgt. York*, 32.
5. Williams, "Alvin C. York."

CHAPTER 13

1. Michael K. Deaver, "The Ronald Reagan I Knew," *Parade*, 22 April 2001, 12.
2. Ibid., 10.
3. "Thirty Years with Reagan: A Chat with Author, Former Reagan Aide Michael Deaver," 20 April 2001 <www.abcnews.com>.
4. Ibid.

CHAPTER 14

1. Joyce Routson, "Nokia CEO Talks About Next-Generation Mobile Technology," 6 March 2001 <www.gsb.stanford.edu/news>.
2. "The Nokia Way," 29 June 2001 <www.nokia.com>.
3. John S. McClenahen, "CEO of the Year," 30 November 2000 <www.industryweek.com>.
4. Anonymous.
5. Proverbs 8:10–11, author's paraphrase.

CHAPTER 15

1. Peter N. Davies, *The Man Behind the Bridge: Colonel Toosey and the River Kwai* (London: Athlone Press, 1991), 56.
2. Ibid., 107–8.
3. Ibid., 99.
4. "A Tale of Two Rivers," *Electronic Recorder*, March 1998 <www.livgrad.co.uk>.

CHAPTER 16

1. "Code Adam," 29 May 2001 <www.ncmec.org>.
2. "Our Story," 29 May 2001 <www.ncmec.org>.

About the Author

John C. Maxwell is an internationally recognized leadership expert, speaker, and author who has sold over 12 million books. His organizations have trained more than one million leaders worldwide. Dr. Maxwell is the founder of Injoy Stewardship Services and EQUIP. Every year he speaks to Fortune 500 companies, international government leaders, and organizations as diverse as the United States Military Academy at West Point and the National Football League. A *New York Times*, *Wall Street Journal*, and *Business Week* best-selling author, Maxwell was one of 25 authors named to Amazon.com's 10th Anniversary Hall of Fame. Two of his books, *The 21 Irrefutable Laws of Leadership* and *Developing the Leader Within You*, have each sold over a million copies.

THE Difference MAKER

MAKING YOUR ATTITUDE
YOUR GREATEST ASSET

JOHN C. MAXWELL

NELSON BUSINESS
A Division of Thomas Nelson Publishers
Since 1798

www.thomasnelson.com

Published in Nashville, Tennessee, by Thomas Nelson, Inc.

Nelson Books titles may be purchased in bulk for educational, business, fundraising, or sales promotional use. For information, please e-mail SpecialMarkets@ThomasNelson.com.

Published in association with Yates & Yates, LLP, Attorneys and Counselors, Orange, California.

Library of Congress Cataloging-in-Publication Data

Maxwell, John C., 1947-

The difference maker : making your attitude your greatest asset / John C. Maxwell.

p. cm.

Includes bibliographical references.

ISBN 0-7852-6098-6 (hardcover)

ISBN 0-7852-8869-4 (I.E.)

1. Attitude (Psychology) 2. Success. I. Title.

BF327.M39 2006

650.1—dc22

2006006618

Printed in the United States of America

06 07 08 09 QW 6 5 4 3 2 1

ACKNOWLEDGMENTS

This book is dedicated to my assistants:
Barbara Brumagin (1981–1992)
&
Linda Eggers (1995–present)

Thanks for your
servant-hearts, people skills,
competence, loyalty, and friendship.
Both of you have been
Difference Makers in my life!

Thank you to
Charlie Wetzel, my writer;
Stephanie Wetzel, who proofs and
edits the manuscript; and
Linda Eggers, my assistant

CONTENTS

ONE

Where Did You Get Your Attitude?

Have you ever heard someone say, "Attitude is everything"? It seems to be a favorite line of some motivational speakers. According to them, a great attitude is all you need to be successful. Unfortunately, it's simply not true.

I do a lot of professional speaking. Each year I communicate at live events to 250,000 people. And I do believe in motivating others. However, I don't think of myself as a motivational speaker. I call myself a motivational *teacher*. That may seem like a technicality, but here's the difference: A motivational speaker makes you feel good, but the next day you're not sure why. A motivational *teacher* also makes you feel good, but the next day you possess something that will actually help you.

The promise that attitude is everything is hollow. In fact, if you believe that attitude is everything, it may actually hurt you more than help you. If attitude were everything, then the only thing that would separate me from a successful singing career would be the belief that I can do it. But trust me, there is another factor that stands in my way: talent. If you've watched the reality show *American Idol*, then you know what I mean. I am amazed at the number of terrible auditioners who respond to blunt criticism from the judges by saying things like, "I know I can sing. That's just your opinion." Truthfully, no attitude is strong enough to compensate for lack of skill.

So does a good attitude make any difference? Absolutely. Attitude is the difference maker! *Attitude isn't everything, but it is one thing that can make a difference in your life*. Businessman, philanthropist, and author W. Clement Stone stated, "There is little difference in people, but the little difference makes a big difference. The little difference is attitude. The big difference is whether it is positive or negative."

The goal of this book is not to *snow* you by saying that attitude is everything, but to *show* you that your attitude is the difference maker in your life. I desire to do that by helping you understand where your attitude comes from, what it *can* and *can't* do for you, and how you can make it an asset. I also want to give you insight into how to deal with the Big Five Attitude Obstacles everybody faces: discouragement, change, problems, fear, and failure. If you're like most people, you have to deal with at least one of those issues *every single day*! Let's take this journey together by first looking at some basics about attitude.

WHAT IS ATTITUDE?

What is an attitude, anyway? When you hear the word, what do you think about? I think of attitude as an inward feeling expressed by outward behavior. People always project on the outside what they feel on the inside. Some people try to mask their attitude, and they can fool others for a while. But that cover-up doesn't last long. Attitude always wiggles its way out.

My father loves to tell the story of a four-year-old boy who was finally put into time-out after battling his mother.

"Sit in that chair until the timer goes off," the mother said in frustration. The boy sat down, fearing greater punishment, but said, "Okay, Mommy. I'm sitting on the outside, but I'm standing up on the inside."

Your attitude colors every aspect of your life. It is like the mind's paintbrush. It can paint everything in bright, vibrant colors—creating a masterpiece. Or it can make everything dark and dreary. Attitude is so pervasive and important that I've come to think of it like this:

It is the vanguard of your true self.
Its root is inward but its fruit is outward.
It is your best friend or worst enemy.
It is more honest and consistent about you than your words.
It is your outward look based on your past experiences.
It is what draws people to you or repels them.
It is never content until it is expressed.
It is the librarian of your past.
It is the speaker of your present.
It is the prophet of your future.

There is not a single part of your current life that is not affected by your attitude. And your future will definitely be influenced by the attitude you carry with you from today forward.

Your attitude colors every aspect of your life. It is like the mind's paintbrush.

WHERE DID I GET MY ATTITUDE?

If your attitude is so important, then you may be asking yourself, *Where did I get it? Am I stuck with it my whole life—for better or worse?* First, let's look at the question of where your attitude comes from.

1. Personality—Who You Are

Two men were out fishing. When the fish stopped biting, they started to talk. One man praised his wife and extolled her many virtues, summing it up by saying, "You know, if all men were like me, they would all want to be married to my wife."

"And if they were like me," the other replied, "none of them would want to be!"

Everybody's different. Each person is born a unique

individual. We're all as different as our fingerprints. That's true even of siblings born of the same parents and brought up in the same household. Even twins who are genetically identical have distinct personalities.

Your personality type—your natural "wiring"—impacts your attitude. That's not to say that you're trapped by your personality, because you're not. But your attitude is certainly impacted by it.

2. ENVIRONMENT—WHAT'S AROUND YOU

The environment you were exposed to growing up definitely has an impact on your attitude. Did your parents go through a divorce? That may cause you to have a mistrustful attitude toward members of the opposite sex. Did someone close to you die? That may prompt you to have an attitude of emotional distancing from others. Did you grow up in a poor neighborhood? That may prompt you to have a tenacious attitude toward achievement. In contrast, it could make you want to give up more easily.

It may be hard to predict exactly *what* will happen to a person's attitude based on his or her early environment, but you can be certain that it made an impact of some kind. My wife and I adopted both of our children, and based on that experience, we believe that genetics is the strongest early predictor of attitude. But we also know for a fact that environment makes a difference.

3. The Expression of Others—What You Feel

Most people can remember the harsh words of a parent or teacher even years or decades after the fact. Some people carry the scars of such experiences their entire lives. In my book *Winning with People*, the Pain Principle states, "Hurting people hurt people and are easily hurt by them." Many times the hurts that cause people to overreact to others come as the result of negative words from others.

Likewise, positive words can have an impact on a person's attitude. Can you remember the positive words of a favorite teacher or other significant adult? A few words can change the way a person thinks of himself and can change the course of his life. Charlie Wetzel, my writer, remembers the words of his sister, Barbara Rensink, when he was eighteen. He had little direction in his life back then, and she told him that she thought he had a talent for cooking and how flavors go together. He had never considered that before. It sent him on a ten-year quest learning everything he could about food, cooking, and the restaurant business. And it led to his first career as a professional restaurant chef.

4. Self-Image—How You See Yourself

How you see yourself has a tremendous impact on your attitude. Poor self-image and poor attitudes often walk hand in hand. It's hard to see anything in the world as positive if you see yourself as negative.

Dwayne Dyer advises, "Examine the labels you apply to yourself. Every label is a boundary or limit you will not let yourself cross." If you are having trouble getting where you want to go, the problem may be inside you. If you don't change your inward feelings about yourself, you will be unable to change your outward actions toward others.

5. Exposure to Growth Opportunities—What You Experience

Enlightenment writer and philosopher Voltaire likened life to a game of cards. Players must accept the cards dealt to them. However, once they have those cards in hand, they alone choose how they will play them. They decide what risks and actions to take.

The growth opportunities people experience are not all equal. When I was growing up, my parents constantly exposed me to new experiences that would shape me. They sent me to Dale Carnegie's "How to Win Friends and Influence People" and other courses while I was in junior high and high school. My father occasionally took me out of school for a week so that I could travel with him as he performed his duties as a leader of our religious denomination. He took me to hear great evangelists and missionaries speak. My parents even paid me to read books that would shape my thinking. They did everything they could to cultivate an attitude open to personal growth. As an adult I have continued to embrace that attitude and to try to pass it along to my children and grandchildren.

Not everyone is as fortunate as I was. If you had an upbringing similar to mine, thank your parents. However, if you were rarely exposed to growth experiences or taken outside of your comfort zone, then you may have to work harder to cultivate a positive attitude toward positive personal growth.

6. Association with Peers—Who You Are With

All the time you hear about young people in trouble who are said to have been nice kids who ended up hanging with the wrong crowd. It's a fact that you start becoming like the people you spend a lot of time with. If a nice kid spends all of his time with people of low moral character, it's only a matter of time before he begins to display low moral character. Likewise, if someone with a good attitude spends all her time with individuals who display negative attitudes, guess what will happen to her? She'll begin to develop a negative attitude. She may think she can change them, but if she's outnumbered and gets no relief from their negativity, they are the ones who will be doing the influencing, not her.

7. Beliefs—What You Think

Many of the factors I've mentioned that have come together to shape your attitude were set in motion in your past. But do you know what forms and sustains your attitude most today? Your thoughts. As author and successful businessman Bob Conklin indicated in the following piece, thoughts make a huge impact on you:

> I can make you rise or fall. I can work for you or against you. I can make you a success or a failure.
>
> I control the way that you feel and the way that you act.
>
> I can make you laugh . . . work . . . love. I can make your heart sing with joy . . . excitement . . . elation.

Or I can make you wretched . . . dejected . . . morbid.

I can make you sick . . . listless.

I can be as a shackle . . . heavy . . . attached . . . burdensome.

Or I can be as the prism's hue . . . dancing . . . bright . . . fleeting . . . lost forever unless captured by pen or purpose.

I can be nurtured and grown to be great and beautiful . . . seen by the eyes of others through action in you.

I can never be removed . . . only replaced.

I am a THOUGHT.

Why not know me better?[1]

Every thought you have shapes your life. What you think about your neighbor is your attitude toward him. The way you think about your job is your attitude toward work. Your thoughts concerning your spouse, the people on the highway during rush hour, and the government create your attitude toward each of those subjects.

The sum of all your thoughts comprises your overall attitude.

8. CHOICES—WHAT YOU DO

Poet, critic, and dictionary writer Samuel Johnson observed, "He who has so little knowledge of human nature as to seek happiness by changing anything but his own disposition will waste his life in fruitless efforts and multiply the grief which he purposes to remove." Most people want to change the world to improve their lives, but the world they need to change first is the one inside themselves. That is a choice—one that some are not willing to make.

In a *Peanuts* cartoon strip by Charles Schulz, Lucy says to her little brother Linus, "Boy, do I feel crabby."

"Maybe I can help you," Linus responds, always willing to be of assistance. "Why don't you just take my place here in front of the TV while I go and fix you a nice snack? Sometimes we all need a little pampering to help us feel better."

Linus returns with a sandwich, chocolate chip cookies, and a glass of milk.

"Now," he asks, "is there anything else I can get you? Is there anything I haven't thought of?"

Lucy takes the tray, saying, "Yes, there's one thing you haven't thought of." And then she screams, "I don't wanna feel better!"

Early in life, you don't have many choices. You don't choose where and when you are born. You don't choose your parents. You don't choose your race, your personality type, or your genetic makeup. You don't choose your health. Everything you are and nearly everything you do is not up to you. You must live with the conditions you find yourself in. As Voltaire would say, you start with the cards you're dealt.

But the longer you live, the more your life is shaped by your choices. You decide what you will eat. (This is one of the most common ways small children begin to assert their independence.) You decide what toys to play with. You decide whether you will do your homework or watch TV. You choose which friends to spend time with. You choose whether to finish high school, whether you will go to college, who you will marry, what you will do for a living. The longer you live, the more choices you make—and the more responsible you are for how your life is turning out.

Represented visually, it looks like this:

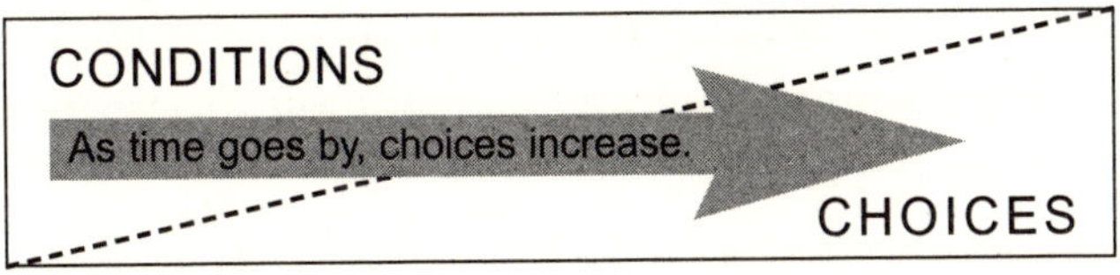

Obviously this graphic does not accurately represent every person's life. But in general, the longer we live, the less conditions dictate how we think and act, and the more our choices determine how we live. And one of those choices is our attitude.

I don't know what kind of circumstances you've had to face in your life. You may have had a really tough time. You may have faced extreme hardship or suffered terrible tragedies. However, your attitude is still your choice.

Perhaps the most remarkable story I've read in the face of horrible circumstances and personal tragedy is that of Viktor Frankl. Born in 1905, Frankl grew up in Vienna and showed an early interest in psychiatry. As a teenager, he corresponded with Sigmund Freud, and one paper he sent Freud so impressed him that the older man sent it to a professional journal, where it was later published.

Frankl became a successful medical doctor in Vienna at age twenty-five, but in 1942, four years after the Nazi invasion of Austria, he was rounded up along with other Austrian Jews and put in a concentration camp. While there, he experienced unspeakable horrors, and he lost his entire family: his pregnant wife, his parents, and his brother.

During the rest of World War II, Frankl was trapped in

concentration camps, including the notoriously brutal Auschwitz. Most of his fellow prisoners either were killed or gave up. Not Frankl. He not only maintained hope, but he helped others to find it. The key, he believed, was to find and hold on to meaning. Years later Frankl told Holcomb B. Noble in the *New York Times* that "the last of the human freedoms [is] to choose one's attitude in any given set of circumstances, to choose one's own way."[2]

Miraculously, Frankl survived his time in the concentration camps. And after the war, he was determined to use his experience to help others. He returned to school and earned a PhD. He developed Logotherapy, often called the "Third Viennese School of Psychotherapy." It is based on a person's will to find meaning and it is expressed, in part, by the attitude we take toward unavoidable suffering.[3]

Until he was eighty-five years old, Frankl taught in Vienna as a professor of neurology and psychiatry. He lectured at 209 universities on five continents. He received twenty-nine honorary doctorates and had more than 150 books published about him and his work in fifteen different languages. During the good years and the bad, his attitude was positive.

"Each man is questioned by life," Frankl once said,

"and he can only answer to life by answering for his own life; to life he can only respond by being responsible."

To change your life, you must make a choice to take responsibility for your attitude, and to do everything you can to make it work for you. Your attitude truly can become a difference maker. It's up to you.

TWO

What Your Attitude *Cannot* Do for You

I read an article in *USA Today* that pointed out issues that university professors and employers are having to address with many young men and women who are now entering adult life. These individuals were products of the self-esteem movement of the 1980s. Many have great attitudes about themselves. However, their high opinions of themselves and their abilities are often disconnected from reality.

Deborah Stipek, dean of education at Stanford University, says, "I often get students in graduate school doing doctorates who made straight A's all their lives, and the first time they get tough feedback, the kind you need to develop skills, [they react badly]. I have a box of Kleenex in my office because they haven't dealt with it before."[1]

Roy Baumeister, a psychology professor at Florida State University, has been studying self-esteem for more than thirty years. He thought it was going to be a key to helping people become successful, but it hasn't. "There is not nearly as much benefit as we hoped," he says. "It's been one of the biggest disappointments of my career."[2]

You cannot disconnect attitude from reality and expect success. I have to admit, I haven't always embraced this view. (A certain sign that we have grown intellectually is that over time our thoughts change.) If you had asked me about the importance of attitude twenty years ago, I'd have said, "Your attitude is the only difference between success and failure. You're only a dream away from success!" Back then, I thought that if you can believe it, you can achieve it, and all you had to do was make it happen.

You cannot disconnect attitude from reality and expect success.

Today I recognize that, while those kinds of statements can motivate you, if you believe that a dream alone can bring success, you will be disappointed. Those statements simply aren't true. I know many people who have a great attitude yet aren't successful. Don't you? When all other things are equal, attitude can be the difference maker, but it alone does not make the difference.

For example, let's say two people apply for the same job. One has great skills and natural talent, ten years of experience, and an okay attitude. The other has a *great* attitude and no experience whatsoever. Who gets the job? Probably the one with the greater skills and experience. Why? Because a great attitude will not make up the gap. However, what if the two job candidates are roughly equal in skill and experience? In that case, the one with the better attitude wins hands down.

WHERE ATTITUDE *CANNOT* MAKE THE DIFFERENCE

Attitude is the difference maker. It is a plus; it gives an edge. It is an additive, but it is not a substitute. Here are some things that your attitude *cannot* make up for:

1. YOUR ATTITUDE CANNOT SUBSTITUTE FOR COMPETENCE

Some people seem to confuse confidence, which is a function of attitude, with competence, which is a function of ability. Or they believe that one can be substituted for the other. But the two are distinctly different. If you *think* you can do something, that's *confidence*. If you *can* do it, that's *competence*. Both are needed for success. A great attitude can help you *personally*. It can make you more content, more pleasant to be around, more likely to tackle difficult problems. But it cannot help you *positionally*. If you don't have competence in your favor, then you're going to be in trouble.

If you think you can do something, that's confidence. If you can do it, that's competence. Both are needed for success.

To see the importance of competence, think about how much we desire it in others. When we hire employees, we certainly desire high competence. We want to find the best people we can. Management expert Peter Drucker once told my friend, Bill Hybels, that the team members he wanted to hire probably were neither unhappy nor unemployed. "If you find someone whose qualifications look good, but he or she is unhappy or unemployed, be very cautious," Drucker said. "The kind of people you're looking for are probably making huge contributions and setting records somewhere. They are probably happy and much loved by the people they work with. Go after that type. Go after proven competence."[3]

In leading and developing people for over thirty-five years, I have discovered that incompetence is a great distraction to people in an organization. When someone on the team is incapable of performing at the appropriate level—even someone with a great attitude—then the leader and the other team members become distracted from their main purpose. They end up spending a lot of time trying to get the incompetent person "on track."

In my book, *The 17 Indisputable Laws of Teamwork*, the Law of the Chain says, "The strength of the team is impacted by the weakest link." That is always true for any team. That problem often cannot be solved merely by adopting a positive attitude. However, it can change if the weak person gets on the ball quickly and develops competence.

2. Your Attitude Cannot Substitute for Experience

A fox, a wolf, and a bear went hunting, and each got a deer. A discussion followed about how they should divide the spoils.

The bear asked the wolf how he thought it should be done. The wolf answered, "That's simple. Each of us should get one deer." As soon as the wolf was done speaking, the bear ate him.

Then the bear asked how the fox proposed to divvy up the spoils. The fox offered his deer to the bear and suggested that the bear take the wolf's as well.

"Where did you get such wisdom?" asked the bear.

"From the wolf," replied the fox.

There are times when there is no adequate substitute for experience. The problem with experience, however, is that you rarely have it until after you need it.

The problem with experience is that you rarely have it until after you need it.

Experience is often a hard teacher because the test is given first and the lessons come afterward. That's probably why the old quote says, "When a person with experience meets a person with money, the person with experience will get the money, and the person with the money will get the experience!"

Back when I thought that attitude was everything, I tried to hire people with the best attitudes and figured I could get them up to speed in their skills. Now that I am older and more experienced, I realize that I had things backward. Now I hire primarily for skill and experience. Here's why: When it comes to talent and skill, a person can grow only a limited amount. On a scale from one to ten, most people can improve in a skill area only about two points. So, for example, if you are naturally a "6" as a leader, you may be able to grow to an "8" if you work at it. However, if you are a "2," you can work as hard as you want and you will never reach even average. The old saying of coaches is true: You can't get out what God didn't put in.

Attitude, however, is a different matter. There is no growth ceiling. Even a person with a "2" attitude can grow to become a "10." So even someone whose attitude isn't the best can turn that around.

On the day that I decided as a leader to hire only people with successful track records to key positions in my organization, my professional life changed. The entire team became more productive, and my organization began going to another level. That's not to say that I began hiring people with bad attitudes; I didn't. It wasn't an either/or decision. It was a both/and decision. Competence, experience, and positive attitude are a winning combination.

3. Your Attitude Cannot Change the Facts

One of the interesting discoveries researchers have made about attitude is that it has an impact on people's health. A study performed by the University of Texas found that elderly people who had a positive attitude remained more physically hardy than those who were pessimistic.[4] That's really good news. But here's the bad news: No matter how good your attitude, it will not stop you from aging. That is just the way it is.

There are certain things in life that are simply facts, and your attitude will not change them. If you're an adult, your height is whatever it is. If you want to play center in the NBA and you're only 5 feet 4 inches tall, forget about it. The most positive attitude in the world isn't going to change that. Problems can be addressed and solved. Facts you just need to learn to live with. I love what poet Maya Angelou says about this, "If you don't like something, change it. If you can't change it, change your attitude. Don't complain."

4. Your Attitude Cannot Substitute for Personal Growth

Ernest Campbell, a former faculty member of the Union Theological Seminary in New York, told the story of a woman who bought a parrot at a local pet store because she was lonely. She took the bird home, but after a couple of days, she returned to the store to complain. "That parrot hasn't said a word yet!"

"Does it have a mirror?" the pet store owner asked. "Parrots like to be able to look at themselves in the mirror." So the lady bought a mirror and returned home.

The next day, she was back at the store because the bird still hadn't made a peep.

"What about a ladder?" the store owner asked. "Parrots enjoy walking up and down a ladder." So she bought a ladder and returned home.

She was back at the store the next day. Still the parrot hadn't said a thing.

"Does the parrot have a swing?" the owner asked. "Birds enjoy relaxing on a swing." She bought a swing and went home again.

The next day she returned to the store to tell the pet store owner that the bird had died.

"I'm terribly sorry to hear that," said the store owner. "Did the bird ever say anything before it died?"

"Yes," answered the lady. "It said, 'Don't they sell any food down there?'"

The lesson of the story, Campbell said, was that we buy mirrors by which to primp, ladders by which we try to climb higher, and swings upon which we seek pleasure, but we neglect food for our souls.

Musician Bruce Springsteen says, "A time comes when you need to stop waiting for the man you want to become and start being the man you want to be."[5] If you possess a good attitude, you have developed competence, and you have gained experience, what will keep you moving forward? Growth. Nothing can substitute for continual learning.

You need to feed your mind and soul to become the person you desire to be.

5. Your Attitude Will Not Stay Good Automatically

I grew up in small-town rural Ohio, and there were plenty of farms nearby. I once heard a farmer say that

the hardest thing about cows is that they never stay milked. A similar thing can be said about a good attitude. The hardest thing about having a good attitude is that it doesn't stay that way on its own.

If you're like most people, just getting to work in the morning is a test of your attitude. I live in the Atlanta area, which is notorious for its bad traffic. The latest report I read stated that we had the fourth worst traffic in the nation behind Los Angeles, San Francisco, and Washington, D.C. Not only that, but on any given day, the person in the vehicle next to you is likely to give you the "you're number one" signal, if you know what I mean. So every time I get in my car, I remind myself, *Today I am going to have a great attitude!*

That doesn't mean I always succeed. I have to remain sensitive to my personal attitude indicators. If I notice myself getting impatient—which is by far my greatest attitude challenge—I try to remind myself to have a good attitude. If I hear myself making cynical remarks, I check my attitude. If I find myself wanting to throw in the towel and stop developing people because they're not catching on quickly enough, I make an attitude correction. And my fail-safe attitude indicator is Margaret, my wife. If it's starting to get out of line, she tells me!

In my book *Today Matters*, one of the concepts I write about is that most people overrate decision making, and they underrate decision managing. It's pretty easy to say to yourself, *From now on, I'm going to have a great attitude*. It's much harder to actually follow through with it. That's why I believe one of the best things you can do for yourself is make the daily *management* of your attitude one of your objectives.

Believing that attitude is everything is really all-or-nothing thinking, and that's a problem. If you make attitude everything, then you are likely to end up with nothing. You cannot expect attitude to fix everything. Attitude is what it is: the difference maker.

There's a story of a young TV journalist that illustrates the limitations of a positive attitude. At age twenty-six, this young man was given an opportunity to anchor a network's evening newscast. He went head-to-head with Walter Cronkite, the most trusted news reporter of the time. The young man was sharp, he had grown up in the home of a newsman, he been a national-level news anchor in Canada prior to getting the job, and he had a good attitude. But it wasn't enough. In 1968, after three years, he stepped down from the job.

"I had the good sense to quit," he later said. But he

did not quit the news profession. What he needed was more experience and more skill. He became a foreign correspondent. For a decade, he took assignments that sent him to hot spots around the world. He went to Vietnam. He reported from the Middle East during the Yom Kippur War and the Lebanese civil war. He was at the Munich Olympics, where Palestinian terrorists murdered Israeli athletes.

In 1978, he returned to the anchor desk. This time he was a seasoned reporter. He was competent, he was experienced, and he had grown into the job. If you haven't already guessed, that reporter was Peter Jennings. When he worked the anchor desk the first time around, he had been called a "glamourcaster" or "anchorboy."[6] By the time he died in 2005, he was one of the most respected and watched reporters on television, having received the Edward R. Murrow Lifetime Achievement Award from Washington State University (2004), the Sol Taishoff Award for Excellence in Broadcast Journalism from the National Press Foundation (2000), fourteen National Emmy Awards, two George Foster Peabody Awards, several Overseas Press Club Awards, Harvard University's Goldsmith Career Award for Excellence in Journalism, the Radio and Television News Directors Paul White

Award (award chosen by the news directors of all three major networks), and the Order of Canada (2005).[7]

If attitude had been enough, then Jennings would have succeeded as ABC's anchor the first time around. Attitude by itself isn't enough. On the other hand, if he had not believed in himself and possessed an attitude of perseverance, he would not have succeeded either.

There are some things that attitude can do for you and others that it can't. To learn more about what it *can* do, turn the page, because that is the subject of the next chapter.

THREE

What Your Attitude *Can* Do for You

What usually separates the best from the rest? Have you ever thought about that? What separates the gold medalist from the silver medalist in the Olympics? What separates the successful entrepreneur from the one who doesn't make it? What makes it possible for one person to thrive after a debilitating accident while another gives up and dies? It's attitude.

Sure, every now and then there are people like Mozart or Lance Armstrong—those whose gifts are so extraordinary that they can achieve things the rest of us can only dream of. (But even they are assisted by the possession of extraordinary attitudes.) Most people at the top of their professions are comparable when it comes to talent. Gold and silver medals are usually separated by hundredths of seconds. Professional golfers win tournaments by a single stroke. As Denis Waitley said in *The Winner's Edge*, "The winner's edge is not in a gifted birth, a high IQ, or in talent. The winner's edge is all in the attitude, not aptitude. Attitude is the criterion for success. But you can't buy an attitude for a million dollars. Attitudes are not for sale."[1]

The greatest difference my difference maker can make is within me, not others.

For years I have tried to live by the following statement: I cannot always choose what happens to me, but I can always choose what happens in me. Some things in life are beyond my control. Some things are within it. My attitude in the areas beyond my control *can* be the difference maker. My attitude in the areas that I do control *will* be the difference maker. In other words, the greatest difference my difference maker can make is within me, not others. That is why your attitude is your greatest asset or liability. It makes you or breaks you. It lifts you up or brings you down. A positive mental attitude will not let you do *everything*. But it can help you do *anything* better than you would if your attitude were negative.

WHAT ATTITUDE CAN DO FOR YOU

A positive attitude is an asset every day in nearly every way. It not only helps with little issues, but it also provides a positive framework from which a person can approach all of life. Here's what I mean:

1. YOUR ATTITUDE MAKES A DIFFERENCE IN YOUR APPROACH TO LIFE

As we neared the end of the twentieth century, much was written about the men and women who survived the Depression and fought World War II, the people Tom Brokaw called "the greatest generation." I recall reading a story about a woman of that generation who followed her husband during the war to a U.S. Army camp in the desert of southern California. The man had advised against it, thinking that she would be more comfortable back East with her family, but the young bride didn't want to be separated from her new husband.

The only living accommodation they could find was a run-down shack near a Native American village. The place was very basic. During the day, temperatures often reached 115 degrees. The wind, which blew constantly, felt like air from a furnace. And the dust made everything miserable.

The young woman found the days to be long and boring. Her only neighbors were Native Americans with whom she could find little in common. When her husband was sent into the desert for two weeks of maneuvers, she broke down. The living conditions and loneliness were too much for her. She wrote her mother to say that she wanted to come home.

A short time later, she received a reply from home. One of the things her mother told her was this:

Two men looked through prison bars;
One saw mud, the other saw stars.

As the young woman read the lines over and over, at first she felt ashamed. Then her resolve grew. She truly wanted to stay with her husband, so she made a decision. She would look for the stars.

The next day, she worked to make friends with her

neighbors. As she got to know them, she also asked them to teach her about their weaving and pottery. At first they were reluctant, but as they saw that her interest in them and their work was genuine, they became more open. The more the woman learned about the Native American culture and history, the more she wanted to know. Her perspective started changing. Even the desert began to look different to her. She began to appreciate its quiet beauty, its tough but beautiful plants, even the rocks and fossilized seashells she found as she explored it. She even began to write about her experiences there.

What had changed? Not the desert. Not the people who lived there. She had changed. Her attitude had transformed—and as a result, so did her outlook.

The happiest people in life don't necessarily *have* the best of everything. They just try to *make* the best of everything. They're like the person in a remote village going to a well every day to get water who says, "Every time I come to this well, I come away with my bucket full!" instead of, "I can't believe I have to keep coming back to this well to fill up my bucket!"

A person's attitude has a profound influence on his approach to life. Ask a coach before a big game whether his attitude and that of his players will make a difference in the outcome of the game. Ask a surgeon if the patient's attitude matters when she's trying to save that life in an emergency room. Ask a teacher if students' attitudes have an impact before they take a test.

One of the things I've learned is that life often gives you whatever you expect from it. If you expect bad things, those are what you get. If you expect good things, you often receive them. I don't know why it works that way, but it does. If you don't believe me, try it out. Give yourself thirty days in which you expect the best of everything: the best parking place, the best table in the restaurant, the best interaction with clients, the best treatment from service people. You'll be surprised by what you encounter, especially if you give your very best to others in every situation as well.

2. Your Attitude Makes a Difference in Your Relationships with People

In August of 2005, I had the privilege to speak at the Willow Creek Leadership Summit. One of the people I met there was Colleen Barrett, president and corporate secretary for Southwest Airlines, who was also a speaker for the event. I was eager to talk to her because while other airlines have lost money and struggled to survive during the last several years, Southwest has succeeded and made a profit.

Colleen and I talked leadership. One of the things that she said the company was most proud of was their reputation for great customer service. When I asked her how they accomplished it, she told me that the company didn't rely on a lot of rules. There were, of course, FAA regulations that they complied with, and they had rules requiring that flight attendants always be on time for their assignments because their staffing is lean. But the company's emphasis is on creating the right kind of attitude among employees. Southwest's workers are empowered to evaluate situations and make decisions. And their focus is on people skills and the golden rule. Even when employees make mistakes, as long as they are attempting to see things from the customer's point of view and trying to give good service, they are supported.

To be successful, a person needs to be able to work well with others. That's why Theodore Roosevelt said, "The most important single ingredient in the formula for success is knowing how to get along with people."

Many factors come into play when it comes to skills working with people, but what makes or breaks that ability is a person's attitude. I recently wrote a book called *Winning with People* in which I describe twenty-five people principles that anyone can use to become better at building relationships and working with others. Many of those principles are attitude-based. Here are some examples:

- *The Lens Principle: Who we are determines how we see others*. Our perception of others depends more on our attitude than it does their characteristics. If we are positive, we see them as positive.
- *The Pain Principle: Hurting people hurt people and are easily hurt by them*. Our negative experiences and emotional baggage color our perception of others' actions. Normal interactions can cause us pain even when another person did nothing to inflict pain.
- *The Elevator Principle: We can lift people up or take them down in our relationships*. People possess a mind-set of either lifting or limiting others.
- *The Learning Principle: Each person we meet has the potential to teach us something*. Some people possess a teachable attitude, and they assume that they can learn something from everyone they meet.

> Others look down on many people and assume that they have nothing to offer.

There are other attitude-based principles in the book, but you get the idea. When it comes to dealing with people, attitude makes a difference. If your track record of dealing with people isn't as good as you would like it to be, maybe you need to look at your attitude. While it's true that some people just seem to have a naturally winning way with others, even someone with limited natural people skills can learn to win with others if he decides to have a positive attitude toward people.

3. Your Attitude Makes a Difference in How You Face Challenges

It's said that when U.S. Marine Chesty Puller found himself surrounded by eight enemy divisions during the Korean War, his response was, "All right, they are on our left. They are on our right. They're in front of us. They're behind us—they can't get away from us this time!"

In life, obstacles, challenges, problems, and failures are inevitable. How are you going to handle them? Will you give up? Will you allow circumstances to make you miserable? Or are you going to try to make the best of things? Which path you choose depends on your attitude.

I once heard a lecturer say that no society has ever developed tough men during times of peace. The old adage is true: What doesn't kill you makes you stronger. Think back to the times in your life when you have grown the most. I'm willing to bet that you grew as the result of overcoming difficulties. The better your attitude, the more likely you will be to overcome difficulties, grow, and move forward.

You can see this pattern in the lives of great men and women:

Demosthenes, called the greatest orator of ancient Greece, possessed a speech impediment. Legend has it he overcame it by reciting verses with pebbles in his mouth and speaking over the roar of the waves at the seashore.

Martin Luther, father of the Reformation, made use of the time he was confined in the castle of Wartburg to translate the New Testament into German.

Composer *Ludwig van Beethoven* wrote his greatest symphonic masterpieces after he had become deaf.

John Bunyan wrote *Pilgrim's Progress* while in prison. *Daniel Defoe* also wrote while in prison, producing *Robinson Crusoe*.

Abraham Lincoln is considered by many to be the best of the United States' presidents, yet he probably would not have stood out as a great leader had he not led the country through the Civil War. Often difficult circumstances seem to be instrumental in the creation of great leaders and thinkers. But that is the case only when their attitudes are right.

I've been told that in the Chinese language two words are often combined to create another word with a very different meaning. For example, when the symbol for the word meaning *man* is combined with the symbol for the word meaning *woman*, the resulting word means *good*.

Possessing a positive attitude can have a similar effect. When a problem comes into contact with someone who has a positive attitude, the result is often something wonderful. Out of the turmoil that problems cause can emerge great statesmen, scientists, authors, or businesspeople. Every challenge has an opportunity. And every opportunity has a challenge. A person's attitude determines how she handles those.

4. Your Attitude Is the Difference Maker

When is attitude most important? When does it make the greatest difference? It's not during a sporting event or when business gets tough. It's when life itself is on the line. And in those instances, it truly is the difference maker.

When I was a pastor, I spent much time with people dealing with tragedies. I've visited with a lot of patients before surgery, and the ones who did the best afterward and recovered the most quickly were the people with the best attitudes. I've visited many nursing homes. The elderly people who thrive are the ones who are still positive about themselves and their situation. I heard from a nursing home official that the new patients who feel like they were forced into nursing homes and had no other options tended to give up and die sooner than those who saw it as just another phase of life to be met with positively.

Many people have written about the power of a positive attitude on health and fitness. Many medical personnel say they have seen a positive correlation between people's attitudes and their ability to recover from illnesses such as cancer. Dr. Ernest H. Rosenbaum and Isadora R. Rosenbaum say that these observations have led to new studies on attitude:

> Researchers are now experimenting with methods of actively enlisting the mind in the body's combat with

> cancer. . . Some doctors and psychologists now believe that the proper attitude may even have a direct effect on cell function and consequently may be used to arrest, if not cure, cancer. This new field of scientific study, called psychoneuroimmunology, focuses on the effect that mental and emotional activity has on physical well-being, indicating that patients can play a much larger role in their recovery.[2]

Seeing a connection between people's thoughts and feelings and their health is nothing new. Rosenbaum points out, "We have known for over 2,000 years—from the writings of Plato and Galen—that there is a direct correlation between the mind, the body and one's health."[3] Poet John Milton wrote,

> The mind is its own place, and it itself
> Can make a heav'n of hell, a hell of heav'n.[4]

Your attitude has a profound influence on how you see the world—and thus on the way you live out your life.

Attitude is important. It is so important that it truly is the difference maker. It isn't everything, but it is one thing that can make a difference in your life. If you want to maximize your attitude and learn how to make it your greatest asset, then turn the page, because that is the subject of the next chapter.

FOUR

How to Make Your Attitude Your Greatest Asset

Former Yankee and Hall of Fame baseball player Yogi Berra has often been quoted as saying, "Life is like baseball; it's 95 percent mental, and the other half is physical." The former catcher and manager's math may not be perfect, but he does understand the power that thinking has on a person's ability to succeed. How many jobs do people lose every day because of attitude issues? How many times are others passed over for promotion because of the way they approach their job and other people? How many marriages fall apart? It would be impossible to calculate.

No one should ever lose a job, miss a promotion, or destroy a marriage because of a poor attitude. Why?

Because a person's attitude is not set; it is a choice. Pastor, professor, and author Chuck Swindoll says,

> Attitude, to me, is more important than education, than money, than circumstances, than failures, than successes, than what other people think or say or do. It is more important than appearance, giftedness, or skill. It will make or break a company . . . a church . . . a home. The remarkable thing is we have a choice every day regarding the attitude we embrace for that day. We cannot change our past . . . we cannot change the fact that people act in a certain way. We cannot change the inevitable. The only thing we can do is play on the one string we have, and that is our attitude. . . . I am convinced that life is 10 percent what happens to me and 90 percent how I react to it. And so it is with you. . . . [W]e are in charge of our attitudes.[1]

HOW TO CHOOSE THE RIGHT TRACK

1. Take Responsibility for Your Attitude

Singer Roberta Flack recalls, "My mother had only gone as far as the tenth grade, and my father had a third-grade education, but they both were very literate. They spoke well, and their values were high. They drummed into our heads that the situation you live in doesn't have to live in you." Our attitudes don't come from our circumstances or personal history. Attitude does not come from outside ourselves. It comes from within.

The first rule of winning is don't beat yourself. If your attitude isn't as good as it could be, and you fail to take personal responsibility for it, then you are beating yourself. However, if you look in the mirror and can with honesty say, "The attitude I possess is my responsibility and no one else's," then you're on your way.

2. Evaluate Your Present Attitude

To improve your attitude, you need to assess where you're starting from. This may take some time. And depending on how self-aware you are, it may even be difficult. The key is to try to look at yourself objectively, to separate yourself from your attitude. Your goal isn't to condemn yourself. It's to see yourself clearly so that you can make positive changes to the way you think. Here's how to proceed:

Identify problem feelings about yourself. Many times our feelings come into play long before we become consciously aware of them intellectually. So let's start with feelings. When do you feel most negative about yourself? Write down your answers.

Identify problem feelings related to others. Attitude issues often relate to other people. What causes you the greatest problems when dealing with others? Once again, write down your answers.

Identify problem thinking. We are the sum of our thoughts. And we cannot for any length of time behave in a way that is inconsistent with our thinking. So the question you must answer is this: What negative thoughts consistently control your mind? Write down your answers.

If you simply read through those questions without actually taking time to think through and write down your answers, then I want to encourage you to do so now. Why? Because you will not be able to change your attitude for the better unless you know what is currently impacting it for the worse. When professional loggers are floating logs down a river and they discover a logjam, they climb a large tree near the river so that they can look over the problem and find the cause. What they're looking for is the key log that is creating the problem. Once they remove that, the river takes care of the rest. An inexperienced person could spend hours, days, even weeks moving around logs without results. Your attitude may be similar. You don't necessarily need to change *all* of your thinking—just the few items that are keeping a positive attitude from flowing in you.

3. Develop the Desire to Change

The desire to change is the key to growth in all areas of life. Ironically, most people desire improvement, yet at the same time they resist change. The problem is that you cannot get one without having the other. Change is possible, but only if you want it badly enough. As Fred Smith observed, "You are the way you are because that's the way you want to be. If you really wanted to be any different, you would be in the process of changing right now."

Comedian Jerry Lewis is reported to have said that the best wedding gift he received was a film of the entire wedding ceremony. Why was that his favorite gift? He said it was because when things got really bad in the marriage, he would go into a room by himself, close the door, run the film backwards, and walk out a free man!

Of course, change is never that easy. It takes lots of time, tremendous amounts of energy, perseverance, and—of course—desire. That's not a decision you make once and forget about. You need to cultivate that desire every day. It's said that when Earl Weaver, one-time manager of major league baseball's Baltimore Orioles, was unhappy with a call by an umpire, he used to charge out of the dugout and shout at him, "Are you gonna get any better, or is *this* it?" If you want to change your attitude, you need to ask yourself a similar question: Are you going to keep working and trying to get better, or is this as good as it gets?

4. Change Your Attitude by Changing Your Thoughts

Norman Vincent Peale, author of *Power of the Plus Factor*, wrote that he once came across a tattoo studio in the twisted streets of Kowloon in Hong Kong. In the window were drawings of the hundreds of choices of tattoos available from the artist who worked there. One in particular really struck him. It said, "Born to lose."

Peale was appalled that anyone might actually ask to have that permanently written on his skin. He went inside and asked the Chinese artist, "Does anyone really have that terrible phrase 'Born to lose' tattooed on his body?"

"Yes, sometimes," the artist answered.

"But, I just can't believe anyone in his right mind would do that."

The artist tapped his forehead, and in broken English said, "Before tattoo on body, tattoo on mind."[2]

The human mind has a tremendous amount of power in our lives. That which holds our attention determines our actions. Because of that, where we are today is the result of the dominating thoughts in our minds. And the way we think determines what our attitudes are. But as I've already said, the good news is that you and I can change that. You can control your thoughts, and because of that, you can control your attitude.

Let's do an experiment that will show you what I mean. First, take a moment to think about the place where you live. No problem. You decided to think about it, and you did it. Okay, now I want you to think of something else. Imagine for a moment that the place where you live has burned to the ground, and everything in it is gone. What kind of emotional response did you have? Maybe you were sad because many irreplaceable things would have been lost in a fire. Maybe you were happy because your current living situation is terrible and a fresh start would do you good. The point is that your thinking prompts your emotion. That's key, and here's why:

Major premise: We can control our thoughts.
Minor premise: Our feelings come from our thoughts.
Therefore: We can control our feelings by changing the way we think.

Why is that important? Because your attitude is your emotional approach to life. It's the framework through which you see events, other people, even yourself. That's why I believe the saying, "You are not what you think you are, but what you think . . . you are."

Sales trainer Brian Azar says, "Sales are not made or unmade inside the prospect's office. They are made or unmade inside you." In sales, if your attitude is positive and you believe you can help the prospect with your product or service, then the most difficult work is already done. It all depends on your thinking. The same thing works in other professions too.

You are not what you think you are,
but what you think . . . you are.

Once while flipping through a copy of ESPN's magazine, I saw an Adidas ad that arrested my attention. Here's what it said:

> Impossible is just a big word thrown around by small men who find it easier to live in the world they've been given than to explore the power they have to change it. Impossible is not a fact. It's an opinion. Impossible is not a declaration. It's a dare. Impossible is potential. Impossible is temporary. Impossible is nothing.[3]

Most of the great work in this world was done by men and women who didn't believe that what they were doing was impossible. Talent is certainly beneficial, but only the right attitude can release it to reach its potential.

5. Develop Good Habits

An annoyed middle-aged woman approached the clerk at her local bookstore. "Every time I come in here to buy a best seller, you're sold out," she criticized. "Why can't you people learn to stock your store more efficiently?"

"I'm so sorry," apologized the clerk. "What is the title of the book you want to purchase?"

"It's called *How to Remain Young and Beautiful*," the woman responded.

"Okay," replied the clerk. "I'll place an order for *How to Remain Young and Beautiful*, and I'll mark the order 'URGENT.'"

Much of what we do every day comes from habitual behaviors. Over the course of time, we have developed a way of approaching life. We treat people a particular way, as the lady in the bookstore did. If we desire to get different results out of life, then it's not enough to change only our thinking. We also need to change our habits. Why? Because if we don't we will revert back to our old thinking. In fact, some people recommend changing behavior first. Psychiatrist William Glasser says, "If you want to change attitudes, start with a change in behavior. In other words, begin to act the part, as well as you can, of the person you would rather be, the person you most want to become. Gradually, the old, fearful person will fade away."

I don't know which has to come first—the thinking or the habits. It's like the chicken or egg question. But I do know this: they are connected. Here's how I think it works:

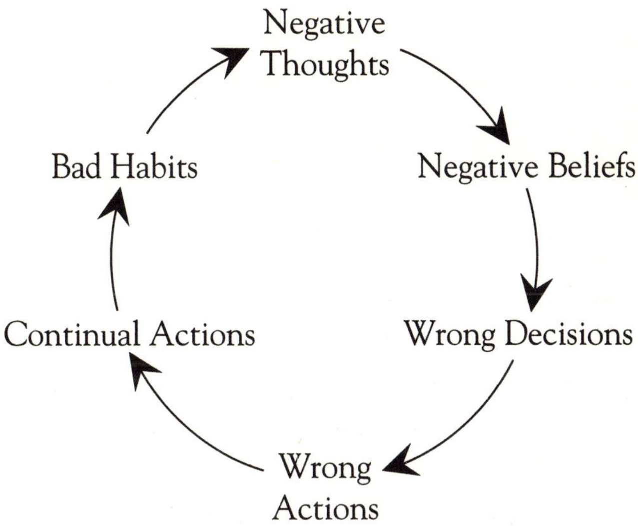

As you can see, negative thoughts lead to negative beliefs. Those beliefs become the basis of wrong decisions, which lead to wrong actions. When those wrong actions are continually repeated, we develop bad habits, which perpetuate a bad attitude. And that bad attitude prompts negative thoughts. It can be a vicious cycle. However, you can break the cycle by cultivating positive thoughts and developing good habits.

Fortunately, habits are not instincts. They are actions

or reactions that we have acquired over time. If you can pinpoint the original cause in your thinking that prompts a bad habit, you can change it.

6. Manage Your Attitude Daily

One of the most significant discoveries of my life was realizing that we often place too much emphasis on making decisions and too little on managing the decisions we've already made. This discovery was so significant to me that I wrote a book about it called *Today Matters*. The thesis of the book is that successful people make right decisions early and manage those decisions daily. You can make a decision to have a good attitude, but if you don't make plans to *manage* that decision every day, then you are likely to end up right back where you started. But here's the good news: *maintaining* the right attitude is easier than *regaining* the right attitude.

How do you do that? A Chinese proverb I came across gives insight: "Assume a cheerfulness you do not feel, and shortly you feel the cheerfulness you assumed." Or as editor and publisher Elbert Hubbard says, "Be pleasant until 10 a.m. and the rest of the day will take care of itself." When you get up in the morning, you need to remind yourself of the decision you've made to have a

FIVE

Discouragement

When it comes to attitude obstacles, let's start with the one that's like the Trojan horse of ancient myth: discouragement. If you let discouragement get inside you, it can conquer you from the inside out, and it will prevent you from achieving the success you desire.

Don't misunderstand; everyone gets discouraged from time to time. Seldom does a day go by in my life without some discouraging thing happening to me. And then there are those times when you know it's going to be *one of those days*. I recently came across a humorous piece that tells about those days when it would be better to just stay in bed:

You know it's going to be a bad day when . . .
You turn on the morning news and it's showing emergency routes out of town.
The sun comes up in the west.
Your boss tells you not to bother taking off your coat.
You jump out of bed and you miss the floor.
The bird singing outside your bedroom window is a buzzard.
You wake up and your dentures are locked together.
Your car's horn gets stuck while you're following a group of Hell's Angels.
You put both contact lenses in the same eye.
You walk to work on a sunny morning and discover the back of your skirt is stuck in your panty hose.
You call to pick up your messages and are told it's none of your business.
Your tax return check bounces.
You put your bra on backwards and it fits better.
You step on the scale and it says "tilt."
You call suicide prevention, and they put you on hold.[1]

As I already mentioned, no one should expect life to be smooth sailing. Sydney J. Harris says, "When I hear somebody sigh, 'Life is hard,' I am always tempted to ask, 'Compared to what?'" Think about the alternative!

If only life could become easier with every day of living! But that's not reality, is it? As you get older, truly some things get harder, but others also get easier. In every stage of life, there are good aspects and bad. The key is to focus on the good and learn to live with the bad. Of course, not everyone does that. In fact, I've found that there are really only two kinds of people in this world when it comes to dealing with discouragement: splatters and bouncers. When splatters hit rock bottom, they fall apart, and they stick to the bottom like glue. On the other hand, when bouncers hit bottom, they pull together and bounce back.

"Ninety percent of those who fail are not actually defeated. They simply quit."—PAUL J. MEYER

Paul J. Meyer, founder of the Success Motivation Institute, says, "Ninety percent of those who fail are not actually defeated. They simply quit." That's what discouragement can do to you if you don't handle it the right way—it can cause you to quit. Since you *will* become discouraged at some point, the question is, Are you going to give up or get up?

DEALING EFFECTIVELY WITH DISCOURAGEMENT

The difference maker between splatters and bouncers is having the right attitude. If you believe in yourself, see discouragement as temporary, and handle it the right way, you can bounce back from nearly anything. Here are five steps you can take that will help you to deal effectively with discouragement:

1. Get the Right Perspective

One of my favorite illustrations on perspective is something I came across years ago and like to use in conferences. It's in the form of a letter home from a girl at college:

> Dear Mom,
>
> Since I have been away at college, one full semester, I think it's time I bring you up to date as to what is going on. Shortly after I arrived at college, I got bored with dormitory life and stole fifty dollars from my roommate's purse. With the money, I rented a motorcycle, which I crashed into a telephone pole a few blocks from the dorm.

I broke my leg in the accident, but I was rescued by the young doctor who lives upstairs in the apartment house on the corner. He took me in, set my leg, nursed me back to health, and thanks to him, I'm up and around again.

We wanted to let you know that we're going to be married as soon as possible. Unfortunately, we're having some trouble with the blood test—they're not sure what the disease is, but it keeps showing up in the test. We hope to get that worked out quickly so that we'll be married before the baby arrives. Shortly thereafter we will all be home to live with you and Dad. And I just know you will learn to love the baby as much as you love me, even though the baby's dad is a different religion and wants us to convert. Please understand, the only reason we're coming back home to stay is that my husband-to-be got tossed out of medical school because he was too busy taking care of me to complete his work.

Really, Mom, I didn't steal any money or rent a motorcycle or hit a telephone pole or break my leg. I didn't meet a young doctor. There's no disease and I'm not expecting a baby. And I won't be coming home to live with you and Dad either. However, I *am* getting a D in algebra and an F in geology, and I wanted you to accept these grades in their proper perspective!

Take a good look at the whole picture. A man stopped to watch a Little League baseball game. He asked one of the players on the bench what the score was.

"We're behind eighteen to nothing," the boy answered.

"Well," remarked the man, "I have to say you sure don't look discouraged."

"Discouraged?" the boy said, puzzled. "Why should we be? We haven't come up to bat yet." For most people, the game of life is long, and we receive many opportunities to learn, to achieve, to serve, and to make amends for our mistakes. Take heart. No matter how dark things may seem at any given moment, there are always reasons to hope.

Take a short look at the problem. After the Civil War, former Confederate general Robert E. Lee visited the beautiful home of a wealthy Kentucky widow. After lunch, she invited Lee to join her on the porch. From there, she pointed to a once-majestic magnolia tree that had been badly burned by Northern artillery fire. The woman began to cry as she described the former magnificence of the tree that had shaded her home for generations. She expected Lee to condemn the Northern troops and sympathize with her loss. Finally, Lee said, "My dear madam, cut it down and forget it."[2]

Someone once said, "To hatch despair, just brood over your troubles."[3] Many people who experience setbacks ask *why*, but never move beyond that. Certainly you can't solve your problems by ignoring them. But you can't solve them by becoming fixated on them either. Once you recognize the problem, you need to focus your attention on solutions.

Take a close look at yourself. A man in his early sixties had just retired in Corgin, Kentucky. During his lifetime, he had worked as a farmer, streetcar conductor, soldier, railroad fireman, ferry boat operator, salesman, and service station operator. His latest venture had been cooking chicken. He had cooked from the time he was a boy of six, when his father died. He sold fried chicken at the gas station, and it had become so popular that he had moved his operation to a motel and restaurant across the street. But in the early 1950s, a planned interstate would bypass his operation. He sold off his operation, paid his bills, and faced living on a $105 a month Social Security check.

He wasn't ready to give up on life—not just yet. He took stock of his assets. He knew that others loved his chicken. In fact, in 1935 Kentucky's governor, Ruby Lafoon, had made the man an honorary Kentucky

Colonel. From then on, he had called himself Colonel Sanders and had dressed the part. Sanders decided to travel across the country cooking his chicken and making deals with restaurant owners. He would provide his blend of eleven herbs and spices, and the restaurant owners would pay him a royalty every time they sold chicken cooked with his recipe.

By 1964 Sanders had more than 600 franchised outlets for his chicken. That was the year he retired again. At the age of 74, he sold his interest in the Kentucky Fried Chicken restaurants for $2 million. But he didn't quit working. He became a marketing representative for the organization, which soon turned into a worldwide operation. He continued working for the restaurant chain, traveling 250,000 miles a year up until his death at age 90![4]

When you face discouragement, you can do one of two things, and the one you choose will color your perspective. You can look at others to place the blame, or you can look at yourself to discover your opportunities. The choice is yours.

Take a long look at successful people. One of the best ways to learn to have a positive attitude and achieve success is to study successful people and learn from them. That's what Napoleon Hill, author of *Think and Grow Rich*,[5] did. He studied the lives of more than five hundred successful people and got to know many of them personally. What he found was that they all shared one trait: persistence. The most successful people had often overcome the greatest obstacles. Their success hadn't come from their circumstances. It had come because of their attitudes.

Take a wide look at the possibilities. In most sets of negative circumstances lie positive possibilities. It's said that when Louis Waterman couldn't get a fountain pen to work when he needed a signature to close a deal, he went away and developed the fountain pen that bore his name. It became the premier writing instrument in the U.S. for fifty years.

When Alexander Fleming had a bunch of cultures he was working on at St. Mary's Hospital in London ruined by an open window, the resulting mold on some of them led him to the discovery of penicillin.

It is very likely that if you are facing something negative right now, there is an opportunity contained in it somewhere, somehow. It may not be easy to find. It may not outweigh the difficulty or lead to a major breakthrough as it did for Waterman and Fleming. But then again, it might. How will you ever know if you don't choose to adopt the right perspective and try to find it?

2. SEE THE RIGHT PEOPLE

Few things are better at helping someone overcome discouragement than spending time with the right person. Some people just lift you up. They help you to have hope or feel good about yourself. Poet Walt Whitman found such a person when he was a young man struggling to get anyone interested in his writing. In 1855 he published *Leaves of Grass*, a small volume of poetry. Because none of the big publishing houses would accept it, he paid neighborhood printers to produce 795 copies of it. It received little notice or acclaim from critics. And it didn't sell.

"He couldn't get rid of them," said Karen Karbiener, a Whitman professor at New York University. "The price was $2, then it went down to $1, then 50 cents."[6]

However, Whitman did receive a note of encouragement from someone. It said, "Dear Sir, I am not blind to the worth of the wonderful gift of *Leaves of Grass*. I find it the most extraordinary piece of wit and wisdom that America has yet contributed. I greet you at the beginning of a great career." Who was this encourager? None other than Ralph Waldo Emerson, the most respected literary figure of the day in America.

I am very fortunate because I grew up in the home of a lifter: my father, Melvin Maxwell. He really understands people and cares about them. When I was a teenager, he used to tell me, "Remember, everyone you come into contact with is fighting a battle." In his eighties and retired from pastoral ministry, he continues to be a lifter. When he moved to a retirement community several years ago, he started to connect with people in his community to encourage them and lend them a hand if they needed it. He had his golf cart and his cell phone, and he was always on the move. That first year, he asked me if I would be willing to speak to the couple of dozen people in his community if he got them together—just to encourage them—which I was glad to do.

Five years later, Dad has enlisted volunteers to help him and is active in thirty-seven retirement communities. This year when I spoke to his group, there were over 600 there! Why has Dad been so successful? Two reasons: first, he's a leader. He has always had the ability to make things happen. Second, he cares about people and lifts them up. If people feel discouraged, all they need to do is spend time with Dad to improve their attitude.

3. Say the Right Words

A main source of discouragement is negative self-talk. D. Martyn Lloyd-Jones, once the greatest heart surgeon in England, says in his book *Spiritual Depression*, "Most of your unhappiness in life is due to the fact that you are listening to yourself rather than talking to yourself."[7] By that, I think he means that we often *passively* allow negative messages from our past to influence our thinking instead of *actively* telling ourselves good things that will help us to think more positively. For years I've used phrases such as these to help me:

- This too shall pass.
- Things could be worse.
- It's not what happens *to* me but what happens *in* me that matters most.
- Keep your chin up.
- Do it anyway.

You need to find your own phrases in a language that works for you. But be sure that the language is positively motivational, not negative or belittling. Nobody can motivate himself in a positive direction by continually using negative words.

4. Have the Right Expectations

Clergyman J. Wallace Hamilton once observed, "Every person's life is a diary in which he or she means to write one story and is forced to write yet another." Haven't you found that to be true? I know I have. Here's the good news: the story you write can actually be *better* than the one you envisioned, but you need to have the right expectations. You have to remain flexible, and you can't expect everything to go perfectly.

Lawrence R. Burns, a psychology professor at Grand Valley State University in Allendale, Michigan, makes the distinction between negative and positive perfectionists. He says that negative perfectionists are "concerned with trying to impress" and as a result are often depressed, anxious, and obsessed with their flaws. Positive perfectionists, on the other hand, set realistic goals and forgive themselves when they fall short. And Burns says it is possible for a person to shift from one to the other. The key is to focus on what you can achieve, not what you can't.[8]

5. MAKE THE RIGHT DECISIONS

Do you ever feel worn out by the end of the day? Maybe it's because you are making decisions that cause you to expend your energy the wrong way. Take a look at the following list of activities reputed to have come from the Southern California Medical Association and the number of calories each burns to see if that may be the problem:

Activity	Calories
Beating around the bush	75
Jogging your memory	125
Jumping to conclusions	100
Climbing the wall	150
Swallowing your pride	150
Passing the buck	25
Beating your own drum	100
Throwing your weight around	300
Turning the other cheek	75
Dragging your heels	100
Throwing in the towel	200[9]

Seriously, the decisions you make and how you make them have a huge impact on your outlook. First, it's important always to do the right thing. Few things increase discouragement the way regret or a guilty conscience can. It's not easy to apologize, admit your faults, forgive, subdue your temper, shoulder a deserved blame, or start over. But making the decision to do these things when they're called for always pays off. Each of us needs to be willing to look at life realistically, see ourselves as we are, and come to terms with what's true.

Second, the timing of the decision is also important. Many people make decisions when things aren't going well. They look for relief in the despair of the valley instead of waiting for the clarity that comes from being on the mountaintop. Why? Because it takes a lot of effort to get to the mountaintop. And when you're experiencing the darkness of the valley, it's always tempting to make changes that you hope will relieve the discomfort.

Robert Schuller, founder of the Crystal Cathedral in Orange, California, calls this the Peak to Peak Principle. It can be represented visually like this:

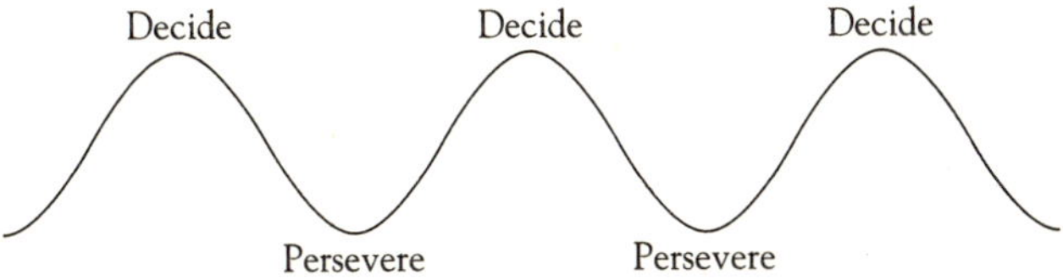

When you are on top of the proverbial mountain, that is the time to make decisions. Here's why:

You can see your situation more clearly.

You are moving to something, not just from something.

You leave those around you in a better position.

You decide using positive data, not negative.

You are more likely to move from peak to peak instead of valley to valley.

On the other hand, when you're in the valley, the most important thing you can do is persevere. If you keep fighting, you're likely to get your second wind, just as distance runners do. And it's said that only when runners are exhausted enough to reach that place do they find out what they can truly accomplish. If you keep persevering while you are in the valley, not only will you likely make it to higher ground where you can make better decisions, but you will also have developed character, which will serve you well throughout life.

Many years ago I came across the poetry of Helen Steiner Rice, and it intrigued me because it seemed to be characterized by hope in the midst of pain or sorrow. When I learned about her story, it made sense to me.

Helen was born in 1900 and grew up on the shores of Lake Erie. Her dream was to study law, but her plans to attend Wesleyan College had to be set aside when her father died during the influenza epidemic of 1918. Instead, she ended up taking a job with an electrical utility company.

In 1928 Helen met a young banker named Franklin Rice. Soon they were married. But their happiness together was short-lived. In the wake of the stock market crash of 1929, Franklin committed suicide.

Helen went back to work, this time taking a job editing greeting cards. For twenty years she worked in the industry, with some of her poems being published by the Gibson Card Company. And she worked and maintained a grateful attitude despite suffering a painful degenerative disease.

Then one day one of her cards was read on *The Lawrence Welk Show*, and her life suddenly changed. People clamored for her poetry. Since then, people have bought more than seven million books of her writing.

She died in 1981, but one of the poems she published before her death describes a discovery she made when facing dark times. The poem is called "The Bend in the Road," and it ends this way:

And together we stand at life's crossroads
And view what we think is the end,
But God has a much bigger vision
And He tells us it's only a bend.

For the road goes on and is smoother,
And the pause in the song is a rest.
And the part that's unsung and unfinished
Is the sweetest and richest and best.

So rest and relax and grow stronger.
Let go and let God share your load,
Your work is not finished or ended,
You've just come to a bend in the road.

If you can maintain that perspective, you can overcome discouragement and move beyond it. No one need be held captive to it. Embrace the difference maker and it will make the difference in you.

SIX

Change

On August 3, 1492, Columbus set sail from Palos in southern Spain in search of a western route to Asia. He was convinced that the world was round, despite the belief by nearly everyone else in Europe that it was flat. Most people believed that a ship sailing due west would fall off the edge of the earth!

Columbus didn't find the route he sought, but he did confirm his suspicions that the earth was a sphere. And after months of exploration and the loss of one ship, he returned to Palos on March 15, 1493—a hero. And in a matter of months, the perspective of everyone in Europe concerning the earth changed drastically. It caused a quick and transforming revolution of the world. Right? Not exactly.

Columbus was considered a hero for returning from his venture. And he was credited with discovering new lands. But people didn't change their minds about the earth. As David Bayles and Ted Orland, authors of *Art and Fear*, state, when Columbus returned from the New World and proclaimed the earth was round, almost everyone else went right on believing the earth was flat. Then they died, and the next generation grew up believing the world was round. That's how people change their minds.[1]

Everyone resists change. For many years, I thought leaders liked change and everyone else didn't. As a visionary leader, I always felt that I was drawing reluctant followers into the future. But I finally realized that leaders don't like change any more than followers do—unless, of course, it's their idea!

WHY DO PEOPLE RESIST CHANGE?

Change is hard for everyone. Novelist Mark Twain said, "The only person who likes change is a wet baby." Truly, change is one of the greatest attitude obstacles you will ever face. Why is that? After all, doesn't progress require change? And doesn't growth? We can't move forward and stay the same at the same time. Yet we resist change. Why? There are several reasons:

1. PEOPLE RESIST CHANGE BECAUSE OF PERSONAL LOSS

Whenever change is imminent, the first question that pops into people's minds is how the change will affect them. For example, imagine that a coworker came up to you today and said, "I just heard that the boss is laying off some people today." Was your first thought, *I wonder what market conditions precipitated such a decision?* Or was it, *Boy, I bet the boss feels bad about having to do that?* Or, *I wonder how that will impact the bottom line of the company?* No, chances are your first thought was, *Am I at risk?* That's just human nature. In the moments that we face change, we can suddenly feel alone and vulnerable.

Optimistic people will more quickly see the good in most changes, and they may try to encourage you by saying something such as, "It's okay. This change is for the better." But the truth is that there is loss even in positive changes. Ralph Waldo Emerson said, "For everything you gain, you lose something." In life, there are wins and losses. Even when change is good, we will give up things that are important to us.

Back in 1996 when I decided to relocate my companies from San Diego to Atlanta, it was a win for the organization. It was the right move for many reasons. Yet it meant leaving many good friends, the place that felt like home, and the best weather in the world. It was a win that contained losses. As poet and literary critic Paul Valéry observed, "Every beginning is a consequence. Every beginning ends something." If not seen correctly, that can be disheartening.

> *"Every beginning is a consequence. Every beginning ends something."*—PAUL VALÉRY

2. PEOPLE RESIST CHANGE BECAUSE OF FEAR OF THE UNKNOWN

I love a story that my friend Zig Ziglar tells: A man from out in the sticks won a bass fiddle in a drawing. He took it home and looked at the beginning music book that had come with it. Unfortunately, the book had been damaged and the only part that survived intact was one page showing the left hand in one position on the strings and the right hand drawing the bow. So he carefully placed his fingers and drew the bow back and forth across the stings, producing an awful sound. And though it was the only sound he could make, he practiced every day. This of course drove his wife crazy.

Then one day his wife went to a concert, and by chance her seat was not very far from the bass fiddle player in the orchestra. She was delighted by the sound *this* player produced with his instrument, and she watched as his fingers traveled up and down the instrument's fret board and the bow moved in various rhythms. It was beautiful.

As she traveled home she decided that she wanted to communicate to old Johnny One Note the potential of his instrument, but she also knew that he was easily upset. As it happened, the man was practicing when she arrived at home.

"Honey," she said, "may I ask you a question?"

"Sure," he answered, continuing to saw at the strings.

"At the concert I noticed that the bass fiddle player kept moving his left hand up and down and left and right while his right hand moved slowly on some occasions and fast on others." She said this gently, not wanting to upset him. "I'm just curious why he moves his hands so much and does so many things while you keep your hands in exactly the same spot all the time."

"That's easy," he answered. "That old boy's still lookin' for his place, and I done found mine!"

People often avoid change because they worry about the unknown. You've probably heard the quote, "The only thing we have to fear is fear itself." Deadpan comedian Pat Paulson said, "The only thing we have to fear is fear itself—and possibly the bogeyman." Ironically, it's the "bogeyman" who often causes us to resist change. It's what we *don't* know that makes us afraid.

> *"The only thing we have to fear is fear itself—and possibly the bogeyman."*—PAT PAULSON

People often cling to what they know, even if they are not satisfied with it. Fear holds them back, yet the only way to overcome the fear is to go out and do the very thing they fear to do.

Fear can be such a difficult problem that I have dedicated an entire section of this book to it, so I don't need to go into it much further here. But I will say this: All the things you love were once unknown to you. Don't be afraid to keep trying something new.

3. People Resist Change Because the Timing Could Be Wrong

Law 19 in *The 21 Irrefutable Laws of Leadership* states, "When to lead is as important as what to do and where to go." What happens when you try to make a change at the wrong time? For that matter, when is the right time to make changes? From a leadership point of view, there actually are better times for change than others. I developed the following checklist to help me navigate the process:

A Checklist for Change

- ○ Will this benefit the followers?
- ○ Is this change compatible with the purpose of the organization?
- ○ Is this change specific and clear?
- ○ Are the top 20 percent (the influencers) in favor of this change?
- ○ Is it possible to test this change before making a total commitment to it?

- Are physical, financial, and human resources available to make this change?
- Is this change reversible?
- Is this change the next obvious step?
- Does this change have both short- and long-range benefits?
- Is the leadership capable of bringing about this change?
- Does everything else indicate the timing is right?

Before implementing a big change, I run through this checklist and answer each question with a yes or no. If too many questions have a no by them, then I conclude that the timing may not be right.

4. People Resist Change Because It Feels Awkward

When was the last time you did something for the first time? Can you name something specific? It has to be something really new. Seeing a new movie doesn't count —because you've seen a movie before. It needs to be a real first. If you can't remember, then you might be in trouble.

I want you to do an experiment. Don't get annoyed by it; just trust me. First, I want you to set this book down and clasp your hands together, palms together with your fingers interlocked. Try it.

If I asked you to do this ten times—which I won't—you will lock your fingers together the same way every time, with one thumb over the other. Now I want you to try something. Clasp your hands together again, but *this* time I want you to interlock your fingers in such a way that the *other* thumb is on top. Try it.

Didn't that feel weird? That's what change does—it makes you feel awkward. It isn't wrong; it's just different, and that takes us out of our comfort zone.

5. PEOPLE RESIST CHANGE BECAUSE OF TRADITION

Cambridge University professor F. M. Cornford said, "Nothing is ever done until everyone is convinced that it ought to be done and has been convinced for so long that it is now time to do something else." Many people cling to tradition. The assumption is that if something is tradition, it must be a better way. But that's not necessarily so. Here's a riddle that shows what I mean: How many traditionalists does it take to change a light bulb? The answer is four: one to change it and three to talk about how wonderful the old bulb was.

If a tradition connects you to other people or to your

personal history, it can be a good thing. If it doesn't, then it may be time to try something else.

PREPARATION POINTS FOR SUCCESSFUL CHANGE

The keys to dealing with change successfully are having a good attitude toward it and being prepared to meet it. The following ideas can help you to do those things:

1. Change Will Happen Whether You Like It or Not

It's said that a duke of Cambridge once said, "Any change at any time for any reason is to be deplored." I feel sorry for people like him. They have a hard time dealing with reality and experience a difficult life. Change is unavoidable. The only thing certain about tomorrow is that it will be different from today. If you doubt that, consider this: My grandfather had a farm, my parents had a garden, and I've got a can opener! It's a different world than it was twenty years ago, and it will be different in another twenty. But the good news is that the world changes so fast that you couldn't stay wrong all the time if you tried!

5. DECIDE WHAT YOU ARE NOT WILLING TO CHANGE

I have to admit that I'm a personal growth fanatic. There are few things I enjoy more than learning something new. My father got me started when I was a kid. He actually paid me to read books that would help me learn and grow. Now I'm in my late fifties, and I still love it when I can see myself improving in an area I've targeted for growth. But as much as I am dedicated to progress, there are some things that I'm not willing to change—no matter what—such as my faith and my values. I'd rather die than forfeit my faith in God or my commitment to integrity, family, generosity, and belief in people. Some things are not worth compromising at any price.

I want to encourage you to think about the nonnegotiables in your life. What are you willing to live and die for? Write down the things you will hold on to no matter what, and take some time to explain why. Once you do that, then *everything* else should be open to change.

6. REMEMBER, IT'S NEVER TOO LATE TO CHANGE

I already mentioned that I am in my late fifties. The older I get, the more I meet people my age who express regret for the way they've lived their lives. Sometimes the regret is for things they've done, but more often it is for things they *didn't* do but felt that they should have. If they ask for my advice, I quote one of my favorite sayings:

Though you cannot go back
And make a brand-new start, my friend.
Anyone can start from now
And make a brand-new end.

It's never too late to change. As the Turkish proverb says, "No matter how far you have gone on a wrong road, turn back."

My friend Dick Biggs, a speaker and author, delivers a program called "The Headache of Changing or the Headache of Not Changing." I just love that title because it really describes the dilemma we all feel when faced with the prospect of change. A positive thinker with a good attitude, Dick has also written a poem on the subject. He has graciously allowed me to share it with you.

Will I Master Change, or Will Change Master Me?
by Dick Biggs

Life's turning points are as sure as the tide
Just a matter of when, so why not decide?

To embrace these transitions as ways to grow
'Tis folly to ignore what you already know.

Make a vow to adapt to the crises of life
There's no reason to suffer more stress or strife.
Quite often change becomes a blessing in time
While making you wiser in pursuit of your prime.
No change is impossible, no one is exempt
You can step out in faith or shrug with contempt.
Life comes in cycles, no two are the same
To claim nothing's new is a naïve game.

Some change is impractical, some things must endure
You need worthwhile values, so profound and pure.
Plus a noble purpose to guide you each day
And give life meaning as you forge your way.

But *most* things do change, it's a natural law
You can believe this is truth or stand there in awe.
It may be uncomfortable, it may cause pain—
Won't a regretful heart be a greater strain?

With *every* change, there's an outcome to bear
So accept the challenge, for life's seldom fair.

Be willing to risk and you're bound to find
More courage and strength from a positive mind.

Be bold, be daring, be receptive to change
For most things are better when you rearrange.
Get out of the rut, seek a new vitality
Move beyond the old to a fresh reality.

Ah, life has turning points, they won't disappear
Rise up to greet them and conquer your fear.
The choice is simple, it's as clear as can be:
Will I master change or will change master me?

In the end, that is really the question. You can allow change to *get* the best of you, or you can harness change and let it help *make* the best of you. To do that, you need to have a positive attitude about it. You need to keep relying on the difference maker.

HOW YOUR ATTITUDE CAN BE THE DIFFERENCE MAKER CONCERNING CHANGE

Think about a change you are currently resisting. It can be a change you feel prompted to make or are currently being asked to make by others. Define the change as clearly as you can here:

Next, write down all the benefits of the change:

Now consider why you are resisting the change. Answer yes or no to each of the following questions:

Yes	No	Question
___	___	1. Are you uncertain of what will happen as a result of the change?
___	___	2. Are you concerned that the timing is wrong?
___	___	3. Does the change violate tradition?
___	___	4. Will it create some kind of loss to you personally?
___	___	5. Will the change make you feel awkward?

If you answered yes to question 1 or 2, use the Checklist for Change from earlier in the chapter to explore the issues at greater depth.

If you answered yes to question 3, explore why you are clinging to the tradition. What real value does the tradition have to you, to others in the organization, or to the people you serve? Write that down. Now weigh that value against the benefits you listed previously.

If you answered yes to question 4 or 5, spend some time thinking about how improvement can come only with change. And think about your motives. Are you putting yourself ahead of the organization or the people you serve? Keeping in mind the value of the change can sometimes help a person to make difficult transitions.

No matter how you answered the questions, keep in mind that for positive change to occur . . .

1. You must make a commitment to pay the price for change;
2. Change must happen within you before it can happen around you; and
3. It's never too late to change.

SEVEN

Problems

Recently I was flipping through a magazine when an ad for a company called Accenture caught my eye. The page showed golfer Tiger Woods on a golf green leaning down to line up a putt. He is holding his putter in his left hand, and he has just set down his ball. His gaze is highly focused—burningly intense—on the hole. At the top of the page are the words, "Waiting for ideal conditions is rarely an option." Only after reading those words did I realize that in the foreground of the picture is a man in heavy rain gear squeegeeing a lot of water off the green in preparation for the putt. Evidently, Woods is plying his craft in the midst of a rainstorm, yet it doesn't seem to be fazing him a bit. Right below the image of Woods it says, "Go on. Be a Tiger."

A PERSPECTIVE ON PROBLEMS

That's the way things are for all of us, isn't it? We try to get things done—whether work, play, family interaction, or something else—and we find ourselves having to do so in the midst of storms. We simply can't avoid them. Here's what I mean:

1. Problems Are Everywhere, and Everybody Has Some

A man living in New York City got up early one morning, and before he was able to leave home for the day, he received four long-distance calls from clients who had problems—every one of whom wanted him to hop on a plane to try to fix them. He finally finished getting dressed and went out to the kitchen where he received two more calls, this time from local clients. He told his wife he was skipping breakfast, and went down and hailed a cab.

"All right, let's get going," he hollered as he jumped in.

"Where do you want me to take you?" asked the cabbie.

"I don't care," replied the man. "I've got problems everywhere."

Do you ever have days that feel like that? Everywhere you turn you see more problems. No one is exempt from the difficulties of life. Having money doesn't protect people from having problems. Neither does social standing, talent, or a good job. In fact, Malcolm Forbes observed, "If you have a job without aggravations, you don't have a job."

Pick any person living or dead, and, if you look, you will see that he had problems.

Problems are simply inescapable. If you're a human being and you're breathing, you will have problems.

2. Our Perspective on the Problem, Not the Problem Itself, Usually Determines Our Success or Failure

Alfred Armand Montapert said, "The majority see the obstacles; the few see the objectives; history records the successes of the latter, while oblivion is the reward of the former." People's perspectives make a huge difference in how they approach their problems. Take a look at the differences between the wrong and right approaches:

A Wrong Perspective	A Right Perspective
Problems are unsolvable	Problems are solvable
Problems are permanent	Problems are temporary
Problems are *not* normal	Problems are a normal part of life
Problems make us bitter	Problems make us better
Problems control us	Problems challenge us
Problems stop us	Problems stretch us

One of the reasons that problem solving is so difficult is that we are often too close to the problems to truly understand them. Novelist John Galsworthy observed, "Idealism increases in direct proportion to one's distance from the problem." By standing back (either literally or figuratively), you can often get a better perspective on a problem. And that better perspective will not only help you to feel better about it, but will also help you to solve it more easily.

3. There Is a Difference Between Problem Spotting and Problem Solving

Cartoonist Ashleigh Brilliant remarked, "I don't have any solutions, but I certainly admire the problem." Isn't that the way some people operate? They're very quick to find any kind of problem and point it out. For example, look at the following remarks, which were taken from actual registration sheets and comment cards returned to the staff in 1996 at the Bridger Wilderness Area in Wyoming:

- Trails need to be wider so people can walk holding hands.
- Trails need to be reconstructed. Please avoid building trails that go uphill.
- Too many bugs and leeches and spiders and spiderwebs. Please spray the wilderness to rid the area of these pests.
- Please pave the trails so they can be plowed of snow during the winter.
- Chairlifts need to be in some places so that we can get to wonderful views without having to hike to them.
- The coyotes made too much noise last night and kept me awake. Please eradicate these annoying animals.
- A small deer came into my camp and stole my jar of pickles. Is there a way I can get reimbursed?
- Reflectors need to be placed on trees every 50 feet so people can hike at night with flashlights.

- Escalators would help on steep hill sections.
- A McDonald's would be nice at the trailhead.
- The places where trails do not exist are not well marked.
- Too many rocks in the mountains.[1]

To become someone who overcomes problems, you need to become a problem solver.

4. The Size of the Person Is More Important Than the Size of the Problem

You can tell the caliber of a person by the amount of opposition it takes to discourage him. Orison Swett Marden, founder of *Success* magazine, observed, "Obstacles will look large or small to you according to whether you are large or small." Big people overcome big obstacles.

There's a world of difference between a person who has a big problem and a person who makes a problem big. It's said that legal immigrants in the United States are four times as likely to become millionaires as native-born Americans. They do this despite the additional obstacles they often face, such as language differences, culture shock, separation from family, and isolation.

Joke writer Robert Orben says that he once saw an ad

in a show business paper that read, "Lion tamer—wants tamer lion." Obviously, that circus performer had room for growth. Instead of working to increase himself, he desired to shrink the problem.

5. PROBLEMS, RESPONDED TO CORRECTLY, CAN ACTUALLY ADVANCE US FORWARD

A young woman was complaining to her father about her problems and how difficult her life was.

"Come with me," he said. "I want to show you something." He took her into the kitchen where he put three pots of water on the stove to heat. Meanwhile, he cut up some carrots and put them into the first pot to boil. Into the simmering water in the second pot he put two eggs. In the third pot he poured some ground coffee. After a few minutes, he strained the carrots into one bowl, peeled the eggs and put them into another, and into a cup he poured the strained coffee. Then he placed them before his daughter.

"What's all this supposed to mean?" she asked somewhat impatiently.

"Each of these items can teach us something about the way we handle adversity," he answered. "The carrots started out hard, but the boiling water turned them mushy. The eggs went into the water fragile but came out hard and rubbery. The coffee, on the other hand, changed the water into something better."

"Sweetheart," he said, "you can choose how you will respond to your problems. You can let them make you weak. You can let them make you hard. Or you can use them to create something beneficial. It's all up to you."

For decades, Victor and Mildred Goertzel have studied the lives of famous people who achieved success. They first published their findings in 1962 in *Cradles of Eminence*, and have since revised and updated it. What did they find to be the greatest commonality between the successful people they studied? Would it surprise you to know that most of them had huge obstacles to overcome? The problems they faced—some physical, some emotional, and some financial—prompted them to achieve. Many likely would not have been driven to succeed without the problems they overcame.

PRINCIPLES FOR HANDLING PROBLEMS

Recognizing problems for what they are—temporary tests of your resolve and ability—won't do you much good if you don't know how to overcome the problems and move forward. After all, the best way to escape a problem is to solve it. Here is some advice concerning how:

1. DEFINE WHAT A REAL PROBLEM IS

Philosopher Abraham Kaplan makes a distinction between problems and predicaments. A problem is something you can do something about. If you can't do something about it, then it's not a problem. It's a predicament. That means it's something that must be coped with, endured.

> *A problem is something you can do something about. If you can't do something about it, then it's not a problem. It's a predicament.*

When people treat a predicament as a problem, they can become frustrated, angry, or depressed. They waste energy. They make bad decisions. And when people treat problems as predicaments, they often settle, give up, or see themselves as victims.

Let me give you a few examples to help you get a handle on what I mean. If you are married, chances are that if you are a morning person, your spouse is a night person (or vice versa). That is a predicament. You can't change that. You can't change the way people are wired internally. If you try to, you and your spouse will experience lots of conflict, and there will be no resolution. However, your difficulty in finding ways to spend time together because of your different bents *is* a problem, and it *can* be solved.

Here is another example. Let's say you go to work one day and find out that the company you work for is going out of business. It's done, and that means your job is gone. That is a predicament—unless you are in a position financially to buy the business. Assuming that you're not, then what are you going to do? Are you going to waste energy complaining about losing your job or trying to talk your boss into restarting the company? You'd be better off working on solving the *problem* of finding a new job or starting your own business. People with a positive attitude often lose a job and use it as an opportunity to transition to something better. People who spend time and energy trying to solve a predicament just get frustrated.

More than twenty-five years ago when I was dealing with some difficult issues, I wrote something to help me see problems in the right light. It became my new "definition" of problems. Maybe it will help you too:

P **redictors**—helping to mold our future.
R **eminders**—showing us that we cannot succeed alone.
O **pportunities**—pulling us out of ruts and prompting us to think creatively.
B **lessings**—opening doors we would otherwise not go through.
L **essons**—providing instruction with each new challenge.
E **verywhere**—telling us that no one is excluded from difficulties.
M **essages**—warning us about potential disaster.
S **olvable**—reminding us that every problem has a solution.

If you can separate the predicaments from the problems, then you put yourself in a much better position to deal with the predicaments and to solve the problems.

2. Anticipate Problems

A young man sent a cryptic e-mail home to his mother at the end of his second college semester. It said, "Flunked out of school and coming home tomorrow. Prepare Dad." It wasn't long before he received an equally brief reply: "Dad prepared. Prepare yourself!"

Al Davis, owner of the NFL's Oakland Raiders, says, "A great leader doesn't treat problems as special. He treats them as normal." If you're working, expect problems. If you're dealing with family, expect problems. If you're just minding your own business and trying to relax, expect problems. If everything goes according to plan, then be pleasantly surprised. If it doesn't and you've planned accordingly, then you won't get so frustrated. A problem not anticipated is a problem. A problem anticipated is an opportunity.

3. Face the Problem

About twenty years ago, a television commercial ran that showed a family at home. The children were playing, the mother was vacuuming, and the father was reading the paper. They could be seen as a typical American family except for one problem: There was a huge elephant in the room with them. Even though you could see that it was making things difficult for them, and they were having to move around it, they seemed to be ignoring the elephant, pretending it didn't exist. The ad was for alcoholism awareness. Difficult problems such as alcoholism create chaos in families, yet people often pretend that everything's fine and won't address the problem.

Author and former economic planner John Perkins believes, "There are three kinds of people in our society: those who can't see or refuse to see the problems; those who see the problems and because they didn't personally create them are content to blame someone else; and those who see the problems and though they didn't create them are willing to assume personal responsibility for solving them."

In my decades of experience working with people, I've found that when people face adversity, they make one of these four decisions:

Flee it—they try to get away, but problems always follow.
Forget it—they hope the problem will go away, but problems left alone only get worse.
Fight it—they resist, but the problems still persist.
Face it—they look at the problem realistically.

People who face their problems understand that the first step in solving a problem is to begin.

4. Evaluate the Problem

It's said that if you keep your head when all about you are losing theirs—then you don't understand the problem. Seriously though, if a serious problem doesn't cause you to pause and take stock, then you probably haven't evaluated it properly. And that will create difficulties for you down the road, because if you've misjudged the size or scope of a problem and try to deal with it anyway, you will have to stop in the middle of trying to solve it, reevaluate, and start all over again.

Mike Leavitt, United States secretary of health and human services under President George W. Bush, says, "There is a time in the life of every problem when it is big enough to see, yet small enough to solve." The trick is to find the right timing and then to be patient when implementing the solution. Inexperienced people expect problems to be settled instantly. Experienced people are like the master sculptor who keeps striking at the chisel on the marble block with steady blows of the hammer. Unlike the rookie who expects to split the stone with one blow of the hammer, he knows that if he keeps working at it, he will eventually succeed.

5. EMBRACE EACH PROBLEM AS A POTENTIAL OPPORTUNITY

President John F. Kennedy was once asked how he became a war hero. His response: "It was quite easy. Somebody sunk my boat!" While it is true that certain individuals have a vision for innovation or change and they pursue it with purpose, the majority of the time adversity paves the way for success. That was the case for King Gillette, who was so tired of sharpening his straight razor that he developed the safety razor with disposable blades. It was true for Chester Greenwood, who suffered from frostbitten ears and consequently developed earmuffs. It was true for Humphrey O'Sullivan, a printer, who tired of coworkers who kept stealing the rubber mat he stood on to work and finally created rubber heels for his shoes. And it was the case for a man whose small shop was in tough straits financially. He recalled,

> I was paying a sheriff $5 a day to postpone a judgment on my small factory. Then came the gas man, and because I could not pay his bill promptly, he cut off my gas. I was in the midst of certain very important experiments, and to have the gas people plunge me into darkness made me

> so mad that I at once began to read up on gas technique and economics, and resolved I would try to see if electricity couldn't be made to replace gas and give those gas people a run for their money.[2]

That man was Thomas Edison, founder of the Edison General Electric Company, which later became General Electric.

Problems are wake-up calls for creativity. If we choose to wake up and get up, problems will prompt us to use our abilities, rally our resources, and move us forward. When a person has the difference maker, adversity causes him to draw on and develop greater strength.

Problems are wake-up calls for creativity.

6. Think of People Who Have Bigger Problems

In a *Peanuts* cartoon, Snoopy sees that everyone in the family is inside the house enjoying Thanksgiving dinner while he receives dog food. *How about that?* he thinks to himself. *Everyone is eating turkey today, but just because I'm a dog, I get dog food.*

He walks to his doghouse, climbs on top, and thinks,

suddenly gaining perspective. *Of course*, Snoopy realizes, *it could have been worse. I could have been born a turkey*.

How big or difficult our problems appear to be is often a matter of perspective. Most difficulties we face are pretty insignificant in the big scheme of things. When a friend gets cancer or loses a loved one, *then* we are reminded of how petty our issues are.

Writer James Agee recalled how he once struck up a conversation with an impoverished elderly woman in the heart of Appalachia during the Great Depression. She lived in a tiny shack with dirt floors, no heat, and no indoor plumbing.

"What would you do," he asked, "if someone came along and gave you some money to help you out?"

The old woman thought for a moment and answered, "I guess I'd give it to the poor."[3]

7. List All the Potential Ways to Solve the Problem

Richard Wirthlin worked as President Ronald Reagan's pollster when he was in the White House. During those years, the president's approval rating varied widely. Right after the assassination attempt on Reagan's life, his rating was about 90 percent. A year later, in the midst of the recession of 1982, his numbers plummeted. Wirthlin recalls having to deliver those low figures to Reagan.

"Well, how was it? How are they? What do the figures look like?" the president asked.

"Well, they're pretty bad, Mr. President."

"How bad are they?"

"Well," answered Wirthlin, "they're about 32 percent."

"Dick, don't worry," said the president with a smile. "I'll just go out there and try to get shot again."[4]

Author and speaker Grenville Kleiser stated, "To every problem there is already a solution whether you know what it is or not." I would take that another step further. I believe every problem has *many* solutions, and no problem can stand the assault of sustained thinking.

To solve problems, we need to fire up our creativity, apply sustained thinking, and pull together our resources. Included in those resources are people. The problems that surround us are not as crucial as the people around us. As you think about solutions, consider the people of your acquaintance who might be able to help you.

8. Determine the Best Three Ways to Solve the Problem

An older woman was being tried for the murder of her

third husband. A lawyer asked, "What happened to your first husband?"

"He died of mushroom poisoning," said the woman.

"How about your second husband?"

"He died of mushroom poisoning too," she replied.

"Well then," the lawyer continued, "what about your third husband?"

"He died of a brain concussion."

"How did that happen?" asked the lawyer.

"He wouldn't eat the mushrooms."

Good thinkers always have more than one way to solve a problem. I believe people make mistakes when they think there is only one solution to any problem. If you identify the *three* best solutions to any problem, you give yourself options—and a backup plan in case the first solution fails.

9. Refocus on the Mission

Ralph Waldo Emerson observed, "Concentration is the secret of strength in politics, in war, in trade, in short, in all management of human affairs." Where should you focus that concentration? On the mission. And when you make a mistake, don't chase after it. Don't try to defend it. Don't throw good money after it. Just refocus your attention on the mission and then move on. You must always keep your eye on what it is you desire to do. I have yet to meet a person focused on yesterday who had a better tomorrow.

John Foster Dulles, secretary of state in the Eisenhower administration, observed, "The measure of success is not whether you have a tough problem to deal with, but whether it is the same problem you had last year." A problem solved is a springboard to future success, to bigger and better things. The key is to focus on what you are learning, not on what you are losing. If you do that, then you will open the door to future possibilities.

"Positive thinking is how you think about a problem. Enthusiasm is how you feel about a problem. The two together determine what you do about a problem."—NORMAN VINCENT PEALE

The difference maker can help you do that. It can help you learn from the present and look to the future. Norman Vincent Peale said, "Positive thinking is how you think about a problem. Enthusiasm is how you feel about a problem. The two together determine what you do about a problem." And that's what really matters in the end.

HOW YOUR ATTITUDE CAN BE THE DIFFERENCE MAKER CONCERNING PROBLEMS

Take one or two minutes to make a list of the top ten things you've done in your life about which you are most proud. Do not take into account what others might say are your greatest accomplishments. This is *your* list. And do not try to rank them. Simply write the first ten you can think of very quickly.

1. ______________________________

2. ______________________________

3. ______________________________

4. ______________________________

5. ______________________________

6. ________________________________

7. ________________________________

8. ________________________________

9. ________________________________

10. ________________________________

Now that you've completed your list, I'm willing to bet that your successes came after you experienced . . .

1. A problem (or challenge)
2. Self-doubt
3. Commitment to persevere

In retrospect, we generally remember the problem and the commitment, but we forget that we also experienced a season of self-doubt. We forget that we had to change our thinking before we could change the problem. And that takes the difference maker—your attitude. When facing problems, remember to always start with yourself.

braces. And he reentered the political arena—fearlessly campaigning to become the governor of New York, which he did in 1929. He went on to become one of the nation's greatest presidents.

FEAR IS PART OF THE HUMAN CONDITION

We tend to think that successful people somehow are exempt from experiencing fear, but nothing could be further from the truth. Every generation in human history has experienced fear. It goes all the way back to Adam and Eve. After they disobeyed God and He called to them, Adam answered, "I heard Your voice in the garden, and I was afraid because I was naked; and I hid myself."[2]

Fear is part of human nature, and it always has been. Trace through human history and you can find plenty of quotes on fear. Here are just a few:

- Lucretius (ca. 60 B.C.) "For as children tremble and fear everything in the blind darkness, so we in the light sometimes fear what is no more to be feared than the things children in the dark hold in terror and imagine will come true."

- Michel Eyquem de Montaigne (1580) "The thing I fear most is fear."
- Francis Bacon (1623) "Nothing is terrible except fear itself."
- Duke of Wellington (1831) "The only thing I am afraid of is fear."

People today are also fearful. According to psychiatrist James Reich, 3 percent of all Americans experience panic, 6 percent agoraphobia, 3 percent generalized anxiety, 2.5 percent simple phobias (fear of a specific situation, object, creature, experience, or activity), and 1.5 percent social phobias (dread of situations that involve interaction with other people).[3] That means one in six people have serious issues with fear. On a lighter note, a psychiatrist who was guest on the original *Tonight Show* told host Steve Allen, "The only two really instinctive fears in men are the fear of loud noises and the fear of falling." He then asked, "What are you afraid of, Mr. Allen?" The host's response: "I have a great fear of making a loud noise while falling."

Of course, most people's fears are more ordinary. Surveys done by the Barna Research Group indicate that four out of five adults face major difficulties in life which really concern them. Their worries break down this way:

Finances 28%
Health 19%
Career concerns 16%
Parenting struggles 11%
Family relationships 7%
Accomplishing personal goals 7%[4]

Your greatest fears may not be included in this list, but I'm certain that you experience some kind of fear.

THE DESTRUCTIVE EFFECTS OF FEAR

Fear can be a very destructive force in a person's life. The root of the word *fear* comes from the Old English word *fǽr*, literally meaning a sudden attack, and is akin to the Old High German word *fāra* meaning ambush or snare.[5] That's what fear does to us: It attacks us and makes us captive. As psychiatrist and Nazi concentration camp survivor Viktor Frankl observed, "Fear makes come true that which one is afraid of."

The destructive power of fear, if left unchecked, can be devastating. Here are just some of the negative things fear can do in a person's life:

1. Fear Breeds More Fear

The most insidious thing about fear is its ability to exaggerate itself. C. Everett Koop, former surgeon general of the Unites States, observed, "People have an inappropriate sense of what is dangerous." If you're not convinced about that statement, then think about this. Are you afraid of flying? Did you know that you are more likely to die choking on a piece of food than in a commercial airline crash? Afraid of dying in a robbery? You are twice as likely to be killed playing a sport than you are to be stabbed to death by a stranger. Are you afraid of sharks? Every year barnyard pigs kill more people than sharks do. Worried about having surgery? You are sixteen times more likely to die in a car crash than you are to die of complications from surgery.

Seldom does the thing we fear come to pass. In our minds, we project coming disasters that will likely never occur. And when they don't come to pass, we think, "Phew, that was a *close* one!" when the reality is that our own thoughts were the only thing creating potential danger for us.

2. Fear Causes Inaction

A census taker was going far into a rural area to finish the work in his territory. Driving down the country roads, he saw many houses with "Beware of Dog" signs. At the gate of the last address on his list, he saw another "Beware of Dog" sign as he entered a farmyard near a barn.

Afraid to get out of his car, he honked his horn, and soon a man came out of the barn with a small Chihuahua at his heels.

When the census taker was done asking his questions and filling out his paperwork, he mentioned how many beware-of-dog signs he had seen and asked, "Is this the dog all the signs are about?"

"Yup, sure is," the farmer replied, picking up the friendly dog.

"But that dog couldn't keep anyone away."

"I know," said the farmer, "but the signs sure do." The lesson is that fear is like a warning sign that makes us afraid of a dog that cannot hurt us!

People who let some kind of fear get hold of them

find themselves increasingly more fearful. It can create a debilitating cycle. Here's how this often works.

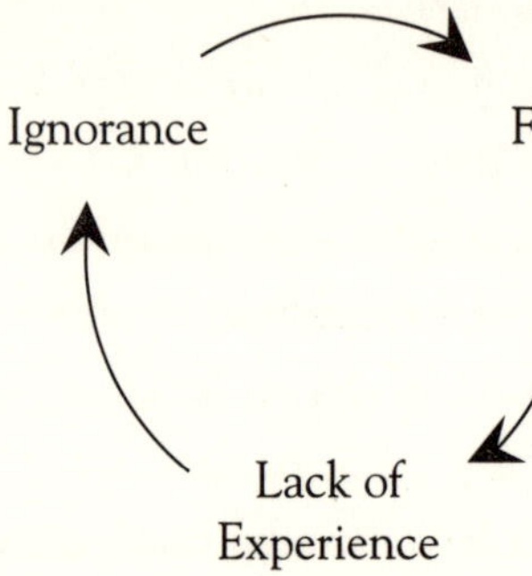

Fear makes us afraid of doing something that might be beneficial for us. Taking action will require us to move into the unknown. That can be scary. But if we give in to our fear, we don't move forward. We don't receive the benefit of what we avoided, nor do we gain the valuable experience that would make us better informed. As a result, we remain ignorant about that area of life, and ignorance almost always breeds more fear, making it that much harder to push ahead and get things done.

We cannot allow fear to paralyze us. As John F. Kennedy observed, "There are risks and costs to a program of action, but they are far less than the long-range risks and costs of comfortable inaction." If we are too afraid of failure, we probably will never win. If we are afraid to die, we will hardly live. Everything in life has some degree of risk.

3. Fear Weakens Us

Harry Truman, thirty-third president of the United States, remarked, "The worst danger we face is the danger of being paralyzed by doubts and fears. This danger is brought on by those who abandon faith and sneer at hope. It is brought on by those who spread cynicism and distrust and try to blind us to our great chance to do good for all mankind."

Fear and anxiety are debilitating emotions. They are interest paid in advance on a debt you may never owe. And they undermine faith—in ourselves, in others, and in God.

Fear	**Faith**
Weakens	Strengthens
Imprisons	Liberates
Paralyzes	Empowers
Disheartens	Encourages
Sickens	Heals

Nineteenth-century preacher and author C. H. Spurgeon stated, "Our anxiety does not empty tomorrow of its sorrows, but only empties today of its strengths." A person cannot allow fear to master him and become the master of his strengths at the same time. It just doesn't happen.

4. Fear Wastes Energy

An old German adage says, "Fear makes the wolf bigger than he is." Because of that, when people let fear get hold of them, they expend valuable energy in ways they shouldn't. How? Sometimes they avoid things that can't really harm them, like the man who returned to his vacation cabin from a hike badly scratched and bruised.

"What happened?" asked his wife.

"I met a snake on the trail," the man answered.

"Don't you remember?" the woman responded. "The ranger told us yesterday that none of the snakes up here are poisonous."

"They don't have to be poisonous if they can make you jump off a twenty-foot cliff!"

Clearly the man's fear—not the snake—was the problem.

Other times people waste energy fantasizing about solutions to problems they fear *will* come their way.

Ironically, what started as an unfounded fear can turn into a real problem because a person wasted energy on wishful thinking instead of productive action. Joe Tye, author of *Never Fear, Never Quit*, says,

> Wishful thinking is the lock that fear puts on the prison gate. Fear lets you indulge yourself, for a while, in flights of wishful thinking. Somehow, you think, something will happen to make the problems go away. By the time you wake up, it's too late. What you feared has happened, and fear has defeated you. The only way to escape from the prison of fear is action. You cannot wish your way out, you cannot wait your way out. You can only work your way out. Every time you escape the prison of fear, you grow stronger.[6]

The bottom line is that fear can push you in the wrong direction by producing nervous energy that causes you to do your worst in a new situation, or it can sap your energy as you fight its paralyzing effects.

5. Fear Keeps Us and Others from Reaching Our Potential

Psychologist Randall B. Hamrock observed, "In twenty years [of practice as a psychologist], I've talked with, tested, and given vocational counsel to at least 10,000 young men and women. One characteristic that almost all had was the tendency to sell themselves short." Fear robs us of our potential. It makes us smaller than we really are. One of the greatest mistakes we can make in life is to be in constant fear that we will make one.

When we give in to fear, we are already beaten. People who are ruled by fear stay where it's safe. And that's sad because people can't reach their potential by staying where it's safe. Worse yet, they keep others from reaching their potential too. When a leader is ruled by fear, he becomes a lid to the people who follow him. Many people fail to reach their potential because their leaders are fearful.

A story from U.S. history illustrates this well. During the American Revolution, the Bahamas were captured by Spain. In April of 1783, Andrew Deveaux, a lieutenant colonel of South Carolina, recruited a handful of militiamen and Harbour Island settlers and planned to take Nassau using a clever strategy.

Deveaux had only two hundred men with him, a far smaller force than that of the Spanish, but he managed to capture the high ground on the island after a brief skirmish. The Spaniards then watched as boats repeatedly ferried load after load of men from Deveaux's ships to his defensive position on shore. What the Spaniards didn't know was that the same men kept going back and forth, standing on their trip over to the island and hiding themselves by lying down in the boat on the trip back to the ships. The leader of the Spanish troops, fearing a defeat at the hands of a large force in a defensible position, surrendered.

Playwright William Shakespeare wrote, "Our doubts are traitors, and they make us lose what we oft might win, by fearing to attempt." That was certainly true in this incident from history.

HOW TO HANDLE FEAR

So how can a person handle fear instead of getting handled by it? If you have been averse to risk and a prisoner of fear, you may be wondering if an individual must possess great courage or exceptional talent. The answer is that fear can be overcome by anyone. Here are the steps I recommend to anyone who is having difficulty moving forward because of fear.

1. Admit Your Fears

Several old-timers sat around talking about their days in the old West, when one said, "I'll never forget the time I killed an Indian."

"Shoot him?" asked another old-timer.

"Nope," said the first.

"Kill him hand to hand with a knife?" asked the second man.

"No, nothing like that," answered the first. "Ran him to death."

"How far did you chase him?"

"Didn't," said the first old-timer. "I was in front."

You can't overcome your fears unless you first recognize they exist. Make a list of what makes you feel fear. If you feel unable to do that, you may be running from those feelings. If that is the case, start paying attention to your feelings. When does your heart race for no apparent reason? When are you paralyzed into inaction? When do you display nervous energy for no apparent reason? These kinds of responses may be due to fear.

2. Discover the Source of Your Fears

A man who had a morbid fear of thunder went to see a noted psychiatrist for treatment.

"You have a condition called brontophobia," the doctor said to the man. "It's silly to be afraid of thunder at your age. Just think of it as a drumroll in the symphony of life."

"What if that doesn't work?" the man asked.

"Well, then do as I do. When you hear thunder, stuff cotton in your ears, crawl under the bed, and sing 'Mary Had a Little Lamb' at the top of your voice until it stops."

Most people's fears are based not on facts, but on feelings. I think of *fear* as **F**alse **E**xpectations **A**ppearing **R**eal. You have to look beyond the irrational feelings you may possess and discover the expectations that lie beneath them. American humorist James Thurber wrote, "All men should strive to learn before they die what they are running from and to and why." That is the next step in the process.

3. Realize How Your Fears Can Limit You

Philosopher and Catholic cardinal J. H. Newman advised, "Fear not that your life will come to an end but that it will never have a beginning." That's what can happen if you let fear take over your life. Honestly, most of our fears are totally unfounded. In fact, studies have shown that 95 percent of what we fear is baseless. The rest are simply things we must learn to live with. Maybe the best approach is to adopt the attitude of poet Gertrude Stein, who said, "Considering how dangerous everything is, nothing is really frightening."

Studies show that 95 percent of what we fear is baseless.

There are no guarantees in life. People look for many things to protect them: burglar alarms, traveler's checks, aspirin, umbrellas, GPS systems, and air bags. But the truth is that life is dangerous, damaging to your health, and will eventually kill you. So you might as well live life to the fullest.

4. Accept Normal Fear as the Price of Progress

One of the secrets of success is not letting what you cannot do interfere with what you can do. Millionaire entrepreneur and philanthropist W. Clement Stone, who started his business career at age five selling newspapers and was selling insurance full-time at age sixteen, never let fear stop him from being successful. A strong proponent of positive thinking, Stone said that the secret to making sales was going where you do not want to go and doing what you do not want to do.

I've found this to be true in my own career. Today I am known most for my public speaking. But when I first started speaking, I wasn't effective. I remember being really fearful. Then when I got the chance to speak at an event as a senior in college, I was terrible. People who knew me then described my speaking style as "stiff." But I kept at it. I began to study effective communicators and spoke to small audiences at every opportunity. It took me seven years to become comfortable while speaking. Only then could I develop and hone my communication style.

In time I got chances to speak to larger audiences. The first time I spoke to over a thousand people was at Veterans Memorial Auditorium in Columbus, Ohio, in the 1970s. In the 1980s, I spoke to an audience of more than 10,000 for the first time during a youth rally at the University of Illinois. In the 1990s, I spoke to 68,000 people at the RCA Dome in Indianapolis. And in the 2000s, I've spoken live in events that were simulcast to even larger audiences.

I don't tell you this to brag. I say it because when I was afraid during that first speaking engagement, I had no idea where it would lead me. But I didn't let my fear rule me. Instead, I accepted it as the price I would have to pay for personal progress.

Shakespeare said, "He is not worthy of the honeycomb that shuns the hive because the bees have stings." Don't let your fear keep you from taking small steps in your development. You never know where they might lead.

5. Convert Fear into Desire

Fight manager Cus D'Amato believed, "The hero and the coward both feel exactly the same fear, only the hero confronts his fear and converts it into fire." Just about every negative emotion we feel can be converted into something positive to help us get further in life.

> Afraid of poverty? Convert it to a positive work ethic.
> Afraid of greediness? Convert it to generosity.
> Afraid of rejection? Convert it to an ability to connect with people.
> Afraid of insignificance? Convert it to the service of others.

Roger Babson, founder of Babson College and Webber International University, remarked, "If things go wrong, don't go with them." Instead, make a new way. People can turn their lives around by taking the very thing that once created fear and using the energy to do something positive and worthwhile.

> *"If things go wrong, don't go with them."*—ROGER BABSON

6. FOCUS ON THINGS YOU CAN CONTROL

Many things in this life you cannot control. There's no good reason to worry about those things. Writer Harold Stephens observes, "There is a great difference between worry and concern. A worried person sees a problem, and a concerned person solves a problem."

How can you become a problem solver? Focus on the things you can control. That usually means two things. The first is your attitude. As you interact with people, you cannot control their actions—no matter how much you might like to. But you can control your attitude. Remember, what happens *to* you isn't as important as what happens *in* you. The second is your calendar. You may not be able to control today's circumstances, but you can do your best to plan the time you have. Most people who fear the future do so because they don't prepare for it.

7. Give Today Your Attention—Not Yesterday or Tomorrow

Yesterday and tomorrow seem to clamor for our attention. Yesterday wants us to second-guess past decisions and worry if we did the right thing. But that is wasted energy. As President Harry Truman said, "If you've done the best you can—if you have done what you have to do—there is no use worrying about it, because nothing can change it."

The future also can cause us to miss present opportunities. I love what former First Lady Barbara Bush said about the future, comparing it to a train ride:

> We get on board that train at birth, and we want to cross the continent because we have in mind that somewhere out there is a station. We pass by sleepy little towns looking out the window of life's train, grain fields and silos, level grade crossings, buses full of people on the roads beside us. We pass by cities and factories, but we don't look at any of it because we want to get to the station. We believe that out there is a station where a band is playing and banners are hung and flags are wav-

ing, and when we get there that will be life's destination. We don't really get to know anybody on the train. We pace up and down the aisles looking at our watches eager to get to the station because we know that life has a station for us.

This station changes for us during life. To begin with, for most of us, it's turning 18, getting out of high school. Then the station is that first promotion and then the station becomes getting the kids out of college, and then the station becomes retirement and then . . . all too late we recognize the truth—that this side of that city whose builder is God, there really isn't a station. The joy is in the journey and the journey is the joy.

Sooner or later, you realize there is no station and the truth of life is the trip. Read a book, eat more ice cream, go barefoot more often, hug a child, go fishing, laugh more. The station will come soon enough. And as you go, find a way to make this world more beautiful.[7]

Most people arrive at a different destination than they expect in life—some better, some worse, but all different. So focusing on the destination is not a good idea. Besides, tomorrow may come; it may not. There are no guarantees.

The only place we really have any power is in the present. Do what you can in the here and now—despite your fear—and you will have the satisfaction of knowing that you are doing everything within your power to reach your potential.

> *"I've been through some terrible things in my life, a few of which actually happened."*—MARK TWAIN

8. FEED THE RIGHT EMOTION AND STARVE THE WRONG ONE

In life, both faith and fear will arise within you, and you choose which one will prevail. Someone once wrote,

> Two natures beat within my breast,
> The one is foul, the other blessed.
> The one I love, the other I hate;
> The one I feed will dominate.

The thing is, both of those emotions will *always* be present in you. The emotion you continually feed is the one that will dominate your life. You can't expect fear simply to disappear. If you continually focus on your fears, entertain them, and give in to them, they will increase. The way to ultimately overcome them is to starve them. Don't give your fears any of your time or energy. Don't feed them with gossip or negative news shows or frightening movies. Focus on your faith and feed it. The more energy and time you give it, the stronger it becomes. And anytime you feel afraid of doing something but go ahead and do it anyway, you will be reprogramming your attitude. When you feel fear, it will mean "go" instead of "stop," and "fight harder" instead of "give up."

I opened this chapter writing about how Franklin D. Roosevelt overcame great obstacles, including fear, to become a world leader. Eleanor Roosevelt, his wife, was also a high achiever and leader in her own right. When her husband was struck down by polio, she not only nursed him back to health, she kept his political aspirations alive by becoming involved in New York state politics on his behalf. She promoted human rights causes while Franklin was president, and after mourning his death became a delegate to the United Nations. She once wrote, "You gain strength, courage and confidence by every experience in which you really stop to look fear in the face. You are able to say to yourself, 'I lived through this horror. I can take the next thing that comes along.' You must do the thing you think you cannot do."

That is what overcoming fear may be to you—doing what you think you can't. But no matter how strong a hold fear may try to take on you, it can be overcome, because fear is in your mind, and your mind can be changed using the difference maker—your attitude.

HOW YOUR ATTITUDE CAN BE THE DIFFERENCE MAKER CONCERNING FEAR

How much of a factor is fear in your life? To what degree does it dominate your attitude? Rate yourself according to the fear index. Circle the number that best corresponds to how you feel about fear:

1. I don't remember the last time I was really afraid even though I take significant risks on a daily basis.
2. I am afraid rarely and only when I or someone close to me is physically in danger; I take reasonable risks and manage my anxiety well.

3. I am a little more fearful than I would like to be, and if I had more courage, I would do more of the things I would really like to do in life.
4. Fear is a significant factor in my everyday life; I avoid anything that I would consider risky or dangerous.
5. I am afraid of many things on a daily basis, and it changes the way I live my life.

Here's what I recommend you do according to how you rated yourself:

If you circled number 1, you are an unusual individual who does not experience normal fear, maybe even when in dangerous situations. You may have to temper your actions with greater discernment and wisdom.

If you circled number 2, you have a good attitude toward fear and possess an excellent handle on it. You should try to encourage others who have a more difficult time with fear than you do.

If you circled number 3 or number 4, you are in an excellent position to improve your life by changing your attitude toward fear. Begin by identifying the source of your fears and determining to turn your fear into fire. For each area of fear, figure out its positive opposite and then create a plan of action to cultivate that quality. Then focus on what you can control *today*. And don't forget that fear is the normal price for progress.

If you circled number 5, then fear is really getting the better of you, and you will have a difficult time overcoming it on your own. Talk to a counselor, clergyman, or doctor to get advice on how to proceed.

NINE

Failure

When it comes to failure, I have to agree with Jan Christian Smuts, a prime minister of South Africa in the first half of the twentieth century who desired to dismantle the country's apartheid system. He said, "A man is not defeated by his opponents but by himself." Most people don't need to learn more about how to overcome their rivals. They need to learn how to get out of their own way.

SELF-SABOTAGING BEHAVIORS

There are three types of people in this world: the "wills," the "won'ts," and the "can'ts." The first type accomplish everything. The second oppose everything. The third fail at everything. People who accomplish much certainly are competent, but their attitude also makes a huge difference. A positive attitude will definitely help you avoid being part of the second group. And if you learn how to handle failure correctly, you'll be able to keep yourself out of the third group.

What tends to pull people into the "can't" group? Most of the time, there are four things:

1. Expecting Failure

The Law of Human Behavior says, "Sooner or later we will get what we expect." Usually, the people who keep failing are the ones who expect to. They're like the pessimist whose tombstone epitaph read, "I expected this."

> *Sooner or later we will get what we expect.*
>
> —THE LAW OF HUMAN BEHAVIOR

In her autobiography, actress Helen Hayes wrote about the Thanksgiving when she cooked her first turkey. Before serving it, she made an announcement to her husband and son.

"Now I know this is the first turkey I've ever cooked," she said. "If it isn't any good, I don't want anybody to say a word. We'll just get up from the table, without comment, and go out to a restaurant to eat."

Hayes then went back to the kitchen and returned to the dining room with the turkey. There she found her husband and son seated at the table—with their hats and coats on.[1]

2. Personalizing Failure

People cannot perform in a way inconsistent with the way they see themselves. Everybody fails. But people who continually fail expect to fail and usually *see themselves as failures*. There's a big difference between failing and being a failure.

Sportswriter Grantland Rice observed, "Failure isn't so bad if it doesn't attack the heart. Success is all right if it doesn't go to the head." If you want to maintain a good attitude and be successful, you cannot take your failures—or your successes—too personally. That's always a danger. But as you get older, more experienced, and more confident, you realize that your failures aren't fatal, and your successes don't completely define you.

3. Refusing to Take a Risk

Life means risk. People who sabotage themselves shouldn't worry about failure as much as they should be concerned about the chances they miss when they don't even try. Speech writer Charles Parnell observed, "Too many people are having what might be called 'near-life experiences.' They go through life bunting, so afraid of failure that they never try to win the big prizes, never knowing the thrill of hitting a home run or even taking a swing at one."

French writer, poet, and art critic Guillaume Apollinaire wrote,

> Come to the edge.
> No, we will fall.
> Come to the edge.
> No, we will fall.
> They came to the edge.
> He pushed them and they flew.

Those who fly always first get out on the edge. If you want to seize an opportunity, you must take a risk. If you want to grow, you must make mistakes. If you want to reach your potential, you will have to take chances. If you don't, you will be resigned to a life of mediocrity. The people who don't make mistakes end up working for those who do. And in the end, they often end up regretting the safe life they lived.

4. Letting Failure Defeat Them

After a particularly bad defeat, legendary baseball manager Casey Stengel remarked, "You gotta lose 'em sometimes. When you do, lose 'em right." Everybody experiences losses. But not everybody allows himself to be stopped by those losses. We must prepare ourselves for failure. We should train for it, preparing to bounce back from it when it occurs. As professional snooker player Steve Davis says, "It may not be your fault for being down, but it is your fault for not getting up." That's what people with the right attitude do—they get back up and keep trying.

> *"It may not be your fault for being down, but it is your fault for not getting up."—Steve Davis*

HOW TO PROFIT FROM FAILURE

If you can't avoid failure, yet you're also not supposed to give in to it and let it color your thinking, what do you do with it? The answer is profit from it. Several years ago I wrote a book called *Failing Forward*. The thesis of the book was that the difference between average people and achieving people is their perception of and response to failure. What creates the right perception and response? The answer is the difference maker. When you have the right attitude, you can actually use failure to your advantage and profit from it. Here's how:

1. CHANGE YOUR ATTITUDE

Cartoon character Homer Simpson summarized the attitude of millions of people when he said, "Kids, you tried your best and you failed miserably. The lesson is, never try." Homer is the classic underachiever. In another episode, he stated, "Trying is the first step toward failure." Homer never tries, and like many real people, he'll be stuck where he is forever.

Business staffing pioneer Robert Half observed, "Laziness is a secret ingredient that goes into failure. But it's only kept a secret from the person who fails."

People who succeed develop an attitude of tenacity. They refuse to quit, and they are determined not to let failure defeat them. If you desire to fulfill your dreams, achieve your goals, and live life to the fullest, that's the kind of attitude you need to cultivate.

2. Change Your Vocabulary

A noted psychiatrist once remarked that the two saddest words in the human vocabulary are "if only." He believed that people who get trapped in their failures spend their whole lives saying "if only—if only I had tried harder, if only I had been more kind to my kids, if only I had been more truthful, if only . . ." The way to correct that mind-set is to change your vocabulary by substituting the words "next time"—"next time I will try harder, next time I will be more kind to my kids, next time I will be more truthful."

Failure isn't failure if you do better the next time. In *Leaders on Leadership*, Warren Bennis interviewed seventy of the nation's top performers in numerous fields. None of them used the word *failure* to describe their mistakes. Instead they referred to learning experiences, tuition paid, detours, or opportunities for growth.[2] You may think that's a small difference, but that small difference can make a big difference. The way you think determines how you act.

Failure isn't failure if you do better the next time.

3. Pay Little Attention to the Odds

You may feel that the odds are stacked against you in life. So what! Every person who has ever achieved something significant had to overcome the odds. The problem for most people isn't the odds. It's that they sell themselves too short. R. H. Headlee observed, "Most people think too small, aim too low, and quit too soon."

When it comes to the thing you love to do, the thing you were made to do, aim high. The odds matter little. Whether you fall down along the way matters little. You fell when learning to walk, didn't you? Maxwell Maltz, developer of psycho-cybernetics, says, "You are a champion in the art of living if you reach only 65 percent of your goals." If the odds say you will make a lot of mistakes on the way to success, so be it. As long as you are eventually successful, isn't that what matters? Remember, if at first you don't succeed, then know that you're running about average.

4. Let Failure Point You to Success

Oliver Goldsmith was born the son of a poor preacher in Ireland in the 1700s. Growing up, he wasn't a great student. In fact, his schoolmaster labeled him a "stupid blockhead." He did manage to earn a college degree, but he finished at the bottom of his class. He was unsure of what he wanted to do. At first he tried to become a preacher, but it didn't suit him, and he was never ordained. Next he tried law but failed at it. He then settled on medicine, but he was an indifferent doctor and was not passionate about his profession. He was able to hold several posts only temporarily. Goldsmith lived in poverty, was often ill, and once even had to pawn his clothes to buy food.

It looked like he would never find his way. But then he discovered an interest and aptitude for writing and translating. At first, he worked as a Fleet Street reviewer and writer. But then he began to write works that came out of his own interests. He secured his reputation as a novelist with *The Vicar of Wakefield*, a poet with "The Deserted Village," and a playwright with *She Stoops to Conquer*.

My friend, Tim Masters, says that failure is the productive part of success. It provides the road you don't have to travel again, the mountain you don't have to climb again, and the valley you don't have to cross again. At the time you're making mistakes, they may not feel like "the kiss of Jesus," which was Mother Teresa's term for failures that drive us to God. But if we have the right attitude, they can lead us to what we ought to be doing.

5. Hold on to Your Sense of Humor

One of the best things you can do for yourself when you fail is to learn to laugh. I love the comment made by a humorist who said he spoke for an organization where they always rated the previous meeting's speaker in their program using little bells. Speakers who received a standing ovation got four bells next to their name. Those who were above average got three. Merely average speakers got two bells, and poor speakers got one. The humorist said that when he spoke to them several months ago, they awarded him the no-bell prize.

There isn't a person alive who wouldn't benefit from a good laugh, especially when he's done something really stupid. When you take your mistakes too seriously, then everything seems to become life-and-death. When that happens, you sure die a lot. The way to solve that is to keep your sense of humor no matter how bad things get.

6. LEARN FROM YOUR MISTAKES

Successful restauranteur and celebrity chef Wolfgang Puck said, "I learned more from the one restaurant that didn't work than from all the ones that were successes." Isn't that usually the way it is? I know that I've learned more from my failures than from my successes—the times that I've had the right attitude about them. When I didn't try to make excuses or place the blame on others, I always learned. That's why I love this quote from Robert Kiyosaki, author of *Rich Dad, Poor Dad*. He says, "Sometimes you win and sometimes you learn."[3] That's the mark of a great attitude! You don't lose—you learn.

> *"Sometimes you win and sometimes you learn."*—ROBERT KIYOSAKI

7. DON'T LOSE YOUR PERSPECTIVE

When ethicist and theologian Reinhold Niebuhr prayed the now famous "Serenity Prayer," he was preaching in a little church in Massachusetts. Only a small group of people was in the audience that day, but one person liked the prayer and after the service asked him for a copy.

"Here," Niebuhr responded, handing over a crumpled piece of paper. "I doubt I'll have any more use for it."

That simple prayer went on to become the most published prayer in America, and Alcoholics Anonymous adopted it.[4] It's ironic that Niebuhr's prayer became so popular. Evidently his perspective wasn't good because he didn't know what he had.

When Football Hall of Fame coach Don Shula was head coach of the Miami Dolphins, he used to practice a twenty-four-hour rule. He allowed himself, his players, and his coaches only twenty-four hours after a game to celebrate a victory or lament a loss. Once the twenty-four hours had passed, it was time to think about getting ready for the next game. That kind of perspective made Shula one of the most successful coaches in NFL history.

Failure is just like success—it's a day-to-day process, not someplace you arrive one day. Failure is not a one-time event. It's how you deal with life along the way. True, you will make mistakes, but you can't conclude that you're a failure until you breathe your last breath. Until then, you're still in the process, and there is still time to turn things around.

8. Don't Become Too Familiar with Failure

In a *Peanuts* comic strip, Lucy misses yet another fly ball. As she approaches Charlie Brown on the mound to explain, she says, "I thought I had it, but suddenly I remembered all the others I've missed." Then Lucy sums up with the ultimate in excuses: "The past got in my eyes." Clearly, Lucy has become way too familiar with failure.

I once heard somebody say that winning is coming in fourth exhausted but excited because you came in fifth last time. That's the right way to think about failure. If you let your mistakes get you down and you stop trying, then you've taken up residence in the house of failure. That's a place nobody ought to live.

9. MAKE FAILURE A GAUGE FOR GROWTH

If you were a baseball fan during the early 1960s, you probably remember a Los Angeles Dodger named Maury Wills. From 1960 to 1966, Wills was a record-making base stealer. In the 1962 season alone, he stole 104 bases!

Wills set another record during that time: most times being thrown out while stealing. In 1965, a year in which he stole more bases than any other player in the major leagues, he also held the record for times caught stealing: thirty-one times.

Most baseball enthusiasts don't remember Wills' failures; they remember only his successes. But if Wills had allowed himself to become discouraged by his outs, he would not have continued to attempt steals, and he never would have set any records.

Successful people understand the role failure plays in achievement. That's true in any life endeavor. Inventor Thomas Edison said, "I'm not discouraged because every wrong attempt discarded is another step forward." And gold-medal-winning gymnast Mary Lou Retton asserted, "Achieving that goal is a good feeling, but to get there you have to also get through the failures. You've got to be able to pick yourself up and continue." Whether it's thousands of experiments that don't work or thousands of falls from a balance beam, the milestones on the road of success are always failures. The farther you go, the more failures you experience.

> *"The person interested in success has to learn to view failure as a healthy, inevitable part of the process of getting to the top."*—JOYCE BROTHERS

Psychologist Joyce Brothers observed, "The person interested in success has to learn to view failure as a healthy, inevitable part of the process of getting to the top." You have to learn to actually see failure as a friend, a companion to success. If you're not failing, then you probably aren't really moving forward. You're just doing what's familiar, comfortable, and safe. As actor Mickey Rooney said, "You always pass failure on the way to success."

10. NEVER GIVE UP

A young man who had just gone off to college decided to bring a female friend he was thinking of dating home to meet his mom. When his friend did not meet his mom's approval, he quickly cooled to the idea of dating her and brought another girl home, hoping for better luck. But this girl didn't meet Mom's standards either. One by one, he brought every girl he knew home, and not a one of them met his mom's approval.

Fed up, he went looking for a girl exactly like his mother. She was the same height, had the same coloring, and even had similar mannerisms. *Surely*, he thought, *she won't have any objections to* this *girl*. And he was right. Mom loved her. There was only one problem: Dad didn't!

Failure doesn't mean you'll never succeed. It just

means it will take longer. John Wayne utters a great line in the movie *The Train Robbers*. He says, "You're going to spend the rest of your life getting up one more time than you're knocked down, so you'd better start getting used to it." That's what success is—getting up one time more than you fall. You have no idea how close you may be to what you desire to achieve. If you give up, you will never know—and you guarantee that you will never get there. Author, lawyer, economist, and actor Ben Stein says, "The human spirit is never finished when it is defeated. It is finished when it surrenders." My advice is: don't ever give up!

Failure doesn't mean you'll never succeed.
It just means it will take longer.

About twenty years ago, *Time* magazine described a study by a psychologist of people who had lost their jobs three times due to plant closings. The writers were amazed by what they discovered. They expected the people being laid off to be beaten down and discouraged. Instead they found them to be incredibly resilient. Why was that? They concluded that people who had weathered repeated adversity had learned to bounce back. People who had lost a job and found a new one twice before were much better prepared to deal with adversity than someone who had always worked at the same place and had never faced adversity.[5]

It may sound ironic, but if you have experienced a lot of failure, you are actually in a better position to achieve success than people who haven't. When you fail, and fail, and fail again—and keep getting back up on your feet and keep learning from your failures—you are building strength, tenacity, experience, and wisdom. And people who develop such qualities are capable of sustaining their success, unlike many for whom good things come early and easily. So if you've failed a lot, celebrate. As long as you don't give up, you're in a really good place.

HOW YOUR ATTITUDE CAN BE THE DIFFERENCE MAKER CONCERNING FAILURE

It's hard to put failure in the right perspective if you are continuing to engage in self-sabotaging behaviors. Answer the following four questions honestly:

1. **Expectations:** What's usually the forecast for your day—cloudy or sunny? Are you someone for whom most things generally go right or wrong? What percentage of the time do you expect to succeed at things you do day to day? Mark your answer on the line below.

0 25 50 75 100

Most things seem to go my way | Nothing goes my way

2. **Self-Image:** How do you see yourself when it comes to failure? This may be a difficult thing to discern. Do you believe you are a highly competent and successful person who sometimes fails, or are you basically a failure who is working to avoid mistakes?

0 25 50 75 100

I am a success who sometimes fails | I am a failure

3. **Risk:** What is the role of risk in your life? Is risk a normal and healthy part of achieving success, or is it something to be avoided at all cost? Perhaps the best

way to discern the way you really feel is to ask the question this way: What percentage of the time do you seek comfort, safety, peace, and the status quo?

0 25 50 75 100

I seek out reasonable risks — I avoid risks at all costs

4. **Tenacity:** Think about the top four or five priorities in your life. If you can't name them off the top of your head, then give the subject some thought and jot them down. In what percentage of those priorities have you lost intensity and stopped fighting to improve and succeed? If you're not sure, use the following as a gauge: If you have not seen a significant improvement in the last year, then you are probably not adequately pushing yourself to succeed in that area.

0 25 50 75 100

I'm still fighting to succeed — I've lost my intensity

If you marked a number higher than 25 percent for any of the questions, then you may be exhibiting self-sabotaging behavior. Use the following list of questions to help change your thinking the next time you experience failure.

- Did I fail because of another person, because of my situation, or because of myself?
- Did I actually fail, or did I simply fall short of unrealistic expectations?
- What part of this "failure" was successful?
- What lessons can I learn from this?
- Am I grateful for the experience despite the outcome?
- Is there a way to turn the failure into a success—for myself or others?
- Have people I know had a similar experience; if so, can they help me?
- How can I use my experience to help others avoid similar problems?
- Where do I go from here?

TEN

The Difference Maker in Your Life Can Help You Make a Difference in the Lives of Others

Attitude isn't everything, but it is one thing that can make a difference in your life. I genuinely believe that, and hopefully by now you have discovered that those words are not only true but also potentially life-changing. People who are successful don't have fewer challenges than anyone else. At this point you probably realize that successful people experience more failure, overcome more problems, navigate more changes, and deal with more potential discouragement and fear than those who don't succeed. How do they do that? They let the difference maker make the difference!

Recently I received a letter from Kevin Keup, president of K. Keup Concrete Construction in Batavia, Illinois, describing how he made some major changes in his life. Here's what he wrote:

Dear Sir,

Two years ago on Father's Day I received your book *The Power of Attitude* as a gift from my wife. As I looked through it, one passage stopped me. On page 23, the quote is, "A pessimist is a person who, regardless of the present, is disappointed in the future." That hit me like a ton of bricks. It referred to the person I had unknowingly become. I didn't know I was at that negative place until I read those words, and I was forced to reckon with who I had become.

I had been in business for 29 years at that point, and for 28 of those years I was an optimist. Whatever difficulties came my way, when I went to bed I knew tomorrow would be a better day. At some point I changed. That phrase in your book was a real trigger for me. Acknowledging that I was living in deep pessimism became a turning point for me and started a journey of change in my life.

I have been renewed spiritually, emotionally, and physically during this journey over the last 2 years. As a business owner, I have a unique opportunity to communicate my thoughts with the people who work with me. One thing that we have implemented here is including a passage from your book and other sources with each week's payroll for about 40 people.

We work in the construction industry, and having these messages go out to our men has been powerful and has brought about positive change. Some of the men keep the quotes on their refrigerators or on bulletin boards to share with their families. . .

All this started with your book and the power of that particular phrase, and I just want to thank you.

Sincerely,
Kevin Keup

When a person recognizes that his attitude isn't right, it opens the door for positive change and tremendous opportunity.

HELPING YOU—HELPING OTHERS

I want to leave you with a few important thoughts as you finish this book and prepare to harness the power of the difference maker in your life and that of others.

1. Make the Decision to Allow the Difference Maker to Make a Difference in Your Life

Never forget that your attitude is a choice. You are the only person who can decide to harness the power of the difference maker. As you ponder that decision, consider this:

> There is a choice you have to make in everything you do.
>
> So keep in mind that in the end, the choice you make makes you.

For many people in this world, the difference maker will never make a difference. Why? They have chosen an attitude that is not an asset to them. If someone isn't purposely choosing to have the right attitude, then she is choosing to have the wrong attitude.

2. Manage Your Decision Every Day of Your Life

The choices we make in life don't *stay* chosen by themselves. In my book *Today Matters*, I point out, "Successful people make right decisions early and manage those decisions daily." Decision making is important. We can't change and grow without it. But decision managing is

highly underrated. We think that our good decisions will automatically stay good, but they won't. Every right decision we make must be managed every day. Remember what Kevin Keup said in his letter? He said he had "unknowingly become" a negative person—even after twenty-eight and a half years of being a positive person!

His was a management issue. He had failed to manage his attitude. And I've learned through experience that it's easier to *maintain* a right attitude than it is to *regain* it! Every day, begin your day by consciously choosing to manage your attitude as a positive influence in your life.

It's easier to maintain a right attitude than it is to regain it.

3. Do Not Allow Adversity to Have an Adverse Effect on Your Attitude

Everybody can have a good attitude when things are going well. But what happens to you when situations in your life go bad? Think back to the Big Five Attitude Obstacles in the book: discouragement, change, problems, fear, and failure. Which one is most likely to affect you negatively? Are you continually preparing

yourself to meet its challenges? You have to be ready mentally to keep difficulties from defeating you.

In September of 2005, Hurricane Katrina left a devastating mark on the southern United States. A few days after the storm hit, an article appeared in *USA Today* containing advice to the people of the American Gulf Coast from people who had suffered similar tragedies. Here's what it said:

> Veterans of some of the nation's worst natural disasters in recent years offer these words of advice for Hurricane Katrina's victims:
>
> Be patient. "It will probably take longer to recover than you think," says Curt Ivy, city manager in Homestead, Fla., ground zero for Hurricane Andrew in 1992. "We thought we would be back in three to five years. We really didn't have a clue."
>
> Beware of shady contractors. "You know there's going to be every Tom, Dick and Harry fly-by-night contractor in New Orleans," says Bob Boucher, whose Houston home was flooded by Tropical Storm Allison in 2001. Don't pay in advance for materials, and don't pay in full before the work is done.
>
> Save your money. If you're out of work, consider call-

ing creditors and putting them on hold rather than paying your bills on time. "What you need is cash until these things pass," says Stan Thomas, who lost his mortgage business in the 1994 Northridge earthquake that hit Southern California.

Prepare for a shortage of labor and materials. Anticipate your needs, such as concrete, Sheetrock, shingles—and people to do the work.

Lean on others, including counselors and churches. "The biggest thing is being able to rely on a close network of friends, family, really pulling together," says Jacob Spenn, who manages the Tropical Storm Allison Recovery Project in Harris County, Texas. "The tighter communities are the communities that seem to come out of it faster."

Go slow and have faith. "Don't do anything real quick," says Phil Halstead, who lost his house to a tornado in Oklahoma City six years ago. "Initially, you think, 'There's just no way I'm going to get out of this,' but you will. You got to stay tough mentally, because it could sure wear you down."[1]

Notice that much of the advice given by people who survived other tragedies focused on attitude issues: Be patient, be wary, prepare yourself, lean on others, have faith, and stay mentally tough. These veterans of adversity are essentially saying, "You couldn't control Katrina, and you can't control your circumstances, but you *can* control your attitude. If you do, it will make a difference in your life. It can be the difference maker between giving up and bouncing back."

4. Once the Difference Maker Makes a Difference in Your Life, Help Others Discover the Difference Maker in Their Lives

I want you to notice one more thing about the letter from Kevin Keup. He's not keeping his discovery about the power of a positive attitude to himself. He's sharing the difference maker with his employees because he knows it will help them. And the result is that the difference maker is starting to spread through the company and make a difference there.

Anyone who helps others discover the impact of the difference maker helps himself, helps others, and makes his little corner of the world a better place to live. Who wouldn't want to be around people who believe in themselves and others, have hope, and work positively to solve problems and overcome difficulties?

I've been writing books for almost thirty years now, and I will keep doing so for one reason: I want to add value to people. Sometimes people like Kevin write me to say that a book I've written has made a difference in their lives. Most of the time, the people whose lives are positively impacted never tell me. That's okay.

Recently my friend Carole Bos shared with me the story of someone who made a difference in her life and how she desperately wants to let him know about the impact he had made. I was so intrigued that I asked her to write it out for me so that I could share it with you. Here is her story:

> It was one of those damp winter nights when the wind, blowing off the North Sea, made me long for a fireplace and a good book. Instead, I had to write a final exam.
>
> We lived in a flat with no fireplace. I was twenty-one years old, trying simultaneously to learn Dutch and German. My professor, on sabbatical from USC, was wrapping up his year of teaching German in the Netherlands. The night of the exam would be the last time I'd see him before he returned to the States.
>
> At the end of class, the prof dismissed everyone but asked me to stay for a few minutes: "I'd like to grade

your exam before you leave." I thought it an odd request but obliged him. I had no idea he was about to change my life.

As he handed my graded exam back to me, that USC prof said, "Carole, I want to talk with you about your future. I've taught at USC a long time. I've had lots of students pass through my classes. You are one of the brightest of those many students, but you do not know that about yourself. As you leave here tonight, I want you to remember my words: You can do anything you want to do. You can be anything you want to be. But you first need to believe in yourself. You need to change your attitude about what you can personally accomplish. Before we part ways, I want you to promise me you will do that."

His words were burned in my memory when I realized he had no motive other than my best interests. I told Jim, my husband, about our conversation.

"He's right," Jim observed. "I think you should study law and become a lawyer." I ultimately took the advice of both.

Working hard in college, juggling both a job and school, I managed to graduate at the top of my class. During law school, I clerked at a firm where I learned to be a courtroom lawyer. After graduation, looking forward to a career with Juris Doctor degree in hand, I was crushed. The firm hired all the male clerks as permanent lawyers. As for me, the only clerk who'd made *Law Review*: "Women shouldn't be trial lawyers." In order to be a courtroom lawyer, I had to start my own firm.

Twenty-five years later, I am blessed with a great team at Bos & Glazier where we work with wonderful clients. I have had the privilege of handling many interesting cases throughout the country, writing inspirational books and giving motivational talks. My great sadness is that I've been unable to carry our children to term. But using my love of storytelling, my degrees in history and Russian studies, and my trial-lawyer skill in finding primary sources, I am able to touch the lives of children everywhere through AwesomeStories.com. It is used in schools throughout the States (as an online teaching/learning tool) and in seventy-five countries (as a fun way for people to improve their English).

I would like to let my USC professor know he became one of the top five most influential people in my life. The problem is . . . I no longer remember his name.

Countless millions of people are like that professor. Every day they add value to others, and there is a very high probability that in most cases they will never be told that they made a difference. That's also okay. This army of difference makers understands that success each day should be judged by the seeds they sow, not the harvest they reap.

Success each day should be judged by the seeds sown, not the harvest reaped.

Won't you join us in this crusade to make a difference in the lives of others? I believe you will. As the author, I hope this book will make a difference in your life. As you lay it down, I am hoping you will make a difference in the lives of others. That is what *The Difference Maker* is all about. Godspeed!

Notes

Chapter 1: Where Did You Get Your Attitude?

1. Bob Conklin, *The Dynamics of Successful Attitudes* (New York: Prentice-Hall, 1963).
2. Howard Baker, "Frankl, Victor E. (1905-1997)," obituary, *Gale Encyclopedia*, http://www.findarticles.com/p/articles/mi_g2699/is_0004/ai_2699000472 (accessed September 15, 2005).
3. Pamela Jessica Runyon, "Viktor E. Frankl," *Empire:zine*, http://www.empirezine.com/spotlight/frankl/frankl1.htm (accessed September 15, 2005).

Chapter 2: What Your Attitude *Cannot* Do for You

1. Sharon Jayson, "Yep, Life'll Burst That Self-Esteem Bubble," *USA Today*, February 15, 2005, http://www.usatoday.com/life/lifestyle/2005-02-15-self-esteem_x.htm (accessed September 14, 2005).
2. Ibid.
3. Bill Hybels, *Courageous Leadership* (Grand Rapids, MI: Zondervan, 2002), 84.
4. "Positive Attitude Delays Aging," BBC News World Edition, September 12, 2004, http://news.bbc.co.uk/2/hi/health/3642356.stm (accessed September 15, 2005).
5. http://www.getmotivation.com/favorites12.html.

6. "Peter Jennings," Wikipedia, http://en.wikipedia.org/wiki/Peter_Jennings (accessed September 19, 2005).
7. Ibid.

Chapter 3: What Your Attitude *Can* Do for You

1. Denis Waitley, *The Winner's Edge* (New York: Berkley, 1986).
2. Ernest H. Rosenbaum and Isadora R. Rosenbaum, "Attitude—The Will to Live," Cancer Supportive Care Programs National and International, reprinted from *Coping with Cancer*, March/April 1999, http://www.cancersupportivecare.com/attitude.html#Mind (accessed September 23, 2005).
3. Ibid.
4. John Milton, *Paradise Lost, Book I*, line 253.

Chapter 4: How to Make Your Attitude Your Greatest Asset

1. quoted at http://www.eyeforbeauty.com/Personal/Philosophy/life.html.
2. Norman Vincent Peale, *The Power of the Plus Factor* (New York: Ballantine, 1996).
3. Adidas ad, *ESPN: The Magazine*, February 16, 2004.

Chapter 5: Discouragement

1. Adapted from "How You Can Tell When It's Going to Be a Rotten Day," http://www.joke-archives.com/toplists/rottendy.html .
2. Charles Bracelen Flood, *Lee: The Last Years* (New York: First Mariner Books, 1998) 136.
3. *The Megiddo Message*.
4. "Colonel Harland Sanders," about KFC, www.kfc.com/about/colonel.htm.
5. Napoleon Hill, *Think and Grow Rich* (New York: Ballantine, 1987).
6. Eliza Strickland, "Happy Birthday 'Leaves of Grass,'" http://jscms.jrn.columbia.edu/cns/2005-02-15/strickland-waltwhitman (accessed November 1, 2005).
7. D. Martyn Lloyd-Jones, *Spiritual Depression: Its Causes and Cure* (Grand Rapids, MI: Wm. B. Eerdmans Publishing Company, 1965), 20.
8. Lucy Maher, "Are You Too Hard on Yourself?"

9. Exercise Regimen for the Workplace," http://www.ucolick.org/~de/humour/exercise.html

Chapter 6: Change

1. David Bayles and Ted Orland, *Art and Fear* (Santa Barbara: Capra Press, 1993), 57.
2. Frances Hodgson Burnett, *The Secret Garden* (New York: Harper Trophy, 1998), 337.

Chapter 7: Problems

1. Tom Zuercher, "And Let it Begin with Me," http://www.brethren.org/AC2001/Zuercher.htm.
2. *Forbes*, October 16, 1920, https://www.keepmedia.com/Auth.do?extId=10022&uri=/archive/forbes/2005/1017/044.html.
3. "Bits and Pieces," August 9, 2001, 21.
4. Richard Reeves, *President Reagan: The Triumph of Imagination* (New York: Simon and Schuster, 2005).

Chapter 8: Fear

1. Franklin D. Roosevelt, Inaugural Address, March 4, 1933, as published in Samuel Rosenman, ed., *The Public Papers of Franklin D. Roosevelt, Volume Two: The Year of Crisis, 1933* (New York: Random House, 1938), 11–16, quoted on http://historymatters.gmu.edu/d/5057/ (accessed November 26, 2005).
2. Genesis 3:10, NKJV.
3. James Reich in *Journal of Nervous and Mental Disease*, March 1986, quoted in Robert Handly and Pauline Neff, *Beyond Fear* (New York: Rawson Associates, 1987), 9.
4. Barna Research Group, "Most Americans Satisfied with Life Despite Having Quality of Life Issues," March 26, 2002, http://www.barna.org/FlexPage.aspx?Page=BarnaUpdate&BarnaUpdateID=109 (accessed November 26, 2005).
5. *Webster's New World Dictionary of American English, 3rd College Edition* (Cleveland, OH: Simon and Schuster, 1991).
6. Joe Tye, author of *Never Fear, Never Quit* (New York: Delacorte Press, 1997).
7. Barbara Bush, Address to Kennebunk (Maine) High School, source unknown.

Chapter 9: Failure

1. Helen Hayes, *On Reflection: An Autobiography* (New York: M. Evans and Company, 1968).
2. Warren Bennis, *Leaders on Leadership* (Boston: Harvard Business School Press, 1992).
3. Robert Kiyosaki, *Rich Dad, Poor Dad* (New York: Warner Business Books, 2000).
4. Harold C. Warlick Jr., *Conquering Loneliness* (Waco, Tex: Word Books, 1979).
5. Arthur Freeman and Rose DeWolf, *The 10 Dumbest Mistakes Smart People Make and How to Avoid Them: Simple and Sure Techniques for Gaining Greater Control of Your Life* (New York: HarperCollins, 1992).

Chapter 10: The Difference Maker in Your Life Can Help You Make a Difference in the Lives of Others

1. Richard Wolf, "Words of Advice from Fellow Survivors," *USA Today*, September 12, 2005, A6.

About the Author

John C. Maxwell, known as America's expert on leadership, speaks in person to hundreds of thousands of people each year. He has communicated his principles to Fortune 500 companies, the United States Military Academy at West Point, international marketing organizations, the NCAA, and professional sports groups such as the NFL.

Maxwell is the founder of Injoy Stewardship Services, as well as several other organizations dedicated to helping people reach their leadership potential. He dedicates much of his time to training leaders worldwide through EQUIP, a non-profit organization. The *New York Times* bestselling author has written more than forty books, including *Winning with People*, *The 360 Degree Leader*, and the million-sellers *Developing the Leader Within You* and *The 21 Irrefutable Laws of Leadership*.

For more information, go to
www.MaximumImpact.com

EQUIP™
Equipping Leaders To Reach Our World
Jesus had a strategy...
Equip leaders.
Founded by leadership expert and
author John C. Maxwell, EQUIP's
passion is the Great Commission
plain and simple.
EQUIP's strategy is developing Christian leaders worldwide with the skills needed to provide leadership to their communities, workplaces, and churches, to ultimately fulfill the Great Commission.
"My vision for EQUIP is that it be continually committed to developing leaders whose potential is great but opportunities for learning leadership have been limited."
John C. Maxwell, Founder of EQUIP
If you share our passion for fulfilling the
Great Commission by empowering great leaders
visit www.iEQUIP.org.

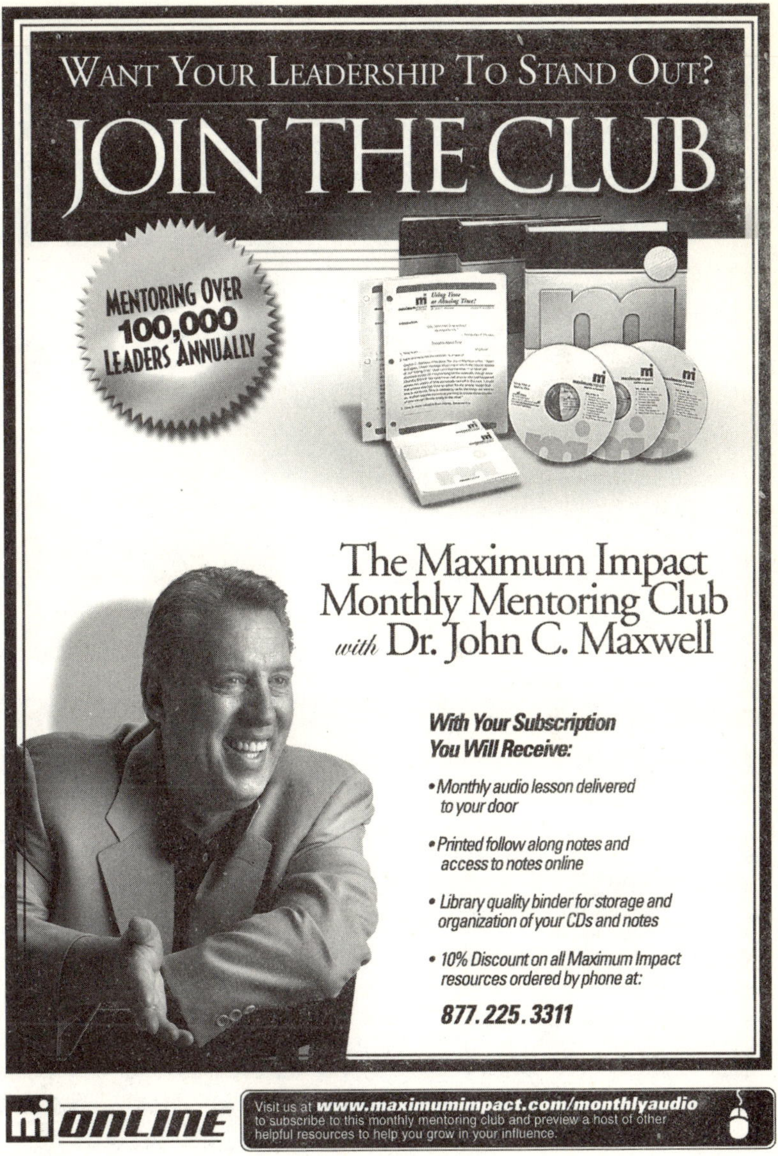
WANT YOUR LEADERSHIP TO STAND OUT?
JOIN THE CLUB
MENTORING OVER 100,000 LEADERS ANNUALLY
The Maximum Impact Monthly Mentoring Club with Dr. John C. Maxwell
With Your Subscription You Will Receive:
• Monthly audio lesson delivered to your door
• Printed follow along notes and access to notes online
• Library quality binder for storage and organization of your CDs and notes
• 10% Discount on all Maximum Impact resources ordered by phone at:
877.225.3311
mi ONLINE
Visit us at www.maximumimpact.com/monthlyaudio to subscribe to this monthly mentoring club and preview a host of other helpful resources to help you grow in your influence.

THE DIFFERENCE MAKER
AVAILABLE IN SPANISH
Autor del éxito de librería
Las 21 leyes irrefutables del liderazgo según el New York Time
JOHN C. MAXWELL
LO QUE MARCA LA Diferencia
Convierta Su Actitud En Su Posesión Más Valiosa
ISBN: 0881133108
Grupo Nelson
Una división de Thomas Nelson Publishers
juntos inspiramos al mundo
www.gruponelson.com

BOOKS BY DR. JOHN C. MAXWELL CAN TEACH YOU HOW TO BE A REAL SUCCESS

RELATIONSHIPS

Becoming a Person of Influence

Relationships 101

The Treasure of a Friend

25 Ways to Win with People

Winning with People

EQUIPPING

Developing the Leaders Around You

Equipping 101

Partners in Prayer

The 17 Essential Qualities of a Team Player

The 17 Indisputable Laws of Teamwork

Success One Day at a Time

Teamwork Makes the Dream Work

Your Road Map for Success

ATTITUDE

Attitude 101

The Difference Maker

Failing Forward

The Journey from Success to Significance

Living at the Next Level

The Winning Attitude

Your Bridge to a Better Future

LEADERSHIP

Developing the Leader Within You

Developing the Leader Within You Workbook

Leadership 101

The Right to Lead

The 360 Degree Leader

The 21 Indispensable Qualities of a Leader

The 21 Irrefutable Laws of Leadership

The 21 Most Powerful Minutes in a Leader's Day

25 WAYS TO WIN WITH PEOPLE

HOW TO MAKE OTHERS FEEL LIKE A MILLION BUCKS

JOHN C. MAXWELL
AND LES PARROTT, PH.D.

NELSON BUSINESS
A Division of Thomas Nelson Publishers
Since 1798

www.thomasnelson.com

Published in Nashville, Tennessee, by Thomas Nelson, Inc.

Nelson Books titles may be purchased in bulk for educational, business, fundraising, or sales promotional use. For information, please e-mail SpecialMarkets@ThomasNelson.com.

Published in association with Yates & Yates, LLP, Attorneys and Counselors, Orange, California.

Library of Congress Cataloging-in-Publication Data

Maxwell, John C., 1947-
25 ways to win with people : how to make others feel like a million bucks / John C. Maxwell and Les Parrott.
p. cm.
Includes bibliographical references.
ISBN 0-7852-6094-3 (hardcover)
ISBN 0-7852-7954-7 (international)
1. Interpersonal relations—Religious aspects—Christianity. 2. Interpersonal communication—Religious aspects—Christianity. 3. Interpersonal relations. 4. Interpersonal communication. I. Title: Twenty-five ways to win with people. II. Parrott, Les. III. Title.
BV4597.52.M393 2005
158.2—dc22

2005000103

Printed in the United States of America

05 06 07 08 09 QW 9 8 7 6 5 4 3

To Tom Mullins,

You are like the Pied Piper. When you walk into a room, people instantly want to follow you. More than anyone I know, you embody the 25 ways to win with people. You make everyone around you feel like a million bucks—including me!

—JOHN C. MAXWELL

To Mike Ingram and Monty Ortman,

Few people build a better business team, win more respect, and achieve bigger results than you two. You both have a winsome way of relating to everyone you meet. Your generous spirits and your investment in people will pay dividends for decades. I'm a better person for having known you both.

—LES PARROTT

CONTENTS

ACKNOWLEDGMENT

Thank you to Charlie Wetzel
for his help in writing this book.

LIFE'S GREATEST JOY

BY JOHN C. MAXWELL

In the spring of 2004, soon after turning in the finished manuscript of *Winning with People*, the publisher sent out a number of advance copies of the book, as they often do, to get feedback and endorsements. One of the people who received a copy was Les Parrott.

Now, you may know Dr. Les Parrott from any one of a number of his successes: he is a professor of psychology at Seattle Pacific University, the founder of the Center for Relationship Development, a nationally successful speaker to Fortune 500 companies, and a best-selling author of books such as *High-Maintenance Relationships* and *Love the Life You Live*. He has been a guest on CNN, *The NBC Nightly News*, *Oprah*, and other programs. But I know Les as a friend. In fact, when I first met Les, he was only a kid. He was just beginning his Ph.D. studies in psychology. And the instant I met him, I could see he was sharp. I knew he would soon be a rising star.

In the summer of 2004, I got a phone call from Les. "John," he said, "I loved *Winning with People*. I think it's going to help a lot of folks. It's going to prompt them to change their attitudes and see their relationships with people in a whole new light. And by the way, I wrote a nice endorsement for it. But I have an idea for you. I think you should write a sequel."

I had put my whole heart and a lifetime of relational learning into *Winning with People*, so I was a bit skeptical. But I have a lot of respect for Les, and he always has great ideas, so I was all ears.

"What's your idea?" I asked.

"I've watched you with people for years," Les continued. "When you spend time with people, you make them feel like a million bucks. You've made *me* feel like a million bucks. I bet you could sit down and come up with a couple of dozen specific things that you've mastered that you could teach others to do." That got my juices flowing. "And John, I think you should call the book *How to Make Others Feel Like a Million Bucks*."

Then Les started to rattle off some of the things he thought I should teach, such as giving others a reputation to uphold, mining the gold of good intentions, telling good stories, and helping people win. The more I thought, the more I liked the idea. *Winning with People* had been written to change the fundamental way people approached relationships. Doing what it suggests would take a period of time to accomplish. On the other hand, the book Les was suggesting would be able to help people learn specific skills that could be mastered in a matter of days.

"You know," I said after a long pause, "it's a great idea. Why don't you write it with me?"

Les was surprised.

"I think we'd make a great team," I told him. "You said yourself that you've watched me for years. You're a trained psychologist. Together we'll figure out what skills to write about. I'll teach how I work with people, and you can help people understand the psychology behind the practices."

And that's how *25 Ways to Win with People* came to be written. Les and I had a great time comparing notes, talking about relationships, and telling stories. My one reservation is that Les insisted on telling so many stories about me. I'm not anywhere near as good as Les makes me out to be. Like everyone, I've done stupid things, stepped on toes, and hurt people's feelings. But I've always tried to do my best. And I'm still working daily to improve my skills with others.

And I can tell you this: these skills really do work! Les and I believe that if you practice the skills in this book, your life will change. Why? Because will be able to help others see themselves in a positive light. You will often make them feel like a million bucks.

I believe there is no greater joy in life than seeing others blossom, grow, and reach their potential. This book can help you have a part in making that happen for the people in your life.

BETTER FOR HAVING KNOWN YOU

BY LES PARROTT

Some people possess an invisible quality that draws others to them like a magnet. They're more than just likable. Their charisma defines everything they do and every encounter they have. Accordingly they build better teams, win more respect, and achieve bigger results. Are they merely lucky in life, blessed with personality traits that spell success without effort? Not on your life!

This alluring and invisible trait is not inherited as much as it is honed. It's a captivating spirit that can be taught and caught. For too long people haven't tried to cultivate these qualities because of the false impression that you either have "it" or you don't. This book will help change that misinformed notion. For here you will find twenty-five of the most compelling keys to unlocking a charismatic spirit—a spirit that will help you win with almost everyone you encounter.

WHY WE'RE WRITING THIS BOOK TOGETHER

No one who has ever come in close contact with John Maxwell has walked away unaffected. That's certainly true for me. As a mentor, John has left a permanent imprint on nearly every aspect of my personal and professional life. More than twenty years ago, before I launched into my graduate training to become a clinical psychologist, I flew from my home in Chicago to spend a week with John in San Diego for the sole purpose of soaking up his wisdom. Some years later, it was John who encouraged me to write books and begin a speaking career. And these days, a dozen books later, when we happen to share the same platform, John is always my biggest fan. It's no exaggeration to say that John believes in me more than I could ever have the right to ask.

I'm a better person because John Maxwell is in my life. John taught me how to summon my courage; how to find my purpose and tap into my passion; how to hone my vision and strive toward my goals. He taught me how to "fail forward," how to make each day count, and how to cultivate a can-do attitude. Interaction with a people person like John can have that kind of an impact on you. Directly and indirectly, John has taught me multiple and invaluable life lessons. But more than anything, John has taught me how to win with people. He has a winsome way of relating to nearly everyone—whether it's a server at a restaurant or the chairman of a major corporation.

The Secrets of Interpersonal Magic

Down through the decades, I've studied John as he lifts people up. And as a friend, I wanted to know how I could personally cultivate more of his interpersonal magic. Anyone who has spent even a short period of time with John knows that he puts you at ease and makes you feel good. Not the kind of "good" that comes from a flippant compliment or insincere affirmation—and certainly not from a smarmy or manipulative slap on the back. I'm talking about the kind of goodness that comes from knowing he genuinely wants the best for you. He's pulling for you and wants you to win.

I've kept my eyes focused on even the most minute of interactions. Time and again, John displays an almost uncanny ability to disarm, entertain, and engage whomever he meets. In other words, he has the ability to make others feel like a million bucks. So as he already told you, one day I approached him with the idea of his sharing the secrets of his magnetic personality to help you learn to do what he does. When John invited me to write this book with him, I spent hours with him to draw out the things he does reflexively on a daily basis. And I also talked extensively to John's friends and staff. I heard story after story about the ways John has won with them and added value to their lives. I tell many of these stories in the book so that you can "see" the practices in action.

Within Your Reach

The twenty-five secrets we include in this book have the potential to change your life. They can help you to become the kind of magnetic person who lights up the room when you arrive. These skills are readily learnable. They are not just for a lucky few who seem to be hardwired with exclusive qualities. They are within reach of anyone who wants them. And they are crucial for anyone wanting to win with people.

1

START WITH YOURSELF

Your relationships can only be as healthy as you are.
—NEIL CLARK WARREN

LES . . . ON STARTING WITH YOURSELF

If you want to win with people, you've got to be a winner yourself—or at the very least be on your way to becoming one. There's no avoiding this simple fact.

As a psychologist specializing in relationships, I've seen hundreds of people in therapy. I've spoken to hundreds of thousands in seminars. I've written more than a dozen books on the subject. People close to me understand that I'm passionate about helping others win with people. But if there is one thing I know, it's that a new tip or technique to win with others will fall flat if you don't start with yourself.

Let me say it straight. If you try to practice the "ways" of winning with people that you are about to learn in the following chapters before you give serious attention to how you can be a winner yourself, you'll be sorely disappointed. However, if you will first take the time to focus on yourself, you'll soon be ready to focus on others.

You've Got to Start with Yourself

William James, the first American psychologist, said, "The hell to be endured hereafter, of which theology tells, is no worse than the hell we make for ourselves in this world by habitually fashioning our characters in the wrong way." If we do not form a winning character, we are sure to lose with other people. That's why this first step is so significant. In fact, there are at least two compelling reasons why winning with people hinges on starting with yourself.

You Can't Be Happy Without Being Healthy

Psychology used to think it was critical to focus on—and then eliminate—negative emotions. We now know there is a better way. A new generation of research has shifted psychology's primary analysis from that of misery to an understanding of wellness.

The new research reveals that you can't be happy simply by being unencumbered by depression, stress, or anxiety. No—you can't be happy unless you are healthy. And there's a lot more to health than not being sick. Emotional health is more than the absence of dysfunctional emotions. Emotional health is at the center of winning with people.

You Can't Give What You Don't Have

One of the oldest psychological truisms in the world is that you cannot give what you do not have. In fact, like every other psychologist-in-training, when I first began my graduate education, I was urged to get into psychotherapy myself. "Les," my advisor said, "as a psychologist, you will only be able to take a person as far as you have gone yourself." Why? Because you cannot give what you do not have. You cannot enjoy others until you enjoy yourself.

Harry Firestone said, "You get the best out of others when you give the best of yourself." So true. But if the best you have isn't any better than what those "others" already possess, you'll never take them any higher than they already are.

The bottom line? If you are not becoming a winner, you'll find it almost impossible to win with others. But here's the good news: your desire and attempts to win with others help to make you a winner. It's what American essayist Charles Warner was getting at when he said, "No one can sincerely try to help another without helping himself."

How to Be a Winner

"There's a period of life when we swallow a knowledge of ourselves," said Pearl Bailey, "and it becomes either good or sour inside." Everyone has little anxieties and insecurities. If I were to ask you to describe a winning person, a person who is whole and healthy, you might say something about this person being confident, warm, kind, stable, giving, and so on. And you'd be right, in a sense. But there's more to becoming a winner than having a list of enviable attributes. Being a winner comes down to one thing: your value.

Winners are valuable. Ask any star athlete or gold medalist who has just signed a multimillion-dollar endorsement deal. But truth be told, being a winner, in the purest sense of the word, has nothing to do with your performance, your salary, or your earning potential. It has to do with your value and whether or not you have *owned* it. When you embrace your own personal value, when you are secure in who you are, then you have become a winner.

Here are a few ways of doing just that:

RECOGNIZE YOUR VALUE. On more than one occasion, I've told the story of being on a speaking platform with my friend Gary Smalley when he did something that captivated the crowd. Before an audience of nearly ten thousand people, Gary held out a crisp fifty-dollar bill and asked them, "Who would like this fifty-dollar bill?" Hands started going up everywhere.

"I am going to give this fifty dollars to one of you," he said, "but first let me do this." He proceeded to crumple up the bill. Then he asked, "Who still wants it?" The same hands went up in the air.

"Well," he continued, "what if I do this?" He dropped it on the ground and started to grind it into the floor with his shoe. He picked it up, all crumpled and dirty. "Now, who still wants it?" Again, hands went into the air.

"You have all learned a valuable lesson," Gary said. "No matter what I do to the money, you still want it because it doesn't decrease in value. It is still worth fifty dollars."

Gary's simple illustration underscores a profound point. Many times in our lives we are dropped, crumpled, and ground into the dirt by the decisions we make or the circumstances that come our way. We may feel as though we are worthless, insignificant in our own eyes and in the eyes of others. But no matter what has happened or what will happen, we *never* lose our value as human beings. Nothing can take that away. Never forget that.

ACCEPT YOUR VALUE. How many times have you heard people say, "He has issues"? What they mean is that the person is stuck. The person is not healthy. He's got a hang-up. He's uncomfortable in his own skin. It's what we psychologists are getting at when we talk about self-acceptance.

Let's face it. All of us walking around on this planet have insecurities and issues that we wish we could change about ourselves. But certain things we can't. Some things about us just *are*. Maybe you weren't born with the kind of looks you would like. Or you aren't as tall as you desire. Your genes dealt you a hand that you've eventually got to accept—either that or you reject your personal value and spend your days trying to compensate for your insecurities. You become hung up, stuck on not being dealt a better hand.

The term *acceptance* comes from the Latin *ad capere* that means "to take to oneself." In other words, inherent in the process of accepting others is the act of self-acceptance. I'll say it again: you will never win with people until *you* become a winner.

INCREASE YOUR VALUE. Perhaps you already recognize and accept your value. Maybe you know at the center of your being, deep in your soul, that you are loved by God and are of inestimable value. Congratulations! The next step is to increase your value to others by solving as many of your problems as you can. In other words, you need to maximize who you are by overcoming or fixing those things that are within your power to change.

You may struggle with a hair-trigger temper, for example. Maybe you have difficulty setting boundaries or taking responsibility. Maybe you have some bad habits, or perhaps your attitude needs an overhaul. All of us have hurdles we can overcome. Forty-five percent of Americans report that they would change a bad habit if they could.[1] The truth is, they can change. Each of us can improve ourselves whenever we decide to.

In his book *Teaching the Elephant to Dance* (Crown, 1990), James Belasco described how trainers shackle young elephants with heavy chains to deeply embedded stakes. In that way the elephant learns to stay in its place. Older, more powerful elephants that have been trained in this way never try to leave—even though they have the strength to pull up the stake and walk away. Their conditioning limits their movements. Eventually, with only a small, unattached metal bracelet on their legs, they stand in place—even though the stakes are actually gone!

It's a story you've probably heard before, but like the powerful elephants, many people are bound by the restraints of previous conditioning. Just as the unattached chain around the elephant's leg keeps it from moving, some people impose needless limits on their personal progress. Don't let this happen to you. Don't mindlessly accept restraints on your abilities. Challenge them and keep growing.

BELIEVE IN YOUR VALUE. Once you've recognized your value, accepted it, and increased it, you've eventually got to believe it. You've got to believe it with such conviction that you'd be willing to bank on it.

Chuck Wepner never learned this lesson. As a boxer, he earned the nickname "The Bayonne Bleeder" because of the punishment he took even while winning. In the boxing world he was what's called "a catcher," a fighter who often uses his head to block the other guy's punches. Wepner continually pressured his opponent until he either won or got knocked out. He never cared how many shots he had to absorb before landing a knockout blow. Trainer Al Braverman called him "the gutsiest fighter I ever met. He was in a league of his own. He didn't care about pain. If he got cut or elbowed, he never looked at me or the referee for help. He was a fighter in the purest sense of the word."

When Wepner knocked out Terry Henke in the eleventh round in Salt Lake City, boxing promoter Don King offered Wepner a title shot against then–heavyweight champion George Foreman. But when Ali defeated Foreman, Wepner found himself scheduled to fight "The Greatest"—Muhammad Ali. On the morning of the fight, Wepner gave his wife a pink negligee and told her she would "soon be sleeping with the heavyweight champion of the world."

Ali scored a technical knockout with just nineteen seconds remaining in the fight. But there was a moment—one glorious moment in the ninth round—when a hamlike paw to Ali's chest knocked the reigning champion off his feet.

Wepner recalled, "When Ali was down, I remember saying to my ringman, Al Braverman, 'Start the car, we're going to the bank, we're millionaires.' And Al said to me, 'You'd better turn around. Because he's getting up.'" After the fight,

Wepner's wife pulled the negligee out of her purse and asked, "Do I go to Ali's room or does he come to mine?" (see www.wepnerhomestead.com)

That story would be nothing more than an odd boxing footnote except for one thing. A struggling writer was watching the fight. And then it suddenly struck him: *There it is*, he said to himself. "So I went home and I started writing. And I wrote for three days straight." That's how writer and actor Sylvester Stallone described the birth of the Academy Award–winning movie *Rocky* to James Lipton on *Inside the Actor's Studio*.

The movie studio offered the struggling writer an unprecedented $400,000 for his script, but Stallone refused the money, choosing instead just $20,000 and the right to play the part of Rocky for actor's minimum wage, a paltry $340 a week. The studio also made an offer to Wepner since the movie was based on his life. He could receive a flat fee of $70,000 or 1 percent of the movie's gross profits. Wanting the guaranteed payday, Wepner took the $70,000, a decision that ultimately cost him $8 million. Today Chuck Wepner lives in Bayonne and works as a liquor salesman.

The same thing happens whenever you sell yourself short. If you don't believe that you have something of great value to offer another person—namely yourself—you'll never truly win with people. Who you are is the greatest asset you'll ever possess. And as long as you recognize this valuable asset, accept it, increase it, and believe it with deep conviction, the ways of winning with people in this book can become a part of your character. And when they come from the heart, they work like a charm.

JOHN . . . WITH A MAXWELL MENTORING MOMENT

If I could meet you in person, one of the first things I would tell you is that I believe in you. You may find that hard to swallow because I don't even know you. But I do know this: everyone has value and something of value to offer others. One of my missions in life is to see that value in others, help them discover it, and encourage them to reach their potential. You can become a winner and help others do the same.

That's why I want to mentor you. I may not be able to sit down with you in person, but I've written this book with Les because I want to help you. In each chapter ahead, I will come alongside you for a mentoring moment and teach you a specific way to make others feel like a million bucks. It's my way of helping you win with people. And when we're done, I want to suggest that you seek out a face-to-face mentor, a winner who can add value to you and walk you through many of life's additional lessons.

LES . . . ON BRINGING IT HOME

Each of the chapters in this book closes with a piece on bringing it home. It's designed to help you put the chapter's "winning way" into action. This little outline has served me well, so I pass it along to you.

To apply John's teaching to your own life . . .

Forget about:

Whatever makes you feel insecure.

Ask:

How can I increase my value in order to benefit others, rather than just myself?

Do it:

List the things you can improve about yourself (bad habits to break, etc.), along with specific steps to take to make the improvements.

Remember:

Your relationships can only be as healthy as you are.

2

Practice the 30-Second Rule

He who waits to do a great deal of good at once, will never do anything.

—Samuel Johnson

LES . . . ON SEEING THE PRACTICE IN ACTION

One of the most valuable lessons in winning with people that I have ever learned from John is the 30-Second Rule: within the first thirty seconds of a conversation, say something encouraging to a person.

John is a master at it. While I was sitting in a meeting at one of his companies a short time ago, John entered the room and within just a few minutes said something encouraging to each person around the table.

"David, I heard you hit it out of the park this morning on that conference call."

"Larry, you are making me look so good with that consultation in Denver. Thank you."

"Kevin, I just saw the numbers for April. Nobody else in the world sees and seizes an opportunity the way you do."

"Les, I'm so glad you made the trip out here to be with us today. I know you're going to add tremendous value to our discussion."

Very early on, John had genuinely encouraged each one of us. And it seemed almost effortless. Since I was trying to learn more about John's winning ways with people, after the meeting I asked John to tell me about what he did. That's when I first heard the term "the 30-Second Rule."

"I learned this from my father," John said. "Years ago, he was the president of a college, and I would often walk across the campus with him. He continually stopped to say encouraging things to the students. When I was tempted to complain, I would look at the students' faces and realize Dad had deposited good words inside of them.

"People never forget that kind of encouragement," John continued. "Yesterday I talked to my dad on the phone, and he excitedly told me about his many former students who keep coming to Florida from all over the United States to see him. He was surprised that they would go out of their way to see him, but I wasn't. The 30-Second Rule that Dad had practiced with everyone every day was returning to him big time."

"I've seen you do this for years," I told John, "but I never knew it was something you picked up from your dad."

"I've learned a lot of great lessons from my dad. He's an incredible leader," John replied. "I practice this rule every day with everyone I meet. You see, someone once said to me, 'Be kind . . . everyone you meet is fighting a hard battle.' People everywhere need a good word, an uplifting compliment to fire their hopes and dreams. It takes very little effort to do, but it really lifts people up."

JOHN . . . WITH A MAXWELL MENTORING MOMENT

When most people meet others, they search for ways to make themselves look good. The key to the 30-Second Rule is reversing this practice. When you make contact with people, instead of focusing on yourself, search for ways to make *them* look good.

Every day before I meet with people, I pause to think about something encouraging I can tell them. What I say can be one of many things: I might thank them for something they've done for me or for a friend. I might tell others about one of their accomplishments. I might praise them for a personal quality they exhibit. Or I might simply compliment their appearance. The practice isn't complicated, but it does take some time, effort, and discipline. The reward for practicing it is huge, because it really makes a positive impact on people.

If you desire to encourage others by practicing the 30-Second Rule, then remember these things the next time you meet people:

The 30-Second Rule Gives People the Triple-A Treatment

All people feel better and do better when you give them *attention*, *affirmation*, and *appreciation*. The next time you make contact with people, begin by giving them your undivided attention during the first thirty seconds. Affirm them and show your appreciation for them in some way. Then watch what happens. You will be surprised by how positively they respond. And if you have trouble remembering to keep your focus on them instead of on yourself, then perhaps the words of William King will help you. He said, "A gossip is one who talks to you about other people. A bore is one who talks to you about himself. And a brilliant conversationalist is one who talks to you about yourself."

"A gossip is one who talks to you about other people. A bore is one who talks to you about himself. And a brilliant conversationalist is one who talks to you about yourself."

—William King

THE 30-SECOND RULE GIVES PEOPLE ENERGY

Psychologist Henry H. Goddard conducted a study on energy levels in children using an instrument he called the "ergograph." His findings are fascinating. He discovered that when tired children were given a word of praise or commendation, the ergograph showed an immediate upward surge of energy in the children. When the children were criticized or discouraged, the ergograph showed that their physical energy took a sudden nosedive.

You may have already discovered this intuitively. When someone praises you, doesn't your energy level go up? And when you are criticized, doesn't that comment drag you down? Words have great power.

What kind of environment do you think you could create if you continually affirmed people when you first came into contact with them? Not only would you encourage them, but you would also become an energy carrier. Whenever you walked into a room, the people would light up! You would help to create the kind of environment everyone loves. Just your presence alone would brighten people's days.

The 30-Second Rule Instills Motivation

Vince Lombardi, the famed Green Bay Packers football coach, was a feared disciplinarian. But he was also a great motivator. One day he chewed out a player who had missed several blocking assignments. After practice, Lombardi stormed into the locker room and saw that the player was sitting at his locker, head down, dejected. Lombardi mussed his hair, patted him on the shoulder, and said, "One of these days, you're going to be the best guard in the NFL."

That player was Jerry Kramer, and Kramer says he carried that positive image of himself for the rest of his career. "Lombardi's encouragement had a tremendous impact on my whole life," Kramer said. He went on to become a member of the Green Bay Packers Hall of Fame and a member of the NFL's All-50-Year Team.

Everybody needs motivation from time to time. Using the 30-Second Rule helps encourage people to be and do their best. Never underestimate the power of motivation:

- Motivation helps people who know what they should do . . . to do it!

- Motivation helps people who know what commitment they should make . . . to make it!
- Motivation helps people who know what habit they should break . . . to break it!
- Motivation helps people who know what path they should take . . . to take it!

Motivation makes it possible to accomplish what you should accomplish.

One of the great side benefits of the 30-Second Rule is that it also helps you. You can't help others without also helping yourself. Benjamin Franklin realized this truth, and he encouraged others with it. In a letter to John Paul Jones, Franklin wrote:

> Hereafter, if you should observe an occasion to give your officers and friends a little more praise than is their due, and confess more fault than you can justly be charged with, you will only become the sooner for it, a great captain. Criticizing and censuring almost everyone you have to do with, will diminish friends, increase enemies, and thereby hurt your affairs.

If you want others to feel good about themselves and to feel glad every time they see you, then practice the 30-Second Rule. Remember this: those who add to us, draw us to them. Those who subtract, cause us to withdraw.

Those who add to us, draw us to them. Those who subtract, cause us to withdraw.

LES . . . ON BRINGING IT HOME

Social psychologists have studied "first impressions" for decades. If you want to make an impression that is lasting and positive, we now know what works and what doesn't. And John's 30-Second Rule is one of the most effective means for finding success in this area. In research it's called the "primacy effect," and its initial impact goes a long way in making others feel connected with you.[1]

To apply John's teaching to your own life . . .

Forget about:

Searching for ways to make yourself look good.
Instead, search for ways to make others look good.

Ask:

What positive, encouraging thing can I say to each person I will see today?

Do it:

Give everyone you meet the Triple-A Treatment—attention, affirmation, and appreciation.

Remember:

Within the first thirty seconds of a conversation, say something encouraging.

3

LET PEOPLE KNOW YOU NEED THEM

The greatest compliment that was ever paid me
was when someone asked me what I thought,
and attended to my answer.
—HENRY DAVID THOREAU

LES . . . ON SEEING THE PRACTICE IN ACTION

One day I asked John the secret to getting people to join a team, and he told me it could be found in a single sentence: "I can't do it without you." He went on to say that great leaders stumble when they believe people need *them* instead of recognizing that the very opposite is true. "Leaders can become great," said John, "only when they realize that *they* are the ones who need people."

As we talked, John pulled a laminated card from his desk drawer and told me he had developed a tool years ago for asking people for help. "Les, I wrote this back in 1974," he said. "I was facing a major building project and I needed to raise more than a million dollars. It was the first time I understood how far over my head I truly was in leadership.

"That's when I realized that if I was ever to achieve something great," John continued, "it would be the result of turning the dream from *me* to *we*." I scribbled down that phrase, intending to "borrow" it for an upcoming lecture. John went on, "I also realized that any dream I could achieve without the help of other people was too small."

Then John handed me the laminated card. On it were these words:

> I Have a Dream
>
> History tells us that in every age there comes a time when leaders must come forth to meet the needs of the hour. Therefore, there is no potential leader who does not have an opportunity to better mankind. Those around him also have the same privilege. Fortunately, I believe that God has surrounded me with those who will accept the challenge of this hour.
>
> My dream allows me to . . .
>
> - Give up at any moment all that I am in order to receive all that I can become.
> - Sense the invisible so I can do the impossible.
> - Trust God's resources since the dream is bigger than all my abilities and acquaintances.

- Continue when discouraged, for where there is no faith in the future, there is no power in the present.
- Attract winners, because big dreams draw big people.
- See my people and myself in the future. Our dream is the promise of what we shall one day be.

Yes, I have a dream. It is greater than any of my gifts. It is as large as the world, but it begins with one. Won't you join me?

—John Maxwell

"Les," he said, "I've given these cards out by the hundreds, and I have seen people time and again join up to help me accomplish my dream for one primary reason—because I let them know I needed them."

JOHN . . . WITH A MAXWELL MENTORING MOMENT

The day that I realized I could no longer do everything myself was a major step in my development as a person and a leader. I've always had vision, plenty of ideas, and vast amounts of energy. But when the vision gets bigger than you, you really only have two choices: give up on the vision or get help. I chose the latter.

> When the vision gets bigger than you, you really only have two choices: give up on the vision or get help.

No matter how successful you are, no matter how important or accomplished, you *do* need people. That's why you need to let them know that you cannot win without them. President Woodrow Wilson said, "We should not only use all the brains we have—but all that we can borrow." Why stop with just their brains? Enlist people's hands and hearts, too! Another president, Lyndon Johnson, was right when he said, "There are no problems we cannot solve together, and very few that we can solve by ourselves."

Asking others for help is a great way to make them feel like a million bucks. Why?

People Need to Be Needed

Have you ever stopped to ask someone for directions? You roll down your car window and ask a passerby, "Can you tell me how to find Larry's Market?" Nearly every time, people stop whatever they are doing and help if they can—even if it means crossing the street or standing in traffic. They may even repeat the directions a couple of times to make sure you get it. Why? Because whenever a person feels that he or she knows something you don't, it gives that person an ego boost. Everyone likes to be an expert, even if it's for a moment. It gives them a great sense of superiority and of accomplishment when they help. That translates into an increased sense of self-worth. And it all stems from the universal need to be needed.

People Need to Know They Need People.

"It marks a big step in your development when you come to realize that other people can help you do a better job than you could do alone," said steel magnate and philanthropist Andrew Carnegie. Sadly, many people never achieve that level of maturity or insight. Some people still want to believe that they can achieve greatness alone.

Every individual's fate is tied to that of many others. We cannot be like the shipwrecked man who sits at one end of a lifeboat doing nothing while everyone at the other end bails furiously, and says, "Thank God that hole isn't in *my* end of the boat!" We all need people, and if we don't know it, we're in trouble.

PEOPLE NEED TO KNOW THEY ARE NEEDED.

Cartoonist Charles Schulz often captured the longings of the human heart in his comic strip *Peanuts*. He really understood the needs of people. In one of his creations, Lucy asks Charlie Brown to help with her homework. "I'll be eternally grateful," she promises.

"Fair enough. I've never had anyone be eternally grateful before," replies Charlie. "Just subtract 4 from 10 to get how many apples the farmer had left."

Lucy says, "That's it? That's it? I have to be eternally grateful for that? I was robbed! I can't be eternally grateful for this—it was too easy!"

With a blank look of discouragement, Charlie replies, "Well, whatever you think is fair."

"How about if I just say 'thanks, bro'?" replies Lucy.

As Charlie leaves to go outside, he meets Linus, who asks, "Where've you been, Charlie Brown?"

"Helping Lucy with her homework."

"Did she appreciate it?" Linus asks.

Charlie responds, "At greatly reduced prices."

Ever felt like Charlie Brown? You're not alone. Every

human being longs for a life of significance. We all need to know we are needed and that what we offer to others is of value.

PEOPLE NEED TO KNOW THAT THEY HELPED.

Whenever someone tells me how valuable the people on my team are to them, I encourage him to tell the individuals who were so helpful. Why? Because people need to know that they helped someone. "Good leaders make people feel that they're at the very heart of things, not at the periphery," says author and leadership expert Warren Bennis. "Everyone feels that he or she makes a difference to the success of the organization. When that happens people feel centered and that gives their work meaning."

> "Good leaders make people feel that they're at the very heart of things, not at the periphery."
>
> —WARREN BENNIS

Walter Shipley of Citibank says, "We have 68,000 employees. With a company this size, I'm not 'running the business' . . . My job is to create the environment that enables people to leverage each other beyond their own individual capabilities . . . I get credit for providing the leadership that got us there. But our people did it." Shipley understands what successful leaders know: people need to know that they made an important contribution to reaching the goal.

It's not a sign of weakness to let others know you value them. It's a sign of security and strength. When you're honest about your need for help, specific with others about the value they add, and inclusive of others as you build a team to do something bigger than you are, everybody wins.

LES . . . ON BRINGING IT HOME

Research proved long ago that when people feel needed, they are far more likely to be productive and creative. In fact, studies of twins with similar IQ scores show that each performs quite differently when they are in differing environments, one supportive (where they know they are needed and appreciated) and the other not. The person who feels needed consistently performs better.[1]

To apply John's teaching to your own life . . .

Forget about:

A prideful attitude that causes you to prove how capable you are without the help of others.

Ask:

Who specifically can help me do a better job than I can do alone? Who is just waiting to be asked to join in what I am doing?

Do it:

Sincerely ask others for input or help and attend carefully to what they have to say.

Remember:

Individuals who win with people make others feel that they are at the very heart of things, not at the periphery.

4

Create a Memory and Visit It Often

Memory is the treasury and guardian of all things.
—Cicero

LES . . . ON SEEING THE PRACTICE IN ACTION

People who spend quality time with John know that they are going to walk away with a memory. It's inevitable. John just has a knack for making memories; it's one of the things that makes him a winner with people.

John also enjoys it when others create a memory for him. One day when we were talking about creating memories, told me this story: he was scheduled to speak to three thousand young leaders in Phoenix at an event, but as he stepped onto the platform that day, he realized his host had something different in mind. "He didn't want me to speak at all," John explained. The group that was gathered had been reading his books and listening to his tapes through the years and had planned a surprise. Instead of having John speak to them, they wanted to speak to John, so they had him sit on the platform and simply listen as they honored him. One after another, twelve preselected leaders from the audience came up to the podium to tell the group about how John's teaching had made an impact on his or her life.

"It was completely unexpected," John said. "And not only did they shower me with kind words, but each speaker presented me with a memento—a tangible remembrance of something they said they had learned from me. I was completely overwhelmed by the experience."

One person gave John a beautiful painting with two images: one of a child reading one of John's books and another of the child as a grown man coaching others.

"Les," John said, tears in his eyes and his voice cracking, "I don't know how many times I've reminisced about that day. I keep the mementos around my office to relive it. That experience meant so much to me. And it renewed my desire to create memories for others."

JOHN . . . WITH A MAXWELL MENTORING MOMENT

Few things bond people together like a shared memory. Soldiers who battle together, teammates who win a championship, and work teams that hit their goals share a connection that never goes away. Married couples who experience rough times can often look back on their earlier experiences together to keep them going. Families bond when they rough it on camping trips or share adventures on vacation and then love recounting their experience years later.

Some memories come as the result of circumstance, but many can be proactively created. Author Lewis Carroll wrote, "It's a poor sort of memory that only works backward." What does that mean to you and me? The richest memories are often those we plan and intentionally create. Here are some hints for creating memories that will help you win with people:

Initiative—Make Something Happen

Memories don't find us—we find them. Even better, if we are intentional, we can *make* memories. If you mention the word *chariot* to friends Dan and Patti Reiland or Tim and Pam Elmore, I can tell you exactly what will come to mind—a crisp autumn day in New York City when we did something that still makes us laugh. After lunch at Tavern on the Green, I hired three "bicycle chariots" with peddling drivers to take each couple on a race through Manhattan to Macy's. It was up to each couple to motivate their driver to win (using whatever financial incentives they wanted). The race was neck-and-neck the entire way, and we laughed the whole time.

We still laugh when we think about it or look at the photos we took that day. But it never would have happened if we hadn't initiated it.

Time—Set Aside Time to Make Something Happen

For years parents have debated the issue of quality time versus quantity of time. As a father and grandfather, I have discovered that it takes quantity time to find quality time. If you don't carve out the time, you can't create the memory.

Haven't you found that most memories you have are with the people you spend the most time with? I know that's true for me. If you want to make memories with your family, spend more time with them. If you want to create memories with your employees, you won't do it behind the door of your office. You simply can't make memories with people if you don't take time to be with them.

PLANNING—PLAN FOR SOMETHING TO HAPPEN

Most people don't lead their lives—they accept their lives. They wait for memorable experiences to happen, never giving a thought to planning an experience that will make a memory. One of the most extravagant memories I ever planned was with Margaret, my wife, for our twenty-fifth wedding anniversary. We decided to share it with thirty of our closest friends. We chartered a yacht and picked everyone up in San Diego Bay. Once on board, we had a delectable meal and then surprised the group by having Frankie Valens entertain us with some of his trademark songs like "Sixteen Candles." Our friends loved it. But the most memorable highlight of the evening was created when Margaret and I said a few words about each person and why that person held such a special place in our hearts. That night is not only a great memory for Margaret and me, but it is a great memory for the people who attended, too.

Most people don't lead their lives—they accept their lives.

Creativity—Find a Way to Make Something Happen

What do you do when you find yourself at an event where you expect to share a memory but nothing seems to happen? You get creative. I've been asked over and over to tell the story of the Holiday Bowl I attended in San Diego with friends about fifteen years ago. The game was so dull that I ended up buying newspapers for everyone in my section so that we would have something to do. Another guy nearby, not to be outdone, bought one hundred bags of peanuts and distributed them to everybody in the section. The two of us got a standing ovation, and soon the news crews were more focused on us than the game. I don't remember the score or much about the game, but it's a night I'll never forget. Neither will the buddies who went with me.

Shared Experiences—Make Something Happen Together

Memories compound when they are experienced with someone you love. Years ago our family went to Jasper Park in Canada for a vacation. While we were there, I took my children, Elizabeth and Joel Porter, fishing. On our way back to our cabin, we called Margaret to let her know we were coming home, and she asked the kids how they did.

"We caught eight trout," Joel said. He was acting low-key about it, but I could tell he was proud. As we drove back, we talked about how great it was going to be to have a dinner of trout we had just pulled from a cold mountain stream. When we arrived, we carried the trout into the kitchen, and there on the counter we saw four steaks ready to be cooked.

"What gives?" Joel asked his mother. "We caught eight trout! And we're looking forward to a trout dinner."

Margaret started to laugh. "I thought you said *a* trout, so I went out and bought steaks." Then I started laughing, and Elizabeth did too. Finally, with a gleam in his eye, Joel said, "Mom's not too good with numbers, is she?"

That happened with our kids when they were eleven and thirteen years old. Every time we've had a cookout since then, the kids have told the trout story. Even now that both of them are married and have kids of their own, they still love to say, "Mom's not too good with numbers," and make us laugh.

Mementos—Show That Something Happened

"Almost anything you do today will be forgotten in just a few weeks," says author and research scientist John McCrone. "The ability to retrieve a memory decreases exponentially unless boosted by artificial aids such as diaries and photographs."

Don't you find that to be true? Do you keep pictures or souvenirs on your desk where you can see them? Do you carry photos of people you love in your wallet? Do you have a trophy, plaque, game ball, or other award on a shelf where you and others can see it? We all have things we love—not because they have any material value but because they remind us of places we've been or things we've done. When you help someone else create a memory, give that person something to remember it by.

Relive the Memory—Talk About What Happened

The most important part of creating a memory is reliving it. It's the payoff! Many times when I travel with others, at the end of our trip I ask them to share a favorite memory. It often leads to rich conversations. Or I write a note to someone soon afterward to share my own favorite memory. It creates a connection that bonds us together and makes both of us feel great.

LES . . . ON BRINGING IT HOME

There isn't a person in the world who doesn't understand the value of positive memories. They can sustain people during the worst of times and inspire them during the best of times. And best of all, anyone can create a memory and visit it often!

To apply John's teaching to your own life . . .

Forget about:

Trying to have quality time to make a memory if you aren't willing to invest the quantity of time it requires.

Ask:

What memories have I already created with people in my life that we need to relive together?

Do it:

Plan an experience that will commemorate an achievement or milestone that people will talk about years from now. And don't forget to create a memento of it.

Remember:

We shouldn't wait for memories to happen to us. We need to make memories happen.

5

Compliment People in Front of Other People

Admonish thy friends in secret, praise them openly.
—Publilius Syrus

LES . . . ON SEEING THE PRACTICE IN ACTION

Complimenting people in front of other people is a John Maxwell trademark. He's known for doing this far and wide. So when I asked a few people around his company to tell me how John does this, I didn't have to look far for stories. Instead, I had to decide which of numerous ones to choose. Many of these stories contained sentiments similar to the ones I heard from Charlie Wetzel, who has worked with John on his books for more than a decade:

For almost twenty years, John has written and recorded leadership lessons, which he used to mentor tens of thousands of people every month, first for the Injoy Life Club and now for Maximum Impact. In 1995, he did a lesson that was designed to teach leaders how to find people with great potential and how to create an environment for them to flourish and emerge as full-fledged leaders. He called it "Searching for Eagles."

John now often records such lessons on-site at corporations and other organizations around the country. But at that time he delivered the teaching to his own church staff and a few people from Injoy, the leadership development company he founded. It was his way of continually developing his people so that they would grow and learn. I sat in the audience that day and took notes as I learned the ten marks of an eagle:

1. Eagles make things happen.
2. Eagles see and seize opportunities.
3. Eagles influence the opinions and actions of others.
4. Eagles add value to you.
5. Eagles draw winners to them.
6. Eagles equip other eagles to lead.
7. Eagles provide ideas that help the organization.
8. Eagles possess an uncommonly great attitude.
9. Eagles live up to their commitments and responsibilities.
10. Eagles show fierce loyalty to the organization and the leader.

It was an inspiring and instructive message. As John wrapped up the lesson, he named some of the eagles that had come into his life through the years. And then John said, "But I want to finish this lesson by telling you about another eagle who has come on board recently. His name is Charlie Wetzel. He's only been working with us a short time, but he makes things happen."

John went on to tell how a connection I made on my own initiative with the editor of a national publication led to the acceptance of a Maxwell article that would be read by over three million subscribers. John then said so many kind and complimentary things about me that it brought tears to my eyes.

John had always said positive things about me in front of my wife and my visiting parents, but this time he was speaking to the entire staff of my church and the president of his company—not to mention the thousands of people who would be listening to the message on tape. It was overwhelming. Before that moment, I'd never thought of myself as an "eagle." Even to this day, it touches my heart when I think about it.

It's been a decade since John paid Charlie that compliment, yet its impact hasn't lessened. That's the power of complimenting people in front of other people.

JOHN . . . WITH A MAXWELL MENTORING MOMENT

The most fundamental and straightforward way of winning with people is to give them a compliment—a sincere and meaningful word of affirmation. If you want to make others feel like a million bucks, you've got to master this elementary skill. And it's essential that you learn to give your compliments in front of others as well as one-on-one. Why? Because that private compliment turned public, instantly and dramatically increases in value. Here are reasons why that's so important:

> A private compliment turned public, instantly and dramatically increases in value.

People Want to Feel Worthwhile in Life

"Everyone has an invisible sign hanging from his neck," says Mary Kay Ash. "It says, 'Make Me Feel Important!'" Mary Kay drilled this principle into her sales team. She told them again and again, "Never forget this message when working with people." She knew compliments and affirmation were critical to enjoying success with others.

And by the way, it's one of the reasons she was so successful. With her life savings of $5,000 and the help of her then twenty-year-old son, she launched Mary Kay Cosmetics in 1963. The company now has more than 500,000 independent beauty consultants in twenty-nine markets worldwide, and Mary Kay Inc., is ranked as one of the 100 best companies to work for in America.

Mary Kay, like every other person who wins with people, knew that people want to feel worthwhile. When you continually keep this in mind, you can't help but give compliments freely.

Compliments Increase in Value When We Value the Person Who Gives Them

Willard Scott, the former longtime weatherman on NBC's *Today Show*, remembers his radio days when he received his all-time favorite letter from a fan:

> Dear Mr. Scott, I think you're the best disc jockey in Washington. You play the best music and have the nicest voice of anyone on the air. Please excuse the crayon—they won't let us have anything sharp in here.

Not all compliments are created equal. Who gives the compliment has a lot to do with how much we prize it. A nice remark from someone who's not allowed to have sharp objects doesn't carry the same weight as a compliment given by your boss in front of people you respect.

Compliments Affirm People and Make Them Strong

To affirm is to make firm. An affirmation is a statement of truth you make firm in a person's heart when you utter it. As a result, it cultivates conviction. For example, when you compliment a person's attitude, you reinforce it and make it more consistent. Because you notice it in a positive way, he will be more likely to demonstrate that same attitude again.

Likewise, when you affirm people's dreams, you help their dreams become more real than their doubts. Like the repetition of a weight-lifting regimen, routine compliments build up people's qualities and strengthen their personalities.

"There are high spots in all of our lives," wrote author George Matthew Adams, "and most of them have come about through encouragement from someone else. I don't care how great, how famous or successful a man or woman may be, each hungers for applause. Encouragement is oxygen to the soul. Good work can never be expected from a worker without encouragement. No one can ever have lived without it."

"Encouragement is oxygen to the soul."

—George Matthew Adams

Compliments in Front of Others Are the Most Effective Ones You Can Give

As commander of a $1 billion warship and a crew of 310, Mike Abrashoff used grassroots leadership to increase retention rates from 28 percent to 100 percent, reduce operating expenditures, and improve readiness. How did he do it? Among other things, he placed supreme importance on public compliments.

"The commanding officer of a ship is authorized to hand out 15 medals a year," he wrote. "I wanted to err on the side of excess, so I passed out 115." Nearly every time a sailor left his ship for another assignment, Captain Abrashoff gave him or her a medal. "Even if they hadn't been star players, they got medals in a public ceremony as long as they had done their best every day. I delivered a short speech describing how much we cherished the recipient's friendship, camaraderie, and hard work." Sometimes the departing sailor's shipmates told funny stories, recalling his or her foibles, trials, and triumphs. But the bottom line was that Abrashoff wanted to make them feel good by complimenting them in front of others.

"There is absolutely no downside to this symbolic gesture," said Abrashoff, "provided it is done sincerely without hype." He knew how to make his sailors feel like a million bucks.

You can do the same thing for the people around you. Whenever you have the opportunity to publicly praise another person, don't let it slip by. Of course, you can create these opportunities, as Captain Abrashoff did, but you can also find countless opportunities if you just look for them.

LES . . . ON BRINGING IT HOME

Think about the last time you received a compliment in the presence of people who mattered to you. How did it make you feel? Few things can lift a person up the way a sincere compliment does.

To apply John's teaching to your own life . . .

Forget about:
Giving compliments only in private. Instead, give public praise whenever you can.

Ask:
Who can I spotlight in front of others?

Do it:
Compliment someone around you in front of other people today.

Remember:
When you give someone a public compliment, you give him or her wings like an eagle.

6

Give Others a Reputation to Uphold

Treat a man as he appears to be and you make him worse. But treat a man as if he already were what he potentially could be, and you make him what he should be.

—Goethe

LES . . . ON SEEING THE PRACTICE IN ACTION

A few years ago, John and Margaret went to London with friends Dan and Patti Reiland, Tim and Pam Elmore, and Andy Steimer. While there, each person had his own must-see destination. For Tim, it was the bunker and war room that Winston Churchill and his advisors used during World War II.

John told me about his experience there. It was not an impressive place: it was basically a basement about twelve feet beneath a building containing a big map room with a large table, a communication room, and some smaller rooms where people could rest. But what had occurred there during the war was impressive. It was from there that Churchill had strategized and rallied the British people.

As we talked, I could tell that John loves history. He talked about Churchill—one of his leadership heroes—and how the prime minister helped to uplift millions of his countrymen in the wake of Britain's June 1940 defeat at the battle of Dunkirk. John quoted part of the speech Churchill used to address the House of Commons upon that occasion:

> We shall not flag or fail . . . We shall fight in France, we shall fight in the seas and oceans, we shall fight with growing confidence and growing strength in the air, we shall defend our island, whatever the cost may be, we shall fight on the beaches, we shall fight on the landing grounds, we shall fight in the fields and in the streets, we shall fight in the hills; we shall never surrender . . .[1]

John explained, "Churchill did a lot of remarkable things during the war, but one of the greatest was his continual ability to give the English people a reputation to uphold. He inspired them; he motivated them; he challenged them. And in response they rose to the occasion. They loved him for it."

John has tried to embody this quality. He says that as he interacts with others, he constantly asks himself, *What is special, unique, and wonderful about this individual?* Then he shares it with others. I've seen John do this time after time. About Linda Eggers, his assistant, he says, "She always represents me well." He calls John Hull, the president of EQUIP,

"Mr. Relationship." He tells everyone that Kirk Nowery, the president of ISS, is "the pastor's best friend."And he points out how Doug Carter, the vice president of EQUIP, "never misses an opportunity to tell the EQUIP story." John thinks the best of people and speaks about the fine qualities he sees in them.

JOHN . . . WITH A MAXWELL MENTORING MOMENT

One of the best ways to inspire others and make them feel good about themselves is to show them who they could be. Years ago, a manager for the New York Yankees wanted rookie players to know what a privilege it was to play for the team. He used to tell them, "Boys, it's an honor just to put on the New York pinstripes. So when you put them on, play like world champions. Play like Yankees. Play proud."

When you give someone a reputation to uphold, you give him something good to shoot for. It's putting something that was beyond his reach within his grasp. By speaking to their potential, you help the people around you to "play proud," as the Yankees do. Why is that important? Because people will go farther than they thought they could when someone they respect tells them they can.

If you desire to give others a reputation to uphold, here are suggestions on how to get started:

Have a High Opinion of People

The opinions you have of people in your life affect them profoundly. Dr. J. Sterling Livingston, formerly of the

Harvard Business School and founder of the Sterling Institute management consulting firm, observed, "People perform consistently as they perceive you expect them to perform."

A reputation is something that many people spend their entire lives trying to live down or live up to. So why not help others up instead of pushing them down? All people possess both value and potential. You can find those things if you try.

Back Up Your High Opinion of Others with Action

When you back up your belief in people with action, their self-doubt begins to evaporate. It's one thing to tell your teenager that you believe he's a good driver; it's another to let him have the keys to your car for the evening. Likewise, if you want a new manager to rise to the high opinion you've expressed about her, then give her significant responsibility. Nothing gives people confidence like seeing someone they respect put his money where his mouth is. Not only does it empower them emotionally, but it also resources their drive toward success.

Look Past Their Pasts and Give Them Reputations for Their Futures

Old negative names, labels, or nicknames can block a person's growth and progress. Perhaps that's why the rites of passage in many cultures include giving a new title or name to the person being honored. A new name gives someone a hope for a new future.

A fun example of this can be found in the movie and play *The Man of La Mancha*, based on Cervantes's classic work *Don Quixote*. The protagonist, Don Alonzo, pursues a life of chivalry and seeks to become a knight-errant long after that age of history has passed. He sees giants where others see windmills and quests where others see rabbit trails. Comically, he "rescues" a common prostitute named Aldonza, whom he sees as a beautiful lady. He calls her Dulcinea and makes her the object of his knightly exploits.

At first she resents him. She thinks he is mocking her, because she hates herself and her life. But with time, his vision of her replaces her own and gives her hope. And as the old man lies on his deathbed, she thanks him for seeing in her what she could not see in herself.

Of course, the most dramatic examples of someone overlooking the pasts of others and giving them reputations for the future can be found in the Bible. The book of Genesis recounts how God changed the life of Abram, an old man with no offspring. God renamed him Abraham,[2] which means "father of many," and made it possible for Abraham to become a father in his old age. And God took Jacob, a trickster who cheated his brother, lied to his father, and constantly schemed to get ahead; and renamed him Israel—his future becoming the inception of the nation of Israel.[3]

Give People a New Name or Nickname That Speaks to Their Potential

Harry Hopman, one of the finest tennis captains and coaches in Australia's history and a member of the International Tennis Hall of Fame, at one time built the Australian team to the point that it dominated the tennis world. How did he do it? By emphasizing what he called "coaching by affirmation." For example, he had a slow player whom he nicknamed "Rocket." Another player, who was not known for his strength or constitution, he called "Muscles." And it certainly gave them a boost. "Rocket" Rod Laver and Ken "Muscles" Rosewall became champions in the tennis world.

I love giving people nicknames that speak to their potential and their greatest strengths. In fact, it's something I'm known for in my family. My own children, Elizabeth and Joel Porter, I call "Apple of My Eye" and "Number One Son." I call my nieces Rachael and Jennifer "Angel" and "Sweet Pea." Grandchildren Madeline, Hannah, John Porter, and Ella are "Sunshine," "Hannah Banana," "JP," and "Peanut."

Each time a child is born in our extended family, the kids want to know what I'm going to call the newest member. It's a tradition we all love. Why? Because everyone enjoys the encouragement that comes from someone seeing—and speaking to—their potential.

LES . . . ON BRINGING IT HOME

I sometimes encounter leaders who believe you shouldn't stroke people's egos by giving them reputations they haven't quite earned. And I always point these folks to the "ten-year rule." It's derived from research showing that elite performers, those whose reputations precede them, usually needed at least ten years of dedicated and consistent practice before they obtained any *recognizable* level of excellence. The research also shows that the process can be cut dramatically when individuals see signs that they are already beginning to achieve a recognizable reputation.[4]

To apply John's teaching to your own life . . .

Forget about:

A person's failures in the past and focus on his or her potential in the future.

Ask:

What is special, unique, and wonderful about this person? How can I show it to others?

Do it:

Back up your high opinion of a person with action that reinforces that opinion.

Remember:

Many people go farther than they thought they could go because someone else believed they could and told them so.

7

Say the Right Words at the Right Time

No man has a prosperity so high or firm, but that two or three words can dishearten it; and there is no calamity which right words will not begin to redress.
—Ralph Waldo Emerson

LES . . . ON SEEING THE PRACTICE IN ACTION

Ask nearly anyone who knows John well, and he will tell you a story of a specific time when John said the right words to him at the right time. One of the most touching I heard while working on this book came from Dan Reiland, John's close friend and former right-hand man. "John has done this so often in my life," explained Dan. "But the time that stands out above all the others is when my mother died."

Her death was sudden and unexpected. Dan promptly got word to John, who was out of town at the time. John and

Margaret quickly changed their plans and flew back home to San Diego. Dan recalled, "John and Margaret came in the door of our house in Rancho San Diego, walked right up to me, gave me a big hug, and said, 'I love you.' That was it. There's nothing anyone could have done that would have been better." Dan told me that John also said many wise things to his brother, Lan, and greatly encouraged his sister, Jean. I could tell that Dan was still touched by it even though it had occurred nearly a decade ago.

"And John gave a beautiful memorial service," remembered Dan. "He gave me his notes afterward, which I cherish. I value everything John did during that time, but nothing quite holds the power of those three words at that very moment when he walked through that door."

People who have not been around John "up close and personal" are sometimes surprised to find out how good he is at saying the right words at the right time. They're used to his public persona as a speaker, where he also excels at communication and timing. But what they may not realize is that John is a genuine encourager who loves to help people and who really understands them, both on- and offstage.

I remember hearing John speak to an audience of managers about the value of what we say and when we say it. He said . . .

- The *wrong words* said at the *wrong time* discourage me.
- The *wrong words* said at the *right time* frustrate me.
- The *right words* said at the *wrong time* confuse me.
- The *right words* said at the *right time* encourage me.

I've certainly found that to be true in my own life. Haven't you? The right words at the right time are like a soothing breeze of encouragement.

JOHN . . . WITH A MAXWELL MENTORING MOMENT

Most people recognize that words have incredible power. Editor and theologian Tyron Edwards observed, "Words are both better and worse than thoughts; they express them, and add to them; they give them power for good or evil; they start them on an endless flight, for instruction and comfort and blessing, or for injury, sorrow and ruin." But saying the right words is not enough. Timing is crucial.

Sometimes, the best thing we can do for someone else is to hold our tongue. When tempted to give advice that's not wanted, to show off, to say "I told you so," or to point out another's error, the best policy is to say nothing. As nineteenth-century British journalist George Sala advised, we should strive "not only to say the right thing in the right place, but far more difficult, to leave unsaid the wrong thing at the tempting moment."

When it is time to speak up, how can you best encourage others using the right words at the right time? Keep these thoughts in mind:

Be Sensitive to Time and Place

It's said that during one of the last major offensives of World War II, General Dwight Eisenhower was walking near the Rhine and came upon a GI who seemed depressed.

"How are you feeling, son?" he asked.

"General," the young man replied, "I'm awful nervous."

"Well," Eisenhower said, "you and I are a good pair then, because I'm nervous too. Maybe if we just walk along together, we'll be good for each other."

The first key to saying the right thing at the right time is paying attention to the context. That is one of the secrets of successful communication to a large audience, and it is just as important when talking with someone one-on-one. King Solomon of ancient Israel was speaking to this truth when he wrote, "Like apples of gold in settings of silver is a word spoken in right circumstances."[1] If you can learn to be sensitive to your setting, you've won half the battle in saying the right words at the right time.

> "Like apples of gold in settings of silver is a word spoken in right circumstances."
>
> —KING SOLOMON OF ISRAEL

SAY IT FROM THE HEART

It's not just what you say and when you say it: it's also *how* you say it. A *Peanuts* comic strip shows Lucy saying to pianist Schroeder, "Do you think I'm the most beautiful girl in the world?" Naturally, she has to ask several times in different ways, until Schroeder, to be finally rid of her, says, "Yes."

Lucy mopes disconsolately and comments, "Even when he says it, he doesn't say it."

People can tell the difference between hollow words and something that is said from the heart. Idaho businessman Don

Bennett was the first amputee to climb to the summit of Mount Rainier. That's 14,410 feet, on one leg and two crutches! During an especially difficult portion of the climb, Bennett and his team had to cross an ice field. To get across the ice, the climbers had to put crampons on their boots, which would give them traction. Unfortunately, one boot didn't help Bennett much. The only way he could get across the ice field was to fall face forward onto the ice, pull himself as far forward as he could, stand up, and then fall forward again.

Bennett's teenage daughter, Kathy, was with him on the climb. She stayed by his side through the entire four-hour struggle. She kept cheering him on, saying, "You can do it, Dad. You're the best dad in the world. You can do it!"[2] His daughter's words, spoken from the heart, helped him to keep going.

Recognize the Power of the Right Words at the Right Time

Saying the right words at the right time can do more than just make a person feel good in the moment. It can have an impact that is positive and lasting.

Painter Benjamin West said that he loved to paint as a youngster. When his mother left the house, he would get out the oils and try to paint. One day when he pulled out paints, brushes, paper, and various other implements, he made quite a mess. When he realized his mother would be home soon, he tried desperately to get everything cleaned up, but he didn't make it. When she walked into the room, he expected the worst.

West said that what she did next completely surprised him. She picked up his painting, looked at it, and said, "My, what a beautiful painting of your sister." She gave him a kiss on the cheek and walked away. With that kiss, West said, he became a painter.

I don't know what kind of experience you had growing up. Perhaps, like me, you had parents who understood the power of encouragement. If not, what would you have given to have someone speak into your life at the right time—a parent, teacher, coach, or pastor? Whether or not you received it then, you can give it now. Look for opportunities to uplift others with your words. It just might change their lives.

LES . . . ON BRINGING IT HOME

Numerous studies back up that when you say the right words at the right time, there are a number of positive outcomes. One of the most important outcomes is trust. When you can offer something to a person at the point of his or her need—even when that person is a stranger—you are very likely to become trusted and seen as honorable. You will be seen as someone who is dependable and considerate.[3] Isn't that encouraging?

To apply John's teaching in your own life . . .

Forget about:

What you want to say and focus on what the other person needs to hear.

Ask:

What would I want to hear if I was in this person's shoes?

Do it:

Change someone's day—or maybe even his entire life—by saying the right words at the right time, from the heart.

Remember:

"Like apples of gold in settings of silver is a word spoken in the right circumstances."

8

ENCOURAGE THE DREAMS OF OTHERS

Keep away from people who try to belittle your ambitions. Small people always do that, but the really great make you feel that you, too, can become great.
—MARK TWAIN

LES . . . ON SEEING THE PRACTICE IN ACTION

When I began talking to John's office staff, one of the things I found out is that he receives dozens of letters every week thanking him for the positive changes that have come as a result of his books, seminars, and lessons on CD. I asked Sue Caldwell if I could see some of the letters, and she handed me a thick folder that contained some that she had shared with the staff. As I flipped through the pages, I noticed how many times people had written about hopes and dreams being rekindled in them.

Two letters jumped out at me because they referred to

things that occurred at a conference for young Christian leaders at which John had spoken. The first, from Kevin, said:

> Thank you! Without being overly dramatic, I cannot begin to tell you how much value you have added to my life over the past six years. I was one of the 5,500 emerging leaders who attended "Catalyst" this past week . . . I feel like God answered my prayer as you poured out your heart to us during your session . . . You said, "I wish you believed in yourself as much as I believe in you." That is the first time I have heard that from anyone in your generation. It was tremendously empowering to hear.

The second one, written by Matt, said:

> Over the past few months, I had become very discouraged and resigned myself to the fact that the dream [I had previously pursued] was dying. Then I came to Catalyst '03. Totally unexpectedly to me, God moved in my heart and reassured me His plan was still alive. When you prayed over us during the session, I could not stop weeping. Your words were directly from God's heart to mine. I will never forget that moment . . . Thanks for impacting my life.

Matt went on to say that he had rededicated himself to his dream and would persevere during this preparation period of his life.

As I talked to John's employees and associates, I discovered that he had repeatedly encouraged their dreams, even when that meant he might lose someone he valued. Often when Tim Elmore—a pastor on John's staff in San Diego for more than ten years—was recruited by another organization, he would go to John and ask him to "take off his employer hat and put on his mentor hat" so that he could ask John's advice. Tim says that John could be remarkably objective, and several times he actually encouraged Tim to pursue it, saying, "This just might be a good fit for you. I don't want you to have regrets if you don't go and see about it. I think you should go."

One of those trips eventually took Tim away when he accepted a position as a vice president of a parachurch organization in Colorado. And John was nothing but encouraging. He truly wanted Tim to realize his dreams and fulfill his potential.

JOHN . . . WITH A MAXWELL MENTORING MOMENT

I consider it a great privilege when people share their dreams with me. It shows a great deal of courage and trust. And at that moment, I'm conscious that I have great power in their lives. That's no small matter. A wrong word can crush a person's dream; the right word can inspire him or her to pursue it.

If someone thinks enough of you to tell you about his or her dreams, take care. And keep these things in mind as you work to encourage that person:

Understand That Dreams Are Fragile

Actress Candice Bergen commented, "Dreams are, by definition, cursed with short life spans." I suspect she said that because there are people who don't like to see others pursuing their dreams. It reminds them of how far they are from living their own dreams. As a result, they try to knock down anyone who is shooting for the stars. By talking others out of their dreams, critical people excuse themselves for staying in their comfort zones.

> "Dreams are, by definition, cursed with short life spans."
>
> —CANDICE BERGEN

Never allow yourself to become a dream killer. Instead, become a dream releaser. Even if you think another person's dream is far-fetched, that's no excuse for criticizing them.

TO LOSE A DREAM IS A GREAT LOSS

Have you given up on one of your dreams? Have you buried a hope that once looked bright and gave you energy? If so, what did it do to you? Norman Cousins, former editor of the *Saturday Review* and adjunct professor of psychiatry at UCLA, believed, "Death is not the greatest loss in life. The greatest loss is what dies inside of us while we live."

> "Death is not the greatest loss in life. The greatest loss is what dies inside of us while we live."
>
> —NORMAN COUSINS

Our dreams keep us alive. Benjamin Franklin observed, "Most men die from the neck up at age twenty-five because they stop dreaming." That's why it's so important that you help keep others' dreams alive. By doing so, you can literally help them live. Encouraging another person's dream can nurture her soul.

Encouraging Others in Their Pursuit of a Dream Is to Give Them a Wonderful Gift

Because dreams are at the center of our souls, we must do everything in our power to help turn dreams into reality. That is one of the greatest gifts we can ever give. How can you do it? Follow these six steps:

1. *Ask them to share their dream with you.* Everyone has a dream, but few people are asked about it.
2. *Affirm the person as well as the dream.* Let the person know that you not only value his or her dream but that you also recognize traits in that individual that can help him or her achieve it.
3. *Ask about the challenges they must overcome to reach their dream.* Few people ask others about their dreams; even fewer try to find out what kinds of hurdles the person is up against to pursue them.
4. *Offer your assistance.* No one achieves a worthwhile dream alone. You'll be amazed by how people light up when you offer to help them achieve their dream.
5. *Revisit their dream with them on a consistent basis.* If you really want to help others with their dreams, don't make it a one-time activity you mark off your list. Check in with them to see how they're doing and to lend assistance.
6. *Determine daily to be a dream booster, not a dream buster.* Everyone has a dream, and everyone needs encouragement. Set your mental radar to pick up on others' dreams and help them along.

PEOPLE WILL LIVE UP TO THEIR DREAMS WHEN THEY HAVE A CHANCE TO FULFILL THEM

Scott Adams, creator of the popular *Dilbert* cartoon, tells this story about his beginnings as a cartoonist:

> You don't have to be a "person of influence" to be influential. In fact, the most influential people in my life probably are not even aware of the things they've taught me. When I was trying to become a syndicated cartoonist, I sent my portfolio to one cartoon editor after another—and received one rejection after another. One editor even called and suggested that I take art classes. Then Sarah Gillespie, an editor at United Media and one of the real experts in the field, called to offer me a contract. At first, I didn't believe her. I asked if I'd have to change my style, get a partner—or learn how to draw. But she believed I was already good enough to be a nationally syndicated cartoonist. Her confidence in me completely changed my frame of reference and altered how I thought about my own abilities. This may sound bizarre, but from the minute I got off the phone with her, I could draw better.

Editor Sarah Gillespie gave Adams a chance to live out his dream, but because so many people had tried to discourage him, he was almost afraid to say yes. But because of her encouragement—and the opportunity she gave him—*Dilbert* has become one of the most popular cartoons in the nation.

There is no telling what might happen if you were to begin encouraging the dreams of the people around you. When you come to the end of your life, wouldn't you love to be the person about whom others say, "I succeeded because this person believed in me when nobody else did"? Start encouraging others. The more you do, the more they will share their dreams with you. And the greater the chance you will get to watch them bloom.

LES . . . ON BRINGING IT HOME

In case you fear that encouraging people's dreams will simply cause them to keep their heads in the clouds, research reveals that this practice does more than cause individuals to seek something positive in the future. It actually causes them to be more engaged in their present activities. Technically speaking, it's called the "resonance performance model," but whatever you call it, you can't go wrong by encouraging the dreams of others.

To apply John's teaching to your own life . . .

Forget about:

Critiquing another person's dream. Instead, affirm his lofty vision and his pursuit to realize it.

Ask:

Who can I encourage today in reaching their dreams?

Do it:

Offer specific help in bringing another person closer to making his or her dream a reality.

Remember:

When a person shares his or her dream with you, it is the center of that person's soul.

9

PASS THE CREDIT ON TO OTHERS

If each of us were to confess his most secret desire, the one that inspires all his plans, all his actions, he would say: "I want to be praised."

—E. M. CIORAN

LES . . . ON SEEING THE PRACTICE IN ACTION

One of my favorite topics of conversation with John is publishing. We've talked about it for nearly two decades now. Whether book ideas, titles, marketing campaigns, publishers, bookstore shelf space, or agents, we have bandied about nearly every conceivable aspect of the industry. And since John has been one of the most successful authors in the area of leadership and sold more than nine million books, I'm always intrigued to learn about the ins and outs of his publishing experiences.

Some time ago John and I were both speaking at a conference in Virginia, and between sessions I asked him to pinpoint a publishing highlight in his career.

"That's a tough one, Les," he told me. "I've been blessed in ways I could have never anticipated."

"Surely something stands out," I gently pressed.

"Well, when *The 21 Laws of Leadership* sold one million copies, Thomas Nelson, the publishing house, hosted a celebration banquet for about 120 people from their company and Injoy to mark the occasion. They gave me some beautiful gifts that night, including these." John pulled up the sleeve of his jacket and pointed to the gold cuff links he was wearing, each bearing the number "21." "What an honor that evening was."

Sometime later, I spoke to a few of the people who attended that banquet, including John's wife, Margaret. She said that when John got up to address everyone, he expressed his gratitude and quickly started crediting the people who had helped make it happen. He told how Victor Oliver had come up with the original concept for the book and had provided the title. He credited a group of key leaders at Injoy who had helped him hone the laws. He thanked Charlie Wetzel, his writer, for being the book's wordsmith. He thanked Ron Land of Thomas Nelson and Kevin Small and the Injoy team for putting together the book tour that helped put *The 21 Laws* on the *New York Times*'s best-seller list. He thanked publisher Mike Hyatt, the Nelson sales and marketing staff, the booksellers, and many other individuals, including his parents. Margaret said that by the time John finished, there wasn't a dry eye in the room.

Making a book successful and getting it into the hands of

people it can help is always a team effort, though not all authors see it that way. Everybody involved in the process has a part to play, and John did his best to pass along the credit by recognizing each person's contribution.

JOHN . . . WITH A MAXWELL MENTORING MOMENT

I'll never forget that night in Orlando. When I wrote my first book in 1979, I never dreamed that anything I wrote would sell a million copies. As Margaret and I went back to our hotel room, she asked me what I considered to be the highlight of the banquet. Without hesitation I replied that it was passing on the credit to the people who helped me so much. Rarely do we get an opportunity to say thank you enough to the people who help us, especially in such a public setting. I really wanted to make the most of it. Not only does it make me feel good to share any success I might have, but it uplifts others—and it makes them feel like a million bucks.

Passing the credit on to others is one of the easiest ways to win with people. If you'd like to practice it, here are a few suggestions to get you started:

Check Your Ego at the Door

The number one reason people don't pass along credit to others is that they think it will somehow hurt them or lessen their value. Many people are so insecure that they constantly feed their egos to compensate for it. But you simply cannot practice this method of winning with people if you can't set your ego aside.

Have you ever heard the saying "An egotist is not a person who thinks too much of himself; it's someone who thinks too little of other people"? If you want to give others credit, put your focus on others. What do they need? How will giving them credit make them feel? How will it enhance their performance? How will it motivate them to reach their potential? If you highlight their contributions, it makes them *and* you look good.

> "An egotist is not a person who thinks too much of himself; it's someone who thinks too little of other people."

DON'T WAIT—PASS THE CREDIT ASAP

I love what H. Ross Perot once said about passing on credit: "Reward employees while the sweat's still on their brow." Isn't it true that one of the very best times to give credit to others is when the amount of work and sacrifice something took is still fresh in their minds? Why wait? You may have heard management expert Ken Blanchard's teaching that you should catch people while they're doing something good. What a great idea! The sooner you give credit to someone else, the bigger the payoff.

In 2003, when I interviewed UCLA basketball coach John Wooden, he told me how he would often teach his players who scored to give a smile, wink, or nod to the player who gave them a good pass. "What if he's not looking?" asked a team member. Wooden replied, "I guarantee he'll look." Everyone enjoys having his contribution acknowledged.

Say It in Front of Others

You've already read the chapter that encourages you to compliment people in front of other people, but it bears saying again. When you give credit to others in front of their peers and loved ones, the value of your compliment multiplies. Former New York Yankees player and manager Billy Martin observed, "There's nothing greater in the world than when somebody on the team does something good and everybody gathers around to pat him on the back." By giving credit in a crowd, you can help to create the kind of environment Martin described.

Put It in Print

When you give people credit verbally, you uplift them for a moment. When you take the time to put it in writing, you have the potential to uplift them for a lifetime. People put plaques on their walls as reminders of their achievements. They save and cherish letters containing recognition and praise for things they've done. Deep down, everyone wants to make a difference, and some days, everyone is in need of some encouragement.

I have a file in my office with letters and notes that have special significance for me. Every now and then, I'll pull out the file and read some of the things people I respect have told me. It allows me to relive that moment of encouragement. It's said that even President Abraham Lincoln used to carry in his pocket a newspaper clipping extolling his accomplishments as president. He was one of the finest leaders in our nation's history, yet he desired something to keep his spirits up.

Please don't underestimate the impact that an article, a public notice, or a personal note can make. What takes you only a few minutes to write may be something that inspires another person for decades.

Only Say It If You Mean It

I love this old joke: As an old man lay dying, his wife of many years sat close by his bed. He opened his eyes and saw her. "There you are, Agnes," he said, "at my side again."

"Yes, dear," she replied.

"Looking back," the old man said, "I remember all the times you were by my side. You were there when I got my draft notice and had to go off to fight in the war. You were with me when our first house burned to the ground. When I had the accident that destroyed our car, you were there. And you were at my side when my business went bankrupt and we lost every cent we had."

"Yes, dear," his wife said.

The old man sighed.

"I tell you, Agnes," he said, "you've been a real jinx."

It may seem obvious, but I want to go ahead and say it anyway so that I'm not misunderstood. You should never say something you don't believe just to uplift someone. If you're not sincere, you don't make people feel good; you make them feel they're being schmoozed. When you pass credit on to others, you need to do it from the heart.

LES . . . ON BRINGING IT HOME

Passing credit along to coworkers or colleagues is more than mere niceness. According to research, when you pass credit along to others, you actually change their biochemistry and create an "emotional stamp" that forever associates you in their minds with their success.

To apply John's teaching to your own life . . .

Forget about:

Your ego. Focus on the people around you and the credit they deserve.

Ask:

Who has made me more successful than I would have been on my own?

Do it:

Publicly pass along credit for a successful endeavor to as many people as you can.

Remember:

If each of us were to confess our most secret desire, we would say: "I want to be praised."

10

OFFER YOUR VERY BEST

I do the very best I know how—the very best I can; and I mean to keep on doing so until the end.
—ABRAHAM LINCOLN

LES . . . ON SEEING THE PRACTICE IN ACTION

For many years now I've received the leadership lessons on tape and CD that John does every month. After listening to one titled "Preparation: The Separation Between Winning and Losing," I had to ask John a question.

"I loved the teaching, and I pulled some nuggets from it that have really helped me," I said, "but I need to ask you a question. Do you really believe preparation is that important in a person's life?"

"Absolutely," John answered. "It really does make the difference between winners and losers. Preparation is more than just a discipline. It's an attitude, a way of life. My father used to quote the Bible verse that says, 'Whatever your hands find to do, do it with all your might.' In other words, in what you do, in what you have, offer your very best. I try to embrace that in everything I do."

I've watched John for years, and I believe that's true. Everything he does, he does with excellence. But it's also more than that. While we were working on this book, we had a meeting in San Diego where John was spending some time while awaiting the birth of his fourth grandchild. When we were done, John took us to dinner at his favorite restaurant in San Diego—Peohe's, which has excellent food and an even better view. It's on Coronado island and is situated on the bay across the water from San Diego's beautiful skyline.

The hostess seated us outside right by the water, and John and Margaret immediately took the two seats facing the restaurant so that everyone else in the party could enjoy the view of the bay. During our meeting earlier in the day in an ocean-view room, John had also sat with his back to the window, allowing others who were visiting from other parts of the country to enjoy the view. And neither time had it been by accident. I know John: he always thinks through what's going to be happening at a meeting and picks his seat carefully. He had taken the worst seat because he wanted to offer all of us the very best.

JOHN . . . WITH A MAXWELL MENTORING MOMENT

For years I've been invited to be the keynote speaker for organizations at their special events. It's something I really enjoy. Communicating to an audience energizes me. It would be easy for me to "wing it" or do a canned speech that I have done elsewhere before. But I never do that because I don't believe it would serve them well. Instead, I spend time researching the company. I find out as much as I can about the particular event they've planned and what they desire to accomplish. You may wonder why I would go to such trouble when I don't necessarily need to. I do it because I have a goal every time I speak. After I'm done communicating with the audience, I want the person who invited me to speak at the event to say, "You exceeded our expectations." I want to deliver for them . . . and then some.

Perhaps you are someone who already possesses an offer-your-best mind-set. If so, I commend you, and I want to encourage you to maintain that attitude. If not, I hope the following thoughts will help you develop that mind-set:

Anyone Can Be an Important Person to Me

We are most likely to give our best to those we love and respect. I think back to my days in school, and I remember loving some teachers and having others who left me cold. I know that I always did my best for the teachers I liked, and for the others I did only what was needed to get a grade. Later, I realized that my off-and-on efforts frequently hurt my relationships with others as well as my potential for success. But then I discovered the antidote: if I saw *everyone* as important—not just the people I liked the most—I would always offer my very best. That change in attitude prompted a change in my actions.

Anything We Do Can Be Made Important

Most moments in life become special only if we treat them that way. The average day is average only because we don't make it something more. The most excellent way to elevate an experience is to give it our best. That makes it special. An average conversation becomes something better when you listen with great interest. A common relationship transforms when you give it uncommon effort. An unremarkable event becomes something special when you spice it up with creativity. You can make anything more important by giving your best to it.

You Can Become Important to Anyone

Who are the most important people in your life? Are they the ones who never give you the time of day, who never seem to be there when you need them? Of course not. Usually the people who are important to you are the ones who treat *you* as important. We naturally value the people who value us. So if you want to be important to others, treat *them* as important. The most effective way to do that is to give them your very best.

Make the Most of Your Gifts and Opportunities

More than thirty years ago I memorized a quote that has shaped the way I live: "My potential is God's gift to me. What I do with my potential is my gift to Him." I believe I am accountable to God, others, and myself for every gift, talent, resource, and opportunity I have in life. If I give less than my best, then I am shirking my responsibility. I believe UCLA coach John Wooden was speaking to this idea when he said,

"Make every day your masterpiece." If we give our very best all the time, we can make our lives into something special. And that will overflow into the lives of others.

"My potential is God's gift to me. What I do with my potential is my gift to Him."

There's a story I love about President Dwight Eisenhower. He once told the National Press Club that he regretted not having a better political background so that he would be a better orator. He said his lack of skill in that area reminded him of his boyhood days in Kansas when an old farmer had a cow for sale. The buyer asked the farmer about the cow's pedigree, butterfat production, and monthly production of milk. The farmer said, "I don't know what a pedigree is, and I don't have an idea about butterfat production, but she's a good cow, and she'll give you all the milk she has." That's all any of us can do—give all that we have. That's always enough.

LES . . . ON BRINGING IT HOME

A tremendous amount of recent psychological research has focused on the value of virtues. And experts are finding that when people strive toward excellence in character traits—for example, when they work to possess a giving spirit—they routinely benefit themselves while in the process of benefiting others. This is known in the field as cultivating "fulfillments."[1] One hardly needs a research study, however, to know that when you give your very best, you are bound to feel fulfilled.

To apply John's teaching to your own life . . .

Forget about:

Doing the minimum required to get by, and focus instead on your maximum effort.

Ask:

What can I do for someone who could never repay me?

Do it:

Voluntarily give beyond what is required.

Remember:

Everybody appreciates a person who gives his very best.

11

Share a Secret with Someone

Conceal not your secret from your friend,
or you deserve to lose him.
—Portuguese Proverb

LES . . . ON SEEING THE PRACTICE IN ACTION

In 1996 John made a major decision concerning his company, and for a time let only a few people in on it. Charlie Wetzel was one of them. Here's what Charlie has to say about what that did for him and his relationship with John:

> One day John asked me to come up to his home office so that we could work on our current book project. We had a very productive work session, and after we were done, John said, "Charlie, before you go, I want to talk to you about something."

When an employee hears those words from his boss, he takes notice. Sometimes the words that follow include the phrases "tough economy," "poor performance," or "you're fired!"

John continued, "In about twelve months, we're going to move the company out of San Diego. We're not going to announce it to all the staff yet, but I'm telling the people on the executive team—my inner circle—about the move so that they can begin processing the information. We're going to be moving to Atlanta."

John went on to explain that flying out of San Diego was taking its toll, not only on him, but also on the consultants who worked for the company. When John had asked his assistant, Linda Eggers, to calculate how many days he spent the previous year just making flight connections from San Diego to Dallas, Chicago, or Atlanta, Linda came back with a mind-boggling figure: thirty days! That's when John knew he had to make a move.

That was a lot of information, so I started processing it. Then John said, "Charlie, I sure hope you'll come with us."

John spoke to me for probably only two minutes, but what he communicated changed my life. At that time I had been working with John for about two years, and we had already written five or six books together. I had worked hard for him, and John had always been lavish with his praise. But I had no idea he valued me as much as he did. Once he shared this secret, my place in his estimation, in my career, and even in my own eyes changed.

John has done a lot of wonderful things for my family and me through the years. He is very generous, and many of

> those things have cost him a lot of time and money. Sharing the secret of our move cost him nothing, yet it made a huge impact on me. It made me feel like a million bucks.

It's not a secret how powerful sharing with another person can be. It's a surefire way to win with people.

JOHN . . . WITH A MAXWELL MENTORING MOMENT

A Sicilian proverb says, "Only the spoon knows what is stirring in the pot." When you allow another person to know what is stirring within you, giving him a "taste" of a plan or idea, you instantly make a meaningful connection with him. Who doesn't want to know what's going on in the mind of someone they care about?

Reading Charlie Wetzel's story might make you think that sharing a secret with someone always has to be a big deal with life-changing ramifications. It doesn't. Of course, when you let people in on something impacting, it makes quite an impression. But you can make sharing a secret part of your everyday life using everyday things. The first time you share something with others, aren't you sharing something that has been secret up to that moment? Why not let the person to whom you're talking know that you're revealing it for the first time? That makes him feel special.

Sharing a secret with someone is really a matter of two things: reading the context of a situation and desiring to build up the other person. If you do those two things, you can learn this skill. As you try it out, keep these three things in mind:

1. Sharing a Secret Means Giving Valuable Information.

When you share a secret, the information needs to be something that the people you're talking to care about. It plays to their interests or meets a felt need they possess. For example, two experienced deep-sea fishermen decided to go ice fishing. They each chopped holes in the ice, put worms on their hooks, dropped their lines into the water, and waited. After three hours, they had caught nothing.

As they sat, they watched a boy come along and cut a hole in the ice midway between them. He put a worm on his hook, dropped his line into the water, and almost instantly he caught a fish. The boy repeated the process and quickly had a catch of more than a dozen fish. The two other fishermen watched and were flabbergasted.

Finally, one of the men approached the boy and said, "Young man, we've been here for more than three hours and haven't caught a single fish. You've caught at least a dozen in just a few minutes. What's your secret?"

The boy mumbled an answer, but the man didn't catch a word of it. Then he noticed a large bulge in the boy's left cheek. "Please, could you take the bubble gum out of your mouth so I can understand what you're saying?" the man said.

The boy cupped his hands, spat it out, and said, "It's not bubble gum; it's my secret. You've got to keep the worms warm."

2. Sharing a Secret Makes People Feel Special.

Letting people in on something always boosts their egos. Charlie's comment says it all: "I had no idea he valued me as much as he did. My place in his estimation, in my career, and even in my own eyes changed." But as I said, the secret doesn't always have to be dramatic to have a positive effect. For example, when I play golf, I usually carry a laminated card with me that contains tips given to me by golf pro Scott Szymoniak. Occasionally if a friend in the group is not playing well, I'll pull him aside and say, "I want to share a secret with you that has really helped my golf game." Then I'll pull out the card and show him the six basic things a golfer must know and do. And I'll let him know that it's my personal golf plan and that I don't share it with everybody.

How does it make you feel when you know that you're the first person being told something? I know it makes me feel special. That's one of the reasons my wife, Margaret, and I have practiced telling each other first about many of the things that happen to us during the day. To help me do that, I carry a note card or small pad and jot down things I want to tell her. Anything I write down I "save" to tell her first. It leads to special times together every day.

3. Sharing a Secret Includes Others in Your Journey.

The bottom line on sharing a secret with others is that it is an act of inclusion. It invites others into your life, into your experience. It includes them in your success. When I speak to an audience—whether it's a roundtable of executives or an arena full of people—I intentionally use inclusive language. I let people in on my personal journey. And when I'm revealing something I've not previously

The bottom line on sharing a secret with others is that it is an act of inclusion.

said publicly, I let them know that I'm doing so. It communicates to people that I care about them and want to help them.

LES . . . ON BRINGING IT HOME

When people are "in the know," according to research, a slew of positive attributes are correlated with their lives. For example, they are far more likely to feel that their jobs fit their ambitions. They are more likely to be active in public service. They have patterns of rich friendships and happier marriages. Researchers call this an "adaptive mental mechanism."[1]

Whatever terminology you use, it turns out that when you share a secret with others, you are doing far more than imparting mere information. You are increasing the odds of a closer relationship.

To apply John's teaching to your own life . . .

Forget about:

Hoarding information for yourself.

Ask:

Whom can I benefit most by letting them in on some otherwise private information?

Do it:

Find someone to let in on a secret today.

Remember:

Sharing a secret with someone is bound to boost their self-esteem.

12

Mine the Gold of Good Intentions

To err is human; to forgive is not company policy.
—Unknown

LES . . . ON SEEING THE PRACTICE IN ACTION

Do you ever struggle to give people the benefit of the doubt—to mine the "gold" of their good intentions? I know I do. Especially when I think they've dropped the ball or tried to hurt me. But if you're like me, you also know that this tendency can be a costly interpersonal mistake if you want to win with people. So when I confessed this faux pas to John one day, he immediately identified with what I said. But he also told me how he had learned to give people the benefit of the doubt: he watched his mother.

"Mom knew my heart and she always evaluated my behavior in light of it," John explained. "Today when I say to someone, 'I didn't mean to do that,' I often wish that they would 'mine the gold of my good intentions' like my mom did. Her ability and willingness to do this in my life was a tremendous gift—and it's helped me to give the benefit of the doubt to others."

"Are you saying your mom looked past all your mistakes?" I asked.

John laughed. "Definitely not. Like every other kid, I got my fair share of reprimands. And trust me, I deserved them! But Mom never seemed to jump to conclusions with me. She never assumed the worst. Instead, she always assumed the best. And that's key to cultivating this quality.

"You see," John continued, "it did so many things for me." He counted them off: "It allowed me to draw close to her. It made her approachable. It brought out the best in me. And it taught me how to do this for others."

"Okay, John," I asked as I considered his words, "do you think that a person who wasn't raised in a home where this kind of quality was modeled is going to have a tougher time doing this for others?"

"Les, I don't really think so," he said. "Sure, a person whose home life wasn't positive won't have seen it modeled, so that person may not do it *naturally*. But when it comes right down to it, giving others the benefit of the doubt is a choice. And I've seen a lot of people who grew up with few advantages rise above that and become winners in every sense of the word."

That gives everyone hope.

JOHN . . . WITH A MAXWELL MENTORING MOMENT

Let's start by being honest. Not everyone has pure intentions. If you mine the gold of good intentions, occasionally people will take advantage of you. They have in my life. And they will in the future. But because I assume the best in others, so many people have done so many wonderful things for me I literally cannot count them all.

I've found that when I am suspicious of others, it causes me to display wrong behavior toward them. And it actually makes any interaction with them worse. In general, you get what you expect from others. So I have chosen to take the high road, expect the best, and be blessed most of the time. If you desire to do the same, do the following:

Believe the Best About People

The first thing you need to do is check your attitude. How do you see others? Do you believe that, deep down, every person desires to be good, to do his best? That matters, because if you don't believe the best in others, you will never believe that their intentions are good. And if you don't believe in their intentions, I imagine you will not exert the effort to "mine" the gold that is in them.

See Things from Their Perspective

The issue of perspective really has to do with maturity. Consider the story of two Cub Scouts whose younger brother had fallen into a lake. They rushed home to Mother with tears in their eyes. One of them sobbed, "We tried to give him CPR, but he kept getting up and walking away."

Without maturity, we lack perspective. The less mature one is, the more difficult it is to see things from another's point of view. Think about the biblical story of the woman caught in adultery where Jesus challenged the people without sin to cast the first stone. The *oldest* people in the crowd were the first to drop their stones and walk away. Why? Their maturity gave them better perspective.[1]

"Since we tend to see ourselves primarily in light of our *intentions*, which are invisible to others," said philosopher J. G. Bennett, "while we see others mainly in the light of their *actions*, which are all that's visible to us, we have a situation in which misunderstanding and injustice are the order of the day." And that's precisely why the ability to see things from another's perspective is essential to finding the gold of their good intentions.

Give People the Benefit of the Doubt

When you were a child, perhaps you were taught the Golden Rule: "Do unto others as you would have them do unto you." I've often found that when my intentions were right but my action turned out wrong, I wanted others to see me in light of the Golden Rule. In other words, I wanted others to give me the benefit of the doubt. Why shouldn't I try to extend the same courtesy to others?

Frank Clark commented, "What great accomplishments we would have in the world if everybody had done what they intended to do." While I'd agree that's true, I'd also add, "What great relationships we would have if everybody was appreciated for what they intended to do—in spite of what they may have done." When you give someone the benefit of the doubt, you are following the most effective interpersonal rule that has ever been written.

"Since nothing we intend is ever faultless, and nothing we achieve without some measure of finitude and fallibility we call humanness, we are saved by forgiveness."

—DAVID AUGSBURGER

REMEMBER THEIR GOOD DAYS, NOT THEIR BAD ONES

We all have good days and bad days. I don't know about you, but I'd like to be remembered for my good ones. And I can only ask to be forgiven for my bad ones. Fuller Theological Seminary Professor David Augsburger observes, "Since nothing we intend is ever faultless, and nothing we achieve without some measure of finitude and fallibility we call humanness, we are saved by forgiveness." If you desire to mine the gold of good intentions in others, then forgiveness is essential. And it's rarely a one-time thing. Civil rights leader Martin Luther King Jr. was right when he said, "Forgiveness is not an occasional act; it is a permanent attitude."

"Forgiveness is not an occasional act, it is a permanent attitude."

—MARTIN LUTHER KING JR.

And remember, it is with the attitude with which you judge others that you will also be judged. If you mine the gold of good intentions in your relationship with others, then people will more likely do the same for you.

LES . . . ON BRINGING IT HOME

If you grew up in an environment where the worst was assumed about you instead of the best, take heart. A research study that followed children for thirty years found that exceptional and caring adults often emerged from difficult childhoods. What made the difference? Two qualities stood out: (1) they found a nurturing relationship somewhere along the line—whether it was a mentor or other kind of role model, and (2) they had a desire to help other people.[2]

To apply John's teaching to your own life . . .

Forget about:

Justice; instead, focus on grace and forgiveness.

Ask:

How would I feel and what would I do if I were in this person's shoes?

Do it:

Practice the Golden Rule by appreciating what others intend, not only what they do—just as you would like for them to do with you.

Remember:

If I fail to believe the best in others, I will not give the effort to "mine" the gold contained in them.

13

KEEP YOUR EYES OFF THE MIRROR

I don't know what your destiny will be,
but one thing I know: the only ones among you who
will be really happy are those who have sought and
found how to serve.

—ALBERT SCHWEITZER

LES . . . ON SEEING THE PRACTICE IN ACTION

Soon after John relocated his companies from San Diego, California, to Atlanta, Georgia, in 1997, he hired researcher George Barna to fly to Atlanta and do some strategic planning with the executive team. Barna is the leading director of the Barna Group, a full-service marketing research company located in Ventura, California. Their expertise is in tracking cultural trends and collecting information on the Christian church.

The leaders and top thinkers from John's companies gathered together in the conference room for an all-day session where they could ask Barna anything they wanted to help them plan business and marketing strategies for the next several years. It took everyone no time at all to dive in and begin picking Barna's brain. He answered question after question. They brainstormed concepts and strategies. And they bounced ideas off of Barna to see if he thought they would fly.

Linda Eggers, John's longtime assistant, noticed that during the long sessions, John listened attentively but rarely chimed in. He seemed content to just listen. At the end of the day, when she and John sat down to attend to calendar items, correspondence, travel arrangements, and the like, Linda noticed that John had an entire legal pad of questions for George Barna that he had never asked.

Linda was surprised—especially since she had booked Barna and she knew exactly how much John had paid for the consultation.

"John, you just let everyone else talk today," she remarked. "Why didn't you ask him any of *your* questions?"

"You know what, Linda?" John said. "Everybody was obviously very excited about meeting with George, and it was so energizing to them, I didn't want to do anything to ruin the momentum. It doesn't matter that I didn't get my questions answered. Some other time."

Linda says that is one of the reasons she loves working for John. "I know that because he seems larger than life and has such charisma in front of an audience," Linda said, "there are people out there who think he has a big ego. They have no idea how much he thinks about others and puts them first."

If you focus on others, continually working to give them what they need, then you are able to keep your eyes off the mirror. And that's a wonderful way to win with people.

JOHN . . . WITH A MAXWELL MENTORING MOMENT

One of the key questions I ask in my book *Winning with People* is the Connection Question: Are we willing to focus on others? The foundational concept for that question is the Big Picture Principle, which states: "The entire population of the world—with one minor exception—is composed of other people." If you've never thought of life in those terms, then it's time to give it a try. If individuals think they are the center of the universe, not only are they in for a big disappointment when they discover it's not true, but they'll also alienate themselves from everyone around them. I've never met a person that truly wins with other people who has not mastered the ability to keep his eyes off the mirror and serve others with dignity.

Most people would readily admit that unselfishness is a positive quality, and even the most egocentric individual possesses the desire, deep down, to help others. The problem, sometimes, is changing our behavior so that we get in the habit of focusing on others instead of on ourselves. Here are a few thoughts to help you remember to keep your eyes off the mirror:

Focusing on Others Can Give You a Sense of Purpose

If you grew up in the 1950s and '60s, you may remember Danny Thomas, the entertainer who starred in the TV show *Make Room for Daddy*. Thomas observed, "All of us are born for a reason, but all of us don't discover why. Success in life has nothing to do with what you gain in life or accomplish for yourself. It's what you do for others."

Not only did Thomas believe that, but he also lived it. As a successful entertainer and television star, he could have done nothing but enjoy the benefits of his achievement. But he desired something more. He founded St. Jude's Hospital, a research facility that focuses on treating children who suffer from catastrophic diseases. And Thomas dedicated much of his life to supporting it. It helped him enjoy a greater purpose.

Focusing on Others Can Give You Energy

Continual focus on yourself can actually drain you of energy, while focusing on others can have the opposite effect. My friend Bill McCartney knew this back when he was head football coach for the University of Colorado Buffaloes. Coach Mac had heard that most people spend 86 percent of their time thinking about themselves, but only 14 percent of their time thinking about others. Yet he knew instinctively that if his players focused their attention on someone they cared about instead of just on themselves, a whole new source of energy would be available to them.

In 1991 Coach Mac decided to use this information when he was facing a great challenge. Colorado was scheduled to play its archrival, the Nebraska Cornhuskers, on Nebraska's home turf. The problem was that Colorado had not won a game there in twenty-three years. But Coach McCartney believed in his team and looked for a way to inspire them to achieve. In the end, he decided to appeal to their love of others.

He did it by challenging each player to call an individual he loved and tell that person he was dedicating the game to him or her. Coach Mac also encouraged the players to ask that person to watch every play, knowing that every hit, every tackle, every block, and every score was being dedicated to him or her.

Coach Mac also took one more step. He arranged to distribute sixty footballs with the game's final score written on them, so that each player could send a ball to the individual he had chosen.

The Colorado Buffaloes won the game. The final score written on the footballs was "27 to 12."

Focusing on Others Can Give You a Sense of Contentment

I'm told that psychological research shows that people are better adjusted and more likely to feel content if they serve others. Serving others actually cultivates health and brings about happiness. People have instinctively known that for centuries—even before the science of psychology was formally developed. For example, look at the wisdom (and humor) found in this Chinese proverb:

> If you want happiness for an hour—take a nap.
> If you want happiness for a day—go fishing.
> If you want happiness for a month—get married.
> If you want happiness for a year—inherit a fortune.
> If you want happiness for a lifetime—help others.

You can actually *help yourself* by helping others.

Remember that, and it will help you to take—and keep—your eyes off the mirror.

LES . . . ON BRINGING IT HOME

Some researchers call it the "ultraself" and consider it the hallmark of wisdom. It refers to a sense of serenity that allows one to focus on others from an emotionally secure place. It is free from petty jealousy and competitiveness. It takes genuine joy in another's success. And study after study shows it to be one of the most important ways to make meaningful connections with others.[1]

To apply John's teaching to your own life . . .

Forget about:

Trying to find happiness by tending to your own needs first.

Ask:

What can I do to forget myself and focus on others?

Do it:

Set your needs aside and do something specific, today, that will help you keep your eyes off the mirror.

Remember:

Success in life has everything to do with what you do for others.

14

Do for Others What They Can't Do for Themselves

You have not lived today until you have done something for someone who can never repay you.

—John Bunyan

LES . . . ON SEEING THE PRACTICE IN ACTION

Early on, John gave a boost to my speaking career when he opened doors I could have never opened myself. On his recommendation, I was standing on speaking platforms around the country, addressing audiences of several thousand at a time. The people who booked the events didn't know me; they knew John and trusted his endorsement of a young speaker who was just getting started.

That was fifteen years ago, and I'm just as grateful now for what John did for me in those early days as I was when it first happened. John gave me something that I could have never gotten without him—a launch to my professional speaking career.

Countless people could tell stories of how John extended himself in some way to help them along personally or professionally. When I talked to Tim Elmore, a longtime friend and employee who is now a vice president of EQUIP, he said, "It's hard for me to narrow it down. John has done so many things for me, and I owe him so much."

He thought for a moment and then told me this:

> Maybe something more personal will really show you John's heart. John and I were in Bangalore, India, to teach leadership—a trip, I might add, that I would not have gotten to take if John hadn't hired me at EQUIP. Before we left the country, my wife, Pam, asked John to keep an eye on me because I'm diabetic. If my blood sugar level drops suddenly, I get disoriented, I have no clue that I'm getting into trouble physically, and I usually need to go to a hospital for help. It can be scary—especially when you're overseas.
>
> When we got to India, John was received like a rock star! You wouldn't believe the way people treated him. Overseas, people wait in lines literally for hours to meet him and have him sign his books. Anyway, John taught a session in Bangalore, and the crowd was going nuts, and the people were all crowding around him, and what does he do? He pushes his way through the crowd, grabs the kit with my diabetic supplies, and checks up on me to make sure I'm not in trouble.
>
> That probably sounds like a small thing but it's hard to

> believe that anybody would not get caught up in that kind of moment and would instead focus on somebody else's needs. It really reveals John's heart and desire to do for others.

Tim got choked up as he told me the last part. I was touched by his story. But there's something that made an even greater impression on me. All the people I talked to about this quality in John said that they desired to do for others what John did for them. Because they have been helped to do things they otherwise couldn't do on their own, they're inspired to give others a boost.

JOHN . . . WITH A MAXWELL MENTORING MOMENT

Ambassador and poet Henry Van Dyke observed, "There is a loftier ambition than merely to stand high in the world. It is to stoop down and lift mankind a little higher." What a great perspective! Doing for others what they can't do for themselves is really a matter of attitude. I believe that whatever I've been given is to be shared with others. And because I have an abundance mind-set, I never worry about running out myself. The more I give away, the more I seem to get to give away.

> "There is a loftier ambition than merely to stand high in the world. It is to stoop down and lift mankind a little higher."
>
> —HENRY VAN DYKE

No matter how much or how little you think you have, you have the ability to do for others what they cannot do for themselves. Exactly how you do that will depend on your unique gifts, resources, and history. However, you can approach the task by thinking in terms of four areas:

1. Introduce Others to People They Can't Know on Their Own.

My dad, Melvin Maxwell, has done many incredible things for me during the course of my life. One of the things that impacted me most was his introducing me to great men. As a teenager, I met Norman Vincent Peale, E. Stanley Jones, and other exceptional men of the faith. And because I had declared my intention to go into the ministry, my father asked these preachers to pray for me. I can't express in words what that did for me.

Today, I am often in a position to do for others what my father did for me. I love introducing young people to my heroes. I love helping people make business contacts. There are often times when I meet someone, and as we talk, it just hits me: I need to introduce this person to so-and-so. That can mean walking somebody across the room, making a phone call on his or her behalf, or arranging a meeting. Several years ago, I was talking to Anne Beiler, the founder of Auntie Anne's, the pretzel company, and she mentioned in passing that Chick-fil-A's founder, Truett Cathy, was one of her heroes. Since I knew Truett, I offered to introduce them to each other. I hosted a dinner party for them at my house, and it was a great night.

Please don't get the impression that you have to know someone famous to help others in this area. Sometimes it's as simple as introducing one friend to another or one business associate to another. Just make connections. Be the bridge in people's relationships with others.

2. Take Others to Places Where They Can't Go on Their Own.

Early in our marriage, Margaret and I were dirt poor. Right out of college, I put in long hours for my career, and Margaret worked three jobs for us to make ends meet. And we did manage to get by, but there was no money left over for luxuries, such as vacations. Fortunately, I had an older brother who loved us and took care of us. The first five or six years of my professional life, any vacation we took was at the invitation of Larry and his wife, Anita. A wonderful trip to Acapulco, Mexico, especially stands out in my mind.

It seems that during the first half of my career, if I got to go anywhere of value to me, it was because someone invited me. Dozens of times I've had experiences that I could not have gained access to on my own: I've gone to ball games, played golf courses, seen churches, attended conferences, and visited countries that appeared to be beyond my reach.

You may have the power to give someone an experience that seems inaccessible to them. If you can't help a friend or colleague, then start with your family. Take your children places they could not go on their own. There's no telling what kind of positive impact it will make.

3. Offer Others Opportunities They Can't Reach on Their Own.

Les mentioned that I helped him to reach larger audiences early in his speaking career. The same thing was done for me. Nearly twenty-five years ago, Professor C. Peter Wagner of Fuller Seminary invited me to speak to audiences of pastors around the country about leadership. He put me on a national stage for the first time and gave me credibility that I didn't possess on my own.

Few things are of greater value to a prepared person than an opportunity. Why? Because opportunities increase our potential. Demosthenes, the great orator of ancient Greece, said, "Small opportunities are often the beginning of great enterprises." An opportunity seized is often a source of success. Help people win by giving them opportunities, and you will win with them.

"Small opportunities are often the beginning of great enterprises."

—DEMOSTHENES

4. SHARE IDEAS WITH OTHERS THAT THEY DON'T POSSESS ON THEIR OWN.

What is an idea worth? Every product begins with an idea. Every service begins with an idea. Every business, every book, every new invention begins with an idea. Ideas are what make the world move forward. So when you give people an idea, you give them a great gift.

One of the things I love about writing books is the process that it takes me through. It usually starts with a concept that I'm anxious to teach. I get a few ideas down on paper, and then I call together a group of good creative thinkers to help me test the concept, brainstorm ideas, and flesh out the outline. Every time we've done this, people have given me great ideas that I never would have come up with on my own. I have to say I'm very grateful.

One of the things I enjoy most about creative people is that they love ideas, and they always seem to have more coming.

The more they give away, the more new ideas they seem to have. Creativity and generosity feed each other. That's one of the reasons I'm never reluctant to share ideas with others. I'm convinced that I will run out of time long before I run out of ideas. It's better to give some away and contribute to another person's success than to have them lying dormant in me.

LES . . . ON BRINGING IT HOME

When you do something for others that they can't do for themselves, you are fostering relationships with those individuals that are sure to be meaningful. Studies on what researchers call the "self-determination theory" have shown that supporting other people's goals cements the relationship, since you are ultimately helping them to align their goals with themselves.[1]

To apply John's teaching to your own life . . .

Forget about:

Focusing on what you can get from others and focus instead on what you can do for others.

Ask:

What opportunity, idea, or experience could I provide that someone might never be able to have without my help?

Do it:

Consider specific things you might be able to do for others by making a list of your unique skills, resources, and connections.

Remember:

We all need others to do for us what we cannot do for ourselves.

15

LISTEN WITH YOUR HEART

The most important thing in communication is to hear what isn't being said.
—PETER DRUCKER

LES . . . ON SEEING THE PRACTICE IN ACTION

As a psychologist, I've been trained to listen for people's feelings, not just their ideas. And I've observed that many leaders—especially strong ones with type-A personalities—are not particularly good at listening. When they do listen, their attitude is usually, *Never mind the delivery story, just show me the baby*.

I would consider John to be a pretty strong person. He can be a take-charge, take-no-prisoners kind of leader. But he is also an effective listener. And he's particularly adept at sensing how people feel. Since that characteristic is unusual for most people like him, I asked him how he came to be such a good listener.

"Failure," was his answer. "Repeated failure. I started out as a terrible listener. Early in my career, I thought I knew it all. The only reason I let people talk was that I knew my turn to talk was coming.

"In my marriage, I was a *little* bit better," John continued. "I very much *wanted* to listen to Margaret because of my love for her. However, that didn't stop me from being Mr. Answer Man. In *Winning with People*, I tell about how I used to win arguments but run over her emotionally. Finally, understanding how I was hurting her feelings caused me to stop what I was doing and learn how to listen—not just to the words, but to the feelings behind her words. I learned to listen with my heart."

"So how did you make the transfer from home to your career?" I asked.

"I saw the value in it from the way Margaret's and my relationship changed. But I also came to realize that it was good leadership too. President Woodrow Wilson said, 'The ear of the leader must ring with the voices of the people.' For a couple of years, whenever I was in a meeting, I wrote a large 'L' at the top of my legal pad to remind myself to listen. In time, it became a skill I mastered."

If you are already a good listener, you are ahead of the game. All you have to do is listen "between the lines" for cues that will tell you how others feel. If you're more like John, it may take you some time to learn the skill of listening with your heart. But anyone can do it—you don't need to be a trained psychologist!

JOHN . . . WITH A MAXWELL MENTORING MOMENT

If you are a poor listener, as I was, then do the following to transform yourself into someone who listens with the heart:

Focus on the Person

Herb Cohen, often called the world's best negotiator, says, "Effective listening requires more than hearing the words transmitted. It demands that you find meaning and understanding in what is being said. After all, meanings are not in words, but in people." Many people put their focus on the ideas being communicated, and they almost seem to forget about the person. You can't do that and listen with the heart.

I am naturally very impatient, so I continually have to fight against the tendency to put my agenda first. I think that is often the case with poor listeners. If that is true for you, slow down and put the person first. Focus on the individual, not just the ideas being expressed.

Unclog Your Ears

Even after you have begun to focus on the person with whom you are conversing, you may still experience many potential barriers to effective listening. Here are a few of them:

Distractions—Phone calls, TV, pagers, and things of that sort can make good listening nearly impossible.

Defensiveness—If you view complaints or criticism as a personal attack, you can become defensive. Once you begin to protect yourself, you will care little about what others think or how they feel.

Closed-mindedness—When you think you have all the answers, you close your mind. And when you close your mind, you close your ears.

Projection—Automatically attributing your own thoughts and feelings to others prevents you from perceiving how they feel.

Assumptions—When you jump to conclusions, you take away your own incentive to listen.

Pride—Thinking we have little to learn from others is, perhaps, the most deadly of distractions to listening. Being full of yourself leaves little room for input from others.

Obviously, your goal is to remove these barriers to good communication. Whenever possible, put yourself in a good physical environment for listening—away from noise and distractions. And also put yourself in a good mental environment for listening—set aside your defenses and preconceived notions so that you are *open* to communication.

Listen Aggressively

There's a difference between listening passively and listening aggressively. To listen with your heart, your listening has to be active. In his book *It's Your Ship* (Warner, 2002), Captain Michael Abrashoff explains that people are more likely to speak aggressively than to listen aggressively. When he decided to become an intentional listener, it made a huge difference in him and his crew. He wrote:

> It didn't take me long to realize that my young crew was smart, talented, and full of good ideas that frequently came to nothing because no one in charge had ever listened to them. Like most organizations, the Navy seemed to put managers in a transmitting mode, which minimized their receptivity. They were conditioned to promulgate orders from above, not to welcome suggestions from below.
>
> I decided that my job was to listen aggressively and to pick up every good idea the crew had for improving the ship's operation. Some traditionalists might consider this heresy, but it's actually just common sense. After all, the people who do the nuts-and-bolts work on a ship constantly see things that officers don't. It seemed to me only prudent for the captain to work hard at seeing the ship through the crew's eyes. Something happened in me as a result of those interviews. I came to respect my crew enormously. No longer were they nameless bodies at which I barked orders. I realized that they . . . had hopes, dreams, loved ones, and they wanted to believe that what they were doing was important. And they wanted to be treated with respect.

As Abrashoff's attitude changed, his crew

There's a difference between listening passively and listening aggressively. To listen with your heart, your listening has to be active.

transformed, his ship turned around, and the results were astounding.

Listen to Understand

The fundamental cause of nearly all communication problems is that people don't listen to understand; they listen to reply. David Burns, a medical doctor and professor of psychiatry at the University of Pennsylvania, says: "The biggest mistake you can make in trying to talk convincingly is to put your highest priority on expressing your ideas and feelings. What most people really want is to be listened to, respected, and understood." If you want to meet others' needs and make them feel like a million bucks, then you need to listen.

One of the ironies of becoming a good listener is that listening to others and making them feel understood also has a side benefit. According to Burns, "The moment people see that they are being understood, they become more motivated to understand your point of view." Listening with the heart produces a win-win situation in relationships.

LES . . . ON BRINGING IT HOME

Few relational topics have had more empirical support than the importance of active listening. Psychologists sometimes call it "listening with the third ear." And the bottom line of most studies shows exactly what John is teaching. When we listen for genuine understanding, we are no longer "playing the role" of listening, but we are fully in the moment, and the person knows it.[1]

To apply John's teaching to your own life . . .

Forget about:

Trying to get your own point across and put your energy into understanding the other person's point.

Ask:

How can I better understand what this person is feeling and thinking?

Do it:

Listen aggressively by eliminating distractions and focusing on the other person's point of view.

Remember:

The best way to persuade is with your ears.

16

Find the Keys to Their Hearts

Coaches who can outline plays on a blackboard are a dime a dozen. The ones who succeed are those who get inside their players and motivate them.

—Vince Lombardi

LES . . . ON SEEING THE PRACTICE IN ACTION

When communicators speak to audiences, a funny thing often occurs. You have a clear purpose in mind, prepare your message carefully, and deliver it. But when people come up to you to talk about what you said—each person seems to have heard a different message. It never fails.

I asked John if he had experienced the same phenomenon. "Absolutely," he answered. "When I first started preaching, I was surprised. I used to wonder if everybody had heard the same sermon. In a way, they hadn't. The words I say may be the same for everyone, but the members of the audience listen differently because they all have different keys to their hearts. That's not only a great lesson for a speaker, but it's also important to remember anytime you work with people."

Whenever I spend time with John, I see him connect with people at the heart level immediately. For example, the other day while I was with him, John met with Kirk Nowery, the president of one of John's companies, ISS. Many times when a leader meets with someone who works for him, he or she immediately gets down to business. But the first thing John did was talk to Kirk about his family. He wanted to know how his wife was doing. He asked about their grown children. John seemed to know all about Kirk's family. And once they had caught up, then they talked business.

John does this intuitively with everyone he knows. He asks about many people's spouses and children by name. He inquires about what's happening at a person's church or business. And he seems to remember the details. Why? Because he makes it his goal to know what's important to the people who are important to him. And by the way, he is able to know these things because he listens with his heart, as we explained in the previous chapter.

JOHN . . . WITH A MAXWELL MENTORING MOMENT

In the 1980s, I had the privilege, along with about thirty other leaders, to spend two days with the father of modern management, Peter Drucker. One of the things he said was,

"Leading people is like conducting an orchestra. There are many different players and instruments that the conductor must know thoroughly." Drucker challenged us to *really* know the key players on our team.

For the last twenty years, I have purposefully tried to discover the keys to the hearts of the people in my life, starting with the people in my family and my inner circle. Here's what I've learned along the way:

Accept the Fact That People Are Different

I've written in previous books about how, when I was young, I used to believe that everyone ought to be like me in order to be successful. I've matured quite a bit since then. Some of my growth has come as a result of traveling and meeting many kinds of people. Books such as Florence Littauer's *Personality Plus* (Revel, 1992) have also helped me. I've come to realize with time that I've got major gaps in my skills and abilities, as everyone does, and if people with different talents and temperaments work together, we all win and get a lot more done. We also enjoy the journey of life much more.

If you have a healthy self-image, you may fall into the same trap I did. However, you cannot win with people if you secretly harbor the belief that everyone ought to be more like you. Accept that people are different, and celebrate that God made us that way.

Find the Keys to Their Hearts by Asking Questions

It may seem fundamental, but asking a good question is essential to discovering the keys to a person's heart. Through the years, I have developed a list of questions that have helped me in this endeavor time and time again. You may want to use them too:

> "What do you dream about?" You can learn about people's minds by looking at what they have already achieved, but to understand their hearts, look at what they dream of becoming.
>
> "What do you cry about?" When you understand people's pain, you can't help but understand their hearts.
>
> "What do you sing about?" What brings people joy is often a source of their strength.
>
> "What are your values?" When people give you access to their values, know that you have entered the most sacred chambers of their hearts.
>
> "What are your strengths?" Whatever people perceive as their strengths makes their hearts proud.
>
> "What is your temperament?" Learn that, and you often discover the way to their hearts.

Obviously, you don't want your questions to feel like an interview, and you don't need to find out all of the answers in one sitting. The process can be natural while being intentional.

Establish Common Ground

Our English word *communication* comes from the Latin word *communis*, which means "common." Effective leaders, communicators, and people persons always find something they have in common with the people they are speaking to. It is on common ground that they connect with others. If you've asked questions and listened, then you will have discovered common ground.

Sometimes in meetings, hidden agendas can make communication ineffective because they make it difficult for people to meet on common ground. When that happens, try suggesting that all parties agree to a simple little ground rule. When one person disagrees with another, before he's allowed to make his own point, he has to understand and be able to articulate his opponent's point. You would be amazed at how quickly this practice puts people on common ground.

Realize That with Time, People Change

It is a major leap for some people to tune into others' dreams and desires and to discover the keys to their hearts. But it's not enough to do that once with a person and then think you've "got it" forever. Time changes all things, including the human heart.

Fred Bucy, former president of Texas Instruments, observed, "It is much easier to assume that what worked yesterday will work today, and this is simply not true." What's effective in motivating people at one point in their careers will not necessarily be effective in motivating them later. What touches their hearts at one stage of life may not be the same as they grow older. Successes and failures, tragedies and triumphs, goals achieved and dreams laid to rest all make an impact on a person's values and desires.

So what does that mean to someone who wants to win with others by finding the keys to their hearts? It means you should . . .

STAY IN CONTINUAL CONVERSATION WITH OTHERS. Keep connecting on the heart level. Ask about what has touched their hearts up to now; if their responses are different, then you know they are changing, and you have a new opportunity to learn about what matters to them now.

LOOK FOR THE "CHANGE INDICATORS" OF A PERSON'S LIFE. There are certain times in people's lives when they are most likely to change: (1) when they *hurt* enough that they *have to*, (2) when they *learn* enough that they *want to*, and (3) when they *receive* enough that they are *able to*.

If you practice these two disciplines, especially with your family and the key players in your organization, you'll be able to stay connected with them.

I need to tell you one more thing about finding the keys to people's hearts, and this is the most important point: Once you have found a key to a person's heart, you must act with integrity, because you have been entrusted with something of great value. Never use it to manipulate someone. "Turn" the key only when you can add value to that person.

LES . . . ON BRINGING IT HOME

Genuine concern for others is a lifestyle more than a technique. Sure, you can practice the tips John suggests and find immediate benefit, but they will never really pay off in your relationships until you practice them consistently. In fact, research shows that

Genuine concern for others is a lifestyle more than a technique.

in learning to develop this quality, you are far more likely to see it become a part of your personality if you work at it on a daily basis, if you make it a reflexive habit with the people around you.[1] In other words, this needs to be something you *are* more than something you *do*.

To apply John's teaching to your own life . . .

Forget about:

Your inclination to believe that everyone is (or should be) just like you.

Ask:

What "change indicators" have I seen in the person whose heart I'd like to understand?

Do it:

Purposefully try to discover the keys to the hearts of your inner circle.

Remember:

Leaders who succeed are those who understand the hearts of their team.

17

Be the First to Help

After the verb "to love," "to help" is the most beautiful verb in the world.
—Berth von Suttner

LES . . . ON SEEING THE PRACTICE IN ACTION

"Les, where are you?"

"I just passed the Hotel del Coronado, and I'm pulling into the complex," I said.

"What color is your rental car?"

"It's silver," I told John over my cell phone.

"Okay, I can see you coming up right now," John said. "Take an immediate right and you'll see a parking space that is just now opening up."

"Where are you?" I asked.

"Look up." John was standing on a balcony of the high-rise building on Coronado island in San Diego. He had rented a condo, and I had just flown in for a day of meetings with him.

"Oh, there you are!" I started to laugh as I saw him waving at me from the balcony. Only John would think of actually scouting out parking spaces from a bird's-eye view so that he could make it easier for me to find a space.

I've long known that offering help to others is a key to winning with people. It's one of the first lessons you'll pick up in any social psychology class. But John puts a new twist on it. He goes out of his way to be helpful, and when someone's in need, he's often the first on the scene.

"Sometimes it's the little things with John," said employee Ken Coleman. "When I'm traveling with him, I've often seen John help someone struggling to get his or her suitcases into the airplane compartment while most other passengers are oblivious and trying to maneuver around the person. John makes a conscious effort to help in the moment. It seems to be an almost reflexive action with him."

John's twenty-six-year career in ministry probably has made a great impact on him in this area. Good pastors seem able to tune in to people's needs. But you don't have to be a professional shepherd to see people's needs and be the first to help. It's the kind of thing that anyone can do—regardless of age, talent, or socioeconomic status.

JOHN . . . WITH A MAXWELL MENTORING MOMENT

My friend Zig Ziglar said, "You can get everything in life you want if you will just help enough other people get what they want." Zig is certainly living proof of that. He has helped so many people, and he has been a success as a result.

> "You can get everything in life you want if you will just help enough other people get what they want."
>
> —ZIG ZIGLAR

I like helping people. I think it's one of the reasons God put us here on earth. But helping others does more than benefit others. It also helps you win with them. I say that because whenever you are quick to help others, it makes a statement. It's like leaving a calling card they will never forget.

So how do you become someone who is the first to help? Follow these guidelines:

MAKE HELPING OTHERS A PRIORITY

We are often so consumed with our own agendas that helping others never becomes important to us. The solution is to make helping others part of your agenda—a top priority. I read recently about something Academy Award–winner Tom Hanks did years ago on the set of *The Green Mile* that shows how helping others is a priority for him. Frank Darabont, director of the film, reflected on Hanks's commitment to helping rising actor Michael Duncan achieve his best, and the impression it had on him. Darabont said:

> Fifteen, twenty years from now, what will I remember [about filming *The Green Mile*]? There was one thing—and I'll never forget this: As we're shooting, [the camera] is on Michael Duncan first, and I'm realizing that I'm getting distracted by Hanks. Hanks is delivering an Academy Award–winning performance, off-camera, for Michael Duncan—to give him every possible thing he needs or can

use to deliver the best possible performance. He wanted Michael to do so well. He wanted him to look so good. I'll never forget that.[1]

Tom Hanks, like some other Hollywood actors, could have been the first to bail out on Duncan. Instead he was the first to help. It obviously paid off. In 1999, Michael Clarke Duncan was nominated for an Academy Award in the Best Actor in a Supporting Role category. And Duncan's career has since taken off.

Make Yourself Aware of People's Needs

This may sound obvious, but you can't meet a need that you don't know exists. Each of us must begin by caring about the people around us and looking for their needs. Sometimes that knowledge can come from listening with your heart. Sometimes it comes from just paying attention to what's going on around you. Other times it comes from mentally putting yourself in another person's place.

There is a Jewish legend that says two brothers once shared a field and a mill, each night dividing the grain they had ground together during the day. One brother lived alone; the other was married with a large family.

One day the single brother thought to himself, *It isn't fair that we divide the grain evenly. I have only myself to care for, but my brother has children to feed.* So each night he secretly took some of his flour to his brother's storehouse.

But the married brother considered his brother's situation, and said to himself, *It isn't right that we divide the grain evenly, because I have children to provide for me in my old age, but my brother has no one. What will he do when he's old?* So every night he secretly took some of his flour and put it in his brother's stores. As a result, both of the brothers found their supply of grain mysteriously replenished each morning.

Then one night they met each other halfway between their two houses. They suddenly realized what the other was doing, and they embraced each other in love. The legend is that God witnessed their meeting and proclaimed, "This is a holy place—a place of love—and here it is that my temple shall be built." The first temple is said to have been constructed on that very site.[2]

Be Willing to Take a Risk

Sometimes helping another person can be a risky proposition, yet that should not keep us from lending a hand. There's a story Ken Sutterfield tells from the 1936 Olympic Games in Berlin, Germany, that illustrates the impact that can be made by taking such a risk. Coming into the games, American sprinter Jesse Owens had set three world records in one day, including a leap of 26 feet 8 1/4 inches in the running broad jump—a record that would stand for twenty-five years. However, Owens faced great pressure during the games. Hitler and his fellow Nazis wanted to use the competition to establish Aryan superiority, and Owens, a black man, could sense the hostility toward him.

As Owens tried to qualify for the finals during the games, he became rattled as he saw a tall, blue-eyed, blond German taking practice jumps in the 26-foot range. On his first jump, Owens leaped from several inches beyond the takeoff board. Then he fouled on the second attempt. He was allowed only one more attempt. If he missed it, he would be eliminated.

The tall German approached Owens and introduced himself. His name was Luz Long. As the Nazis watched, Long encouraged Owens and offered him some advice: since the qualifying distance was only 23 feet 5 1/2 inches, Long suggested that Owens make a mark several inches before the takeoff board to make sure he didn't foul. Owens qualified on his third jump. In the finals, he set an Olympic record and earned one of his four gold medals. And who was the first person to congratulate Owens? Luz Long!

Owens never forgot the help Long had given him, though he never saw Long again. "You could melt down all the medals and cups I have," Owens wrote, "and they wouldn't be plating on the 24-carat friendship I felt for Luz Long."[3]

Follow Through Once You Begin to Help

Philanthropist Andrew Carnegie was approached by members of the New York Philharmonic Society, one of Carnegie's favorite charities, for financial support. He was about to write a check to wipe out the Society's entire deficit when suddenly he stopped. "Surely there must be other rich, generous music lovers in this town who could help out," he said. "Why don't you raise half this amount, and come back to me for the other half," said the great philanthropist.

The next day, the treasurer came back and told Carnegie that he had raised $30,000 and would like now to get Carnegie's check. The patron of the arts was immensely pleased at this show of enterprise and immediately handed it over. But he was curious. "Who, may I ask, contributed the other half?"

"Mrs. Carnegie," came the reply.

Sometimes when we are the first to offer help, we discover that the person to whom we made the offer isn't in as great a need as we first expected. Follow through anyway. Being the first to help is a great way to win with people. Offering to help and then not following through is a sure way to lose.

LES . . . ON BRINGING IT HOME

Studies on altruism fill volume after volume of academic journals. If there is one thing the professional community of psychologists knows, it's that being helpful is one of the shortest distances between two people—especially when you are the *first* to help. And like John says, helping others speaks volumes about you.[4]

To apply John's teaching to your own life . . .

Forget about:

Thinking only about what's in it for you and think about how you can offer a hand.

Ask:

How can I help you?

Do it:

Be the first to volunteer your services, offer assistance, or lend a hand.

Remember:

If you help enough people get what they want, you'll get what you want too.

18

Add Value to People

Try not to become a man of success,
but rather try to become a man of value.
—Albert Einstein

LES . . . ON SEEING THE PRACTICE IN ACTION

I've heard John speak to all kinds of audiences all over the globe, and a theme that runs like a ribbon through many of his talks has to do with adding value to people. Whatever the conference or topic, he often weaves the importance of "adding value" into it. I've also been in meetings around a conference table where John focuses on value added—to him from others and by him to others. It's a John Maxwell trademark.

So when I started researching the subject for this book, I went to Dan Reiland, a friend and colleague of John's for more than twenty years.

"John has desired to add value to people for as long as I've known him," said Dan, "but in recent years he has identified that as his primary purpose in life. And he does it in so many ways. He takes members of his staff to conferences and training events to make them better. He sets aside time for individuals to personally mentor and coach them. He gives the people he leads freedom to risk and succeed and a safe place to fail and learn. He even adds value by paying his people well."

"But how has he added value to you personally?" I asked Dan.

"Where do I start?" exclaimed Dan. "I could give you a list." And he did:

> Believing in me.
> Speaking the truth in love to me.
> Stretching me—way beyond my comfort zone but not outside of my gift zone.
> Opening the world to me through foreign travel.
> Modeling leadership in both the tough times and the fun times.
> Speaking to others more highly of me than I deserve.
> Opening doors in life that I could never have opened myself.
> Consistently having my best interest at heart.
> Allowing me into his inner circle.
> Treating me like a younger brother—a gift of immeasurable value.

"If I had never met John, my whole life would be different—my career, my skills, my relationships," Dan explained. "He has added value to me every step of the way for two decades. How do you measure that?"

John never seems to miss an opportunity to add value to people. And that priority, as much as anything else, has made him a winner with people.

JOHN . . . WITH A MAXWELL MENTORING MOMENT

At the core of my being, I believe that there is nothing in this life more important than people. Having embraced that truth, I try to live it out with integrity. To me that means doing everything in my power to add value to people.

If you desire to become a value adder, then take these things to heart:

VALUE PEOPLE

It all starts with your attitude toward people. Human relations expert Les Giblin remarked, "You can't make the other fellow feel important in your presence if you secretly feel that he is a nobody." Isn't that true? Don't you find it difficult to do something kind for people when you dislike them?

> "You can't make the other fellow feel important in your presence if you secretly feel that he is a nobody."
>
> —LES GIBLIN

The way we see people is often the difference between manipulating and motivating them. If we don't want to help people, yet we want them to help us, then we get in trouble. We manipulate people when we move them for our *personal* advantage. However, we motivate people when we move them for *mutual* advantage. Adding value to others is often a win-win proposition.

How do you see people? Are they potential recipients of value you can give, or do they tend to be nuisances along your path to success? Author Sydney J. Harris said, "People want to be appreciated, not impressed. They want to be regarded as human beings, not as sounding boards for other people's egos. They want to be treated as an end in themselves, not as a means towards the gratification of another's vanity." If you want to add value to people, you have to value them first.

Make Yourself More Valuable

We've talked about the phrase "you cannot give what you do not have." There are people who possess good hearts and the desire to give, yet they have very little to offer. Why? Because they have not first added value to themselves. Making yourself more valuable is not an entirely selfish act. When you acquire knowledge, learn a new skill, or gain experience, you not only improve yourself, but you also increase your ability to help others.

In 1974 I committed myself to the pursuit of personal growth. I knew that it would help me to be a better minister, so I began to continually read books, listen to tapes, attend conferences, and learn from better leaders. At the time, I had no idea that this commitment would be the most important thing I would ever do to help others. But that has turned out to be the case. As I improve myself, I am better able to help others improve. The more I grow, the more I can help others grow. The same will be true for you. If you want to add value to people, you must make yourself more valuable.

Know What People Value

Since you have read the chapters "Listen with Your Heart" and "Find the Keys to Their Hearts," you have a good grasp on the principle behind this practice. If you've already begun to practice it, then you know that it can be very time-consuming. But you also know it can be the most important step in adding value to others. Once we know what people value, with some effort we can add value to them.

I make it standard practice to note what the people in my life value from me, and you should too. Here are some examples from my own life:

Margaret, my wife, values my time with her, and my attention.

My children, Elizabeth and Joel Porter, value the legacy Margaret and I are leaving them.

Larry, my brother, values my prayers and our time together.

Eric and Troy, my nephews, value the fatherly advice and unconditional love I give them.

Linda, my assistant, values my time and effectiveness, because she is an integral part of it.

John, the president of my nonprofit organization, EQUIP, values the leadership and opportunities I give him.

Kirk, the president of my company ISS, values my friendship and partnership.

Tom values my friendship and mentoring.

Rick values my "big brother" relationship with him.

Joel values the networking opportunities I can give him.

I could go on, but I don't want to bore you. The point is that we must take the time to know what our most valuable people value.

By the way, adding value to others is not only a gift to them; it is a gift to you. The people I have just listed continually add value to my life. Some have given so much to me that no matter how much I do for them, I will never even the score.

LES . . . ON BRINGING IT HOME

Adding value to people is one of the reasons God put us here on earth. You cannot go wrong by helping others to live a better life or to reach their potential.

To apply John's teaching to your own life . . .

Forget about:

Trying to become a person of success, and instead become a person of value.

Ask:

Who adds value to my life, and to whom would I most like to add value?

Do it:

Make a list of the people in your life and note exactly what they value most from you.

Remember:

If you don't truly value the person, he or she will never feel important in your presence.

19

REMEMBER A PERSON'S STORY

Many a man would rather you heard his story than granted his request.

—PHILLIP STANHOPE, EARL OF CHESTERFIELD

LES . . . ON SEEING THE PRACTICE IN ACTION

"Les," John will say, "tell me about your dad. How are he and your mom doing since they moved to Phoenix?"

It's just like John to recall that my parents recently moved.

"And tell me about your brothers," he'll continue. "What's the latest with them?"

John always seems to remember my story—just as he does with so many people. He does it well, often, and consistently. When he has met people, I've heard him flat-out ask them to tell him their stories. So I asked him how he learned to be a collector of people's stories.

"To begin with, I love a good story—whether I'm learning about someone I've just met or hearing about an adventure from someone I've known my whole life. In fact, when I spend time with my dad, who is now eighty-two, our time is always filled with storytelling. We talk about the new things that are happening in our lives, but often the stories are ones I have heard dozens of times. Some Dad loves to tell over and over. Others I ask him to tell. Some I love retelling."

"But you seem to go out of your way to get the story of someone you just met," I commented.

"That's true. Whenever I have a few minutes with someone," John said, "I ask him to tell me his story, because I know that time in the conversation will focus entirely on him, his interests, dreams, uniqueness, disappointments, questions, hopes—his journey. While that person enjoys the personal attention, I gain insight into the keys to his life. Learning a person's story is a great way to connect with him. Remembering his journey and building on it is the greatest way to develop a strong relationship.

"Just the other day I took a taxi from the San Diego airport over to Coronado. And I talked to the cab driver," said John. "His name was Raphael. I asked him his story, and he told me that he had lived on Coronado thirty-five years, and there he had found something he'd not found anywhere else in his life: community. Every afternoon he meets his friends at a local market, where they talk and play games. He was so pleased that I asked and he was so delighted to tell his story that he invited me to the market."

That shows how great a connection you can make in a

short time by simply asking people to tell you their stories. And just imagine the impression it will make when you remember each story: it will help you to reconnect with people very quickly.

JOHN . . . WITH A MAXWELL MENTORING MOMENT

There are so many good reasons to learn a person's story. Here are just a few that keep motivating me to continue this practice with others:

Requesting a person's story says, "You could be special."
Remembering a person's story says, "You are special."
Reminding a person of his or her story says, "You are special to me."
Repeating a person's story to others says, "You should be special to them."

The result? You become special to the person who shared a story with you.

There are really just three small steps when it comes to embracing this practice in order to win with people. The key is to cultivate the habit of actually taking these steps with the people in your life.

1. Ask

When you meet someone new, after the introductions and initial pleasantries, don't hesitate. Dive in and ask to hear the person's story. You can do it any number of ways: you can flat-out ask, "What's your story?" You can request that he tell you about himself. You can ask where he is from or how he got into the field he's in. Use your own style.

If you've never tried this kind of thing before and you worry that it might be awkward the first few times you do it, then practice with people you are unlikely to see again—the driver in a cab, a passenger on a plane, a waitress in a restaurant. Once you become comfortable asking questions of total strangers, the rest will be easy.

2. LISTEN

Years ago I came across a list of suggestions for good listening. (I think I clipped it from *Bits and Pieces*.) Here were some of the tips:

Look the speaker in the eye.

Be attentive—don't roll your eyes or grimace when you hear something you don't agree with.

Don't interrupt—try phrases like "Go on" or "I see" instead of "Now, that reminds me . . ."

Tell the speaker what you think you heard; begin by saying, "Let me see if I understand . . ."

The main idea is to really focus on the other person. The problem many people have is that while the other person speaks, they are thinking more about what they want to say when it's their turn instead of focusing on listening. When you give people your undivided attention, then you are in a better position to achieve the next step.

3. REMEMBER

Some people have a knack for numbers, others for names or faces. But just about everyone has the capacity to remember stories. Small children remember them. And stories have been recited and sung from memory for thousands of years. Even long stories, such as the Iliad and the Odyssey—believed to have been created nearly three thousand years ago—were sung for three centuries before being written down. Stories stay with us.

A couple of years ago, the conference department at Injoy received a letter from Ellis Brust, formerly of St. Michael and All Angels Episcopal Church, that tells the power of remembering a person's story. Here's what it said:

> One of my leaders in the church has just opened a franchise fast-food place in the small East Texas town of Gilmer. He is in business with two other men in the church and they are committed to running the business with sound Christian principles. I took him to hear John three or four years ago and he recalled John's Nordstrom's stories [about how their employees go the extra mile]. He has tried to train his employees using these principles.
>
> On the first week of operation, he overheard two little old ladies talking about the soft drink selection and one of them was disappointed that there was no Diet Dr. Pepper offered. He spoke with the woman who was diabetic and preferred Diet Dr. Pepper to other diet drinks. He got in his car, drove to the 7-11, purchased a six-pack of Diet Dr. Pepper, took the woman a cup of ice and a can of the drink. He told her that there would always be a case

of Diet Dr. Pepper in the refrigerator with her name on it, and she just needed to tell the person at the counter who she was and what her beverage preference was and she would get it.

The shocked woman said, "Young man, I have been in this town my whole life. I have many influential friends and they will all hear what you just did for me. Thank you, and we will be regular customers."

I thought you would want to know one small way your work is changing lives. Keep up the good work.

Was what the restaurant owner did a big deal? Did it change the lady's life? No. In fact, we don't know if he ever talked to her again or learned anything else about her story. But he made her feel special, and it served her well. If we care about people, really listen to them, and try to remember their stories, we can make an impact on them. And we can make them feel like a million bucks.

LES . . . ON BRINGING IT HOME

Researchers call it a "commitment script." It's part of a person's life narrative that is particularly meaningful and personal. From my own experience and from numerous studies, I can attest to the fact that when you tap into it with another person, when you take the time to explore it and remember it, you will make an extremely valuable connection.[1]

To apply John's teaching to your own life . . .

Forget about:

Telling your own story and listen to the story of others.

Ask:

What's your story?

Do it:

Bring up some aspect of a person's story the next time you see him or her.

Remember:

Everyone loves to tell his story.

20

Tell a Good Story

The universe is made of stories, not atoms.
—Muriel Rukeyser

LES . . . ON SEEING THE PRACTICE IN ACTION

I spotted John on the curb at the Seattle airport and pulled up to get him. After tossing his bag into the back of my Jeep, I slid in behind the wheel. Then off we went to dinner at a hotel before a speaking engagement.

After a few minutes of catching up, we arrived at the hotel. As we walked through the lobby, John said, "Hold on a second. I want to tell you a story." He took me down a hallway, and we ducked into a meeting room.

"This place is very special to me," John explained. He pointed to a chair at the end of a conference table. "I was sitting in this chair right here when ISS evolved into the company it is today," John began, referencing one of his organizations. He pointed to each chair and explained who had been seated in it. Then he laid out the entire process of what happened that day: how he had flown to Seattle to get advice from a business executive; how his dream to help pastors raise money to expand their churches crossed over from vision to reality that day; how he recruited that business leader to assist churches on a national level.

The way John told it, I could easily visualize the whole thing and feel his enthusiasm. "I tell you, Les, coming back to a place where something good happened always renews my gratitude."

The lesson of this story stuck. John told me that story eight years ago, and I still remember it vividly. In fact, I can't help but think of it every time I drive by that hotel. It was an important point of connection to John for me at the time. He included me in a private part of his life—sharing his heart, his dreams, and his personal history. It made me feel good—and still does.

As a communicator, I'm always watching to see how people speak to an audience. John always tells a good story—in front of an audience as well as one-on-one. And he uses lots of stories when he communicates. So I asked him why.

"That's easy: stories stick; principles fade," said John. "If you want people to remember what you said, tell a story.

"Let me tell you something else," he continued. "It took a while for me to learn the lesson about stories in my writing. I'm so bottom-line that I used to just teach principles without many stories. But a friend convinced me to change my style. And it's made a big difference for my readers. As a writer, you've got to ask yourself, 'Will the reader turn the page?' The person most likely will if I am telling a good story."

I haven't met a person yet who doesn't love a good story. That's one of the reasons storytellers are so magnetic!

JOHN . . . WITH A MAXWELL MENTORING MOMENT

In the fall of 1999, Margaret, some friends, and I visited the small town of Jonesborough, Tennessee. More than seven thousand people from all over the country, many at considerable expense, came there to sit for hours on end on blankets, on folding chairs, sometimes even in the rain. Why? They wanted to attend the annual National Storytelling Festival.

We watched one storyteller after another captivate listeners. The stories were diverse—sad, happy, funny, sentimental, historical, fictitious, mythical. Some had a great message; others simply entertained. But all the stories and storytellers had one thing in common: they had the power to captivate their listeners.

At the end of the conference, my friends and I discussed why these storytellers were so effective. "What traits did they have that made them so successful?" we asked. Here's the list we came up with:

Enthusiasm—They enjoyed what they were doing and expressed themselves with joy and vitality.

Animation—The presentations were marked by lively facial expressions and gestures.

Audience participation—Nearly every storyteller involved the audience in some way, asking listeners to sing, clap, repeat phrases, or do sign language.

Spontaneity—The storytellers responded freely to their listeners.

Memorization—Telling their stories without notes allowed for eye contact.

Humor—Humor was interjected in both serious and sad stories.

Creativity—Classic themes were told from a fresh perspective.

Personal—Most stories were told in the first person.

Heartwarming—Their stories made people feel good for having heard them.

Storytelling is very effective one-on-one, in small group conversation, and in front of large audiences. Invariably, the person who tells the best stories becomes the one to whom others turn their attention.

Storytelling is a skill that comes with practice, and anyone can learn to develop it. If you don't have much experience with it, or you would like to improve, then allow me to give you a few tips:

Share Something You've Experienced

The stories we tell the best are the ones we've lived. We care about them, we know the material, and we know how they have affected us. And we can shape and embellish them any way we want. Everybody has had experiences that others would be interested in.

The stories we tell the best are the ones we've lived.

Tell It with the Goal of Connecting

The people who have the toughest time telling stories are the ones who try to impress others with them. If that describes you, then change your goal. Tell stories with the purpose of connecting with others. Put the focus on the listener, and your storytelling skills will improve overnight.

Put Your Heart into It

People love humor, but not everyone can tell a funny story. If you can, go with it. But never underestimate the power of a story from the heart. (If you want evidence, look at the sales figures of the *Chicken Soup for the Soul* books!) If you want to tell a connecting story, make it warm. Put your heart into it. And don't be afraid to show people that you care about what you're talking about.

Assume That Others Want to Hear It

One of the biggest mistakes novice storytellers make is being tentative. Nothing makes a story go flat more quickly than a timid delivery. If you're going to tell a story, be bold. Be energetic. Be engaging. Go for it, or don't go at all.

I've read that the "elite" often criticized President Lincoln for telling too many stories. But he didn't let it stop him, because he knew what worked with people. He remarked, "They say I tell a great many stories; I reckon I do, but I have found in the course of a long experience that common people, take them as they run, are more easily informed through the medium of a broad illustration than in any other way, and as to what the hypercritical few may think, I don't care."

Follow the lead of Lincoln and other great leaders who knew how to win with people. Tell a good story, engage them at the heart level, and win them over.

LES . . . ON BRINGING IT HOME

Research supports the value of being able to relate your thoughts and ideas through stories. In fact, one recent study revealed that those who use storytelling as a means of relating to others engender greater authenticity and self-esteem. It turns out their self-expression makes others feel good, and they feel better about themselves in the process.[1]

To apply John's teaching to your own life . . .

Forget about:

Being a professional storyteller.

Ask:

How can I make my point come through stronger with a story?

Do it:

Tell a story instead of relaying only facts.

Remember:

Stories stick—principles fade.

21

Give with No Strings Attached

Life's most persistent and urgent question is:
What are you doing for others?
—Martin Luther King, Jr.

LES . . . ON SEEING THE PRACTICE IN ACTION

Whenever I visit John at his office in Atlanta, one of the people I always see is Linda Eggers, John's assistant. On a recent trip as I chatted with her, I began querying her for stories to illustrate the idea of giving with no strings attached.

"Who's got a good story?" I asked. "Who should I go talk to?"

"How about me?" Linda responded. She began telling me one story after another, but one in particular seemed to mean the most to her. It occurred when her youngest daughter, Kim, was getting ready to graduate from high school. It was an especially hectic time at the office too. And Linda's middle child, Jennie, who was living in California, had recently given birth under difficult circumstances.

The day before Kim's graduation, Linda got word that Jenny was having serious complications that would require surgery.

"I'm a very steady person," said Linda. "There aren't too many things that can get to me. But I was totally overwhelmed by the situation."

Linda said that when she sat down and told John about all that was happening, after some kind words and prayer, John offered to step in and help her. The first thing he did was buy her a ticket so that she could be with Jennie that day for the surgery—a ticket with a return flight on the red-eye so that Linda could get back for Kim's graduation. And he bought her another ticket so that Linda could go back out again to be with Jennie during her recovery.

"How many employers do you know who would do something like that?" said Linda. "Because of his busy schedule, it was a real inconvenience for John to lose me during that time. But he just said, 'You take whatever time you need and do what needs to be done,' and he really meant it. I was gone for another whole week."

Linda's wasn't the only story I heard. Charlie Wetzel, John's writer for more than a decade, told me about the time John offered to send him to a weeklong writer's conference after he had worked for John only a year. When Charlie explained that he couldn't go because it was his first wedding anniversary, John offered to send Charlie and his wife. And more than one person told about a time when they were barely making it financially and John slipped them money so that they could go out for a nice dinner with their spouse.

Generosity is an extremely appealing quality. When someone gives to others—with no strings attached—it really makes them feel special.

JOHN . . . WITH A MAXWELL MENTORING MOMENT

Jesuit theologian Pierre Teilhard de Chardin said, "The most satisfying thing in life is to have been able to give a large part of one's self to others." Anyone who has unselfishly helped another person knows this to be true. Yet not everyone is able to adopt an ongoing mind-set of giving toward others. Why is that? First of all, I believe it has nothing to do with circumstances. I've met generous people with almost nothing who were willing to share what little they possessed. And I've met well-off people who were stingy with their time, money, and talents.

The issue is really attitude. I've found that people who enjoy giving with no strings attached usually exhibit two characteristics that anyone can embrace:

1. They Have an Abundance Mentality

If you've read Stephen Covey's book *The Seven Habits of Highly Effective People* (Free Press, 1989), then you are familiar with the concepts related to scarcity and abundance mind-sets. In a nutshell, people with a scarcity mind-set believe that in life, there's only a limited supply of anything to go around, whether it's money, resources, opportunity, and so forth. They see the world as a pie with a limited number of slices. Once they're gone, they're gone. As a result, they fight to get their piece—and once they have it, they protect it.

People possessing an abundance mind-set believe that there is plenty of everything to go around. If life is a pie, and others are helping themselves to pieces, the solution of the person with the abundance mind-set is to bake another pie. There is always more money to be made, more (or different) resources to be discovered, additional opportunities to be pursued. An old solution isn't working anymore? Don't worry: someone will find a new one. The inventors, entrepreneurs, and explorers of the world are continually creating new "pies" so that everyone can get a slice.

My own take on this is that people tend to fall into one of two categories: they are either takers or makers. Takers are people who take, grab, and consume whatever they can to meet their own needs. They see life as a rat race. Of course, the main problem with that is that even if you win, you're still a rat. Makers, on the other hand, are people who give, create, and make things happen. They create progress and foster success for others. They are just as likely to give as to take because they are continually helping to create more for everyone.

People who habitually give with no strings attached almost always have an abundance mentality. They are generous because they believe that if they give, they will not run out of

"When we refrain from giving, with a scarcity mentality, the little we have will become less. When we give generously, with an abundance mentality, what we give away will multiply."

—Henri Nouwen

resources. Pastor and former college professor Henri Nouwen states, "When we refrain from giving, with a scarcity mentality, the little we have will become less. When we give generously, with an abundance mentality, what we give away will multiply."

I have found this to be true. Someone once asked me why he should adopt an abundance mentality, and he was surprised by my answer. I told him that if you believe in abundance, that's what life gives you. If you believe in scarcity, then that's what you get. I don't know why that is, but after fifty years of paying attention to people's attitudes and watching how life unfolded for them, I know it to be true. So if you desire to be more generous, change your thinking and your attitude when it comes to abundance. Not only will it allow you to be more generous, but also it will change your life.

2. They See the Big Picture

People who give with no strings attached are usually aware of the help *they* have received along the way. They recognize that they are standing on the shoulders of previous generations. The progress they make is due, at least in part, to the work and sacrifice of those who have gone before them. Because of this, they are determined to do for the next generation what was done for them.

I came across a poem by W. A. Dromgoale called "The Bridge Builder." It beautifully illustrates this desire to give to others:

> An old man walking a lonesome road,
> Came at the evening, cold and gray,
> To a chasm vast and wide and deep.

The old man crossed in the twilight dim,
The rolling stream had no fears for him;
But he turned when safe on the other side,
And built a bridge to span the tide.

"Old man," said a fellow traveler near,
"You are wasting your strength with building here,
Your journey will end with the passing day,
You never again will pass this way.
You've crossed the chasm, deep and wide,
Why build you this bridge at eventide?"

The builder lifted his old gray head,
"Good friend, in the path I have come," he said,
"There followeth after me today,
A youth whose feet must pass this way.
The chasm that was nought to me,
To the fair headed youth may a pitfall be.
He too must cross in the twilight dim—
Good friend, I am building this bridge for him."[1]

To become better givers, we need greater perspective. When we realize how much we have benefited from the kindness of others, it becomes much easier for us to be generous. And one of the best things is that giving is so rewarding. College president and educational reformer Horace Mann commented, "We must be purposely kind and generous or we miss the best part of existence. The heart that goes out of itself gets large and full of joy. This is the great secret of the inner life. We do ourselves the most good doing something for others." When we give unselfishly, we will gain something in return.

LES . . . ON BRINGING IT HOME

This lesson certainly rings true in my therapy sessions with clients. And it's backed up by plenty of research. Studies have shown that the higher one's level of helpfulness to others, the greater well-being one will experience. Researchers call it "generativity," and it is consistently linked to greater personal growth and even physical health.[2]

Studies have shown that the higher one's level of helpfulness to others, the greater well-being one will experience.

To apply John's teaching to your own life . . .

Forget about:

Scarcity; instead, focus on abundance.

Ask:

Whom can I help that will give nothing in return?

Do it:

Be purposely kind and generous to a specific person.

Remember:

You do yourself the most good when you are doing something good for others.

22

Learn Your Mailman's Name

Remember that a person's name is to that person the sweetest and most important sound in any language.
—Dale Carnegie

LES . . . ON SEEING THE PRACTICE IN ACTION

John tells the story about how he used to memorize the names of people who attended his church when he was the senior pastor of Skyline Wesleyan Church in San Diego, California. He used to make an offer to visitors: if they would allow someone to take their pictures on Sunday after the service, John promised to learn their names by the following Sunday. John did that until he finished his tenure at the church in 1995. Fulfilling that promise, John was able to memorize the names of more than twenty-two hundred people and greet them by name.

In the summer of 2004, Skyline Church celebrated its fiftieth anniversary, and John and Margaret were delighted to return and be a part of the celebration. John told me that thousands of people attended, many of whom he had not seen in nine years. He was thankful that each person had a name tag. "But as I approached one couple," John told me, "the husband covered his name tag. When I called him by name he laughed and said, 'I was just checking to see if you could still remember names.'"

"That doesn't surprise me," I said, "but it still impresses me."

"You know," John replied, "at fifty-seven, it's not as easy as it once was, but I still work at remembering names."

I've long admired this skill and personal approach of John's. In fact, it inspired me in my work as a professor to learn the names of several hundred students in my classes each semester at the university. Why do we do it? Because we know that a person's name is his personal signboard to the world, his most intimate, distinctive possession. And when you remember a person's name, it can make him or her feel like a million bucks.

A person's name is his personal signboard to the world, his most intimate, distinctive possession.

JOHN . . . WITH A MAXWELL MENTORING MOMENT

In 1937 the granddaddy of all people-skills books was published. It was an overnight hit, eventually selling more than fifteen million copies. That book was *How to Win Friends and*

Influence People (Simon & Schuster, 1981), by Dale Carnegie. What made that book so valuable was Carnegie's understanding of human nature. I love his simple words of wisdom. Something that I learned early from Carnegie was this: remember and use a person's name. "We should be aware of the *magic* contained in a name . . . The name sets the individual apart; it makes him or her unique among all others. The information we are imparting or the request we are making takes on a special importance when we approach the situation with the name of the individual. From the waitress to the senior executive, the name will work magic as we deal with others."

What was true in 1937 is even more applicable in our fast-paced world. These days an account number or a title too often replaces a person's name. Remembering names can help enhance your personal image, improve your style, and, most importantly, increase your impact on others. And when you take the time to learn the names of not only your clients and important acquaintances, but also the everyday people you interact with—such as your postal worker or neighborhood store owner—you go to another level of relational connectivity.

If you desire to improve your skill with names, here are a few suggestions:

Recognize the Value of a Name

How do you feel when someone calls you by the wrong name? How about when you kindly correct the person and spend time with him, and he still gets your name wrong? How about when people haven't seen you for a long time, and they still remember your name? Doesn't it make you feel good? (And doesn't it also impress you?) When people care enough to know your name, they make you feel valued.

Playwright William Shakespeare wrote, "Good name, in man or woman, is the immediate jewel of their souls.—Who steals my purse steals trash; but he that filches from me my good name, robs me of that which not enriches him, and makes me poor indeed."[1]

Use the SAVE Method

My friend Jerry Lucas is known as "Dr. Memory." He has spent the years following his hugely successful run in the NBA helping schoolchildren and adults improve their memories through a variety of innovative techniques. One of the things he teaches is called the SAVE Method. Here's how it works:

S—Say the name three times in conversation.

A—Ask a question about the name (for example, how it is spelled) or about the person.

V—Visualize the person's prominent physical or personality feature.

E—End the conversation with the name.

Years ago Jerry showed how useful his method could be by remembering the names of every guest in the audience at the *Tonight Show*. I believe it can also help you remember the first and last names of the people you meet.

In Case of Memory Failure . . .

Almost everyone has trouble recalling names on some occasions. When this happens, try to recall the situation in which you met the person or last saw him or her. If you can't recall even that, then ask, "How long has it been?" Perhaps that will jog your memory.

If you're meeting people along with a friend or colleague, sometimes you can help each other out. Introduce the person whose name you do remember to the person whose name you don't, and perhaps the individual will volunteer his name. Or you can agree with your friend ahead of time to come to each other's aid. My wife and I do this. When we make introductions, Margaret knows that if I don't introduce someone by name, I'm not sure I remember it correctly. And she will quickly introduce herself and get the other person's name in return.

When all else fails, just say, "I'm so sorry; I remember you well, but I'm afraid your name has slipped my mind." Then after the individual reminds you, use the SAVE method so that you are less likely to forget it again in the future.

Go Easy on Yourself If You Forget

If you work at it, you *will* become better at remembering people's names. Don't be too hard on yourself, however, when you blow it. That's what I did recently when meeting a couple whose last name was Lake. One of the things I do when learning a name is to link the name to a mental image. When I was introduced to the Lakes, I immediately placed a mental image of a lake on their heads and thought of Hargus Lake where I grew up. A few days later when I saw them again, I mistakenly asked, "How are you doing tonight, Mr. and Mrs. Hargus?" Sometimes even our best practices fail us!

LES . . . ON BRINGING IT HOME

One hardly needs a research study to validate the points John is making about the value of remembering people's names. However, if you want to know whether it is substantiated by studies, I could point you to a mountain of research that shows exactly how a person's mood and self-evaluation are consistently improved when another person remembers him or her personally.[2] There is simply no question of the value of remembering people's names.

To apply John's teaching to your own life . . .

Forget about:

Blaming your "bad" memory and exert some effort to remember people's names.

Ask:

What can you tell me about the origin of your name or how it's spelled?

Do it:

Use the SAVE Method with each new person you meet this week.

Remember:

A person's name is one of his or her most valuable possessions.

23

Point Out People's Strengths

The praises of others may be of use in teaching us, not what we are, but what we ought to be.
—August W. Hare

LES . . . ON SEEING THE PRACTICE IN ACTION

I am constantly amazed by the number of high-caliber people John has on his staff. He seems to be surrounded by all-stars. When asked about his secret, he responded, "Two things. First, I try to hire the best leaders I can find. If I can hire a few '9s' and '10s,' then they will attract and hire '8s' and '9s.' Second, I always try to put people in their areas of strength."

"Okay," I said, "let me quiz you on some of the people in your circle. I'll give you a name, and you tell me their strength."

"Okay, shoot," John answered.

"Tim Elmore."

"There's nobody better than Tim at examining a passage of Scripture, searching it thoroughly, and pulling out teaching points from it."

"Linda Eggers."

"Linda's attention to detail is off the charts; she runs my whole life. But I'd have to say that her greatest strength is the confidence she instills in others. When someone talks to Linda, they feel that they've talked to me."

"Dan Reiland."

"Dan's greatest skill is leading and developing leaders on his staff. You know, back at Skyline he was my executive pastor; he led the staff and ran the church day to day while I traveled nationally."

"Did Dan come to you with experience as an executive pastor?" I asked.

"No, no, when I met Dan, he was an intern," John explained. "He had worked briefly as a youth pastor, and when he started working for me as a regular employee after seminary, I put him in charge of children's education. But over the years, he did a lot of different things. Anytime I wanted to start a new ministry, Dan was my man.

"As we worked together, a pattern of strength emerged. Dan always had the big picture, championed the vision, and possessed influence with his peers and volunteers. And he had a particular knack for developing people. As those strengths emerged, it became obvious that he was the right person to become my executive pastor."

Jim Collins, in his book *Good to Great* (Harperbusiness,

2001), writes about the concept of getting the right people on the bus and then making sure each is in the right seat. That's essentially what John was saying. When you look for and point out people's strengths, then you are able to help people take the place that's best for them and the organization. And that helps everyone win!

JOHN . . . WITH A MAXWELL MENTORING MOMENT

People often make a mistake in their personal development when they focus too much on their weaknesses. As a result, they spend all their time trying to shore up those weaknesses instead of maximizing the strengths they possess. Similarly, it's a mistake to focus on the weaknesses of others. The self-proclaimed "experts" who spend their time telling others what's wrong with them *never* win with people. Most people simply avoid them.

Instead, we need to focus on finding people's strengths and pointing them out. Here's why:

Pointing Out Strengths Underlines People's Uniqueness

Most people have strengths that they rarely get to use. Those strengths may be job skills, knowledge, general abilities, personality characteristics, or other attributes. I once read an interesting fact based on research, saying that every person can do at least one thing better than ten thousand other people. Think about that! You possess an ability that can't be matched by anyone in your town or neighborhood . . . or in your college or university . . . or in your company or maybe even in your industry.

Have you discovered that ability? If so, you are probably well on your way to pursuing your life's purpose. If you haven't, wouldn't you love it if someone came alongside you and pointed it out? How would you feel about that person? I bet you'd be pretty grateful.

Why not try to become that kind of person in someone else's life? When you do, you just might be helping others to discover the thing God created them to do.

People Are Motivated in Their Areas of Strength

I once read that a survey was taken of workers across the United States in which it was found that nearly 85 percent of those interviewed said that they could work harder on the job. More than half of them claimed they could double their effectiveness if they wanted to. Why would that be? It is because so few people are working in their areas of strength. Do you get excited when asked to work in an area of weakness? I certainly don't.

Marcus Buckingham and Donald O. Clifton have done tremendous research in this area. If you want to learn more, I suggest you read their book: *Now, Discover Your Strengths* (Free Press, 2001). But know this: when you work in your areas of strength, you don't need much external motivation. If people have been grinding away at tasks in their weak areas, and they are reassigned to work in areas of strength, watch their motivation, enthusiasm, and productivity skyrocket.

People Add the Most Value in Their Strength Zones

People often ask me what the key to my success is. And I tell them that I think it can be attributed to three things:

(1) the goodness of God; (2) the excellent people around me; and (3) my ability to stay in my strength zone. It took the first five years of my professional life to figure out what my strengths were. But with the passing of years since then, I've narrowed my focus down to fewer and fewer things.

The Law of the Niche in my book *The 17 Indisputable Laws for Teamwork* states, "All players have a place where they add the most value." That place is their "strength zone." I'm worthless at most things. But I do four things really well: lead, create, communicate, and network. And as much as possible, I stick to those things.

As a leader and employer, I try to help others do the same. I help them find their strength zones, and I try to position them there as much as possible. You see, a successful person finds the right place for himself. But a successful leader finds the right place for others. How do I do that?

A successful person finds the right place for himself. But a successful leader finds the right place for others.

First, I look for the best in others. Anybody can see weaknesses, mistakes, and shortcomings in others. That's no unique skill. Seeing only the good things is harder. Hall of Fame baseball player Reggie Jackson said that the best major-league baseball leaders possess that ability. He observed, "A great manager has a knack for making ballplayers think they are better than they think they are. He forces you to have a good opinion of yourself. He lets you know he believes in you. He makes you get more out of yourself. And once you learn how good you really are, you never settle for playing anything less than your very best." That's true in any area of life: business, parenting, marriage, ministry, and so forth. Don't look for the flaws, warts, and blemishes in others. Look for their best.

Second, I speak up. You can think the world of others, but if you never actually tell them, then you don't really help them. I have always believed that all people have a "success seed" within them. Most never find it and therefore fail to reach their potential. I often look at other people and ask, "What are their success seeds?" When I discover them, I point them out to those individuals. Then I fertilize those seeds with encouragement and water them with opportunity.

LES . . . ON BRINGING IT HOME

One of the most cutting-edge aspects of contemporary research in psychology has to do with what are termed "signature strengths." Everyone has a number of positive qualities that represent his or her strengths, but some of those are more important and more central to a person's identity. When you can point them out to others, research shows, a person is far more likely to use them, to put them on display, and to embrace them as a key component of his or her identity.

To apply John's teaching to your own life . . .

Forget about:

The weaknesses of others.

Ask:

What does this individual do exceptionally well?

Do it:

Every day this week, tell at least one person what strength you see in him or her.

Remember:

Every person in the world possesses the seeds for success.

24

Write Notes of Encouragement

The power of words is immense. A well-chosen word has often sufficed to stop a flying army, to change defeat into victory, and to save an empire.

—Emile De Girardin

LES . . . ON SEEING THE PRACTICE IN ACTION

I always love to see the inner sanctums of great leaders. You can learn much about people when you see where they work. Recently I was in John's home office, where he does most of his thinking, dreaming, writing, and creating. Among the memorabilia that is important to him, one cannot help but notice an impressive collection of John Wesley's works. In fact, it may be one of the most extensive privately held historical collections of its kind. And as a student of Wesley myself, I was intrigued.

"What's your most prized piece in this collection, John?" I asked, pointing to a shelf of antique books.

"It would have to be a letter I have that was signed by John Wesley and postscripted by his brother Charles," John said as he took me around the corner to see it hanging in a frame on the wall.

"Is it an important letter?" I asked, trying to decipher Wesley's spidery handwriting.

"It's a letter to a friend, giving him parenting advice. I prize it because it is written in Wesley's hand and signed by him," John said. "But if you want to talk about *important* letters by Wesley, then you have to consider the letter he wrote to William Wilberforce.

"In 1791, William Wilberforce was facing one more discouraging defeat in his attempt to abolish Britain's slave trade," explained John. "Then he received a letter from John Wesley. That now-famous letter would prove to be a continuing source of strength for the rest of his life."

John went quickly into his files under the topic of "encouragement" and found the text of that Wesley letter and read it aloud to me:

> London, February 26, 1791
>
> Dear Sir:
> Unless the divine power has raised you up . . . I see not how you can go through your glorious enterprise, in opposing that execrable villainy, which is the scandal of religion, of England, and of human nature. Unless God has raised you up for this very thing, you will be worn out

> by the opposition of men and devils. But, "if God be for you, who can be against you?" Are all of them stronger than God? O "be not weary in well doing!" Go on, in the name of God and in the power of His might, till even American slavery (the vilest that ever saw the sun) shall vanish away before it.
>
> . . . That He who has guided you from your youth up, may continue to strengthen you in this and all things, is the prayer of,
>
> Your affectionate servant,
> J. Wesley

"Four days after writing that letter," John recounted, "Wesley was dead. And once again Wilberforce was defeated when the vote was taken in Parliament. Ultimately Wilberforce prevailed, but in the intervening years, he was vilified and faced so many disappointments. His opponents even arranged for him to be challenged to a duel and made an attempt to kill him."

John continued, "He was tempted to give up the fight more than once. But every time he became discouraged, he returned to Wesley's letter. Each time he read it, it was like the first time. It never failed to encourage and strengthen him.

"If you don't believe in the encouraging power of the written note after hearing about that," John said, "you probably never will."

I can attest to the fact that John believes in that power. I've received several notes of encouragement from him over the years, and I still have many of them. They may not hold the historical value of Wesley's note to Wilberforce, but their value to me is priceless.

JOHN . . . WITH A MAXWELL MENTORING MOMENT

If you haven't already guessed it, I'm a real history buff. Let me tell you the rest of the story: in 1806, after working tirelessly for twenty years, Wilberforce finally succeeded in getting a bill passed that abolished the slave trade. Twenty-eight years later, on July 31, 1834, slavery itself was outlawed throughout the British Empire, freeing approximately 800,000 slaves. Although he did not live to see the realization of his dream, having died on August 5, 1833, no one was more responsible than William Wilberforce for the demise of slavery in the British Empire.

Wilberforce died one of the most esteemed men of his day and was buried in Westminster Abbey. His epitaph reads in part:

> Eminent as he was in every department of public labour,
> And a leader in every work of charity,
> Whether to relieve the temporal or the spiritual wants of his fellow men
> His name will ever be specially identified
> With those exertions
> Which, by the blessing of God, removed from England
> The guilt of the African slave trade,
> And prepared the way for the abolition of slavery in every colony of the Empire.

Wilberforce had devoted his entire life and political career to a great cause: ending slavery. Yet he might not have prevailed had it not been for the encouraging note of John Wesley.

I have believed in the power of written notes of encouragement for many years—beginning before I received the Wesley letter as a gift from the people of Skyline Church after serving as their pastor. In fact, it was while leading Skyline that I asked my staff members to devote time every Monday to handwriting notes to people.

Written notes don't have to come from someone famous to be encouraging. A kind word given from the heart is always well received. If you've never mastered the practice of sending handwritten notes to people, then I want to encourage you to try this often neglected way of winning with people. Here's why:

Encouraging Notes Have a Personal Touch

Today we communicate by telephone, digital pager, cell phone, fax machine, e-mail, and the Internet. In the hectic pace of our busy lives, who has time to correspond the old-fashioned way? Yet the more convenient our communication becomes, the more temporary it is. We forget how meaningful that personal touch can be. Few things beat opening a mailbox and pulling out a real note written by a real person. When you see the thoughts of someone you respect written in his or her own hand, it really means something.

Six days a week, regular mail service is provided by the United States Postal Service. Annually postal workers handle 170 billion pieces of mail. Yet, in this huge sea of mail, officials say personal letters account for less than 4 percent of the total. So on average, you will have to wade through twenty-five pieces of mail before you put your hands on one that contains a personal word. More than ever in this day and age, a handwritten note communicates that you care.

NOTES REPRESENT AN INVESTMENT BY THE WRITER

In his book *The Power of Encouragement* (Multnomah, 1997), my friend David Jeremiah says, "Written encouragement comes directly from the heart, uninterrupted and uninhibited. That's why it's so powerful." Haven't you known that to be true?

"Written encouragement comes directly from the heart, uninterrupted and uninhibited. That's why it's so powerful."

—DAVID JEREMIAH

Nineteenth-century writer Walt Whitman struggled for years to get anyone interested in his poetry. He became very discouraged. Then he received a note that read: "Dear sir, I am not blind to the worth of the wonderful gift of *Leaves of Grass*. I find it the most extraordinary piece of wit and wisdom that America has yet contributed. I greet you at the beginning of a great career." It was signed by Ralph Waldo Emerson.

I can't help but wonder what might have happened to Whitman had Emerson not invested in him by writing those kind words. That note was like fresh air to Whitman, who breathed in that encouragement and was inspired to keep writing. But you don't have to be a professional writer to make a difference in someone's life. Just taking the time to write is evidence of your willingness to invest in that person.

Notes Are Remembered Long After the Writer Has Forgotten Them

For years I have made it a practice to write personal notes to others. I often forget what I have written, but occasionally someone who has received a note from me will show it to me and tell me what an encouragement it was. It is in those moments that I am reminded of the sustained and repeated encouragement people receive from the written word.

You never can tell when something you write to others will light them up in down times or sustain them when life gets difficult. In the first *Chicken Soup for the Soul* (Health Communications, 1993) book, teacher Sister Helen Mrosla recounted how a spur-of-the-moment assignment in class became a source of encouragement for her students. On a day when her junior high math students were especially ornery, she asked them to write down what they liked about each of their fellow students. She then compiled the results over the weekend and handed out the lists on the following Monday.

Years later when one of those students, Mark, was killed in Vietnam, she and some of those former students got together for the funeral. Afterward, Mark's father told the group, "They found this on Mark when he was killed," and he showed them a folded, refolded, and taped paper—the one he had received years before from his teacher. Right after that, Charlie, one of Mark's classmates, said, "I keep my list in my desk drawer." Chuck's wife said, "Chuck put his in our wedding album." "I have mine, too," Marilyn said, "in my diary."

Standing there, Vicky reached into her pocketbook and brought out her frazzled list, showing it to her teacher and former classmates. Each person cherished the kind words of encouragement they had received. That's the power of a few kind words.

LES . . . ON BRINGING IT HOME

You may be reluctant to take time writing notes to others because you believe that complimenting people verbally is enough. If so, you may be surprised by recent research into the topic of authenticity, which found that when a word of encouragement is written down for another person, it is often perceived to be more genuine than when it is spoken.[1] That leaves little doubt about the value of writing notes of encouragement to others.

When a word of encouragement is written down for another person, it is often perceived to be more genuine than when it is spoken.

To apply John's teaching to your own life . . .

Forget about:

Being a perfect writer and focus on writing from the heart.

Ask:

What can I say that will be an encouragement now, as well as someday in the future?

Do it:

Take one hour today to write several notes to people for the sole purpose of encouraging them.

Remember:

Words have the power to give encouragement long after the writer has forgotten them.

25

Help People Win

The most important measure of how good a game I played was how much better I'd make my teammates play.

—Bill Russell, winner of more NBA championships than any other player

LES . . . ON SEEING THE PRACTICE IN ACTION

If I've ever met anyone who loves to see people win, it's John Maxwell. That's the reason he writes books and leads seminars and conferences. He believes he has something to offer to others to help them succeed. But John also helps people win on a smaller scale, whether it's teaching his daughter how to sell candy door-to-door for school when she was little, taking time to give a struggling pastor advice to help him through a tough time, or giving a young person with potential tremendous responsibility. John loves to win, and he enjoys seeing others win even more.

For many years, John did a one-day seminar that taught pastors and their church members how to partner in volunteer ministry. At the end of the session, he used to tell one of my favorite stories. It really typifies John's attitude toward helping others.

When John's nephew, Eric, was seven years old, he got ready to play his first game in his first season of Little League baseball. John and Margaret went to see the game, and of course, John wanted to help Eric win. Here's the story as John often tells it:

> You've got to understand, Eric had never played baseball before. He's intimidated, he's scared, he's fearful, he's frightened. And his coach thinks it's the World Series! So Eric walks up to the plate. His helmet is way down over his ears, his uniform is way too big for him, and he can hardly hold the bat. He's petrified. So there he stands, facing the other team's pitcher, who is always the biggest kid. His name is Butch; he's got a big wad of bubble gum in his jaw, and peach fuzz all over his face.
>
> Eric just kind of hugged the bat and closed his eyes and prayed. And that ball went whoosh! Strike one. Whoosh! Strike two. Whoosh! Strike three. I mean, just like that; and when the umpire said, "You're out," Eric just looked glad to be alive.
>
> As he walked back to the dugout, parents started yelling at him and the coach was hollering at him. And I'm sitting there thinking, *This is my nephew, and he's scared.* So I went down to that little fence where Eric was, and I said, "Sweetheart, I don't know what they've told

you about baseball, but let your Uncle John teach you something. Baseball is a very simple game."

He said, "What do you mean?"

I said, "You only have to do one thing. The next time you go up to bat, every time Butch throws the ball, you just swing the bat. That's all you have to do. Butch throws the ball; you swing the bat. Butch throws the ball; you swing the bat."

He looked at me and said, "That's all I gotta do?"

I said, "That's all. Don't worry about hitting that ball; just swing the bat." And all of a sudden a smile broke out on his face, and he said, "I can do that."

I said, "Sure you can do that! Go get 'em, boy."

The next time Eric got up to bat, Butch threw the ball and Eric swung the bat. He missed it by a mile. In fact, he swung so late the ball was already in the catcher's glove. I am now beginning to clap my hands. I am saying, "Wonderful swing, Eric, wonderful swing. That-a-boy! Every time Butch throws the ball, you swing the bat."

Butch throws the ball; Eric swings the bat. Butch throws the ball; he's missing it by about three feet. Finally, he strikes out on the third strike. I'm on my feet shouting, "Eric McCullogh, that is the finest strikeout I have ever seen in my life. Way to go!"

At that point, the coach looks up into the bleachers and gives me a dirty look. And the parents aren't too happy either. Margaret says, "Sweetheart, I'm gonna go to the car and read a book." But I don't care, because after this at bat, Eric is smiling.

Now, to be honest, I didn't think Eric was going to get

a hit that day. Besides, in Little League baseball, there's no such thing as a hit. If there's any kind of contact, it's not the bat hitting the ball; it's the ball hitting the bat. And if there's one thing I know, it's this: if the ball hits the bat, it doesn't have to go far; it just has to go fair. And in Little League baseball, if the ball goes anywhere in fair territory, you never stop running.

Well, I didn't think it was gonna happen, but it did. The third time up, Butch threw the ball; Eric swings; the ball hits the bat. It wasn't a crack out into center field; it was a thud. As soon as I saw the ball was fair, I'm out of the bleachers and I'm running down the first base line, saying, "Eric, keep on running, keep on running!"

As Eric goes around first base, I cut across the infield as fast as I can. I'm now at third base and I'm saying, "Come on, Eric! Come on, Eric!" Eric rounds third base, and together we slide safe into home. Eric gets up and brushes off his uniform, I get up and brush off my suit; and as we walked off the field, I just looked at the coach and gave him a smile.

We went home that day to Eric's house. His parents had to work and didn't get to see the game; but we replayed it for them. I stood in the middle of the living room and I pretended to be Butch, and Eric stood by the piano bench, which was home plate. I threw that pitch; he hit that ball. He went around the bases and Eric slid safe under the piano bench. We all stood up and gave him a standing ovation, and that day we launched Eric into his Little League baseball career.

Eric is all grown up now. But at about the time he was

> ready to graduate from high school, Eric came out to visit me. And he said, "Uncle John, I've got something exciting to tell you. You remember my first Little League baseball game?"
>
> "Of course I do," I said, and we reminisced about it.
>
> "I've never forgotten it," Eric said. "And I just wanted to tell you, this year I'm going to college on a baseball scholarship."

You don't have to be rich, famous, or talented to help others win. You just need to care and do your best to help them. And know this: when you have the ability to help someone win, you will be that person's friend for life.

JOHN . . . WITH A MAXWELL MENTORING MOMENT

Helping another person to win is one of the greatest feelings in the world. I haven't met a person yet who doesn't like to win. And everyone I know who's made the effort to help others has said that it is the most rewarding part of life. As poet Ralph Waldo Emerson said, "It is one of the most beautiful compensations of life that no man can sincerely try to help another without helping himself."

"It is one of the most beautiful compensations of life that no man can sincerely try to help another without helping himself."

—Ralph Waldo Emerson

If you want to help people win, then take the following steps:

Believe in People

After a conference in Toledo, a man came up to me and asked a pointed question: "How do I get unbelievable results from a person?"

"Have unbelievable expectations about that person," was my answer.

If you don't believe in people, then you are unlikely to do everything you can to help them win. People know when someone doesn't believe in them. They see right through pretense and insincere backslapping. But when they know you believe in them, magic begins to happen. What writer John Spalding said is true: "Those who believe in our ability do more than stimulate us, they create for us an atmosphere in which it becomes easier to succeed."

Give People Hope

A reporter asked Prime Minister Winston Churchill, who led Britain during the dark moments of the Second World War, what was the greatest weapon his country possessed against the Nazi regime of Hitler. Without pausing for even a moment, Churchill said, "It was what England's greatest weapon has always been—hope."

Hope is one of the most powerful and energizing words in the English language. It is something that gives us power to keep going in the toughest of times. And its power energizes us with excitement and anticipation as we look toward the future.

It's been said that a person can live forty days without food, four days without water, four minutes without air, but only four seconds without hope. If you want to help people win, then become a purveyor of hope.

Focus on the Process, Not Just the Win

Many of us desire the win so much that we forget what it takes to get there. We're like the kid who plays chess with his grandfather. When he loses, he says, "Oh no! Not again! Grampa, you always win!"

"What do you want me to do, lose on purpose?" the old man replies. "You won't learn anything if I do that!"

"I don't wanna learn anything," the boy says. "I just wanna win!"

That's the way we often feel, but let's be honest. Which wins are the most satisfying: the easy ones or the ones we really have to work for? When you help somebody win, don't just hand it to him, even if it's in your power to do so. Help *him* win. If you assist him in the process, then you're not just giving him the victory; you're giving him the means for additional future victories. He can win and win again. And the only thing sweeter than a win is a whole bunch of wins.

Understand That When You Help Others Win, You Also Win

In 1984, Lou Whittaker led the first all-American team to the summit of Mt. Everest. After months of grueling effort, five members of the team reached the final campsite at twenty-seven thousand feet. With two thousand feet to go, they met in a crowded tent. Whittaker had a tough decision to make: he knew how highly motivated all five climbers were to stand on the highest point on earth. But two would have to go back to the previous camp, load up food, water, and oxygen, then return to the camp where they now met. After completing this support assignment, these two climbers would be in no condition to make a try for the summit. The others would stay in the tent that day to drink water, breathe oxygen, and rest, preparing them for the summit attempt the next day.

The first decision Whittaker made was to stay at the twenty-seven-thousand-foot camp to coordinate the team's activities. The next was to send the two strongest climbers down the mountain to get the supplies; it was the tougher job. The two weaker climbers would rest, renew their strength, and receive the glory of the summit.

When asked why he didn't assign himself the summit run, his answer showed his understanding of people and the strength of his leadership. He said, "My job was to put other people on top."

Whittaker understood that when people make the right decisions that help the team to achieve its goal, everybody wins. You can't help winning when you help others win.

LES . . . ON BRINGING IT HOME

When I think back, I can remember many people in my life who have helped me to win. The chair of the psychology department at the college I went to honed my vision for graduate school. He showed me what steps to take and how to succeed. George, a friend of mine, helped me win by showing me how to land and host a radio show. Janice, my publicist, helps me win every time she gets me on a national television show to talk about one of my books. Kevin, another friend, helped me win by showing me how to craft a meaningful mission statement for my life. Of course, John has helped me win in my career on several fronts. Everyone likes to win. And nobody wins without help.

More than three decades ago, a research study examined the kinds of people who relate well to others. It looked at 268 Harvard sophomore men, considered to be "the best and the brightest," and followed them for forty years. Among the findings was the fact that men who were emotionally healthiest recognized that a good life was not about the absence of problems, but about how one chooses to react to problems. In other words, these men perceived themselves as winners and helped others to win in spite of their circumstances. Not surprisingly, they also had far more meaningful relationships with others.[1]

To apply John's teaching to your own life . . .

Forget about:

Approaching life as a competition where you have to beat everyone else in order to win.

Ask:

Whom would I most like to help win and how can I do it?

Do it:

Make a game plan. Chart the road you will travel together on your way to victory.

Remember:

Once you help someone win, you will have a friend for life.

A CLOSING WORD FROM JOHN

All my life, I've believed that anyone can learn to win with people. All it takes is a belief in people and a sincere desire to help them. I hope that after reading this book, you believe that too.

We also hope that you will embrace the practices Les and I have endeavored to teach. If you have already tried some of them out, then you've probably already discovered that they really do work. If you want to learn to master all of them, then here's how I suggest you proceed: put yourself on a twelve-week program for winning with people. After starting with you, select two of the practices and do them every day for an entire week. If you do that, you will go through a process where you will . . .

1. Become conscious of how that winning way works,
2. Learn the basics of how to do it,
3. Practice it until you master it, and
4. Begin to make it a habit.

You may not feel instantly comfortable doing some of them, but there isn't a single one you can't master. And of course, keep adding other practices that you learn on your own or from others. You can never learn too many ways to win with people.

Here's to your success: may you keep winning by helping others win.

NOTES

CHAPTER 1

1. James Patterson and Peter Kim, *The Day America Told the Truth* (East Rutherford, NJ: Prentice Hall Press, 1991).

CHAPTER 2

1. Wes Smith, *Hope Meadows: Real-Life Stories of Healing and Caring from an Inspiring Community* (New York: Berkley, 2001).

CHAPTER 3

1. J. G. Nicholls, "Creativity in the person who will never produce anything original and useful: The concept of creativity as a normally distributed trait," *American Psychologist*, 27 (8) (1972), 717–27.

CHAPTER 6

1. James C. Humes, *The Wit and Wisdom of Winston Churchill* (New York: Harper Perennial, 1994), 119–20.
2. Genesis 17:5.
3. Genesis 32:28.
4. Howard Gardner, *Creating Minds: An Anatomy of Creativity Seen Through the Lives of Freud, Einstein, Picasso, Stravinsky, Eliot, Graham, and Gandhi* (New York: Basic Books, 1993).

CHAPTER 7

1. Proverbs 25:11.
2. James Kouzes and Barry Posner, *Encouraging the Heart: A Leader's Guide to Rewarding and Recognizing Others* (San Francisco: Jossey-Bass Publishers, 1999).
3. H. S. Leonard, "The many faces of character," *Consulting Psychology Journal*, 49 (4) (1997), 235–45.

CHAPTER 10

1. M. E. McCullough and C. R. Snyder, "Classical source of human strength: Revisiting an old home and building a new one." *Journal of Social and Clinical Psychology*, 19 (1) (2000), 1–10.

CHAPTER 11

1. G. E. Vaillant, "Adaptive mental mechanisms: Their role in a positive psychology," *American Psychologist*, 55 (1) (2000), 89–98.

CHAPTER 12

1. John 8.
2. E. E. Werner, "Resilience in development," *Current Directions in Psychological Science*, 4 (3) (1995), 81–85.

CHAPTER 13

1. D. A. Kramer, "Wisdom as a classical source of human strength: Conceptualization and empirical inquiry," *Journal of Social and Clinical Psychology*, 19 (1) (2000), 83–101.

CHAPTER 14

1. R. M. Ryan and E. L. Deci, "Self-determination theory and the facilitation of intrinsic motivation, social development, and well-being," *American Psychologist*, 55 (1) (2000), 68–78.

CHAPTER 15

1. J. W. MacDevitt, "Therapist's personal therapy and professional self-awareness," *Psychotherapy*, 24 (1987), 693–703.

CHAPTER 16

1. Les Parrott, *Counseling and Psychotherapy*, 2nd ed. (Pacific Grove, CA: Brooks/Cole/Thomson Learning, 2003).

CHAPTER 17

1. "Walking the Mile: A Behind-the-Scenes Documentary" (Warner Home Video, 1999).
2. Belden Lane, "Rabbinical Stories," *Christian Century*, 98:41 (16 December 1981).
3. Ken Sutterfield, *The Power of an Encouraging Word* (Green Forest, AR: New Leaf, 1997).
4. J. J. Campos and K. C. Barrett, "Toward a new understanding of emotions and their development," *Emotions Cognition, and Behavior*, eds. C. Izard, J. Kagan, and R. Zajonc (New York: Cambridge University Press, 1988).

CHAPTER 19

1. D. P. McAdams, A. Diamond, E. de St. Aubin, and E. Mansfield, "Stories of commitment: The psychosocial construction of generative lives," *Journal of Personality and Social Psychology*, 72 (3) (1997), 678–94.

CHAPTER 20

1. I. K. M. Sheldon, R. M. Ryan, L. J. Rawsthorne, and B. Ilardi, "Trait self and true self: Cross-role variation in the big-five personality traits and its relations with psychological authenticity and subjective well-being," *Journal of Personality and Social Psychology*, 73 (1997), 1380–93.

CHAPTER 21

1. Source Unknown.
2. D. P. McAdams and Ed de St. Aubin (ed.), *Generativity and Adult Development: How and Why We Care for the Next Generation* (Washington, DC: APA Books, 1998).

CHAPTER 22

1. Othello, Act III, Scene 3.
2. J. D. Brown and T. A. Mankowski, "Self-esteem, mood and self-evaluation: Changes in mood and the way you see you," *Journal of Personality and Social Psychology*, 64 (1993), 421.

CHAPTER 23

1. M. E. P. Seligman and M. Csikszentmihalyi, "Positive psychology: An introduction," *American Psychologist*, 55 (1) (2000), 5–14.

CHAPTER 24

1. S. Harter, "Authenticity," C. R. Snyder and S. J. Lopez, eds., *Handbook of Positive Psychology* (New York: Oxford University Press, 2002), 382–94.

CHAPTER 25

1. Vaillant, *Adaptation to Life* (Boston: Little Brown, 1977).

ABOUT THE AUTHORS

John C. Maxwell, known as America's expert on leadership, speaks in person to hundreds of thousands of people each year. He has communicated his principles to Fortune 500 companies, the United States Military Academy at West Point, international marketing organizations, the NCAA, and professional sports groups such as the NFL. Maxwell is the founder of several leadership organizations dedicated to helping people reach their personal and leadership potential, such as Injoy Stewardship Services. He dedicates much of his time to training leaders worldwide through EQUIP, a non-profit organization. A *New York Times* bestselling author with more than 8 million books in print, Dr. Maxwell has written more than thirty books, including *Developing the Leader Within You*, *Today Matters*, and *The 21 Irrefutable Laws of Leadership*, which has sold more than one million copies.

Les Parrott, Ph.D., is founder of the Center for Relationship Development on the campus of Seattle Pacific University and the best-selling author of *High-Maintenance Relationships*, *The Control Freak*, *Shoulda Coulda Woulda*, and *Love Talk*. Dr. Parrott is a sought after speaker to Fortune 500 companies and holds relationship seminars across North America. He communicates annually to a wide variety of audiences, including professional athletes, government agencies, military personnel, and business leaders. He also hosts the national radio broadcast "Love Talk." Dr Parrott has been featured in *USA Today*, the *Wall Street Journal*, and the *New York Times*. His television appearances include *The View*, *The O'Reilly Factor*, CNN, *Good Morning America*, and *Oprah*.

To learn about his speaking availability and seminar schedules, as well as all of Dr. Parrott's resources, contact: www.RealRelationships.com.

Step 1: Reinforce Your Foundation

Relationships — The First Step to Success

Winning with people isn't a natural gift; it's a nurtured one. That's why it is so important to continually expose your mind to material that reinforces the importance of relationship building in *your* life. When you visit **www.WinningWithPeopleBook.com,** you will receive access to a free lesson on relationships by John Maxwell entitled, *Relationships — The First Step to Success.* This entertaining lesson contains valuable information on building, nurturing and enjoying successful relationships and will effectively prepare you to take the next step in relationship construction.

Relationships — The First Step to Success is available to you free of charge in streaming audio format online or on CD (for a minimal shipping charge of $2.00).

mi online

Visit us at www.WinningWithPeopleBook.com to receive your FREE training lesson, as well as information on other valuable training materials.

Step 3: Build Your Leadership Development Program

Now that you have built up your ability to create and manage strong, healthy relationships, it's time to ramp up your leadership training curriculum. To facilitate your leadership skills training, Maximum Impact has two monthly audio programs — **The Maximum Impact Club** and the **Leadership Today Audio Series.** With these programs you will learn from some of the greatest leadership minds of our day: **John C. Maxwell, Pat Williams, Mark Sanborn, Pat Summitt,** and many more. Make a significant difference in your life today by joining one of these stellar programs. You will be amazed at the results and excited about awakening the potential within you!

The Maximum Impact Monthly Mentoring Club brings John C. Maxwell to you each and every month. Turn your drive time into a "leadership university" by subscribing to this powerful monthly resource. John will present relevant, insightful content to you each month in a CD or audiocassette format.

To learn more about Maximum Impact's monthly mentoring programs, visit us at www.WinningWithPeopleBook.com!

Step 4: Furnish Your Relationship and Leadership Home

Step four introduces you to the most powerful leadership training that Maximum Impact currently offers. **Maximum Impact's Corporate Training** takes John C. Maxwell's principles to the next level using workshops in leadership, teamwork, and personal development.

Values-based Leadership Development

The Developing the Leader Within You™ two-day workshop is a values-based, facilitator-lead interactive experience that allows you to raise your level of influence. This course takes content from John's best-selling books *The 21 Irrefutable Laws of Leadership, Developing the Leader Within You,* and *Developing the Leader Around You* and allows you to see who you really are in terms of your personal leadership behaviors and chart a course that will yield outstanding results.

Teamwork

In addition to leadership development training, you can build your business or organization with our **Teamwork Training Workshops.** These highly interactive and fun experiences explore the dynamics of great teams and teach these principles with tactile and textbook instruction. These workshops are available by appointment and are held at your location or at

Step 4: Furnish Your Relationship and Leadership Home

your planned retreat or conference. We illustrate John Maxwell's teambuilding principles and bring them to life for you to bring to your team. Based on John's books *The 17 indisputable Laws of Teamwork* and *The 17 Qualities of a Team Player*, these dynamic workshops put a framework in place that you can replicate with confidence at your organization.

TRAINING

Leadership and Teamwork PowerShops

Does your organization have a meeting event, conference, or management retreat that needs to introduce or reinforce leadership or teambuilding principles? A **Maximum Impact PowerShop** may be the perfect solution. Whether a breakout session, a keynote, or class, a **Leadership PowerShop** or a **Teamwork PowerShop** takes John Maxwell's principles and abbreviates and tailors the message for your audience. The PowerShop is hands-on teaching that sticks in the minds of the participants. This training ranges in scope and duration based on your event's needs. Perfect for introducing a new leadership or teambuilding initiative, the PowerShop will bring a high-energy and tangible experience to your group.

AVAILABLE IN SPANISH
How to Make Others Feel Like a Million Bucks
Autor de éxitos de librería según el New York
JOHN C. MAXWELL
Y LES PARROTT, PH.D.
25 MANERAS DE GANARSE A LA GENTE
Cómo hacer que los demás se sientan valiosos
ISBN: 0881139017
Caribe-Betania Editores
Una división de Thomas Nelson Publishers
www.caribebetania.com

LEADERSHIP

PROMISES FOR YOUR WORK WEEK

JOHN C.
MAXWELL

COUNTRYMAN®

Nashville, Tennessee

Published by J. Countryman®, a division of Thomas Nelson, Inc., Nashville, Tennessee 37214

Published in association with Yates & Yates, LLP, Attorneys and Counselors, Orange, California.

Design: The DesignWorks Group | www.thedesignworksgroup.com

ISBN 1 4041 0429 1

Printed and bound in the United States of America

www.thomasnelson.com | www.jcountryman.com

www.maximumimpact.com

TABLE OF CONTENTS

INTRODUCTION

Leadership is essential to accomplishing every goal in life, and as a leader, you must grow in order to succeed. Think you're not a leader? Think again. First and foremost, you lead yourself. Then, through your influence—official or unofficial, personal or professional—you lead others. You even show leadership through the attitude and ethics with which you follow those with authority over you.

You are a leader, and this book is for you. It's a collection of fifty–two devotionals following a new theme every week. Each chapter includes a promise that God has made to leaders, a promise good leaders make to their teams, a quick lesson, and a thought or activity to help carry you through the week.

Leadership Promises for Your Work Week provides biblical principles to help you develop as a leader, build stronger team players, and develop successful teams. Don't start your week without it!

GOD'S PROMISE TO LEADERS

The LORD shows mercy and is kind.
He does not become angry quickly, and he has great love.
He will not always accuse us,
and he will not be angry forever.
He has not punished us as our sins should be punished;
he has not repaid us for the evil we have done.
The LORD has mercy on those who respect him,
as a father has mercy on his children.

PSALM 103:8–9, 13 (NCV)

A LEADER'S PROMISE TO THE TEAM

I AM HUMBLY AWARE OF HOW MUCH I'VE ALREADY BEEN FORGIVEN, AND I WILL CONTINUE OWNING UP TO MY MISTAKES.

WEEK 1

ACCEPT RESPONSIBILITY

And David said to God, "Was it not I who commanded the people to be numbered? I am the one who has sinned and done evil indeed; but these sheep, what have they done? Let Your hand, I pray, O LORD my God, be against me and my father's house, but not against Your people that they should be plagued."

1 CHRONICLES 21:17

Times of failure not only reveal a leader's true character, but also present opportunities for significant leadership lessons.

After a major victory over the Philistines, King David made a major mistake. The king stopped trusting God for the defense of his nation and undertook a census to measure his military power. David's willingness to take responsibility for his foolish action demonstrated his depth of character. He repented and accepted punishment from the hand of God, trusting in the grace of God. Even so, David's error snuffed out the lives of seventy thousand Israelites. When leaders mess up, many people suffer.

Many leaders attempt to hide failures, blame others, or run from God. But David admitted his failure and repented. Although he faced many difficulties, David worked to restore his relationship with God and did whatever he could to minimize the consequences of his failure in the lives of others.

The Maxwell Leadership Bible

Lifting the Lid

"Also, in time past, when Saul was king over us,
you were the one who led Israel out and brought them in;
and the LORD said to you, 'You shall shepherd My people Israel,
and be ruler over Israel'."

2 SAMUEL 5:2

Why did Saul fail as Israel's king, while David succeeded? The answer can be found in the Law of the Lid. Leadership ability is the lid that determines a person's level of effectiveness. And to reach the highest level of effectiveness, you have to raise the lid on your leadership ability. David had many lids on his life, but they did not stop him:

1. His family
2. His leader
3. His background
4. His youthfulness and inexperience

Ultimately, David became a great leader—yet not because he lacked limitations in life. He achieved much because he became a lid lifter.

Every leader has lids on his life; nobody is born without them. And they don't disappear when a person receives a title, achieves a position, or gets invested with power. The issue is not whether you have lids, but what you are going to do about them.

The Maxwell Leadership Bible

Following in Your Footsteps

So Aaron and his sons did all the things that the LORD had commanded by the hand of Moses.

LEVITICUS 8:36

Aaron, like many leaders through history, received a divine calling. God chose Aaron and his sons to serve as Israel's priests and charged them with carrying out rituals and sacrifices on behalf of all Israelites. Scripture gives meticulous detail to their ordination and calling. Their conduct was to be beyond reproach—God made it crystal clear that failure to uphold His established guidelines would result in death.

Despite his high calling, Aaron at times struggled with his authority. He once caved in to the depraved wishes of the people and led Israel in a pagan worship service, an abomination that led to the deaths of many Israelites. Aaron had been set apart for God's service, but on that occasion, he chose to live and lead otherwise.

The failure of a leader usually results in consequences far more grave that the fall of a nonleader; on the day Aaron failed, "about three thousand men of the people [died]" (Exodus 32:28). When leaders fall, followers also pay the price.

The Maxwell Leadership Bible

THIS WEEK: Are you letting any of the lids on your life hold you down? Who has suffered because of your failures? Ask key people for forgiveness, and see if there's any way to repair the damage.

GOD'S PROMISE TO LEADERS

The mouth of the righteous speaks wisdom,
And his tongue talks of justice.
The law of his God is in his heart;
None of his steps shall slide.

Psalm 37:30–31

A LEADER'S PROMISE TO THE TEAM

I know how much I need God's help,
and I turn to Him daily
for counsel and encouragement.

WEEK 2

ACKNOWLEDGE GOD'S ROLE

When I consider Your heavens, the work of Your fingers, the moon and the stars, which You have ordained, what is man that You are mindful of him, and the son of man that You visit him? For You have made him a little lower than the angels, and You have crowned him with glory and honor. You have made him to have dominion over the works of Your hands; You have put all things under his feet . . . O LORD, our Lord, how excellent is Your name in all the earth!

PSALM 8:3–6, 9

Have you ever asked, "When does a leader's confidence become arrogance? What does humility look like in a leader's life?" Psalm 8 shows leaders how to balance their identity with their self–esteem. Consider how David maintains both confidence and humility.

1. David sees his own weakness and humanity. David realizes that in the sweep of the galaxy, man accounts for only a very small part.

2. David sees his God–given position and privileges. David knows that God has made humankind a little lower than Himself.

3. David sees a balance by giving all the glory to God. David closes the psalm the way he began. He magnifies the Lord and gives Him the credit for the good that has come from his life and leadership.

The Maxwell Leadership Bible

SECURITY IS FOUND IN GOD, NOT IN FOLLOWERS

Unless the LORD builds the house, they labor in vain who build it; unless the LORD guards the city, the watchman stays awake in vain.

PSALM 127:1

Unless God remains at the center of your efforts, you labor in vain. Whether we lead in the military, in construction, or sit behind a desk, we cannot fight, build, or plan well enough to gain anything permanent. Smart leaders not only include God in their strategy, they place Him at its center. Consider the following list of rules regarding security and people.

1. People cannot provide permanent security for a leader.
2. Leaders should never put their emotional health in the hands of someone else.
3. Spiritual and emotional health requires the truth.
4. Leaders must remember that hurting people naturally hurt people.
5. Trouble arises when leaders depend on people to do what only God can do.

In trouble? Turn to God. "I waited patiently for the LORD; and He inclined to me, and heard my cry. He also brought me up out of a horrible pit, out of the miry clay, and set my feet upon a rock, and established my steps" (Psalm 40:1–2). God is rich in grace and mercy. He not only forgives, but restores and redeems. When times of trouble arrive—even trouble we bring on ourselves—we must turn to God and wait patiently for His help. He'll never fail us.

The Maxwell Leadership Bible

Guide the Way

I will instruct you and teach you in the way you should go;
I will guide you with My eye.

Psalm 32:8

Leaders must closely observe the flock for its needs and problems. God expects spiritual leaders to serve as guides. A guide takes a person or group safely to a planned destination. The Hebrew word for "guide" gives us several clues as to what God expects from those He uses as leaders. A guide . . .

is a spiritual head who unites and directs people in their walk with God.

takes people on the straight path that leads to fellowship with God.

gives accurate and godly counsel to those who need it.

leads with gentleness and trustworthiness, making others feel safe.

bases his or her direction on the Spirit and the Word of God.

The Maxwell Leadership Bible

This Week: Meditate daily on Psalm 23. Then notice what happens to your stress level. Psalm 23 reminds us of what God alone can control and what we can control. It distinguishes between problems (things we can change) and facts (things we cannot change). It defines God as our . . .

possession	provision	peace
pardon	partner	preparation
praise	paradise	

The Maxwell Leadership Bible

GOD'S PROMISE TO LEADERS

If my people who are called by my name
will humble themselves and pray and seek my face
and turn from their wicked ways,
I will hear from heaven and will forgive their
sins and heal their land. I will listen to
every prayer made in this place.

2 Chronicles 7:14–15 (NLT)

A LEADER'S PROMISE TO THE TEAM

I UNDERSTAND THAT THE QUALITY OF MY LEADERSHIP SPRINGS FROM THE QUALITY OF MY HEART. I WILL GUARD MY HEART.

WEEK 3

ACHIEVE VICTORY OVER SELF

Surely the princes of Zoan are fools; Pharaoh's wise counselors give foolish counsel . . . Let them know what the L*ORD* *of hosts has purposed against Egypt. The princes of Zoan have become fools; the princes of Noph are deceived; they have also deluded Egypt, those who are the mainstay of its tribes.*

Isaiah 19:11–13

Most natural leaders don't aspire to be great leaders; they aspire to be great persons. Personal qualifications lead to leadership qualifications. When leaders lead their own lives well, others naturally want to follow.

Consider Mother Teresa of Calcutta, India. It's doubtful she ever said, "I am going to set out to be a great leader!" Yet that is what she became by determining to be the person God created her to be.

If we want our leadership to last, we must pay attention to four crucial elements:

Character enables us to do what is right even when it seems difficult.

Perspective enables us to understand what must happen to reach a goal.

Courage enables us to initiate and take risks to step out toward a worthy goal.

Favor enables us to attract and empower others to join us in the cause.

The Maxwell Leadership Bible

Win Within

How does a leader seek victory over self? Consider how King Josiah conquered himself (2 Chronicles 34:31).

1. *He remained open and teachable.* Josiah humbled himself. He departed from the ways of his arrogant father and sought God.

2. *He removed obstacles carried forward from the past.* Josiah swept the country clean of idols.

3. *He realized what he needed to give and gave it.* Victory always carries a personal cost. For Josiah, that meant repairing the temple and reinstating the Passover.

4. *He recognized the key to victory.* For Josiah, the key to victory was repentance.

5. *He retained a personal commitment to succeed.* People never become more committed than their leader. Josiah's personal commitment inspired the people to be faithful despite their evil desires and history.

What qualities should every leader possess? Psalm 15 lists many of the necessary traits. David pictures a godly leader as one who . . .

possesses integrity.
does not participate in gossip.
does not harm others.
speaks out against wrong.
honors others who walk in truth.
keeps their word even at personal cost.
isn't greedy to gain at the expense of others.
is strong and stable.

The Maxwell Leadership Bible

Alarm Bells for Leaders

Do not be deceived, God is not mocked; for whatever a man sows, that he will also reap. For he who sows to his flesh will of the flesh reap corruption, but he who sows to the Spirit will of the Spirit reap everlasting life. And let us not grow weary while doing good, for in due season we shall reap if we do not lose heart. Therefore, as we have opportunity, let us do good to all, especially to those who are of the household of faith.

Galatians 6:7–10

We can't pull a fast one on God. He sees all and cannot be deceived. To ensure that we live by this truth, seek others to act as your "alarm bells" and ask you tough questions, such as the following:

Is your personal walk with God up–to–date?

Are you keeping your priorities straight?

Are you asking yourself the hard questions?

Are you accountable to someone in authority?

Are you sensitive to what God is saying to the whole body of Christ?

Are you over–concerned with building your image?

Do you put more stock in "events" rather than "process"?

Are you a loner in your leadership and personal life?

Are you aware and honest about your weaknesses?

Is your calling constantly before you?

The Maxwell Leadership Bible

This Week: Consider what victories over yourself you still need to achieve, What's your battle plan? What victories are already accomplished or well in hand?

GOD'S PROMISE TO LEADERS

If we say we have no sin, we are fooling ourselves, and the truth is not in us. But if we confess our sins, he will forgive our sins, because we can trust God to do what is right. He will cleanse us from all the wrongs we have done.

1 John 1:8–9 (NCV)

A LEADER'S PROMISE TO THE TEAM

I TAKE MY CHARACTER SERIOUSLY. MY MORAL COMPASS IS SET. SOMETIMES I DO FALL, HOWEVER, AND WHEN THAT HAPPENS, I'LL APOLOGIZE AND WORK QUICKLY TO REPAIR THE DAMAGE DONE BY MY MISTAKES.

WEEK 4

BALANCE YOUR GIFTS WITH CHARACTER

For people who hate discipline and only get more stubborn, there'll come a day when life tumbles in and they break, but by then it'll be too late to help them.

PROVERBS 29:1 (MSG)

How many leaders have ruined their lives and damaged the lives of others through immorality? Character has become a crucial issue today precisely because of the myriad leaders in the political, business, and religious worlds who have fallen morally. Leaders need to remember that they influence many others beyond themselves; they never fall in a vacuum. They also need to realize that replacing fallen leaders is a slow and difficult process.

So how can we guard against falling? First, we must take care not to emphasize the gifts of a leader over his or her character. We have an unhealthy tendency to see and reward the gift more than the character; but both are to be developed. We must strike the following balance if we are to finish well:

What I Am—Humble, Convicted, Visionary

What I Do—Rely on God, Do the Right Thing, Set Goals

What I Gain—Power from God, High Morale, Credibility

The Maxwell Leadership Bible

Broken to Be Better

Even leaders gifted with tremendous natural leadership can have a very difficult time, especially with issues of character. That was true for Jacob. From the very beginning he wielded great influence. Wealthy, strong, and blessed with a large family, Jacob seemed to have everything. But a leader who goes his own way cannot be an effective instrument in God's hands. God had to break Jacob to make him useful (Genesis 32:24–25). In the breaking process, Jacob—the deceiving "heel–catcher"—became Israel, a "prince of God" who purposed to serve God rather than himself.

Natural leaders often need to be broken. Consider your natural ability to lead a gift from God, but your character a gift to present back to God. Every time you stand up under the weight of adversity, you are being prepared, as Jacob was, to better serve God and lead people.

Warning signs. Throughout the book of Esther, Haman gives us a clear picture of a leader out of control.

1. He lost joy over little problems.
2. He needed friends to build his self–image.
3. His greed made him unhappy.
4. He listened to the wrong people.
5. He thought too highly of himself.
6. He set himself up for a fall.
7. He reaped what he sowed.

The Maxwell Leadership Bible

Repair Character Faults

Now about that time Herod the king stretched out his hand to harass some from the church. Then he killed James the brother of John with the sword. And because he saw that it pleased the Jews, he proceeded further to seize Peter also.

Acts 12:1–3

Ego drove King Herod of Paul's day, just as it had driven his father and grandfather. They all desperately lacked character. Herod's lack of character provides many examples of what not to do as a leader:

1. He mistreated his own citizens.
2. He made decisions based on popularity.
3. He acted irrationally in difficult times.
4. He harbored anger toward others.
5. He sought power out of insecurity.
6. He projected an infallible image.
7. He was blinded by his ego.

To improve your character and build a solid foundation of your own leadership, you must:

Identify where you're weak or have taken shortcuts.

Look for patterns.

Apologize to those you've wronged.

Stay teachable and rebuild.

The Maxwell Leadership Bible

This Week: Pay particular attention to your character. In what ways are you living up to the standards to which you aspire? How are you falling short? How can you improve? What character victories have you had recently?

GOD'S PROMISE TO LEADERS

Who are those who fear the LORD?
He will show them the path they should choose.
They will live in prosperity,
and their children will inherit the Promised Land.
Friendship with the LORD is reserved
for those who fear him.
With them he shares the secrets of his covenant.

PSALM 25:12–14 (NLT)

A LEADER'S PROMISE TO THE TEAM

I RESPECT GOD. I SEEK TO BE HIS FRIEND AND LIVE IN HIS WISDOM. THIS EMPHASIS WILL MAKE ME A BETTER LEADER FOR OUR TEAM.

WEEK 5

BE A MENTOR

So it was, whenever Moses went out to the tabernacle, that all the people rose, and each man stood at his tent door and watched Moses until he had gone into the tabernacle.

EXODUS 33:8

Modeling provides the basis of all true leadership. Leaders must set the example for their followers. The number one management principle in the world is this: People do what people see.

Moses demonstrated this truth. The people watched him as he spent time with God, interceding for them in intimate, personal communion—and it changed them more than any sermon could have. If you want to enjoy an intimate relationship with God, as Moses did, you must practice what he did:

1. Separate yourself regularly.
2. Seek God with all your heart.
3. Risk being watched and scrutinized.
4. Learn to listen and obey God's voice.
5. Enter covenant partnership with God.

Remember, the number one management principle in the world is, "People do what people see." If they want to succeed, leaders must incarnate the life they desire in their followers.

The Maxwell Leadership Bible

Play Favorites

One of the biggest mistakes a coach can make is to believe that he must treat all of his players the same. Coaches are hired to win—not to make everyone happy or give everyone equal time, money, or resources. Every player must be given support and encouragement, but poor or mediocre performance should not be rewarded the same as the outstanding contributions.

Great coaches give opportunities, resources, and playing time according to players' performance records. The greater the performer, the greater the opportunities. When you have a player like Michael Jordan, you want to put the ball in his hands as often as possible.

When you aren't sure about a player's performance level, especially with a "rookie," give that player frequent but small opportunities to determine his or her caliber of play, and that will show you how to respond.

Developing the Leaders Around You

See the heart and the potential. Every person carries the seed of success. To find it, you have to look at their gifts, temperament, passions, successes, joys, and opportunities. And once you find that seed, you need to fertilize it with encouragement and water it with opportunity. Remember . . .

Everyone wants to feel worthwhile.

Everyone needs and responds to encouragement.

People are naturally motivated.

People buy into the person before buying into their leadership.

The more you understand people, the greater your chance of success in mentoring.

Your Road Map for Success

Share the Game Plan

And He said to them, "Go into all the world and preach the gospel to every creature."

Mark 16:15

Every good coach I've watched has worked from a game plan. He's got one not only for each individual game, but a plan for the development of the whole team over the course of the current and upcoming seasons. Once the game plan has been drawn up, he then communicates it to his team on an almost continual basis. Paul "Bear" Bryant, the legendary Alabama football coach, had five points that explained what he believed a coach should do.

1. Tell players what you expect of them.
2. Give players an opportunity to perform.
3. Let players know how they're getting along.
4. Instruct and empower players when they need it.
5. Reward players according to their contribution.

The process must begin with communicating the game plan. That is the key to productivity. But it must continue with the exchange of information. As Sydney J. Harris said, information is "giving out" while communication is "getting through." When there is interactive communication between the team leader and his people, it empowers them to succeed.

Developing the Leaders Around You

This Week: Psalm 119 is the longest chapter in the Bible, and a main theme is the writer's passion for God's mentoring. Read Psalm 119, and consider how your passion for God's mentoring compares to the writer's.

GOD'S PROMISE TO LEADERS

And Christ gave gifts to people—he made some to be apostles, some to be prophets, some to go and tell the Good News, and some to have the work of caring for and teaching God's people. Christ gave those gifts to prepare God's holy people for the work of serving, to make the body of Christ stronger.

Ephesians 4:11–12 (NCV)

A LEADER'S PROMISE TO THE TEAM

I WILL VALUE EVERYONE ON THIS TEAM AND THEIR UNIQUE CONTRIBUTIONS TO THE QUALITY AND ENJOYMENT OF OUR WORK.

WEEK 6

BE CLEAR ABOUT ROLES

Where the word of a king is, there is power; and who may say to him, "What are you doing?" He who keeps his command will experience nothing harmful; And a wise man's heart discerns both time and judgment . . .
All this I have seen, and applied my heart to every work that is done under the sun: There is a time in which one man rules over another to his own hurt.

ECCLESIASTES 8:4–5, 9

Solomon makes points about our relationship to the people who lead us. We are to submit to them, not because the person deserves it, but because the office deserves it and God decrees it. And what about leaders in authority? Solomon also issues a warning. When leaders try to exercise authority without a servant's heart, they eventually hurt themselves. Consider what he says.

ROLE OF THE FOLLOWER

1. Submit to God–given authority.
2. Trust God to accomplish His purpose.
3. Don't quit or become divisive.

ROLE OF THE LEADER

1. Exercise authority with wisdom and caution.
2. Recognize that no human controls all of life.
3. Lead others by serving, not bossing them.

The Maxwell Leadership Bible

Call in the Reserves

After this the Lord appointed seventy–two others and sent them two by two ahead of him to every town and place where He was about to go.

Luke 10:1 (NIV)

If you look at the roster of any successful team, you will see that the starters are always outnumbered by the other players on the team. Teams that win championships have strong backups ready and waiting on the bench.

You find similar situations in every field. In the entertainment industry, the actors are often known, but the hundreds of necessary crew members aren't. For any politician or corporate executive or big–name fashion designer that you know about, hundreds of people are working quietly in the background to make their work possible. Nobody can neglect the majority of the team and hope to be successful.

Any team that wants to excel must have good substitutes as well as starters. You may be able to do some wonderful things with a handful of top people, but if you want your team to do well over the long haul, you've got to build your bench. A great team with no bench eventually collapses.

The 17 Indisputable Laws of Teamwork

Honor Everyone on the Team

And those members of the body which we think to be less honorable, on these we bestow greater honor . . .

1 Corinthians 12:23

People who build successful teams never forget that every person's role is contributing to the bigger picture.

One of the best examples of this involves Winston Churchill. During World War II when Britain was experiencing its darkest days, the country had a difficult time keeping men working in the coal mines. Many wanted to give up their dirty, thankless jobs in the dangerous mines to join the military service, which got much public praise and support. Yet without coal, the military and the people at home would be in trouble.

So Churchill faced thousands of coal miners one day and passionately told them of their importance to the war effort, how their role could make or break the goal of maintaining England's freedom. It's said that tears appeared in the eyes of those hardened men. And they returned to their inglorious work with steely resolve. That's the kind of mindset it takes to build a team.

The 17 Indisputable Laws of Teamwork

This Week: Who are your starters? Your reserves? Does everyone know their role and their importance in it? Find a way to remind the reserves that they are appreciated and valued.

GOD'S PROMISE TO LEADERS

Command those who are rich in this present age not to be haughty, nor to trust in uncertain riches but in the living God, who gives us richly all things to enjoy. Let them do good, that they be rich in good works, ready to give, willing to share, storing up for themselves a good foundation for the time to come, that they may lay hold on eternal life.

1 Timothy 6:17–19

A LEADER'S PROMISE TO THE TEAM

I WILL TRAIN MYSELF TO BE GENEROUS IN BOTH RELATIONSHIPS AND RESOURCES.

WEEK 7

BE GENEROUS

If there is among you a poor man of your brethren, within any of the gates in your land which the Lord your God is giving you, you shall not harden your heart nor shut your hand from your poor brother, but you shall open your hand wide to him and willingly lend him sufficient for his need, whatever he needs.

DEUTERONOMY 15:7–8

If great leaders err, they do so on the side of generosity. They are givers, not takers. They feel motivated to:

1. Serve others to help them grow and thrive.
2. Solve problems that prevent potential from being reached.
3. Save causes that benefit mankind.

God instructs His leaders and the entire nation of Israel to imitate His generosity and grace. At the end of every seventh year, every Israelite was to cancel all debts owed by fellow citizens. If they would indeed cancel debts, model graciousness and forgiveness, and care for the poor, God would favor their land with abundant crops and freedom from invasion. Imagine! They simply needed to trust that God was in control and let Him worry about rain and sun and fruitful harvest times.

The Maxwell Leadership Bible

Give Yourself Away

Speak up for the people who have no voice,
for the rights of all the down–and–outers. Speak out
for justice! Stand up for the poor and destitute!

Proverbs 31:8–9 (Msg)

Nothing has such a positive impact on a person as giving to others. That's because giving is the highest level of living. Generous people focus their time and energy on what they can give to others rather than what they can get from them. And the more a person gives, the better his attitude.

Most unsuccessful people don't understand this concept. They believe that how much people give and their attitude about it are based on how much they have. But it's not what you have that makes a difference. It's what you do with what you have. And that is based completely on attitude.

Sow a seed, change a life. It's been said that we make a living by what we get, but we make a life by what we give. Helping others is something you can start doing today, whether it's spending more time with your family, developing an employee who shows potential, helping people in the community, or putting your own desires on hold to benefit your team. The key is to find your purpose and help others while you're pursuing it. As entertainer Danny Thomas said: "All of us are born for a reason, but all of us don't discover why. Success in life has nothing to do with what you gain in life or accomplish for yourself. It's what you do for others."

Your Road Map for Success

Giving Is the Highest Level of Living

Then Abram gave him a tenth of everything.

Genesis 14:20 (NIV)

Nothing speaks to others more loudly than generosity from a leader. True generosity isn't an occasional event. It comes from the heart and permeates every aspect of a leader's life, touching their time, money, talents, and possessions. Effective leaders don't gather things just for themselves; they do it in order to give to others.

To cultivate the quality of generosity in your life, do the following:

1. Be grateful for whatever you have.
2. Put people first.
3. Don't allow the desire for possessions to control you.
4. See money as a resource.
5. Develop the habit of giving.

The only way to maintain an attitude of generosity is to make it your habit to give—your time, attention, money, and resources. As Richard Foster says, "Just the very act of letting go of money, or some other treasure, does something within us. It destroys the demon 'greed'."

The 21 Indispensable Qualities of a Leader

This Week: Consider what you're already giving, what you're being asked to give, and what you'd like to give even though you haven't been asked. Your reasons for accepting or denying requests might be good, but are they godly? How does it feel when you give?

GOD'S PROMISE TO LEADERS

A light shines in the dark for honest people,
for those who are merciful and kind and good.
It is good to be merciful and generous.
Those who are fair in their business
will never be defeated.
Good people will always be remembered.

PSALM 112:4–6 (NCV)

A LEADER'S PROMISE TO THE TEAM

I WILL MAKE OUR WORKPLACE AND OUR TEAM INTERACTIONS AS POSITIVE AS POSSIBLE. I WILL PRAISE THE GOOD IN OUR TEAM EVEN WHEN WE MUST CONFRONT THE BAD.

WEEK 8

BE POSITIVE

I remind you to stir up the gift of God which is in you through the laying on of my hands. For God has not given us a spirit of fear, but of power and of love and of a sound mind.

2 TIMOTHY 1:6–7

People rise or fall to meet our level of expectations for them. If you express skepticism and doubt in others, they'll return your lack of confidence with mediocrity. But if you believe in them and expect them to do well, they'll wear themselves out trying to do their best. And in the process, both of you benefit.

If you've never been one to trust people and put your faith in them, change your way of thinking and begin believing in others. Your life will quickly begin to improve. When you have faith in another person, you give him or her an incredible gift, maybe the best gift you can give another person. Give others money, and it's soon spent. Give resources, and they may not be used to the greatest advantage. Give help, and they'll often find themselves back where they started in a short period of time. But give them your faith, and they become confident, energized, and self–reliant. They become motivated to acquire what they need to succeed on their own. And then later if you do share money, resources, and help, they're better able to use them to build a better future.

Becoming a Person of Influence

Boosting Low Morale

Nothing is more unpleasant than being on a team when nobody wants to be there. When that is the case, the team is usually negative, lethargic, or without hope. If you find yourself in that kind of situation, then do the following:

Investigate the situation. Address what the team is doing wrong and begin fixing what's broken.

Initiate belief. The only way for a team to change is if people believe in themselves. As the leader, you must initiate that belief.

Create energy. To bring a greater level of energy to the team, you need to be energetic. Eventually, your energy will spread.

Communicate hope. The greatest need of players at this stage is hope. Help them see the potential of the team.

To give the team a boost when morale is low, the leader must do productive things and pick up some speed. After all, you can't steer a parked car! To get the team moving . . .

Model behavior that has a high return. People do what people see.

Develop relationships with people of potential. Start with the people who have the potential to be productive. Remember, leaders touch a heart before they ask for a hand.

Set up small victories and talk teammates through them. Nothing helps people grow in skill and confidence like having some wins under their belts.

Communicate vision. Keep the vision before your team continually because vision gives team members direction and confidence.

The 17 Indisputable Laws of Teamwork

You're a 10!

I've never known a positive person yet who didn't love people and try to see the best in them. And one of the most effective ways to help you see the best in others is to do what I call putting a "10" on people's heads. Here's what I mean: We all have expectations of others, but we can choose whether those expectations are positive or negative. We can think that others are worthless or wonderful. When we make the decision to expect the best and actually look for the good instead of the bad, we're seeing them as a "10."

The ability to do this is important for a couple of reasons. First, we usually see in others what we expect to see. Second, people generally rise to meet our level of expectations.

Your Road Map for Success

THIS WEEK: The Pauline epistles are filled with instructions for growing in Christ, but Paul also made sure to encourage the young churches. Read Philippians 1:3–6 (NCV), and consider how you can similarly encourage your team members. "I thank my God every time I remember you, always praying with joy for all of you. I thank God for the help you gave me . . . God began doing a good work in you, and I am sure he will continue it until it is finished when Jesus Christ comes again."

GOD'S PROMISE TO LEADERS

He who endures to the end shall be saved.

MATTHEW 24:13

A LEADER'S PROMISE TO THE TEAM

WE WILL HAVE DIFFICULT TIMES, BUT I WILL NOT LET THEM DETER US FROM OUR GOALS. WE WILL ENDURE, IMPROVE, AND OVERCOME.

WEEK 9

BECOME A MOMENTUM MAKER

And all Israel heard of the judgment which the king had rendered; and they feared the king, for they saw that the wisdom of God was in him to administer justice.

1 Kings 3:28

It takes a leader to create momentum. Followers catch it. And managers are able to continue it once it has begun. But creating momentum requires someone who can motivate others, not someone who needs to be motivated. Just as every sailor knows you can't steer a ship that isn't moving forward, strong leaders understand that to change direction, you first have to create forward progress. Without momentum, even the simplest tasks can seem insurmountable. But with momentum on your side, nearly any kind of change is possible.

Consider the ways young Solomon created momentum:

- He started with what David provided.
- He made wise decisions that won him credibility.
- He maintained the peace.

No leader can ignore the impact of momentum. If you've got it, you and your people will be able to accomplish things you never thought possible. The choice to build momentum is yours.

The Maxwell Leadership Bible

Do the Little Things to Maintain Momentum

These things I have spoken to you, that in Me you may have peace. In the world you will have tribulation; but be of good cheer, I have overcome the world.

John 16:33

When your people are winning and morale is high, you still have an important role as a leader. To help the team maintain high morale and momentum . . .

Keep the team focused and on course. If team members lose focus or get off course, then they'll stop winning.

Communicate successes. Nothing boosts morale like winning and then celebrating it.

Remove morale mashers. Once the team is rolling in the right direction, keep it rolling. Leaders see before others do, so they need to protect the team from the things that will hurt the team.

Allow other leaders to lead. When a leader prepares other team members to lead and then turns them loose to do it, two things result. First, it uses the existing momentum to create new leaders for the team. It's easier to make new leaders successful if they are part of a successful team. Second, it increases the leadership of the team. And that makes the team even more successful.

The process of building high morale is simple, but it isn't easy. It takes strong leadership, and it takes time.

The 17 Indisputable Laws of Teamwork

Go to the Very End

I have fought the good fight, I have finished the race, I have kept the faith.

2 Timothy 4:7

Even people who lack talent and fail to cultivate other vital qualities can contribute if they possess a tenacious spirit. Being tenacious means . . .

1. *Giving all that you have, not more than you have.* Some people mistakenly believe that being tenacious demands from them more than they have to offer. As a result, they don't push themselves. However, being tenacious requires that you give 100 percent—not more, but certainly not less.

2. *Working with determination, not waiting on destiny.* Tenacious people don't rely on luck, fate, or destiny for their success. They know that trying times are no time to quit trying.

3. *Quitting when the job is done, not when you're tired.* If you want your team to succeed, you have to keep pushing beyond what you think you can do. The victory isn't won until the last step in the relay race, the last shot in the basketball game, the last yard into the end zone.

The 17 Essential Qualities of a Team Player

This Week: Consider your track record of persistence and discipline. Where in your life and work do you need to improve? Read Hebrews 11 to review the list of some of the Bible's most amazing people of persistent faith. What could be said about you? "By faith, I, ________, persisted in ________________."

GOD'S PROMISE TO LEADERS

Fools will die because they refuse to listen;
they will be destroyed because they do not care.
But those who listen to [wisdom] will live in safety
and be at peace, without fear of injury."

PROVERBS 1:32–33 (NCV)

A LEADER'S PROMISE TO THE TEAM

I RECOGNIZE THAT EVERYONE ON OUR TEAM HAS INFLUENCE. YOUR INSIGHTS MATTER! I WILL LISTEN TO YOU, AND I WILL HELP YOU GROW.

WEEK 10

BEGIN LEADING BY LOVING

A good leader motivates, doesn't mislead, doesn't exploit.

Proverbs 16:10 (Msg)

If you desire to influence another person, the way to start is by nurturing them. What clergyman John Knox said over four hundred years ago is still true: "You cannot antagonize and influence at the same time."

At the heart of the nurturing process is genuine concern for others. And as we try to help and influence the people around us, we must have positive feelings and concern for them. If you want to help people and make a positive impact on them, you cannot dislike or disparage them. You must give love to them and give them respect.

You may be wondering why you should take on a nurturing role with the people you want to influence, especially if they are employees, colleagues, or friends. You may be saying to yourself, "Isn't that something they can get somewhere else, like at home?" The unfortunate truth is that most people are desperate for encouragement. If you become a major nurturer in the life of another person, then you have an opportunity to make a major impact on them.

Becoming a Person of Influence

Unequal in Influence

Influence is a curious thing. Even though we make some kind of impact on nearly everyone around us, we need to recognize that our level of influence is not the same with everyone. To see this principle in action, try ordering around your best friend's dog the next time you visit.

You may not have thought much about it, but you probably know instinctively which people you have great influence with and which ones you don't. One person may think all your ideas are great. Another may view everything you say with a great deal of skepticism. Yet that same skeptical person may love every single idea presented by your boss or one of your colleagues. That just shows your influence with him may not be as strong as that of someone else.

Becoming a Person of Influence

A position doesn't make a leader. A title may give someone authority, but not influence. Influence comes from the person; it must be earned. For instance, David was leading Israel long before Saul lost his throne (1 Chronicles 11:1–2). David had earned influence and Saul had not. Why was this so?

Unity. David rallied the people and created unity.

Identification. David identified with his followers as family.

Credibility. David effectively led military campaigns.

Anointing. David enjoyed God's hand and power on his life.

Partnership. David worked cooperatively with key leaders.

The Maxwell Leadership Bible

SEE THE LEADER, KNOW THE FOLLOWERS

People reflect their leader. We cannot expect followers to grow beyond their leader. We cannot expect followers to turn out fundamentally different from their leader. Consider what Proverbs 29 tells us about the influence of good and bad leaders:

Attitudes. When good leaders rule, people rejoice; when the wicked reign, people groan (v. 2).

Stability. When moral leaders rule, they establish justice; compromising leaders tear things down (v. 4).

Compassion. Good leaders express concern for the poor; bad leaders reflect no compassion for anyone (v. 7).

Honesty. When leaders pay attention to lies, their staff begins to esteem the same deceptions (v. 12).

Vision. Solid vision keeps everyone on track; chaos reigns wherever the vision lapses (v. 18).

The Maxwell Leadership Bible

THIS WEEK: Evaluate yourself according to the following formula: Competence + Character + Connection = Influence

How strong are you in each of those areas with regard to your work? Your family? Your community? Do you connect well with people? Do you exhibit excellence in your tasks? Is your character in line with your values? Do you see how all these elements cooperate to create your level of influence?

GOD'S PROMISE TO LEADERS

Through Christ we feel certain before God. . . .
It is God who makes us able to do all that we do.

2 CORINTHIANS 3:4–5 (NCV)

A LEADER'S PROMISE TO THE TEAM

I'M CONFIDENT IN YOU,
AND I BELIEVE THAT TOGETHER
WE CAN ACCOMPLISH
WHAT WE NEED TO DO.

WEEK 11

BELIEVE IN YOURSELF

"Let no man's heart fail because of him; your servant will go and fight with this Philistine."

1 Samuel 17:32

People will not follow a leader who does not have confidence in himself. In fact, people are naturally attracted to people who convey confidence.

An excellent example of this can be seen in an incident that occurred in Russia during an attempted coup. Army tanks surrounded the government building that housed President Boris Yeltsin and his pro–democracy supporters. As the army rolled into position, Yeltsin strode from the building, climbed up on a tank, looked the commander in the eye, and thanked him for coming over to the side of democracy. Later the commander admitted that although they had not intended to go over to his side, Yeltsin had appeared so confident that the soldiers decided to join him.

Confidence is a characteristic of a positive attitude. The greatest achievers remain confident regardless of circumstances. Strong leaders recognize and appreciate confidence in others. Confidence is not simply for show. Confidence empowers. Good leaders have the ability to instill within their people confidence in their own leadership. Great leaders have the ability to instill within their people confidence in themselves.

Developing the Leaders Around You

Are People Drawn to You?

Charisma is the ability to draw people to you. And like other character traits, it can be developed. Watch out for these roadblocks to charisma:

Pride. Nobody wants to follow a leader who thinks he is better than everyone else.

Insecurity. If you are uncomfortable with who you are, others will be too.

Moodiness. If people never know what to expect from you, they stop expecting anything.

Perfectionism. People respect the desire for excellence, but dread unrealistic expectations.

Cynicism. People don't want to be rained on by someone who sees a cloud around every silver lining.

If you can stay away from those qualities, you can cultivate charisma.

The 21 Indispensable Qualities of a Leader

Anointed to lead. When Moses brought the commandments, his face shone with the glory of God (Exodus 34:29). The Israelites perceived God's presence in Moses' leadership. Anointed leadership is characterized by:

1. *Charisma.* The anointed enjoy a sense of giftedness that comes from God. It seems magnetic.

2. *Character.* People see God's nature in your leadership. They trust you.

3. *Competence.* You have the ability to get the job done. Your leadership produces results.

4. *Conviction.* Your leadership has backbone. You always stand for what is right.

The Maxwell Leadership Bible

Who You Are Is Who You Attract

Then [Elisha] arose and followed Elijah,
and became his servant.

1 Kings 19:21

Effective leaders are always on the lookout for good people. But who you get is not determined by what you want, but by who you are. In most situations, you draw people who possess the same qualities you do.

What enabled Elijah to draw like-minded people to his side? This truth: who you are is who you attract.

1. Every leader has a measure of magnetism.

2. A leader's magnetism may impact others intellectually, emotionally, or volitionally.

3. Magnetism is neither good nor bad in itself—it depends on what a leader does with it.

4. Secure leaders draw both similar and complementary followers.

5. A leader's magnetism never remains static.

It is possible for you to go out and recruit people unlike yourself, but it's crucial to recognize that people who are different will not naturally be attracted to you. Their quality depends on you. If you think the people you attract could be better, then it's time for you to improve yourself.

The Maxwell Leadership Bible

This Week: Consider how optimistic or pessimistic you are about yourself, your team, your current situation, and your mission. Who shares your mind? Who on your team is a positive influence on the others?

GOD'S PROMISE TO LEADERS

My child, do not reject the LORD's discipline,
and don't get angry when he corrects you.
The LORD corrects those he loves,
just as parents correct the child they delight in.

PROVERBS 3:11–12 (NCV)

A LEADER'S PROMISE TO THE TEAM

WHEN THERE'S A PROBLEM, I WILL DEAL WITH IT DIRECTLY, PROMPTLY, AND RESPECTFULLY, AND I WILL HELP US CORRECT THE SITUATION TO GET BACK ON TRACK.

WEEK 12

CARE ENOUGH TO CONFRONT

Then Nathan said to David, "You are the man!"

2 Samuel 12:7

Many people avoid confrontation. Some fear being disliked and rejected. Others are afraid confrontation will make things worse by creating anger and resentment in the person they confront. But avoiding confrontation always worsens the situation. Confrontation can be a win–win situation, a chance to help and develop your people—if you do it with respect and with the other person's best interests at heart. Here are ten guidelines to help you confront positively.

1. Confront ASAP.
2. Address the wrong action, not the person.
3. Confront only what the person can change.
4. Give the person the benefit of the doubt.
5. Be specific.
6. Avoid sarcasm.
7. Avoid words like "always" and "never."
8. If appropriate, tell the person how you feel about what was done wrong.
9. Give the person a game plan to fix the problem.
10. Affirm him or her as a person and a friend.

Positive confrontation is a sure sign that you care for a person and have their best interests at heart.

Developing the Leaders Around You

Everyone's a Critic

Leaders can bank on two truths. First, they will be criticized. Second, criticism always changes the leader. Unhappy people tend to attack the point person. Notice what God and Moses teach us on how to handle criticism (Numbers 12).

1. Maintain your humility (v. 3).
2. Face the criticism squarely (v. 4).
3. Be specific about the issue (vv. 5–8).
4. Lay out consequences (vv. 9, 10).
5. Pray for the criticizers (vv. 12, 13).
6. Restore them when appropriate (v. 14).

Confrontation results in purity and security. Confrontation is not a punishment, but a redemptive act of leadership. The goals of healthy confrontation are . . .

Clarification. I will get a better understanding of the person and what happened.

Change. I hope to get improvement from it. And it may be me!

Relationship. I will likely deepen my relationship with this person.

Purity. As word gets out, the organization will be purified and sobered.

Respect. The organization will likely raise the members' level of respect for the leadership.

Security. People feel safe knowing leaders are strong enough to take a stand.

The Maxwell Leadership Bible

The Velvet–Covered Brick

The apostle Paul loved his Corinthian brothers and sisters in Christ, but when he received reports that divisions, immorality, and pride had crept into the church, he knew he had to confront their sin (1 Corinthians 1:11). It was as if Paul were hitting them on the head with a velvet–covered brick—the brick being his condemnation of their sin, the velvet being his love for those whom God had set apart for good works. Paul practiced "The 101% Principle"—finding the 1 percent you can affirm, and giving it 100 percent of your attention. Remember, affirmation comes before confrontation. Good leaders look for the good in people and affirm it. Only then do they address the problems.

Paul's integrity also drove him to stand up to Peter, his fellow leader, in front of several Jewish and Gentile believers (Galatians 2:14). Consider his checklist for critiquing someone.

- Check your motive.
- Make sure the issue is worthy of criticism.
- Be specific.
- Don't undermine the person's self–confidence or identity.
- Do not postpone needed criticism.
- Look at yourself before looking at others.
- End criticism with encouragement.

The Maxwell Leadership Bible

This Week: Think about some recent or current conflicts. How promptly do you deal with conflicts? Are you good at confrontation? Review the checklists in this chapter several times before a confrontation. How did the confrontation go when you had the principles fresh in your mind?

GOD'S PROMISE TO LEADERS

When people are tempted and still continue strong, they should be happy. After they have proved their faith, God will reward them with life forever. God promised this to all those who love him.

JAMES 1:12 (NCV)

A LEADER'S PROMISE TO THE TEAM

I'M NOT PERFECT, BUT I KNOW WHO IS. AND I'M DOING MY BEST TO BECOME MORE AND MORE LIKE HIM IN BOTH MY PROFESSIONAL LIFE AND IN MY PERSONAL LIFE.

WEEK 13

CHARACTER IS CRUCIAL

Live right, and you will eat from the life-giving tree.
And if you act wisely, others will follow.

PROVERBS 11:30 (CEV)

All leaders desire results, but being must precede doing.

• To achieve higher goals, you must be a more effective leader.

• To attract better people, you must be a better person yourself.

• To achieve greater results, you must be a person of great character.

A common problem occurs when a leader's real identity and the desired results don't match up. But when leaders display consistency of character, competence, and purpose, it makes a powerful statement to the people around them—and it draws those people to them.

If you desire to do great things with your life, then seek to become a better person and a better leader. Nothing great can be achieved alone. Any task worth doing requires the help of others. And if you want to attract good people, you've got to become a better person yourself. If you're willing to do that, then you can leave the results to God.

The 21 Most Powerful Minutes in a Leader's Day

Count on Character

A thick bankroll is no help when life falls apart, but a principled life can stand up to the worst.

Proverbs 11:4 (Msg)

Crisis doesn't necessarily make character, but it certainly does reveal it. Adversity makes a person choose one of two paths: character or compromise. Every time leaders choose character, they become stronger even if that choice brings negative consequences. The development of character is at the heart of our development, not just as leaders, but as human beings.

What must every person know about character?

- Character is more than talk.
- Talent is a gift, but character is a choice.
- Character brings lasting success with people.
- Leaders cannot rise above the limitations of their character.

The 21 Indispensable Qualities of a Leader

Don't value talent above character. The enemy has targeted leaders for attack, and myriad leaders in the political, business, and religious worlds have fallen morally. Leaders need to remember that they influence many others beyond themselves; they never fall in a vacuum. We must take care not to emphasize the talents of a leader over his or her character. We have unhealthy tendency to see and reward the gift more than the character, but both are to be developed. We must strike the following balance if we are to finish well: Gift Deposited = Character Built.

The Maxwell Leadership Bible

Guard Your Thinking

For as he thinks in his heart, so is he . . . Do not speak in the hearing of a fool, for he will despise the wisdom of your words . . . Apply your heart to instruction, and your ears to words of knowledge . . . Do not let your heart envy sinners, but be zealous for the fear of the Lord *all the day; for surely there is a hereafter, and your hope will not be cut off. Hear, my son, and be wise; and guide your heart in the way.*

Proverbs 23:7, 9, 12, 17–19

Leaders understand the importance of their minds to the future of their organizations. Consider some of these timeless principles offered in Proverbs 23 about our minds and a godly vision for tomorrow.

• Your thoughts determine your character.

• Don't waste your thoughts on those who don't hunger for them.

• The first person you lead is you, and the first organ you master is your mind.

• Don't let your mind drift away from God's truth and into vain envy.

• Stay confident that your vision will come to pass.

• Discipline your thoughts to remain steadfast in what you know is right.

The Maxwell Leadership Bible

This Week: Consider the evidence of your character. Where is your character strong? Weak? Note how you respond in character-revealing and character-building situations this week.

GOD'S PROMISE TO LEADERS

For the LORD gives wisdom;
From His mouth come knowledge and understanding;
He stores up sound wisdom for the upright;
He is a shield to those who walk uprightly;
He guards the paths of justice,
And preserves the way of His saints.
Then you will understand righteousness and justice,
Equity and every good path.

PROVERBS 2:6–9

A LEADER'S PROMISE TO THE TEAM

AS I CHART THE COURSE FOR OUR TEAM,
I'M GUIDED BY THE TRUE NORTH STAR—
THE LORD—AND I'M EVALUATING OUR JOURNEY
ACCORDING TO HIS WISDOM.

WEEK 14

CHART THE COURSE

The preparations of the heart belong to man,
But the answer of the tongue is from the LORD.
All the ways of a man are pure in his own eyes,
But the LORD weighs the spirits.
Commit your works to the LORD,
And your thoughts will be established.

PROVERBS 16:1–3

Effective leaders practice the Law of Navigation, which says that anyone can steer the ship, but it takes a leader to chart the course. The verses in Proverbs 16 remind leaders to:

- Check the source of their wisdom.
- Check their motives.
- Check the outcome they are pursuing.

Consider five key words to understanding how God helps leaders navigate their way through life:

Process. What is God revealing progressively?

Purpose. Why were you created?

Potential. God will use your gifts and passion. Does this goal fit who you are?

Prioritize. God will ask you to adjust your time and energy. What steps must you take?

Proceed. God will eventually require you to act. When should you start?

The Maxwell Leadership Bible

Charting Your Own Course

As a good leader, Moses methodically arranged the tribal camps in the wilderness (Numbers 2:34). We would do well to plan and organize as he did.

• Give time for planning and organizing. Determine your primary purpose.

• Understand where you are before trying to develop a strategy.

• Prioritize the needs and goals of the team by asking the right questions.

• Write goals that are realistic, measurable, and convicting.

• Clarify goals and communicate with your team.

• Identify possible obstacles. Have an open system approach to your planning.

• Budget your cost and time by scheduling everything you can and setting deadlines.

• Study the results. Evaluation prevents stagnation and exaggeration.

Remember, anyone can steer the ship, but it takes a leader to chart the course.

The Maxwell Leadership Bible

Navigators do more than steer. They plan the whole trip in their minds before they leave the dock. They have a vision for their destination, they understand what it will take to get there, they know who they'll need on the team to be successful, and they recognize the obstacles long before they appear on the horizon. Leaders who prepare well can take their people just about anywhere.

The 21 Irrefutable Laws of Leadership

Moving Your Team in the Right Direction

Do you remember what it was like when you first got your driver's license? Just going for a drive was probably a thrill. It didn't really matter where you went. But as you got older, having a destination became more important. The same is true with a team.

Getting the team together and moving it are accomplishments, but where you're going matters. You've got to begin doing the difficult things that help the team to improve and develop high morale. Among other things, you must:

- Make changes that make the team better.
- Receive the buy–in of team members.
- Communicate commitment.
- Develop and equip members for success.

The two toughest stages in the life of a team are when you are trying to create movement in a team that's going nowhere, and when you must become a change agent. Those are the times when leadership is most needed.

The 17 Indisputable Laws of Leadership

THIS WEEK: Consider your team's journey. Is your team moving? Is it moving in the right direction? Does everyone know the destination? Is everyone aware of the challenges that await along the way? Is the morale of your team members an indicator of how prepared they are for the journey? Are you a good navigator?

GOD'S PROMISE TO LEADERS

In the past God spoke to our ancestors through the prophets many times and in many different ways. But now in these last days God has spoken to us through his Son. God has chosen his Son to own all things, and through him he made the world.

HEBREWS 1:1–2 (NCV)

A LEADER'S PROMISE TO THE TEAM

IT IS IMPORTANT THAT WE UNDERSTAND EACH OTHER. I WILL BE AS CLEAR, CONSISTENT, AND COURTEOUS AS POSSIBLE IN COMMUNICATING MY EXPECTATIONS, INTENTIONS, CONCERNS, AND PRAISE.

WEEK 15

COMMUNICATE TO LEAD

And so it was, when Jesus had ended these sayings, that the people were astonished at His teaching, for He taught them as one having authority, and not as the scribes.

MATTHEW 7:28–29

John W. Gardner observed, "If I had to name a single all–purpose instrument of leadership, it would be communication." If you cannot communicate, you will not lead others effectively. Give yourself three standards to live by as you communicate to your team.

Be consistent. Nothing frustrates team members more than leaders who can't make up their minds.

Be clear. Your team cannot execute if they don't know what you want. Don't try to dazzle anyone with your intelligence; impress them with your simple straightforwardness.

Be courteous. Everyone deserves to be shown respect, no matter what their position or what kind of history you might have with them. If you are courteous to your people, you set a tone for the entire organization.

Never forget that as the leader, your communication sets the tone for the interaction among your people.

The 17 Indisputable Laws of Teamwork

Make Communication Clear

The success of your marriage, job, and personal relationships all depend greatly on communication. You can be more a more effective communicator if you follow these four truths.

1. *Simplify your message.* Forget about impressing people with big words or complex sentences. If you want to connect with people, keep it simple.

2. *See the person.* As you communicate with individuals or groups, ask yourself these questions: Who is my audience? What are their questions? What needs to be accomplished?

3. *Show the truth.* Credibility precedes great communication. Believe in what you say. Then, live what you say. There is no greater credibility than conviction in action.

4. *Seek a response.* Never forget that the goal of all communication is action. Give people something to feel, something to remember, and something to do.

The 21 Indispensable Qualities of a Leader

Give yourself, not just your opinion. Note how communicators differ from public speakers.

Public Speaker	**Communicator**
1. Seeks to be understood and liked	1. Seeks to understand and connect
2. Asks: What do I have?	2. Asks: What do they need?
3. Focuses on techniques	3. Focuses on atmosphere
4. Is self–conscious	4. Is audience–oriented
5. Wants to complete the speech	5. Wants to complete the people
6. Is content–oriented	6. Is change–oriented

The Maxwell Leadership Bible

Leaders Touch a Heart Before They Ask for a Hand

A leader can't connect with people only when he is communicating among groups; he must connect with individuals. The stronger the relationship and connection between individuals, the more likely the follower will help the leader. Successful leaders always initiate; they take the first step and make the effort to continue building relationships.

Connecting with people isn't complicated, but it takes effort. Observe the truths about connection that Rehoboam, son of David, ignored (1 Kings 12:16):

- Your people are more willing to take action when you first move them with emotion.
- When you give first, your people will give in return.
- When you connect with individuals, you gain the attention of crowds.
- When you reach out to your people, they will reach back toward you.
- Whether you have just taken over a leadership position or are well established, you must connect with your people if you are to succeed.

The Maxwell Leadership Bible

THIS WEEK: Consider the communication flow among your team members. Where does the information flow clearly and quickly? Where does information become muddied? As the chief communicator, do you connect well with your team?

GOD'S PROMISE TO LEADERS

Then Jesus said to his followers, "If people want to follow me, they must give up the things they want. They must be willing even to give up their lives to follow me. . . . The Son of Man will come again with his Father's glory and with his angels. At that time, he will reward them for what they have done."

MATTHEW 16:24, 27 (NCV)

A LEADER'S PROMISE TO THE TEAM

I'VE CONSIDERED THE COST OF THIS ENDEAVOR, AND I COMMIT MYSELF TO FOLLOW THROUGH, BECAUSE I BELIEVE WE WILL SEE REWARDS.

WEEK 16

THE COST OF COMMITMENT

Thus Hezekiah did throughout all Judah, and he did what was good and right and true before the LORD *his God. And in every work that he began in the service of the house of God, in the law and in the commandment, to seek his God, he did it with all his heart. So he prospered.*

2 CHRONICLES 31:20–21

The Bible describes King Hezekiah as a leader who "did what was good and right and true before the Lord his God. And in every work that he began . . . he did it with all his heart." Hezekiah paid the price to get the job done. But what is the price of commitment?

1. *Change of lifestyle.* Hezekiah couldn't live the way his father lived.

2. *Loneliness.* Hezekiah alone obeyed God at first.

3. *Faith in God.* Hezekiah believed that God would bless his efforts.

4. *Criticism.* Hezekiah weathered the harsh questions of an older generation.

5. *Hard work and money.* The king gave up time, energy, and budget to reach his goal.

6. *Daily discipline.* Hezekiah had to instill a daily regimen to bring about reform.

7. *Constant pressure.* The king endured the pressure of potential failure and misunderstanding.

The Maxwell Leadership Bible

Be Careful What You Promise

Do not be rash with your mouth, and let not your heart utter anything hastily before God. For God is in heaven, and you on earth; therefore let your words be few. . . . When you make a vow to God, do not delay to pay it; for He has no pleasure in fools. . . . Do not let your mouth cause your flesh to sin, nor say before the messenger of God that it was an error. Why should God be angry at your excuse and destroy the work of your hands? For in the multitude of dreams and many words there is also vanity. But fear God.

Ecclesiastes 5:2, 4, 6–7

Do you make promises to God? Scripture advises caution before we commit something to God—good advice for any decision a leader must make. Solomon describes three major pitfalls lying in wait for careless leaders:

- *Hasty speech.* Leaders must listen as much as they speak.
- *Empty promises.* Leaders tend to say what others want to hear. Don't promise what you can't deliver.
- *Lame excuses.* Leaders diminish their influence when they try to reverse a mistake with a lame excuse.

The Maxwell Leadership Bible

Ask for commitment. Don't equip people who are merely interested. Equip the ones who are committed. Without commitment, there can be no success. To determine whether your people are committed, make sure they know what it will cost them. If they won't commit, don't go any further in the equipping process. Don't waste your time.

Developing the Leaders Around You

The Commitment Crucible

Then Jesus said to the twelve, "Do you also want to go away?" But Simon Peter answered Him, "Lord, to whom shall we go? You have the words of eternal life."

John 6:67–68

People often associate commitment with their emotions. If they feel the right way, then they can follow through on their commitments. But true commitment doesn't work that way. It's not an emotion; it's a character quality that enables us to reach our goals. Human emotions go up and down all the time, but commitment has to be rock solid.

There are some things every leader needs to know about being committed:

1. It usually is discovered amid adversity.
2. It does not depend on gifts or abilities.
3. It comes as the result of choice, not conditions.
4. It lasts when it's based on values.

The 17 Essential Qualities of a Team Player

This Week: Review the commitments pressing upon you. How did you prepare before accepting the commitments? Did you really know what you were getting into? What new commitments currently await your response? Who on your team is consistently good at accepting and following through on commitments? Who lets you down? Have you let down your team?

GOD'S PROMISE TO LEADERS

But I will send you the Counselor—
the Spirit of truth. He will come to you from the
Father and will tell you all about me.
And you must also tell others about me because
you have been with me from the beginning.

JOHN 15:26–27 (NLT)

A LEADER'S PROMISE TO THE TEAM

I WILL SEEK GOD AND GOOD ADVICE FROM OTHERS AS I LEAD.

WEEK 17

CREATE A STRONG INNER CIRCLE

Now these were the heads of the mighty men whom David had,
who strengthened themselves with him in his kingdom,
with all Israel, to make him king,
according to the word of the LORD concerning Israel.

1 CHRONICLES 11:10

There are no Lone Ranger leaders. If you're alone, you're not leading anybody. Examine the way King David pulled together the core people who made him great:

1. He built a strong inner circle before he needed it. David began building his team long before he was crowned king.

2. He attracted people with varied gifts. David attracted men of diverse abilities. We read of experienced warriors with a variety of skills, many men of valor, and hundreds of captains. With the help of these men, David felt ready for anything.

3. He engendered loyalty. David's followers displayed incredible loyalty to him throughout his life. Those closest to him seemed willing to put their lives on the line for him.

4. He delegated responsibility based on ability. David continually gave authority to others. He designated Joab as commander of the army, and he felt equally secure in giving others civil authority.

The Maxwell Leadership Bible

Those Closest To You . . .

Some of David's first followers were misfits, yet he transformed his ragtag supporters into a winning team (1 Samuel 22:1–2). As David gained experience and grew in his leadership, he continued to attract stronger and stronger people. David made his inner circle great, and his inner circle made him great.

The 21 Most Powerful Minutes in a Leader's Day

No leader succeeds alone. Even David needed his Jonathan (1 Samuel 19:2–3). Do you have someone who "strengthens your hand in God"? All leaders need loyal friends who can help them persevere.

Choose your circle carefully. King Rehoboam had the benefit of his father's wise inner circle, but the foolish young king instead heeded advice that agreed with his own opinion (2 Chronicles 10:8). Horrible move! He should have gone with a core team with these qualities of a solid inner circle.

1. *Experience.* People who have been down the road of life and understand it.
2. *Heart for God.* People who place God first and uphold His values.
3. *Objectivity.* People who see the pros and cons of the issues.
4. *Love for people.* People who love others and value them more than things.
5. *Complementary gifts.* People who bring diverse gifts to the relationship.
6. *Loyalty to the leader.* People who truly love and are concerned for the leader.

The Maxwell Leadership Bible

Be First to Take Your Good Advice

My son, pay attention to my wisdom; Lend your ear to my understanding. That you may preserve discretion, And your lips may keep knowledge. For the lips of an immoral woman drip honey, And her mouth is smoother than oil; Remove your way far from her, And do not go near the door of her house, Lest you give your honor to others, And your years to the cruel one.

Proverbs 5:1–3 & 8–9

It doesn't take a leader very long to realize that it's easier to give good advice than to follow it. Solomon proves the point. He tells us repeatedly and with great conviction that only fools fall into adultery. And yet, somehow, this same leader failed to heed God's explicit warning against kings taking many wives (Deuteronomy 17:17). Solomon blatantly disobeyed this command and married seven hundred women. The result? "His wives turned his heart after other gods; and his heart was not loyal to the Lord his God" (1 Kings 11:4).

Wise leaders not only give good advice; they heed it. How different the fortunes of Israel might have turned out had Solomon acted on the wisdom he so forcefully expressed to others!

The Maxwell Leadership Bible

This Week: Consider who sits in your inner circle. Do they share your vision? Do they have complementary gifts, useful where you need them most?

GOD'S PROMISE TO LEADERS

Then Jesus came to them and said, "All power in heaven and on earth is given to me. So go and make followers of all people in the world. Baptize them in the name of the Father and the Son and the Holy Spirit. Teach them to obey everything that I have taught you, and I will be with you always, even until the end of this age."

MATTHEW 28:18–20 (NCV)

A LEADER'S PROMISE TO THE TEAM

I TRUST YOU. I NEED YOU.
I WILL HELP YOU BECOME READY TO TAKE ON MORE RESPONSIBILITIES, AND WHEN I DELEGATE TO YOU I WILL MAKE SURE YOU HAVE THE RESOURCES TO EXCEL IN YOUR TASKS.

WEEK 18

DELEGATE TO TEAM MEMBERS

Abraham said to the oldest servant of his house . . . "Go to my country and to my family, and take a wife for my son Isaac."

GENESIS 24:2, 4

Delegation is the most powerful tool leaders have. Delegation increases individual productivity according to the number of people to whom leaders can delegate. It increases the productivity of their department or organization. Leaders who can't or won't delegate create a bottleneck to productivity. So why do some leaders fail to delegate effectively?

1. Insecurity
2. Lack of confidence in others
3. Lack of ability to train others
4. Personal enjoyment of the task
5. Habit
6. Inability to find someone else to do it
7. Lack of time
8. An "I do it best" mind-set

If you recognize yourself in any of the issues above, you probably aren't doing enough delegating. Here are some other indicators that you need to delegate: When deadlines are missed often; crises become frequent; someone else could do the job; or those under your leadership need another world to conquer.

Developing the Leaders Around You

Decide to Delegate

One of the most common mistakes a coach can make is to misjudge the level of a player. If the leader doesn't work with each player according to where he is in his development, the player won't produce, succeed, and develop. According to management consultant Ken Blanchard, all team members fit into one of four categories with regard to the type of leadership they need:

Players who need direction. These players don't know what to do or how to do it. You need to instruct them every step of the way.

Players who need coaching. Players who are able to do more of the job on their own will become more independent, but they still rely on you for direction and feedback.

Players who need support. Players able to work without your direction still may require resources and encouragement.

Players to whom you delegate. When these players are given a task, you can be confident that it will be done. They only need you to lead. Provide them with vision on the front end and accountability on the back end, and they will multiply your efforts toward success.

Developing the Leaders Around You

It takes a team. God's answer to Moses' cry for help was for Moses to share the responsibilities of leadership with a select group (Numbers 11:14). When a leader called by God has a burden that becomes too great, God provides help . . . if the leader will ask for it. He also will anoint them with His power, just as He did the seventy elders of Israel.

The Maxwell Leadership Bible

Share the Burden

Moreover you shall select from all the people able men . . . And let them judge the people at all times. Then it will be that every great matter they shall bring to you, but every small matter they themselves shall judge. So it will be easier for you, for they will bear the burden with you.

Exodus 18:21–22

Easing people into delegation is important. You can't simply dump tasks on people, not if you want them to succeed. Delegate according to the following steps:

1. Ask them to be fact finders only. It gives them a chance to become acquainted with the issues and objectives.

2. Ask them to make suggestions. This gets them thinking and it gives you a chance to become acquainted with their thought processes.

3. Ask them to implement one of their recommendations, but only after you give your approval. Set them up for success, not failure.

4. Ask them to take action on their own, but to report the results immediately. This will give them confidence, and you will still be able to perform damage control if necessary.

5. Give complete authority. This is what you've been working toward.

Developing the Leaders Around You

This Week: Consider some specific tasks that you and/or your team must do. Per task, is the responsible person someone who needs direction, coaching, support, or delegation?

GOD'S PROMISE TO LEADERS

Each one of us did the work God gave us to do.
I planted the seed, and Apollos watered it.
But God is the One who made it grow. . . .
The one who plants and the one who waters have
the same purpose, and each will be
rewarded for his own work.

1 Corinthians 3:5–6, 8 (NCV)

A LEADER'S PROMISE TO THE TEAM

I cannot fulfill our mission alone.
I want to empower you.
I invite you to share your desire to grow,
so we can make it happen together.

WEEK 19

EMPOWER YOUR PEOPLE

I want to share a secret with you. It's the greatest principle I've ever learned in the area of developing others. Here it is: Never work alone. I know that sounds too simple, but it is truly the secret to developing others. Whenever you do anything that you want to pass along to others, take someone along with you.

This isn't necessarily a natural practice for many of us. The most common learning model in the United States is when a leader asks questions or lectures while the follower listens and tries to comprehend the instructor's ideas. But craftsmen use a different model for developing others. They take apprentices who work alongside them until they master their craft and are able to pass it along to others. Their model looks something like this:

I do it.
I do it—and you watch.
You do it—and I watch.
You do it.

In all the years I've been equipping and developing others, I've never found a better way to do it than this.

Your Road Map for Success

Evaluate, Then Empower

If anyone wants to provide leadership in the church, good!
But there are preconditions.

1 Timothy 3:1 (Msg)

The way to start empowering people is by evaluating them. With inexperienced people, if you give them too much authority too soon, you can be setting them up to fail. With people who have lots of experience, if you move too slowly you can frustrate and demoralize them.

Remember that everyone has the potential to succeed. Your job is to see the potential, find out what he lacks, and equip him with what he needs. As you evaluate the people you intend to empower, look first at three areas:

1. *Knowledge.* Think about what people need to know in order to do anything you intend to give them.

2. *Skill.* Nothing is more frustrating than being asked to do things for which you have no ability.

3. *Desire.* No amount of skill, knowledge, or potential can help a person succeed if he doesn't have the desire to be successful.

Becoming a Person of Influence

Invest to empower. To be an empowering leader, you must do more than believe in emerging leaders. You need to take steps to help them become the leaders they have the potential to be. Empowering people takes a personal investment. It requires energy and time. But it's worth the price. And when you empower others, you create power in your organization.

The Maxwell Leadership Bible

The Power to Change the World

All the training in the world will provide only limited success if you don't turn your people loose to do the job. The way to do that is to give them responsibility, authority, accountability, and resources.

Responsibility may seem like the easiest to give, but some leaders find it difficult to allow their people to keep the responsibility after it's been given. Poor managers want to control every detail of their people's work. When that happens, the potential leaders who work for them become frustrated and don't develop. Rather than desiring more responsibility, they become indifferent or avoid responsibility altogether.

With responsibility must go authority. Winston Churchill said, "I am your servant. You have the right to dismiss me when you please. What you have no right to do is ask me to bear responsibility without the power of action."

Once responsibility and authority have been given to people, they become empowered to make things happen. But we also have to be sure that they are accountable for making the right things happen.

Resources are necessary for fulfilling responsibilities. This includes much more than just equipment. It includes training and professional development. Be willing to spend money on books, tapes, conferences, and the like. Be creative in providing tools. It will keep your people growing and equip them to do the job well.

Developing the Leaders Around You

This Week: Reflect on your own journey. Who empowered you along the way? How can you be more deliberate in empowering your team?

GOD'S PROMISE TO LEADERS

Be of good courage,
And He shall strengthen your heart,
All you who hope in the LORD.

PSALM 31:24

A LEADER'S PROMISE TO THE TEAM

I WILL BE AN ENLARGER. I WILL ENCOURAGE THE BEST QUALITIES IN INDIVIDUALS AND IN THE TEAM AS A WHOLE.

WEEK 20

ENLARGE YOUR PEOPLE

Good leadership is a channel of water controlled by GOD; he directs it to whatever ends he chooses.

PROVERBS 21:1 (MSG)

With good leadership, everything improves. Leaders are lifters. They push the thinking of their teammates beyond old boundaries of creativity. They elevate others' performance, making them better than they've ever been. They improve people's confidence in themselves and others. While managers are often able to maintain a team at its current level, leaders are able to lift it to a higher level than it has ever reached before. The key to that is working with people and bringing out the best in them. For example:

Leaders transfer ownership for work to those who execute the work.

Leaders create an environment where each team member wants to be responsible.

Leaders coach the development of personal capabilities.

Leaders learn quickly and encourage others to learn efficiently also.

If you want to give a team a lift, then provide it with better leadership.

The 17 Indisputable Laws of Teamwork

Give Them Themselves

Team members always love and admire a person who is able to help them go to another level, someone who enlarges them and empowers them to be successful. Players who enlarge their teammates have several things in common.

1. Enlargers value their teammates. People's performances usually reflect the expectations of those they respect.

2. Enlargers know and relate to what their teammates value. Players who enlarge others understand what their teammates value. That kind of knowledge, along with a desire to relate to their fellow players, creates a strong connection between teammates.

3. Enlargers add value to their teammates. An enlarger looks for the gifts, talents, and uniqueness in other people, and then helps them increase those abilities for their benefit and for that of the entire team.

4. Enlargers make themselves more valuable. You cannot give what you do not have. If you want to increase the ability of a teammate, make yourself better.

The 17 Essential Qualities of a Team Player

When people are esteemed, relationships are redeemed. Leaders know that people are an organization's most appreciable asset; therefore, people skills are a leader's most important attribute. Proverbs 27 presents some fundamentals on relationships.

1. Don't brag.
2. Don't envy.
3. Be forthright.
4. Don't forsake your roots.
5. Stay close.
6. Add value.
7. Don't be moved by flattery.

The Maxwell Leadership Bible

Blessed for Success

And he blessed Joseph, and said, " . . . The Angel who has redeemed me from all evil, bless the lads;
Let my name be named upon them, and the name of my fathers Abraham and Isaac; and let them grow into a multitude in the midst of the earth."

Genesis 48:15–16

Not everyone you influence will think the same way you do. You have to help them not only believe that they can succeed, but also show them that you want them to succeed. How do you do that?

Expect it. People can sense your underlying attitude no matter what you say or do. If you have an expectation for your people to be successful, they will know it.

Verbalize it. People need to hear you tell them that you believe in them and want them to succeed. Become a positive prophet of their success.

Reinforce it. You can never do too much when it comes to believing in people.

Once people recognize and understand that you genuinely want to see them succeed and are committed to helping them, they will begin to believe they can accomplish what you give them to do.

Becoming a Person of Influence

This Week: Make a point to enlarge everyone on your team. Note how they react—both immediately and in the successive hours and days. How can you enlarge people on a more consistent basis?

GOD'S PROMISE TO LEADERS

We know that in everything God works for the good of those who love him. They are the people he called, because that was his plan.

ROMANS 8:28 (NCV)

A LEADER'S PROMISE TO THE TEAM

WHEN I FAIL,
I WILL ACCEPT RESPONSIBILITY,
LEARN FROM MY MISTAKES,
AND GET BACK IN THE GAME.

WEEK 21

FAIL FORWARD

Have mercy upon me, O God,
According to Your lovingkindness;
According to the multitude of Your tender mercies,
Blot out my transgressions.
Wash me thoroughly from my iniquity,
And cleanse me from my sin.
For I acknowledge my transgressions,
And my sin is always before me . . .
Create in me a clean heart, O God,
And renew a steadfast spirit within me.

PSALM 51:1–3, 10

Mistakes are a part of life. Successful leaders recognize their errors, learn from them, and then work to correct their faults. A study of 105 executives determined many of the characteristics of successful executives, but one particular trait they shared was identified as the most valuable. It was that they admitted their mistakes and accepted the consequences rather than trying to blame others.

Most people don't want to reap the consequences of their actions. You can see this type of attitude everywhere. A leader who is willing to take responsibility for their actions and be honest or "transparent" with their people is someone they will admire, respect, and trust. That leader is also someone they can learn from.

Developing the Leaders Around You

Accept Responsibility and Get Back in the Game

When things go wrong, the natural tendency is to look for someone to blame. You can go all the way back to the Garden of Eden on this one. When God asked Adam what he'd done, he said it was Eve's fault. Then when God questioned Eve, she blamed it on the snake. The same thing happens today.

The next time you experience a failure, think about why you failed instead of who was at fault. Try to look at it objectively so that you can do better next time. Ask yourself:

What lessons have I learned?

How can I turn the failure into success?

Where did I succeed as well as fail?

People who blame others for their failures never overcome them. They simply move from problem to problem. To reach your potential, you must continually improve yourself, and you can't do that if you don't take responsibility for your actions and learn from your mistakes.

In life, you will have problems. Are you going to give up and stay down, wallowing in your defeat, or are you going to get back on your feet as quickly as you can?

When you fall, make the best of it and get back on your feet. Learn what you can from your mistake, and then get back in the game. View your errors the way Henry Ford did his. He said, "Failure is the opportunity to begin again more intelligently."

Your Road Map for Success

Don't Take Yourself Too Seriously

A merry heart does good, like medicine.

Proverbs 17:22

I work with a lot of leaders. And one thing I've found is that many times they take themselves much too seriously. Of course, they're not alone. I meet people in every walk of life who have too much doom and gloom in their attitudes. They simply need to lighten up. No matter how serious your work is, that's no reason to take yourself seriously.

If any person had a reason to take his job and himself seriously, it would be a president of the United States. Yet it's possible for even people holding that position to maintain their sense of humor and keep their egos in check. For example, when Calvin Coolidge was asked if he was attending the Sesquicentennial Exposition in Philadelphia, the president answered, "Yes."

"Why are you going, Mr. President?" a reporter asked.

"As an exhibit," answered the rotund Coolidge.

If you tend to take yourself too seriously, give yourself and everyone else around you a break. Recognize that laughter breeds resilience. Laughing is the quickest way to get up and get going again when you've been knocked down.

Failing Forward

This Week: Think about your recent failures at work and at home. What have you learned from those experiences? Did you take your share of responsibility? Did you blame others unduly? How can you begin again more intelligently? Can you laugh at yourself?

GOD'S PROMISE TO LEADERS

It is my family God has chosen!
Yes, he has made an everlasting covenant with me.
His agreement is eternal, final, sealed.
He will constantly look after my safety and success.

2 Samuel 23:5 (NLT)

A LEADER'S PROMISE TO THE TEAM

MY FAMILY COMES FIRST, AND BECAUSE I DO A GOOD JOB LEADING THE PEOPLE WHO MEAN THE MOST TO ME, YOU CAN TRUST ME TO TAKE SIMILAR CARE IN LEADING THIS TEAM.

WEEK 22

FAMILY FIRST

But if anyone does not provide for his own,
and especially for those of his household, he has denied the faith
and is worse than an unbeliever.

1 TIMOTHY 5:8

Every day parents and spouses leave their families in the pursuit of success. It's almost as though they're driving down the road, and they get pretty far along before they realize they've left members of their family behind. The tragedy is that many value their careers, success, or personal happiness more than they do their families. They decide that it's too much work to go back, so they just keep driving.

But what many are now realizing is that the hope of happiness at the expense of breaking up a family is an illusion. You can't give up your marriage or neglect your children and gain true success.

To build a strong family, you have to make your home a supportive environment. Psychologist William James said, "In every person from the cradle to the grave, there is a deep craving to be appreciated." Feeling appreciated brings out the best in people. And when that appreciation comes in the home and is coupled with acceptance, love, and encouragement, the bonds between family members grow, and the home becomes a safe haven for everyone.

Your Road Map for Success

Leadership Begins at Home

As a leader, where should your influence begin? A good answer can be drawn from the life of Joshua. To him, leading his family was more important than leading his country (Joshua 24:15). It may sound ironic, but when leaders put their families first, the community benefits. When leaders put the community first, both their families and the community suffer. Starting at home is always the key to affecting others in a positive way. Because Joshua had his priorities right and had led his household well, he gained credibility to lead the entire house of Israel.

If you have a family, put them first in your leadership. There's no legacy like that of the positive influence leaders can exercise with their family.

The 21 Most Powerful Minutes in a Leader's Day

Lead your children well. Eli's failure to lead his family eventually led to his downfall as a religious leader (1 Samuel 2:22–36). He lost his credibility, his job, and eventually his life. He missed the mark by making some crucial errors.

1. *Emphasis.* Eli emphasized teaching his colleagues and clients, not his family.

2. *Expectations.* Eli thought his sons would "get it" just because they lived in the house of the Lord.

3. *Example.* Eli failed to live out in his home what he taught in his work.

4. *Entanglements.* Eli got so caught up with his profession, he blinded himself to his failure.

The Maxwell Leadership Bible

Leadership Is More Example Than Power

Leadership in the home is not about power or control; it's about giving up yourself for someone else. Evaluate your home leadership in each of the following categories:

Initiative. Do I give direction and take responsibility for my primary relationships?

Intimacy. Do I experience intimacy with God and others through open conversations?

Influence. Do I exercise biblical influence by encouraging and developing others?

Integrity. Do I lead an honest life?

Identity. Am I secure in who I am?

Inner circle. Do I exhibit the fruit of the Spirit in my life, including self–discipline?

"Train up a child in the way he should go, and when he is old he will not depart from it" (Proverbs 22:6). God calls parents to lead their children, and focusing on three key words can help.

Modeling. A good example is worth a thousand sermons.

Management. Good management is the ability to discern the uniqueness of a child and teach him or her accordingly.

Memories. The verse says, "When he is old, he will not depart . . ." This implies that the child has special memories of his early experiences.

The Maxwell Leadership Bible

THIS WEEK: Evaluate the leadership in your home. Are you giving your best to the people you love? Are you modeling what you want your family to do, too? What were the leaders like where you grew up? How is that modeling experience affecting you today as a leader?

GOD'S PROMISE TO LEADERS

The humble He guides in justice,
And the humble He teaches His way.
All the paths of the LORD are mercy and truth,
To such as keep His covenant and His testimonies.

PSALM 25:9–10

A LEADER'S PROMISE TO THE TEAM

AS I LEAD YOU, I AM ALSO ENDEAVORING TO LEARN AND GROW AS A LEADER MYSELF.

WEEK 23

FIND A MENTOR

Then Moses spoke to the LORD, saying: "Let the LORD . . . set a man over the congregation . . . that the congregation of the LORD may not be like sheep which have no shepherd." And the LORD said to Moses: "Take Joshua the son of Nun with you, a man in whom is the Spirit."

NUMBERS 27:15–18

Joshua was an impressive leader. One of the major factors in Joshua's increase in influence was the impact of Moses on his life. Wherever Moses went, Joshua went with him, whether it was up Mount Sinai or to meet with God in the tabernacle.

After the Hebrews refused to enter the Promised Land, the mentoring relationship between the two men continued. In fact, the process continued for forty years and culminated with Moses imparting his authority to the younger man. And after Moses died, no one questioned Joshua's leadership.

Pastor A. W. Tozer said, "God is looking for people through whom He can do the impossible—what a pity that we plan only the things we can do by ourselves." Moses' investment in Joshua released God's power in him.

The 21 Most Powerful Minutes in a Leader's Day

Choosing a Leadership Model

Give great thought to which leaders you follow because they determine your course as a leader. Here are six questions to consider before picking a model to follow.

1. Does my model's life deserve a following?

2. Does my model's life already have a following?

3. What is the main strength that influences others to follow my model?

4. Does my model reproduce other leaders?

5. Is my model's strength reproducible in my life?

6. If my model's strength is reproducible in my life, what steps must I take to develop and demonstrate that strength?

Remember, studying national or historical figures can certainly benefit you, but not the way a personal mentor can.

Be a worthy follower. Use these guidelines to help develop a positive mentoring relationship.

Ask the right questions. Make the questions strategic for your growth.

Don't let ego get in the way of learning.

Respect mentors but don't idolize them.

Put into effect immediately what you are learning.

Be disciplined in relating to mentors. Arrange for ample time, select the subject matter in advance, and do your homework.

Don't threaten to give up. Let mentors know they're not wasting their time.

Developing the Leaders Around You

Choose Your Mentor Well

Every leader needs mentors, especially emerging leaders. God took Elisha through the preparation necessary under Elijah. Note several principles outlined in 1 Kings 19 and 2 Kings 2 underlying his preparation:

Elisha's Preparation	**Leadership Principle**
1. He was anointed to replace Elijah.	1. Leaders must understand their call and role.
2. Elisha touched Elijah's mantle long before he entered his ministry.	2. Leaders must wait patiently on God's perfect timing for their authority.
3. Elisha burned his farming tools.	3. Leaders must surrender former ambitions.
4. Elisha stuck with Elijah wherever he went.	4. Leaders must pursue good mentors.
5. Elisha absorbed all he could from Elijah.	5. Leaders must hunger to grow and develop.

The Maxwell Leadership Bible

This Week: Consider how God is mentoring you. Who and what has He used to grow you in faith? In servant leadership? What do you hunger to learn? Can you think of other leaders who might be good mentors for you? Will you ask them to teach you?

GOD'S PROMISE TO LEADERS

When people's steps follow the LORD,
God is pleased with their ways.
If they stumble, they will not fall,
because the LORD holds their hand.

PSALM 37:23–24 (NCV)

A LEADER'S PROMISE TO THE TEAM

I KNOW WHO MY LEADER IS,
AND I'M ALERT TO HIS CALL.

WEEK 24

FOLLOW THE ULTIMATE LEADER

Then God said, "Let us make man in our image, in our likeness, and let them rule over the fish of the sea and the birds of the air, over the livestock, over all the earth . . ."

GENESIS 1:26 (NIV)

God is the Ultimate Leader, and He calls every believer to lead others. God could have arranged His creation in any number of ways, but He chose to create human beings who possess spirits and the capacity to relate to Him and follow Him, yet who are not forced to do so.

When mankind fell into sin, God could have executed a plan of redemption that did not include sinful people, but He has called us to participate and to lead others as we follow Him. God made that clear from the beginning when He stated, "have dominion" (Genesis 1:28).

The call to leadership is a consistent pattern in the Bible. When God decided to raise up a nation of His own, He didn't call upon the masses. He called out one leader—Abraham. When He wanted to deliver His people out of Egypt, He didn't guide them as a group. He raised up a leader to do it—Moses. When it came time for the people to cross into the Promised Land, they followed one man—Joshua.

Every time God desired to do something great, He called a leader to step forward. Today He still calls leaders to step forward for every work, both large and small.

The Maxwell Leadership Bible

Fire of God

"Who among us shall dwell with the devouring fire?
Who among us shall dwell with everlasting burnings?"
He who walks righteously and speaks uprightly, he who despises
the gain of oppressions, who gestures with his hands,
refusing bribes, who stops his ears from hearing of bloodshed,
and shuts his eyes from seeing evil.

Isaiah 33:14–15

Isaiah lays out a list of traits for the kind of people who can stand up in a crisis. Ponder his description:

Integrity. The leader's life and words match.

Justice. The leader rejects dishonest gain.

Convictions. The leader's values won't allow him or her to accept bribes.

Positive focus. The leader rejects destructive thinking.

Pure. The leader disciplines his or her mind to remain clean and pure.

Secure. The leader is firm, stable in his or her identity and source of strength.

Calling all leaders! When the Lord wanted someone to speak to the people for Him, Isaiah answered the call (Isaiah 6) because of three factors that still call leaders today.

Opportunity. We see a specific place where we can make a difference. This has to do with timing.

Ability. We recognize that we have the God-given gifts to do something about the need. This has to do with competence.

Desire. We want to step out and address the need; our hunger pushes us. This has to do with passion.

The Maxwell Leadership Bible

Follow My Lead

Look at every phase of Joshua's life, and you see a man who gave himself wholeheartedly to completing whatever task was assigned to him. From the first, he immediately obeyed the instruction of Moses (Exodus 17:9–10). Thereafter Joshua took on the role of Moses' assistant. Joshua again displayed his obedience when he agreed to spy out the Promised Land. Upon his return from the reconnaissance mission, he and Caleb, alone among the spies, were ready to obey God and enter Canaan. Forty years later when Moses handed the reins of power to his protégé, Joshua again obeyed the call (Joshua 1:5–11).

In the end, the people of Israel followed Joshua's example and did what God asked of them—and as a result inherited the land God had promised.

By the time of his death, Joshua was known simply as "the servant of the Lord" (Judges 2:7–8). That is high praise! While today we consider Joshua an exceptional leader, nowhere does Scripture describe him as a man of extraordinary might, intellect, or talent. Obedience made him extraordinary. And when you're a servant of the Lord, that's all you really need.

The Maxwell Leadership Bible

This Week: Consider your call to leadership. How were you called? Can you see God's hand in your preparation? How have you been refined along the way? Is your call the same today as it was in the beginning? How has it changed? Is it changing now?

GOD'S PROMISE TO LEADERS

For the kingdom of God is . . . righteousness and peace and joy in the Holy Spirit. For he who serves Christ in these things is acceptable to God and approved by men.

ROMANS 14:17–18

A LEADER'S PROMISE TO THE TEAM

I'M HERE TO SERVE THIS TEAM SO TOGETHER WE CAN FULFILL OUR PURPOSE.

WEEK 25

GIVE YOURSELF AWAY

But whoever desires to become great among you, let him be your servant. And whoever desires to be first among you, let him be your slave.

Matthew 20:26–27

As a team leader, how do you cultivate an attitude of selflessness among your people? Begin this way:

1. *Being generous.* Saint Francis of Assisi said, "All getting separates you from others; all giving unites you to others." If team members are willing to give of themselves generously to the team, then it is being set up to succeed.

2. *Avoiding internal politics.* One of the worst forms of selfishness can be seen in people who are playing politics on the team. That usually means posturing or positioning themselves for their own benefit, regardless of how it might damage the team. But good team players worry about the benefit of their teammates more than themselves.

3. *Displaying loyalty.* If you show the people on your team loyalty, they will return loyalty in kind. Loyalty fosters unity, and unity breeds team success.

4. *Valuing interdependence more than independence.* In the United States, we value independence highly, because it is often accompanied by innovation, hard work, and a willingness to stand for what's right. But independence taken too far is a characteristic of selfishness.

Let God Worry About Your Promotion

Don't work yourself into the spotlight;
Don't push your way into the place of prominence.
It's better to be promoted to a place of honor
Than face humiliation by being demoted.

Proverbs 25:6–7 (Msg)

In his first letter to Timothy, the apostle Paul tells us that aspiring to a position of leadership is a good thing (3:1). However, there's a difference between stepping forward to accept the responsibility of leadership and stepping forward to put yourself into the spotlight for the benefit of self–promotion.

The road to biblical leadership comes through service. Leaders may find themselves in the spotlight, but they also take the heat that often comes with that place of prominence. They speak up for the sake of the mission, but they are also willing to remain silent when it serves the organization. And at any moment, they must be willing to make all kinds of sacrifices for the sake of their people.

Leaders lose the right to be selfish. Romans 15:1–6 reminds us that leadership is about serving others, not wielding power. A servant . . .

1. denies self. We are to please others, not ourselves.
2. develops others. We are to add value to others.
3. accepts mistreatment. We are to forgive wrongs.
4. imitates Christ. We are to look to Jesus as our model.
5. is a student. We are to remain teachable.
6. pursues the harmony of relationships. We are to pursue unity and peace.

The Maxwell Leadership Bible

Oh, It's Nothing

Then news of these things came to the ears of the church in Jerusalem, and they sent out Barnabas to go as far as Antioch. When he came and had seen the grace of God, he was glad, and encouraged them all that with purpose of heart they should continue with the Lord. For he was a good man, full of the Holy Spirit and of faith. And a great many people were added to the Lord.

Acts 11:22–24

If any early church leader could be called a servant, it is Barnabas. He initiated and did whatever it took to raise morale, men, or money. What allowed Barnabas to demonstrate such a lifestyle? He had . . .

Nothing to prove. Barnabas didn't have to play games. He never sought the limelight. When he mentored Paul, he happily let the emerging apostle rise above him.

Nothing to lose. Barnabas didn't have to guard his reputation or fear that he would lose popularity. He came to serve, not to be served. This enabled him to focus on giving, not getting.

Nothing to hide. Barnabas didn't maintain a facade or image. He remained authentic, vulnerable, and transparent. He could rejoice with other's victories.

The Maxwell Leadership Bible

This Week: In what ways are you an effective servant of your team? In what ways do you struggle? Seek out an opportunity to quietly serve someone on your team, and take note of the results.

GOD'S PROMISE TO LEADERS

A man's heart plans his way,
But the LORD directs his steps. . . .
He who heeds the word wisely will find good,
And whoever trusts in the LORD, happy is he.

PROVERBS 16:9, 20

A LEADER'S PROMISE TO THE TEAM

ALTHOUGH I VALUE EVERYONE'S OPINION, I WILL GIVE EXTRA CONSIDERATION TO THOSE WHO HAVE PROVEN THEMSELVES TO BE WISE, RELIABLE, AND COMMITTED TO THE WELLBEING OF OUR TEAM AND OUR MISSION.

WEEK 26

GOOD ADVICE CAN MAKE YOU GREAT

Blessed is the man who walks not in the counsel of the ungodly, nor stands in the path of sinners, nor sits in the seat of the scornful; But his delight is in the law of the Lord, and in His law he meditates day and night. He shall be like a tree planted by the rivers of water, that brings forth its fruit in its season, whose leaf also shall not wither; And whatever he does shall prosper.

PSALM 1:1–3

The brilliant first psalm contrasts the righteous and the wicked. Leaders, take note, because the difference between the two seems to be where they get their counsel! Observe how a foolish leader can be led astray by a corrupt inner circle.

1. The leader begins to browse for the wrong counsel.
2. The leader begins to listen to the wrong voices.
3. The leader joins the wrong inner circle.

A wise leader meditates on God's Word day and night. Note the results of receiving counsel from the right inner circle.

1. Stability
2. Inward nourishment and refreshment
3. Fruitfulness and productivity
4. Strength and durability
5. Success

The Maxwell Leadership Bible

YOUR ADVISORS WILL MAKE OR BREAK YOU

Every leader ought to build an inner circle that adds value to him or her and to the leadership of the organization. But choose well, for the members of this inner circle will become your closest confidantes; your inner circle will make you or break you. So who belongs in the "council" in this inner circle? Strive for the following:

Creative people
Loyal people
People who share your vision
Wise and intelligent people
People with complementary gifts
People with influence
People of faith
People of integrity

The Maxwell Leadership Bible

Where does God fit in? Leaders and organizations constantly make plans. Yet Isaiah issues a warning to every leader who develops plans without consulting God's design (Isaiah 30:1–5). Leaders must remember just how tentative strategic plans need to be. No one knows the future except God. Keep in mind the following equation as you plan:

Our Preparation + God's Providence = Success

Leaders must constantly ask if their plans fit God's revealed will for them and their organization. Then they must ask if their plans remain relevant to the needs of their mission, their values, their vision, and their long–range objectives. Finally, they need to ask if their plans fit the needs of their culture and time.

The Maxwell Leadership Bible

The Priority of God's Word

The longest chapter in the Bible is a song about the priority of the Word of God. For 176 verses, Psalm 119 holds high the words and wisdom of God and convinces us to treasure it more than anything else in life.

Why is this so crucial for us? Leaders in our world face two realities:

1. Change happens faster than ever, so leaders must remain adaptable.

2. We need timeless values more than ever, so leaders must remain principle driven.

Consider what Psalm 119 teaches about God's Word as our source for leadership principles. Our leadership will . . .

be blessed.
remain pure and ethical.
be strengthened and revitalized.
insightfully answer criticism.
enjoy liberty.
gain wise counsel when needed.
remain steady even when afflicted.
be enlightened, intuitive.
have a reliable guide.

The Maxwell Leadership Bible

This Week: Consider the members of your team. Whose counsel do you trust? Why? Consider your superiors? Do you trust all of them? Why or why not? Do your advisors know how you esteem them? In what areas could you use more or better counselors? Are you a good advisor for others? Remember, "Where there is no counsel, the people fall; but in the multitude of counselors there is safety" (Proverbs 11:14).

GOD'S PROMISE TO LEADERS

Blessed is the man who trusts in the LORD,
And whose hope is the LORD.
For he shall be like a tree planted by the waters,
Which spreads out its roots by the river,
And will not fear when heat comes;
But its leaf will be green,
And will not be anxious in the year of drought,
Nor will cease from yielding fruit.

JEREMIAH 17:7–8

A LEADER'S PROMISE TO THE TEAM

I WILL CONTINUALLY GROW MY LEADERSHIP SKILLS IN ORDER TO BETTER SERVE OUR TEAM AND OUR CUSTOMERS.

WEEK 27

GROWTH STARTS WITH THE LEADER

So when Peter saw it, he responded to the people . . . Many of those who heard the word believed; and the number of the men came to be about five thousand.

ACTS 3:12, 4:4

A company cannot grow without, until its leaders grow within. I often am amazed at the money, energy, and marketing that organizations focus on areas that will not produce growth. Slick brochures and catchy slogans will never overcome incompetent leadership.

In 1981 I became senior pastor of a church whose attendance was obviously on a plateau. When I called my first staff meeting, I drew a line across a marker board and wrote the number "1,000." I shared that although I knew the staff could lead one thousand people effectively, I did not know whether they could lead two thousand people. When the leaders changed positively, I knew the growth would become automatic. First, though, I had to help them change themselves.

The strength of any organization is a direct result of the strength of its leaders.

Weak leaders = weak organizations.

Strong leaders = strong organizations.

Everything rises and falls on leadership.

Developing the Leaders Around You

Sharp Focus Sharpens Leadership

What does it take to have the focus required to be a truly effective leader? The keys are priorities and concentration. To focus your time and energy use these guidelines to help you:

Focus 70 percent on developing strengths. Effective leaders who reach their potential spend more time focusing on what they do well than on what they do wrong.

Focus 25 percent on new things. If you want to get better, you have to keep changing and improving. That means stepping out into new areas. If you dedicate time to new things related to your strength areas, then you'll grow as a leader.

Focus 5 percent on areas of weakness. Nobody can entirely avoid working in areas of weakness. The key is to minimize it as much as possible, and leaders can do it by delegating.

The 21 Indispensable Qualities of a Leader

Encourage others' strengths. If you start trying to help your people grow by correcting their weaknesses, you will demoralize them and unintentionally sabotage the enlarging process. Instead, give your attention to people's strengths. Sharpen skills that already exist. Compliment positive qualities. Bring out the gifts inherent in them. Weaknesses can wait unless they are character flaws. Only after you have developed a strong rapport with the person and they have begun to grow and gain confidence should you address areas of weakness. And then those should be handled gently and one at a time.

Becoming a Person of Influence

Growth = Change

Be transformed by the renewing of your mind.

Romans 12:2

Change is hard for most people, but growth is impossible without change. Most people fight against change, especially when it affects them personally. As novelist Leo Tolstoy said, "Everyone thinks of changing the world, but no one thinks of changing himself."

Change is inevitable. Everybody has to deal with it in their lives. On the other hand, growth is optional. You can choose to grow or to fight it. But know this: people unwilling to grow will never reach their potential.

Making the change from being an occasional learner to someone dedicated to personal growth is tough. It goes against the grain of the way most people live. Most people celebrate when they receive their diploma or degree and say to themselves, "Thank goodness that's over. I'm done with studying." But that kind of thinking doesn't take you any higher than average.

Your Road Map for Success

THIS WEEK: Reflect on who you are and face your flaws. You can reach your potential tomorrow if you dedicate yourself to growth today. Remember, to change your world, you must first change yourself. To do that:

1. See yourself clearly.
2. Admit your flaws honestly.
3. Discover your strengths joyfully.
4. Build on those strengths passionately.

Failing Forward

GOD'S PROMISE TO LEADERS

I will instruct you and teach you
in the way you should go;
I will guide you with My eye.

PSALM 32:8

A LEADER'S PROMISE TO THE TEAM

I KNOW WHERE WE NEED TO GO,
AND I CAN GET US THERE.
THIS IS OUR PATH.

WEEK 28

IDENTIFY THE VISION

Where there is no vision, the people perish.

PROVERBS 29:18 (KJV)

Have you ever been part of a team that didn't seem to make any progress? Maybe the group had plenty of talent, resources, and opportunities, and team members got along, but the group just never went anywhere. There's a strong possibility that the situation was caused by lack of vision.

Great vision precedes great achievement. Every team needs a compelling vision to give it direction. If a team doesn't have one, then the group is liable to suffer the fate expressed by baseball Hall-of-Famer Yogi Berra: "You've got to be very careful if you don't know where you're going, because you might not get there." A team without vision is, at worst, purposeless. At best, it is subject to the personal—and sometimes selfish—agendas of various teammates. As those agendas work against each other, it saps the team's energy and drive. On the other hand, a team that embraces a vision becomes focused, energized, and confident. It knows where it's headed and why it's going there.

If you lead your team, then you are responsible for identifying a worthy and compelling vision and articulating it to your team members.

The 17 Indisputable Laws of Teamwork

Leading the Leader

Vision is indispensable. It leads the leaders. It paints the targets, sparks and fuels the fire within, and draws them forward. And it is also the fire–lighter for others who follow those leaders. Show me a leader without vision, and I'll show you someone who isn't going anywhere. To get a handle on vision, understand these things:

1. *Vision starts within.* If you lack vision, draw on your calling and your natural gifts and desires. If you still don't sense a vision of your own, then consider partnering with a leader whose vision resonates with you.

2. *Vision draws on your history.* Vision isn't some mystical quality that comes out of a vacuum. It grows out of your past and the history of the people around you.

3. *Vision meets others' needs.* True vision goes beyond what one individual can accomplish. It also does more than just include others; it adds value to them. If your vision doesn't serve others, it's probably too small.

4. *Vision helps you gather resources.* Vision acts like a magnet. It attracts, challenges, and unites people. It also rallies finances and other resources. The greater the vision, the more winners it has the potential to attract. The more challenging the vision, the harder the participants fight to achieve it.

The 21 Indispensable Qualities of a Leader

Know the way, then show the way. Leaders do more than control the direction in which they and their people travel. They see the whole trip in their minds before they set forth. Leaders see *farther* than others see, *more* than others see, and *before* others see.

The Maxwell Leadership Bible

Let These Voices Guide Your Vision

The Inner Voice. What's your mission? What stirs your heart? If what you're pursuing in life doesn't come from within, you will not be able to accomplish it.

The Unhappy Voice. Discontent with the status quo is a great catalyst for vision. Are you on complacent cruise control? Or do you itch to change your world?

The Successful Voice. Nobody can accomplish great things alone. To fulfill a big vision, you need a good team. But you also need good advice from someone who is ahead of you in the leadership journey. If you want to lead others to greatness, find a good mentor.

The Higher Voice. A truly valuable vision must have God in it. Only He knows what you're really capable of. Have you looked beyond yourself, even beyond your own lifetime as you've sought your vision? If not, you may be missing your true potential and life's best for you.

The 21 Indispensable Qualities of a Leader

This Week: Draw a "map" of where your team is, where you've been, and where you're going. Note some of the mountains, valleys, deserts, and rivers you've encountered. Does your team know the history of the journey? Are they clear about where you're going and what challenges await?

GOD'S PROMISE TO LEADERS

I have taught you in the way of wisdom;
I have led you in right paths.
When you walk, your steps will not be hindered,
And when you run, you will not stumble.
Take firm hold of instruction, do not let go;
Keep her, for she is your life.

PROVERBS 4:11–13

A LEADER'S PROMISE TO THE TEAM

OUR JOURNEY TOGETHER WILL HAVE DIFFICULT TIMES, BUT I WILL STAY ON A PATH OF ONGOING GROWTH TO HELP US MEET THE CHALLENGES AHEAD.

WEEK 29

KEEP IMPROVING

Everyone who competes in the games goes into strict training.

1 CORINTHIANS 9:25 (NIV)

We live in a society with destination disease. Too many people want to do enough to "arrive," and then they want to retire. My friend Kevin Myers says it this way: "Everyone is looking for a quick fix, but what they really need is fitness. People who look for fixes stop doing what's right when pressure is relieved. People who pursue fitness do what they should no matter what the circumstances are." People who are constantly improving themselves make three processes an ongoing cycle in their lives.

1. *Preparation.* When individuals are intentional about learning something every day, then they become better prepared to handle whatever challenges they meet.

2. *Contemplation.* Time alone is essential to self–improvement. It allows you to gain perspective on your failures and successes so that you can learn from them. It gives you the time and space to sharpen your personal or organizational vision. And it enables you to plan how you can improve in the future.

3. *Application.* Musician Bruce Springsteen said, "A time comes when you need to stop waiting for the man you want to become and start being the man you want to be." In other words, you need to apply what you've learned.

The 17 Essential Qualities of a Team Player

Leaders are Learners

A wise man will hear and increase learning.

Proverbs 1:5

If you continually invest in your leadership development, the inevitable result is growth over time. Although it's true that some people are born with greater natural gifts than others, the ability to lead is really a collection of skills, nearly all of which can be learned and improved. But that process doesn't happen overnight. Leadership is complicated. It has many facets: respect, experience, emotional strength, people skills, discipline, vision, momentum, timing—the list goes on. That's why leaders require so much seasoning to be effective.

Successful leaders are learners. And the learning process is ongoing, a result of self–discipline and perseverance. The goal each day must be to get a little better, to build on the previous day's progress.

The 21 Irrefutable Laws of Leadership

When Naaman sought Elisha's help in curing his leprosy, Elisha's response enraged Naaman (2 Kings 5:11). He struggled with pride, faulty expectations, and inflexibility. Yet as a strong leader, Naaman had surrounded himself with individuals who could speak up and disagree with him, and his inner circle provided good counsel. Naaman changed his mind, followed the prophet's directives, and was healed. Leaders who remain teachable receive ongoing blessings.

The Maxwell Leadership Bible

Lift Your Lid

When good people run things, everyone is glad,
but when the ruler is bad, everyone groans.

Proverbs 29:2 (Msg)

Success is within the reach of just about everyone. But personal success without leadership ability brings only limited effectiveness. A person's impact is only a fraction of what it could be with good leadership. The higher you want to climb, the more you need leadership. The greater the impact you want to make, the greater your influence needs to be. Whatever you will accomplish is restricted by your ability to lead others.

Leadership ability is the lid that determines a person's level of effectiveness. The lower a person's ability to lead, the lower the lid on his potential. The higher the leadership, the greater the effectiveness. Your leadership ability—for better or for worse—always determines your effectiveness and the potential impact of your organization. To reach the highest level of effectiveness, you have to raise the lid on your leadership ability. The good news is that you can—if you're willing to pay the price to change.

The 21 Irrefutable Laws of Leadership

This Week: Evaluate your personal growth journey. Do you have a strategic plan or are you just learning whatever comes your way? List three ways you want to grow, and then list three possible ways to facilitate each growth goal. Are you encouraging your team members to grow strategically?

GOD'S PROMISE TO LEADERS

So know that the LORD your God is God, the faithful God. He will keep his agreement of love for a thousand lifetimes for people who love him and obey his commands.

DEUTERONOMY 7:9 (NCV)

A LEADER'S PROMISE TO THE TEAM

I'M COMMITTED TO THE SUCCESSFUL FULFILLMENT OF OUR STATED MISSION. WORK WITH ME, AND WE'LL GET IT DONE RIGHT.

WEEK 30

KEEP YOUR COMMITMENTS

And it happened, when all our enemies heard of it, and all the nations around us saw these things, that they were very disheartened in their own eyes; for they perceived that this work was done by our God.

Nehemiah 6:16

Commitment comes before anything else in a leader's life. Because Nehemiah had it and drew it out of others, the people finished the wall in fifty–three days, despite much adversity. Their great accomplishment so thrilled Nehemiah that he wrote, "When all our enemies heard of it, and all the nations around us saw these things . . . they were very disheartened in their own eyes; for they perceived that this work was done by our God."

Leaders who complete a task possess these characteristics:

Compelling purpose. They make a great commitment to a great cause.

Clear perspective. They don't let fear cloud their view of the future.

Continual prayer. They pray about everything and gain God's favor.

Courageous persistence. They move ahead despite the odds.

If you're facing a God–sized challenge, cultivate these characteristics to give yourself the best opportunity for success.

The Maxwell Leadership Bible

Commitment Precedes Resources

But Ruth said: "Entreat me not to leave you,
Or to turn back from following after you;
For wherever you go, I will go; And wherever you lodge,
I will lodge; Your people shall be my people,
And your God, my God."

Ruth 1:16

While every leader needs financial and human resources to reach his or her goals, commitment should always precede those resources. When a leader demonstrates a commitment to the mission and goals of the organization, then God moves and a whole stream of events begin to flow.

In the very first chapter of the book that bears her name, Ruth chooses to stay with Naomi, her mother–in–law, even after she loses her husband. She didn't know it, but her commitment would lead to all kinds of open doors. Ruth finds work during a difficult time, makes friends in a foreign land, and eventually gains a new husband, Boaz. Most impressively, God includes her—a Moabite adopted into the family of Israel—in the line of Christ. The child she bore became part of the lineage of the Messiah.

The key? Commitment. Once a leader definitely commits, God moves and all manner of unforeseen incidents, meetings, persons, and material assistance begin to stream forth.

The Maxwell Leadership Bible

Go the Distance

Genesis 11:31 tells us that Abraham's father, Terah, set out for Canaan from Ur of the Chaldeans long before Abraham made a similar trip. But for some reason, Terah stopped in Haran and never continued his journey. Did Terah receive an original call from God . . . but neglect to follow through? We don't know.

We do know that Abraham never made such a mistake. Although he made other leadership errors, Abraham always seemed to follow through on his commitments. When God called him to depart to an unknown land, he went the distance. When enemies abducted Lot and his goods, Abraham pursued the kidnappers and subdued them (Genesis 14:14–16). When commanded to circumcise the males of his household, Abraham did it that very day (Genesis 17:23). And when God asked Abraham to sacrifice his beloved son, Isaac, only a last-second angelic intervention spared the young man's life (Genesis 22:1–9). No wonder that God, the Ultimate Leader, called Abraham "My friend" (Isaiah 41:8)!

The Maxwell Leadership Bible

This Week: List some of your commitments at work, at home, and in the community. Are you going the distance in all of them? Which commitments do you wish you could drop or change? Is your team confident in your commitment to them and to your mission? What are the boundaries of your commitments?

GOD'S PROMISE TO LEADERS

Let heaven fill your thoughts. Do not think only about things down here on earth. For you died when Christ died, and your real life is hidden with Christ in God. And when Christ, who is your real life, is revealed to the whole world, you will share in all his glory.

COLOSSIANS 3:2–4 (NLT)

A LEADER'S PROMISE TO THE TEAM

I WILL ASK QUESTIONS, SEEK ANSWERS, AND KNOCK ON ALL DOORS UNTIL I'M CONFIDENT THAT WE'RE PURSUING THE RIGHT PURPOSE.

WEEK 31

KNOW YOUR PURPOSE

For we are His workmanship, created in Christ Jesus for good works, which God prepared beforehand that we should walk in them.

EPHESIANS 2:10

Nothing in life can take the place of knowing your purpose. If you don't try to discover your purpose, you're likely to spend your life doing the wrong things.

I believe that God created every person for a purpose. As psychologist Viktor Frankl said, "Everyone has his own specific vocation or mission in life. . . . Thus everyone's task is as unique as his specific opportunity to implement it." Each of us has a purpose for which we were created. Our responsibility—and our joy—is to identify it.

Here are some questions to ask yourself to help you identify your purpose:

For what am I searching? All of us have a strong desire set in our hearts, something that speaks to our deepest thoughts and feelings, something that sets our souls on fire.

Why was I created? Think about the unique mix of abilities you have, the resources available to you, your own personal history, and the opportunities around you.

Do I believe in my potential? No one can consistently act in a manner inconsistent with the way he sees himself.

When do I start? The answer to that question is "NOW."

Your Road Map for Success

The Power of Purpose

The apostle Paul might have been forgiven had he chosen to take a little sabbatical as he sat in prison, awaiting his trial. Yet he used even this opportunity to advance the gospel (Philippians 1:12–14). Paul was a leader who never drifted from his mission. He determined to leave his mark wherever he went.

How did Paul's sense of purpose keep him in the battle as he sat in prison? What did he learn behind bars? Consider the following:

A purpose will motivate you.

A purpose will keep your priorities straight.

A purpose will develop your potential.

A purpose will give you power to live in the present.

A purpose will help you evaluate your progress.

The Maxwell Leadership Bible

Seek God, then ask these questions. Most people can prioritize when faced with right or wrong issues. The challenge arises when we are faced with two good choices. If you're having trouble deciding between two good things, then look at these suggestions.

Ask your overseer or coworkers their preference.

Can one of the options be handled by someone else?

Which option would be of greater benefit to the customer?

Make your decision based on the purpose of the organization.

Developing the Leader Within You

Trading For Something Greater

Poet Rudyard Kipling said, "If you don't get what you want, it is a sign either that you did not seriously want it, or that you tried to bargain over the price." How badly do you want to reach your potential and fulfill your purpose in life? It will take passion on your part to keep growing, learning, and trading up.

Over the years I've found that you have to make tradeoffs throughout life in order to succeed, and only through wise exchanges can you reach your potential.

The problem of many unsuccessful people is that they haven't worked to develop much in their lives worth trading. You can only make a trade when you've got something worth giving up. And when you do trade, you don't trade from the lowest level to the highest, skipping over all the levels in between. Usually you're only able to move one level at a time—either up or down.

Your Road Map for Success

This Week: Meditate on Revelation 12:12–13: "And behold, I am coming quickly, and My reward is with Me, to give to every one according to his work. I am the Alpha and the Omega, the Beginning and the End, the First and the Last." What does this say about how God wants us to prioritize Him? Is He in every part of your life? In other words, does your priority list read like this: God and family, God and job, God and church, God and community, and so forth?

GOD'S PROMISE TO LEADERS

There is going to come a time of testing at the judgment day to see what kind of work each builder has done. Everyone's work will be put through the fire to see whether or not it keeps its value. If the work survives the fire, that builder will receive a reward. But if the work is burned up, the builder will suffer great loss. The builders themselves will be saved, but like someone escaping through a wall of flames.

1 Corinthians 3:13–15 (NLT)

A LEADER'S PROMISE TO THE TEAM

I WILL VALUE YOU AS PEOPLE, PRAISE YOUR EFFORTS, AND REWARD YOU BASED ON YOUR PERFORMANCE.

WEEK 32

LEAD FROM THE INSIDE OUT

So he shepherded them according to the integrity of his heart, and guided them by the skillfulness of his hands.

PSALM 78:72

David's leadership succeeded through a two-sided coin: his outward skill and his inward integrity. Every great leader must have this combination. Leaders must . . .

1. Value excellence.
2. Not settle for average.
3. Pay attention to detail.
4. Remain committed to what really matters.
5. Display integrity and sound ethics.
6. Show genuine respect for others.
7. Go the second mile.
8. Demonstrate consistency.
9. Never stop improving
10. Always give 100%.
11. Make excellence a lifestyle.

The first person you lead is you—and you can't lead effectively without self-discipline. Leaders must . . .

1. Develop and follow your priorities.

2. Challenge your excuses.

3. Remove rewards until you finish the job.

4. Stay focused on results, and never trade what you want at the moment for what you want most.

The Maxwell Leadership Bible

Competence Doesn't Compensate for Insecurity

So from that time on Saul kept a jealous eye on David.

1 Samuel 18:9 (NLT)

Insecure leaders are dangerous—to themselves, their followers, and the organizations they lead. That's because a leadership position becomes an amplifier of personal flaws. Whatever negative baggage you have in life only gets heavier when you're trying to lead others.

Unsure leaders have several common traits:

1. *They don't provide security for others.* To become an effective leader, you need to make your followers feel good about themselves.

2. *They take more from people than they give.* Insecure people are on a continual quest for validation, acknowledgment, and love. Because of that, their focus is on finding security, not instilling it in others.

3. *They continually limit their best people.* Show me an insecure leader, and I'll show you someone who cannot genuinely celebrate victories. The leader might even take credit personally for the best work of the team.

4. *They continually limit their organization.* When followers are undermined and receive no recognition, they become discouraged and eventually stop performing at their potential. And when that happens, the entire organization suffers.

The 21 Indispensable Qualities of a Leader

Love People, Reward Performance

"Well done, good and faithful servant; you have been faithful over a few things, I will make you ruler over many things. Enter into the joy of your lord."

Matthew 25:23

Educators in the United States have been seeking ways to increase students' test scores. One popular theory states that the best way to improve children's ability is to puff up their self–esteem because high achievers tend to have high self–esteem. However, researchers have found that simply building children's egos breeds many negative traits: indifference to excellence, inability to overcome adversity, and aggressiveness toward people who criticize them.

Now, I place high value on praising people, especially children. But I also believe that you have to base your praise on truth. Here's the approach I use to encourage and lead others:

Value people. Praise effort. Reward performance.

I use that method with everyone, including myself.

Failing Forward

This Week: Do you have clearly defined standards of excellence for you and your team? Does everyone understand what those standards are? How well are you meeting those standards? In what ways are you struggling? What can you as a leader do to improve performance? What does your team think?

GOD'S PROMISE TO LEADERS

Have I not commanded you?
Be strong and of good courage;
do not be afraid, nor be dismayed, for the LORD
your God is with you wherever you go.

JOSHUA 1:9

A LEADER'S PROMISE TO THE TEAM

I KNOW THE DANGERS ALONG OUR PATH,
AND I KNOW WE CAN OVERCOME THEM.

WEEK 33

LEAD WITH COURAGE

"Be strong and of good courage . . ."

DEUTERONOMY 31:7

Whenever you see significant progress in an organization, it's because the leader made courageous decisions. The leadership position itself doesn't give people courage, but courage can give them a leadership position. As you approach the tough decisions that will challenge you, recognize these truths about courage:

1. Courage begins with an inward battle. Courage isn't an absence of fear; it's doing what you are afraid to do.

2. Courage is making things right, not just smoothing them over. Martin Luther King, Jr. said, "The ultimate measure of a man is not where he stands in moments of comfort and convenience, but where he stands at times of challenge and controversy."

3. Courage in a leader inspires commitment from followers. "Courage is contagious," says evangelist Billy Graham. "When a brave man takes a stand, the spines of others are stiffened."

4. Your life expands in proportion to your courage. Roman historian Tacitus said, "The desire for safety stands against every great and noble enterprise." But courage opens doors, and that's one of its most wonderful benefits.

The 21 Indispensable Qualities of a Leader

Where Is Your Confidence?

It's always a good idea to have a battle plan if you intend to lead an army into war. Moses possessed a plan for the army of Israel, a set of instructions that came straight from the very top (Deuteronomy 20:1). Imagine the confidence a field commander could instill in his troops knowing that he could not lose. That was just the kind of guarantee God gave Moses and the people of Israel. God assured them they had nothing to fear—as long as they remembered that He would remain with them always.

Christian leaders today can bank on the same promise that gave Moses such courage: "For the Lord your God is He who goes with you, to fight for you against your enemies, to save you" (Deuteronomy 20:4). And so God gives us the same words He gave to Moses: "Do not be afraid."

Take the necessary risks. True leadership may mean standing alone and speaking difficult truth. The prophet Elijah knew this well as he prayed for judgment on his own people, confronted a wicked king, then challenged hundreds of false prophets. He risked his life to lead Israel back to God (1 Kings 18:37). Risks are tough for most people. This is why leaders must both model courage and call it forth from others.

The Maxwell Leadership Bible

Falling Short

Then Saul said to Samuel, "I have sinned, for I have transgressed the commandment of the Lord and your words, because I feared the people and obeyed their voice."

1 Samuel 15:24

King Saul never won the inward battles. When faced with a challenge he panicked. He lacked the courage necessary to lead the people of Israel.

Some lessons about courage we learn from Saul are that:

Courage and cowardice are both contagious. When Saul fled, so did his men.

Without courage, it doesn't matter how good your intentions are. Saul had good intentions when he presented burnt offerings to the Lord. But he let his fear that people would desert him control his actions.

Without courage, we're slaves of our own insecurity and possessiveness. Saul was captive to his fears of being replaced by David.

A leader without courage will never let go of the familiar. Saul employed a medium to ask counsel of Samuel's spirit.

Lack of courage will eventually sabotage a leader. Saul's lack of courage cost him everything.

The Maxwell Leadership Bible

This Week: Consider the risks before you. What does your team fear? What do you fear? How can you increase your courage and model it more for your team?

GOD'S PROMISE TO LEADERS

Now He who searches the hearts knows what the mind of the Spirit is, because He makes intercession for the saints according to the will of God. And we know that all things work together for good to those who love God, to those who are the called according to His purpose.

ROMANS 8:27–28

A LEADER'S PROMISE TO THE TEAM

I GENUINELY CARE ABOUT EVERYONE ON THIS TEAM AND ABOUT WHAT WE'RE ACCOMPLISHING TOGETHER.

WEEK 34

LEADERSHIP BEGINS IN THE HEART

No longer do I call you servants . . .
but I have called you friends.

JOHN 15:15

What can a person do to manage and cultivate good relationships as a leader? It requires three things:

1. *Understand people.* Marketing expert Rod Nichols says, "If you deal with every customer in the same way, you will only close 25 percent to 30 percent of your contacts, because you will only close one personality type. But if you learn how to effectively work with all four personality types, you can conceivably close 100 percent of your contacts."

2. *Love people.* Businessman Henry Gruland says, "Being a leader is more than just wanting to lead. Leaders have empathy for others and a keen ability to find the best in people . . . not the worst . . . by truly caring for others." You cannot be a truly effective leader unless you love people.

3. *Help people.* If your focus is on what you can put into people rather than what you can get out of them, they'll love and respect you—and those attributes are great foundations for building relationships.

The 21 Indispensable Qualities of a Leader

A Leader's Heart

The selection of David to be Israel's king illustrates how God often disregards human customs and traditions to accomplish His purposes (1 Samuel 16:7). God saw the heart of this young man and knew that His people needed a leader with a tenderness of spirit. David might have become a warrior, but gentleness was his defining trait. David's life illustrates that faithfulness in small things often results in much larger assignments and greater responsibility down the road. David loved the Lord and lived his life as a man after God's own heart.

Who you are precedes what you do. As Paul spoke to the Ephesians in Acts 20:22–24, he described the ingredients of an effective leader. Paul made tough calls, yet shed tears in front of his people. One thing is sure: Leadership begins with the heart. Paul had a heart that was . . .

Consistent. He lived steadily while moving among the people he led.

Contrite. He acted humbly and willingly showed his weakness.

Courageous. He didn't shrink from doing the right thing.

Convictional. He communicated his convictions boldly.

Committed. He left for Jerusalem, willing to die for Jesus.

Captivated. He showed that a surrendered man doesn't have to survive.

The Maxwell Leadership Bible

WHOLE–HEARTED DEVOTION

Whatever you do, work at it with all your heart, as working for the Lord, not for men.

COLOSSIANS 3:23 (NIV)

Experts spend a lot of time trying to figure out what makes people successful, and more than anything else, passion is what makes the difference.

Take a look at four truths about passion and what it can do for you as a leader:

1. *Passion is the first step to achievement.* Your desire determines your destiny. The stronger your fire, the greater the desire—and the greater the potential.

2. *Passion increases your willpower.* There is no substitute for passion. It is fuel for the will. If you want anything badly enough, you can find the willpower to achieve it.

3. *Passion changes you.* If you follow your passion you can't help but become a more dedicated, productive person. In the end, your passion will have more influence than your personality.

4. *Passion makes the impossible possible.* Human beings are so made that whenever anything fires their soul, impossibilities vanish. A fire in the heart lifts everything in your life A leader with great passion and few skills always outperforms a leader with great skills and no passion.

The 21 Indispensable Qualities of a Leader

THIS WEEK: Give your heart a checkup. About what are you passionate? Is your heart consistent, contrite, courageous, convictional, committed, and captivated?

GOD'S PROMISE TO LEADERS

Therefore, LORD God of Israel, now keep what You promised Your servant David my father, saying, "You shall not fail to have a man sit before Me on the throne of Israel, only if your sons take heed to their way, that they walk in My law as you have walked before Me."

2 CHRONICLES 6:16

A LEADER'S PROMISE TO THE TEAM

I WILL HELP PREPARE OTHER LEADERS TO RISE TO NEW LEVELS OF RESPONSIBILITY AND INFLUENCE.

WEEK 35

LEAVE A LEADERSHIP LEGACY

And the LORD said to Moses: "Take Joshua the son of Nun with you, a man in whom is the Spirit, and lay your hand on him; set him before Eleazar the priest and before all the congregation, and inaugurate him in their sight. And you shall give some of your authority to him, that all the congregation of the children of Israel may be obedient.

NUMBERS 27:18–20

Of all the wonderful ways Moses expressed his leadership, the most strategic had to be his training of Joshua. Moses passed along his authority, abilities, and anointing to Joshua. He gave Joshua his time, his insight, a learning environment, an opportunity to prove himself, and a strong belief in his future.

The interaction of Moses and Joshua demonstrates that reproducing leaders is not a quick, simple process. It requires time, emotional investment, and sacrifice.

When you begin developing the next generation of leaders, recognize that your protégés will need certain things:

1. From themselves: Conviction, courage, and obedience
2. From their mentor: Equipping
3. From God: Vision
4. From the people: Buy–In

With time, investment, and sacrifice, you will build a legacy of leadership.

The Maxwell Leadership Bible

Leave More than an Inheritance

A huge difference exists between a legacy and an inheritance. Anyone can leave an inheritance. An inheritance is something you leave to your family or loved ones. (It also fades.) A legacy is something you leave in your family and loved ones. Consider these differences:

Inheritance	Legacy
1. Something you give to others	1. Something you place in others
2. Temporarily brings them happiness	2. Permanently transforms them
3. Eventually fades as it is spent	3. Lives on long after you die
4. Your activity may or may not pay off	4. Your activity becomes achievement

The Maxwell Leadership Bible

You reap what you sow. In trying to encourage the Corinthian church to give generously, the apostle Paul instructs the church to view its resources as a farmer views his sowing seed (2 Corinthians 9:10–11). You can't harvest what you haven't planted. Some leaders, like the Corinthians, find it hard to invest resources because they fear their commodities will run out. Good leaders see the same resources as sufficient seed to be sown—knowing the harvest will come and more will be created. We must guard against poverty; we should give our life because it is plentiful.

The Maxwell Leadership Bible

A House Divided

Saul's death led to all kinds of turmoil over who would become the next king. Despite David's anointing by Samuel, others saw a tempting opportunity to seize power (2 Samuel 2:10).

Transitions often bring difficult times. Leaders who fail to plan for their departure invite trouble. Saul could have been a hero had he cooperated with God in preparing David to succeed him. He didn't have a more submissive staff person in his entire palace than David. Saul could've helped himself had he recognized these truths:

1. Leaders must see ahead and prepare for change.

2. People can live without certainty, but not without clarity regarding future direction.

3. Wise choices today put "change in the pocket" of a leader regarding future choices.

4. Problem–solving skills and effective communication earn the leader trust and credibility.

The Maxwell Leadership Bible

This Week: Consider your leadership heritage. What legacies are you fulfilling? Read the first nine chapters of 1 Chronicles to see a genealogy of Israel's leaders. How can you apply the following lessons from that lineage to your life?

They remained connected to their heritage.
They gained perspective from their place in history.
They were able to honor their forefathers.
They saw their lineage as a family blessing.
They sensed tendencies of ancestral giftedness and calling.
They could retain their identity even when exiled.

The Maxwell Leadership Bible

GOD'S PROMISE TO LEADERS

Blessed is the man who listens to me,
Watching daily at my gates,
Waiting at the posts of my doors.
For whoever finds me finds life,
And obtains favor from the LORD.

PROVERBS 8:34–35

A LEADER'S PROMISE TO THE TEAM

YOU ARE IMPORTANT TO ME, TO THIS TEAM, AND TO OUR MISSION. I WANT TO HEAR WHAT YOU HAVE TO SAY. I WILL LISTEN.

WEEK 36

LISTEN UP

. . . and after the earthquake a fire, but the LORD was not in the fire; and after the fire a still small voice. So it was, when Elijah heard it."

1 KINGS 19:12–13

Someone once asked Joan of Arc why God spoke only to her. She responded, "Sir, you are wrong. God speaks to everyone. I just listen."

When God spoke to Samuel, it was as the boy lay down quietly in the middle of the night. Even then, Samuel did not at first recognize that the voice belonged to God. He needed the wisdom of his experienced mentor, Eli, to understand who was communicating with him. But based on how often Samuel heard God's voice as an adult, it's clear that he did learn to identify, listen to, and obey God's voice.

Leaders are often very busy people. And they can easily get caught up in the activity of their obligations. If you're a leader, that's why it's important to set aside times to quiet yourself and listen for God's direction.

The 21 Most Powerful Minutes in a Leader's Day

When a Leader Speaks

When somebody asks a question in a meeting, whom do people look to for the answer? This person is the real leader.

Identifying a real leader can be easy if you remember what you're looking for. Don't listen to the claims of the person professing to be the leader. Instead, observe the reactions of the people around him. The proof of leadership is found in the followers. People listen to what someone has to say not necessarily because of the message, but because of their respect for the messenger.

So I must ask you this: How do people react when you communicate? When you speak, do people really listen? Or do they wait to hear what someone else has to say before they act? You can find out a lot about your level of leadership if you have the courage to ask and answer that question.

The 21 Irrefutable Laws of Leadership

To communicate, listen. For one whole week, Job's friends just sat with him and listened (Job 2:11–13). They realized an important truth: People don't lose intimacy when they stop talking, but when they stop listening. Leaders seldom realize how much their listening empowers the other person. Because they are leaders, the sheer act of listening speaks volumes that even a great speech can't communicate.

The Maxwell Leadership Bible

Speak Up to Your Leader

Good leaders cultivate honest speech;
they love advisors who tell them the truth.

Proverbs 16:13 (Msg)

Good team leaders never want yes–men. They need direct and honest communication from their people. I have always encouraged people on my team to speak openly and directly with me. Our meetings are often brainstorming sessions where the best idea wins. Often, a team member's remarks or observations really help the team. Sometimes we disagree. That's okay, because we've developed strong enough relationships that we can survive conflict. Getting everything out on the table always improves the team. The one thing I never want to hear from a teammate is, "I could have told you that wouldn't work." If you know it beforehand, that's the time to say it.

Besides directness, the other quality team members need to display when communicating with their leaders is respect. Leading a team isn't easy. It requires making tough and sometimes unpopular decisions. We should respect the people who take on leadership roles and show them loyalty.

The 17 Indisputable Laws of Teamwork

This Week: Take the time to listen—really listen—to several of your key team members. If they're not coming to you, ask them questions about something. Then ask yourself why they weren't coming to you in the first place. Are you a good listener? Do people really listen to you in meetings or do they listen more to someone else?

GOD'S PROMISE TO LEADERS

But those who wait on the LORD
Shall renew their strength;
They shall mount up with wings like eagles,
They shall run and not be weary,
They shall walk and not faint.

ISAIAH 40:31

A LEADER'S PROMISE TO THE TEAM

I WILL MANAGE MY TIME
TO THE BEST OF MY ABILITY.
I WILL ENDEAVOR TO MAKE DECISIONS
TO BEST BENEFIT THE TEAM.

WEEK 37

MAKE THE MOST OF YOUR TIME

Lord, make me to know my end, and what is the measure of my days, that I may know how frail I am. Indeed, You have made my days as handbreadths, and my age is as nothing before You; certainly every man at his best state is but vapor.

Psalm 39:4–5

In Psalm 90, David shows his mindfulness of his brief time on earth. He asks God to help him number his days, which ought to be the prayer of every leader. Wise leaders work to redeem the time they have.

A leader needs to wonder if the task is worth the time investment. What would happen if the leader wasn't the one doing it? Is there someone else who could do it just as well, and for whom the task would be time better spent? A good leader knows that time is like gold, and good "spending habits" are essential. It's just that in this case the units are minutes, not dollars.

If you don't know where your time goes—that's a danger signal. If you can save small bits of time and consolidate them into a chunk of time that can be spent on something worthwhile—that's like "found money." If leaders can number their minutes and hours, "numbering their days" will be easier.

The Maxwell Leadership Bible

Do the Right Thing at the Right Time

Good leaders understand that timing is everything. Nehemiah began praying about the ruined wall in December, but not until April did he approach the king about rebuilding them. What was he waiting on?

No one knows for sure, but Nehemiah might well have been waiting on . . .

1. His ownership of the vision and burden.
2. A foundation of prayer to be laid.
3. His own readiness with a plan.
4. The king's mental and emotional mood.
5. The season when he could move quickly.
6. A trust to deepen between him and the king.

Moses felt weary of the complaining, the stagnation, and the lack of progress among his people. He was running on empty. And in his weakened condition he made a decision that cost him his future in the Promised Land (Numbers 20:12). This sad incident teaches us at least two lessons. First, never make a major decision during an emotionally low time. Second, choose to be proactive, not reactive, in your leadership. Get your cues from God and the mission He has given you. Ask yourself these questions:

1. Am I a reactor or a creator when I lead?
2. Do I play defense or offense when I lead?
3. Am I a people–pleaser or a God–pleaser when I lead?
4. Do I boss my calendar, or does someone else choose where I give my time?

The Maxwell Leadership Bible

Guard Against the Sluggard

The lazy man will not plow because of winter;
He will beg during harvest and have nothing.

Proverbs 20:4

King Solomon had plenty to say about the "sluggard," or the habitually lazy person. The sluggard's only commitment is to his leisure. He avoids honest labor. He contributes nothing to the world; instead, he just pillages some of its resources. When leaders become lazy and lose their diligence in doing good for God, they become spiritual sluggards and worthless to the kingdom.

Wise leaders know their time is limited. They know they have no way to retrieve misused or wasted time (John 9:4). Leaders in the body of Christ must remain diligent in doing good and in encouraging others to do likewise.

The Maxwell Leadership Bible

This Week: How do you know when to move in leadership? How does asking at the right time increase your chance for success? Read Ecclesiastes chapter 3, which begins with the famous line, "To everything there is a season . . . a time to be born, and a time to die." Consider also how that passage ends: "God shall judge the righteous and the wicked, for there is a time for every purpose and for every work" (v. 17). Is your use of time righteous or wicked?

GOD'S PROMISE TO LEADERS

Trust in the LORD, and do good;
Dwell in the land, and feed on His faithfulness.
Delight yourself also in the LORD,
And He shall give you the desires of your heart.

PSALM 37:3–4

A LEADER'S PROMISE TO THE TEAM

I WILL GUARD MY CHARACTER, TAKE RESPONSIBILITY FOR DECISIONS, AND CONSISTENTLY TRY TO DO THE RIGHT THING. I WON'T PRETEND TO BE PERFECT, BUT I WILL DEMONSTRATE THAT I AM RELIABLE AND WORTHY OF YOUR TRUST.

WEEK 38

PASS THE TRUST TEST

Among leaders who lack insight, abuse abounds,
but for one who hates corruption, the future is bright.

PROVERBS 28:16 (MSG)

People today are desperate for leaders, but they want to be influenced by someone they can trust, a person of good character. If you want to become someone who can positively influence other people:

Model consistency of character. Solid trust can only develop when people can trust you all the time

Employ honest communication. To be trustworthy, you have to be like a good musical composition: your words and music must match.

Value transparency. If you're honest with people and admit your weaknesses, they appreciate your honesty. And they are able to relate to you better.

Exemplify humility. People won't trust you if they see that you are driven by ego, jealousy, or the belief that you are better than they are.

Demonstrate your support of others. Nothing develops or displays your character better than your desire to put others first.

Fulfill your promises. One of the fastest ways to break trust with others is in failing to fulfill your commitments.

Becoming a Person of Influence

Accept the Responsibility of a Leader's Trust

A leader can delegate anything except responsibility. Leaders simply cannot give it away. They can model it; they can teach it; they can share it. But in the words of Harry Truman, the buck stops with the leader. Then especially in times of crisis, we find out the quality of our leadership.

1. *Dropouts* give up and fail to take responsibility.
2. *Cop–outs* make excuses for why they aren't responsible.
3. *Hold–outs* waiver too long to take responsibility.
4. *All–outs* own the responsibility and take action.

Be a good follower first. Before David became king, he showed respect for his predecessor (1 Samuel 26:9). Saul failed to practice this principle, and lost his kingdom. The Bible provides a vivid contrast between the leadership of Saul and David.

Saul	**David**
Was self–conscious from the beginning	Displayed God–confidence from the beginning
Presumed the priestly office	Didn't assume any right or privilege
Disobeyed God in the little things	Obeyed God in the little things
Lost integrity by covering his sin	Maintained integrity by respecting Saul
Failed to submit to God–given authority	Consistently submitted to authority
Was preoccupied with his own fame	Desired to increase God's reputation

The Maxwell Leadership Bible

Trust Buster

Samson learned the hard way that trust provides the foundation for all genuine leadership. This impetuous, volatile, lustful, moody, emotional, and unpredictable man provides a very good example of a very bad leader. Because no one could trust him, none followed his leadership (Judges 15:11–12).

Leaders who erode the solid ground of trustworthy leadership usually exhibit one or more of the following signs—Samson displayed them all. Leaders in trouble . . .

1. fail to address glaring character weaknesses.
2. count on deception to safeguard themselves.
3. act impulsively.
4. are overcome by an area of weakness.
5. misuse their God-given gifts.

Samson's self-centered, undisciplined, and arrogant nature made him an ineffective leader.

The Maxwell Leadership Bible

This Week: Consider the trustworthiness of the Ultimate Leader. God expects us to obey Him. Why? Because His Word not only keeps us clean—or holy—before Him, but it also protects us and qualifies us for greater blessings. The Father always knows what is best for us and for our relationship with Him. *"If you walk in My statutes and keep My commandments, and perform them, then I will give you rain in its season, the land shall yield its produce, and the trees of the field shall yield their fruit . . . I will walk among you and be your God, and you shall be My people"* (Leviticus 26:3, 4, 12).

GOD'S PROMISE TO LEADERS

I, the LORD, search the heart,
I test the mind,
Even to give every man according to his ways,
According to the fruit of his doings.

JEREMIAH 17:10

A LEADER'S PROMISE TO THE TEAM

I RECOGNIZE THAT THE SMALL MATTERS OF MY HEART CAN MAKE A BIG DIFFERENCE IN OUR SUCCESS OR FAILURE, SO I'M GUARDING MY HEART TO KEEP IT IN LINE WITH HIGH VALUES.

WEEK 39

PEOPLE WILL FOLLOW THE LEADER

He did evil in the sight of the LORD,
and walked in the way of Jeroboam, and in his sin
by which he had made Israel sin.

1 KINGS 15:34

Leadership ability is the lid on the success of a nation or organization. When Israel or Judah lived under good kings, things went well. Under bad kings, things went sour. The heart and skill of a leader will always tremendously affect the life of the people under his direction. This is a law, both timeless and universal. See how this law played out under the Hebrew kings of the Old Testament:

GOOD KINGS	**BAD KINGS**
1. Drew loyalty from their people	1. Drew rebellion from their people
2. Enjoyed victory over sin	2. Saw bondage to sin
3. Enjoyed peace within the kingdom	3. Suffered turmoil within the kingdom
4. Were affirmed by God's prophets	4. Were rebuked by God's prophets
5. Enjoyed prosperity	5. Often endured natural disasters and war
6. Opposed evil kings	6. Opposed good kings

The Maxwell Leadership Bible

Differences That Make a Difference

Why was David able to stand against Goliath when the army of Israel pulled back in fear? Because in the following ways, he differed from others:

1. *Perspective.* He saw an opportunity.

2. *Methods.* He decided to use proven weapons that he knew would work.

3. *Conviction.* He heard Goliath's threats against the God of Israel and knew God could beat him.

4. *Vision.* He wanted to make Yahweh known to the world as the most powerful God on earth.

5. *Experience.* He brought to the battlefield past victories over a lion and bear, not months of paralyzing fear.

6. *Attitude.* He saw Goliath not as a threat too big to hit, but a target too big to miss.

Deception, more often than mistakes, disqualifies leaders. David wrote Psalm 51 shortly after he committed adultery with Bathsheba and had Uriah killed (2 Samuel 11). When Nathan confronted him about his sin (2 Samuel 12), the king publicly sought restoration, so God allowed him to remain in office until he died. Leaders who do not repent after some failure—or who do so only for public show—often lose their positions. History teaches that people usually forgive a leader who owns up to his mistakes, but they refuse to forgive those who remain unrepentant.

The Maxwell Leadership Bible

Leadership in God's Economy

Some leaders step into positions of power out of love and a sense of mission. Others seek leadership merely to gain power over others and feel superior. Normally it doesn't take long to determine which sort of leader you've got. Leaders are not given authority in order to better themselves, enlarge their income or social status, or improve their standard of living. They are first and always servants of others. This idea appears throughout the Scripture.

Human Economy	God's Economy
1. Pursuit of power and prestige.	1. Pursuit of love and service to others.
2. Improve wealth and status of the leader.	2. Improve the welfare of the people.
3. See others as enemies and competitors.	3. See others as brothers who complement.
4. Motive is to remove or kill opposition.	4. Motive is to meet needs and grow the cause.
5. The result: the leader is glorified.	5. The result: God is glorified.

The Maxwell Leadership Bible

This Week: Reflect on your team. By looking at them, would you say you're a good king? How are you helping your team to be an army of Davids? Are you burdened by some deception? What's your "economic status" according to God?

GOD'S PROMISE FOR LEADERS

God is fair; he will not forget the work you did and the love you showed for him by helping his people. And he will remember that you are still helping them. We want each of you to go on with the same hard work all your lives so you will surely get what you hope for. We do not want you to become lazy. Be like those who through faith and patience will receive what God has promised.

HEBREWS 6:10–12 (NCV)

A LEADER'S PROMISE FOR THE TEAM

I WON'T JUST FOLLOW UP ON OUR MISSION;
I'LL FOLLOW THROUGH WITH IT
ALL THE WAY TO THE END,
AND I WILL HELP YOU DO THAT, TOO.

WEEK 40

PERSISTENCE PAYS OFF

And it happened, when our enemies heard that it was known to us, and that God had brought their plot to nothing, that all of us returned to the wall, everyone to his work.

NEHEMIAH 4:15

One of the great tests of leadership is how you handle opposition. Nehemiah faced the usual tactics of the opposition: ridicule, resistance, and rumor. Nehemiah modeled the right response to all three of these challenges by . . .

Relying on God.
Respecting the opposition.
Reinforcing his weak points.
Reassuring the people.
Refusing to quit.
Renewing the people's strength continually.

Nehemiah had to deal with problems from without—ridicule, resistance, and rumor—and within—disputes about food, property, and taxes.

Persistence is the ultimate gauge of our leadership; the secret is to outlast our critics. Nehemiah taught us this lesson by staying committed to his ultimate calling.

The Maxwell Leadership Bible

The Will to Do What's Right

Discipline is doing what you really don't want to do, so that you can do what you really want to do. It's paying the price in the little things so that you can buy the bigger thing. Disciplined leaders must possess . . .

1. *Disciplined Thinking.* Keep your mind active and regularly take on mental challenges to develop the kind of disciplined thinking that will help you with whatever you endeavor to do.

2. *Disciplined Emotions.* You must master your emotions or they'll master you. Don't let your feelings prevent you from doing what you should or drive you to do things you shouldn't.

3. *Disciplined Actions.* Action separates the winners from the losers. Your actions always reflect your degree of discipline.

The 17 Essential Qualities of a Team Player

Pay now, play later. When it comes to self–discipline, people choose one of two things—either they choose the pain of discipline, which comes from sacrifice and growth, or they choose the pain of regret, which comes from taking the easy road and missing opportunities. Each person in life chooses. Every person on the planet is given the same allotment of minutes in a day. But each person's level of self–discipline dictates how effectively those minutes are used. Disciplined people maximize the use of their time.

Developing the Leaders Around You

The Longest Way is a Short–Cut

One of the most common obstacles to success is the desire to cut corners. But shortcuts never pay off in the long run.

If you find that you continually give in to your moods or impulses, then you need to change your approach to doing things. Cutting corners is really a sign of impatience and poor self–discipline. But if you are willing to follow through, you can achieve a breakthrough. The best method is to set up standards for yourself that require accountability. Any time you suffer a consequence for not following through, it helps you stay on track. Once you have your standards in place, work according to them, not your moods. That will get you going in the right direction. Self–discipline is a quality that is won through practice

Failing Forward

This Week: Make a reasonable to–do list with goals for the week involving both your professional and your personal life. At the end of the week, check off what you actually accomplished. Why did some things happen and others not? Do you see areas where better discipline could help you accomplish more? What steps can you take to improve?

GOD'S PROMISE TO LEADERS

Blessed is the man You choose,
And cause to approach You,
That he may dwell in Your courts.
We shall be satisfied with the goodness of Your house,
Of Your holy temple.

PSALM 65:4

A LEADER'S PROMISE TO THE TEAM

I WILL NOT MAKE HASTY DECISIONS, BUT WILL CAREFULLY SELECT THE PEOPLE I INCLUDE ON OUR TEAM. I WILL CONSIDER THE TEAM'S NEEDS AND OPINIONS, NOT JUST MY OWN.

WEEK 41

PICK THE RIGHT PEOPLE

Therefore, brethren, seek out from among you seven men of good reputation, full of the Holy Spirit and wisdom, whom we may appoint over this business.

ACTS 6:3

Red Auerbach, long–time president of the Boston Celtics, said, "How you select people is more important than how you manage them once they're on the job. If you start with the right people, you won't have problems later on." You have to begin with the right raw materials in order to create a winning team.

I want each of the people close to me to . . .

Know my heart. This takes time for both of us and desire on their part.

Be loyal to me. They are an extension of me and my work.

Be trustworthy. They must not abuse authority, power, or confidences.

Be discerning. They make decisions for me.

Have a servant's heart. They carry a heavy load because of my high demands.

Be a good thinker. Our two heads are better than my one.

Be able to follow through. They take authority and carry out the vision.

Have a great heart for God. My heart for God is my driving force in life.

Developing the Leaders Around You

An Investment for the Future

Most people recognize that investing in a team brings benefits to everyone on the team. Here are ten steps you can take to invest in your team.

1. Decide to build a team.
2. Gather the best team possible.
3. Pay the price to develop the team.
4. Do things together as a team.
5. Empower team members with responsibility and authority.
6. Give credit for success to the team.
7. Watch to see that the investment in the team is paying off.
8. Stop your investment in players who do not grow.
9. Create new opportunities for the team.
10. Give the team the best possible chance to succeed.

One of the great things about investing in a team is that it almost guarantees a high return for the effort, because a team can do so much more than individuals. Or as Rex Murphy, one of my conference attendees, told me: "Where there's a will there's a way; where there's a team, there's more than one way."

The 17 Indisputable Laws of Leadership

Recruit people who seize opportunities. The best people to take with you on the leadership journey don't simply sit back and wait for opportunities to come to them. They make it their responsibility to go out and find them. Good potential leaders don't rely on luck. Of the people around you, who always seems able to recognize opportunities and grab hold of them?

Take Care of Those Closest to You

Just before the Passover Feast, Jesus knew that the time had come to leave this world to go to the Father. Having loved his dear companions, he continued to love them right to the end.

John 13:1 (Msg)

If you lead your team, you are responsible for making sure that better players are joining the team than are leaving. One of the ways you can facilitate that is to place high value on the good people you already have on the team. Every team has three groups of players.

Starters directly add value to the organization or directly influence its course.

Bench players add value to the organization indirectly or support the starters who do.

Inner–circle members are a core group within the starters, and without them the team would fall apart.

Your job is to make sure each group is continually developed so that bench players are able to step up to become starters, and starters are able to step up to become inner–circle members. If your treatment of key people doesn't match their value, you run the risk of losing them.

The 17 Indisputable Laws of Teamwork

This Week: Who are your starters, bench players, and inner–circle members? Are these people aware of their importance? Have you made any bad investments in adding to your team? What can you do to minimize the losses or even turn things around to post some gains? What benefits does each person bring to your team? What drawbacks?

GOD'S PROMISE TO LEADERS

Now if you walk before Me as your father David walked, in integrity of heart and in uprightness, to do according to all that I have commanded you, and if you keep My statutes and My judgments, then I will establish the throne of your kingdom over Israel forever, as I promised David your father, saying, "You shall not fail to have a man on the throne of Israel."

1 Kings 9:4–5

A LEADER'S PROMISE TO THE TEAM

I WILL TEACH MY SUCCESSORS WHAT I KNOW. LEADERSHIP DOES NOT END WITH ME.

WEEK 42

PREPARE YOUR SUCCESSOR

And everyone who was in distress, everyone who was in debt,
and everyone who was discontented gathered to [David].
So he became captain over them.
And there were about four hundred men with him.

1 SAMUEL 22:2

The men who David attracted while he fled from Saul eventually became like him. Some even killed giants as he did—showing that what you are is what you reproduce. Observe what David teaches us about his leadership:

1. David attracted men even without pursuing them.
2. David drew deep loyalty from them without ever trying to get it.
3. David transformed these men without disenchanting them over their initial state.
4. David fought alongside these men and turned them into winners.

Consider the astounding exploits of some of these men. Second Samuel 23:8 tells us that Adino slew 800 men with a spear in one battle (v. 8); Eleazar struck down the enemy until his hand clung to his sword (vv. 9, 10); Shammah defended a plot of ground against an enemy army (vv. 11, 12). David attracted men like him—souls in distress. He also reproduced men like him—warriors and conquerors.

The Maxwell Leadership Bible

Create a Climate for Developing Leaders

We can conclude from the list of warriors who joined David in Ziklag that his ragtag team was diverse, loyal, and hungry for victory (1 Chronicles 12:38). So what did David do to reproduce his leadership in them?

1. *He was relational.* David's approachable manner enticed hundreds of misfits to serve him. David accepted anyone.

2. *He was resourceful.* David made the best of every situation. He resourced his team to become all it could be and enabled it to succeed.

3. *He was rewarding.* David quickly shared both rewards and recognition for victory. He affirmed his men and motivated them with words of encouragement and spoils from battle.

4. *He was respectable.* David modeled a leadership style that others wanted to imitate. Friends and foes alike respected him.

A leader passes the baton. King David was determined to ensure his legacy by preparing the next leader, Solomon, and committing him to the care of God (1 Chronicles 28–29). Look closely at what he did:

1. He rallied all the people together.
2. He affirmed God's choice of his successor.
3. He identified the great need for help.
4. He reminded the people of his own commitment.
5. He declared that the people were well on their way to the goal.
6. He asked for commitment.

The Maxwell Leadership Bible

Leadership Transitions Can Be Tricky

Transitions in leadership often cause significant problems for groups and organizations.

Solomon had to make some tough but crucial leadership decisions at the beginning of his reign. First, he had to deal with men scheming for power—one of his own brothers, Adonijah, even tried to set up his own kingdom (1 Kings 1:5). One by one, King Solomon discerned the loyalties of his associates, then removed all who refused to cooperate with him.

Solomon knew he could never work with renegades, no matter how influential or strategic they might seem. The young king ensured that his inner circle would include only loyal men who wanted to work with him.

David had seen these troubles brewing on the horizon. He knew he was placing his successor in a precarious leadership situation, but he confidently declared that Solomon would know what to do. David understood that those closest to Solomon would greatly hinder or improve his level of success. Solomon understood the same thing—and wisely acted on it.

The Maxwell Leadership Bible

This Week: Has your predecessor or superior affirmed your leadership? How do you affirm your successors or other team members? Is your team prepared for transition?

GOD'S PROMISE TO LEADERS

Therefore do not worry, saying, "What shall we eat?" or "What shall we drink?" or "What shall we wear?" For after all these things the Gentiles seek. For your heavenly Father knows that you need all these things. But seek first the kingdom of God and His righteousness, and all these things shall be added to you.

MATTHEW 6:31–33

A LEADER'S PROMISE TO THE TEAM

I WILL NOT LET LESS–SIGNIFICANT DETAILS AND SITUATIONS GET IN THE WAY OF OUR ACCOMPLISHING OUR CHIEF PURPOSE.

WEEK 43

PRIORITIZE YOUR LIFE

I have finished the work which You have given Me to do.

John 17:4

When Peter was a young fisherman in Galilee, no one would have thought he was destined to become the passionate leader of a world movement. After all, he had almost no education and probably would have been happy to live the remainder of his life in obscurity. But God had something else in mind, and when Peter met Jesus, his priorities began to change.

Like many leaders, Peter had to learn how to put first things first. In fact, Scripture reveals a lot about the inconsistencies of his behavior and his many irrational decisions. But the more time Peter spent with Jesus, the more he learned the difference between mere activity and accomplishment.

Like Peter, great leaders sift through the many things that demand their time, and they discern not only what needs to be done first, but also what doesn't need to be done at all. That starts with a passion to excel. When you focus your passion on what's most important, your leadership climbs to new heights.

The 21 Most Powerful Minutes in a Leader's Day

When Your Priorities Are Right

Every leader must establish a list of priorities, then learn to put first things first. When Solomon became king of Israel, he was given the opportunity to ask God for anything (2 Chronicles 1:7–12). No doubt, King Solomon faced the same options we have today:

1. *Easy things first.* He could've chosen to focus on the easy tasks ahead of him.

2. *Fun things first.* He could've chosen to focus on riches or fame.

3. *Urgent things first.* He could've asked for help in building the temple.

4. *Hard things first.* He could've sought favor with those who didn't like him.

5. *First things first.* Instead, he chose to seek wisdom so he could glorify God.

Keep the main thing the main thing. Moses attempts this in Deuteronomy 6:5–7 by reminding the Israelites that their existence revolves around loving God. He also tells family leaders how to transfer truth to their children. Reggie Joiner notes the principles Moses develops:

1. Relationship comes before rules.
2. Truth must be in you before it can be in them.
3. Each day offers natural opportunities for teaching.
4. Repetition is the teacher's best friend.

Make use of all of these opportunities. Decide on issues you can discuss and ask questions of each other. Pray about your priorities together.

The Maxwell Leadership Bible

Choose Achievement over Affirmation

If you want to make an impact during your lifetime, you have to trade the praise you could receive from others for the things of value that you can accomplish.

A friend once explained something to me that illustrates this concept very well. He told me that as people catch crabs, they'll toss the crustaceans into a basket. If you have only one crab in the basket you need a lid to keep it from crawling out, but if you've got two or more, you don't. When there are several crabs, they will drag one another down so that none of them can get away.

A lot of unsuccessful people act the same way. They'll do things to keep others from getting ahead. But the good news is that if you observe someone trying to do that, you don't have to buy into their belief system. You can get out and stay out of the basket by refusing to be a crab.

Your Road Map for Success

THIS WEEK: In your interactions with people, ask yourself: "What priority is this serving? The importance of relationships? The value of our work? The growth of our faith? Other?" If the interaction is not benefiting a priority, what do you think you should do about it?

GOD'S PROMISE TO LEADERS

For God has not given us a spirit of fear,
but of power and of love and of a sound mind.

2 Timothy 1:7

A LEADER'S PROMISE TO THE TEAM

I will not let fear paralyze me from making decisions. I'd rather break new ground than let the status quo become our burial ground.

WEEK 44

RISK GREATNESS

Therefore, if anyone is in Christ, he is a new creation; old things have passed away; behold, all things have become new.

2 CORINTHIANS 5:17

Status quo is Latin for "the mess we're in." Leaders see what is, but they also have a vision for what could be. They are never content with things as they are. To be leading, by definition, is to be in front, breaking new ground, conquering new worlds, moving away from the status quo.

Dissatisfaction with the status quo does not mean having a negative attitude or grumbling. It has to do with a willingness to be different and to take risks. A person who refuses to risk change fails to grow. A leader who loves the status quo soon becomes a follower. Raymond Smith of the Bell Atlantic Corporation once remarked, "Administrators are easy to find and cheap to keep. Leaders—risk takers—are in very short supply. And ones with vision are pure gold."

Risk seems dangerous to many people because they are more comfortable with the old problems versus what it takes to come up with new solutions. The difference is attitude. When you seek out potential leaders, seek people who seek solutions.

Developing the Leaders Around You

Secure Leadership

Psalm 91 is one of the most comforting chapters in the Bible. It describes the security believers can enjoy through faith in God. Leaders especially can benefit from this set of promises. Study them and enjoy them:

Promise	**Leader's Benefit**
1. God's presence	1. It doesn't have to be lonely at the top.
2. God's protection	2. As you take initiative and risks, God keeps you safe.
3. God's peace	3. You don't have to feel insecure in unknown territory.
4. God's perspective	4. God gives an eternal view of life that keeps you steady.
5. God's provision	5. Regardless of your needs, God meets them.
6. God's power	6. In adversity, God delivers and helps you reach your goal.

Security is the foundation. We must feel secure even when people stop liking us, when funding drops, when morale dips, or when others reject us. If we don't feel secure, fear will eventually cause us to sabotage our leadership. David had covered up his sins after his affair with Bathsheba, so Nathan had to feel utterly secure in his plan of confrontation (2 Samuel 12:9). In God, we have every reason to feel secure as leaders.

The Maxwell Leadership Bible

Trade Your Fears for Faith in God

Brokenness involves removing inappropriate pride and self–reliance and building healthy God–reliance. God tamed Moses' self–reliance and pride in the desert, but to create trust He had to break the man's fears (Exodus 3:1–4:17). Moses dealt with different kinds of fear in his encounter with God:

Fears concerning himself. God responded by assuring Moses of his purpose.

Fears concerning God. God responded by overwhelming Moses with His presence.

Fears concerning others. God responded by demonstrating His power and commitment.

Fears concerning his ability. God responded by proving him with a partner, his brother, Aaron.

With his willfulness broken, his fears overcome, and his purpose affirmed, Moses finally placed himself in the hands of God (Exodus 4:20).

Life is filled with tradeoffs. Moses sacrificed his status and material possessions to prepare for his life purpose. And then to fulfill it, he had to sacrifice again, relinquishing the security and safety of obscurity in the desert. If you desire to lead, then you must be ready to make sacrifices.

The Maxwell Leadership Bible

This Week: Consider the risks that accompany your opportunities. Do you fear lack of resources or cooperation? Do you think the opportunities are beyond your capabilities? Are you secure in your leadership? What risks are you and your team willing to take? What assurance will help you risk more?

GOD'S PROMISE TO LEADERS

And my God shall supply all your need according to His riches in glory by Christ Jesus.

PHILIPPIANS 4:19

A LEADER'S PROMISE TO THE TEAM

I WILL NOT ASK YOU TO SACRIFICE MORE THAN I'M WILLING TO. I WILL PLACE THE TEAM'S INTERESTS ABOVE MY OWN PROFESSIONAL INTERESTS.

WEEK 45

SACRIFICE TO STEP UP

My brethren, count it all joy when you fall into various trials.

JAMES 1:2

What price are you willing to pay to be a more effective leader?

One of the finest examples of sacrifice by a leader in the Bible can be seen in the life of Moses. He could easily be the "poster child" for leadership sacrifice. He grew up like a son of Pharaoh, a prince. As a boy, he enjoyed every privilege and pleasure of the palace.

Yet Moses risked all of that to try to help his people. And in fact, he lost everything. After murdering an Egyptian, he faced exile in the desert of Midian, and for forty years he lived with the sacrifice he had made before learning that God intended to use him as a leader. By then, Moses had undergone the breaking and remaking process required for him to be used by God.

As a leader you may not be asked to leave your country or give up all your possessions as Moses was. But you can be sure that leading others will have a price.

The 21 Most Powerful Minutes in a Leader's Day

Give Up Your Rights

Have you been wronged? If so, you're faced with a decision. Are you going to spend your time and energy on what should have been, or are you going to focus on what can be?

Even when truth and justice are on your side, you may never be able to right your wrongs. Continually fighting for your rights will just make you resentful, angry, and negative. And besides, when you focus on your rights, you're often looking backward rather than forward.

When you stop worrying about your rights, you're released to move forward on the journey. You recognize the wrongs, but you forgive them and focus on what you can control—your responsibilities. This increases your energy, builds your potential, and improves your prospects.

Your Road Map for Success

As responsibilities increase, rights decrease. In a world of perks and privileges that accompany the climb to success, little thought is given to the responsibilities of the upward journey. John D. Rockefeller, Jr., said, "I believe that every right implies a responsibility; every opportunity, an obligation; every possession, a duty." Jesus said, "For everyone to whom much is given, from him much will be required; and to whom much has been committed, of him they will ask the more" (Luke 12:48).

Developing the Leader Within You

A Living Sacrifice

For even the Son of Man did not come to be served, but to serve, and to give His life a ransom for many.

Mark 10:45

Teams fail to reach their potential when they fail to pay the price for achieving it. If you lead a team, then one of the difficult things you must do is convince your teammates to sacrifice for the good of the group. The more talented the team members, the more difficult it may be to convince them to put the team first. Begin by modeling sacrifice. Show the team that you are willing to . . .

- Make financial sacrifices for the team.
- Keep growing for the sake of the team.
- Empower others for the sake of the team.
- Make difficult decisions for the sake of the team.

Once you have modeled a willingness to pay your own price for the potential of the team, you have the credibility to ask others to do the same. Then when you recognize sacrifices that teammates must make for the team, show them why and how to do it. Then praise their sacrifices greatly to their teammates.

The 21 Indisputable Laws of Teamwork

This Week: What have you sacrificed to be a leader? Are these the right sacrifices? What sacrifices are you asking of your team members?

GOD'S PROMISE TO LEADERS

Teach the wise, and they will become even wiser;
teach good people, and they will learn even more.
Wisdom begins with respect for the LORD,
and understanding begins
with knowing the Holy One.

PROVERBS 9:9–10 (NCV)

A LEADER'S PROMISE TO THE TEAM

I WILL SEEK OUT PEOPLE WHO CHALLENGE ME
TO STRETCH MY CURRENT ABILITIES,
SO THAT I CAN BE CONSTANTLY PUSHED TO
IMPROVE IN HOW I LEAD AND
SERVE THIS TEAM AND OUR MISSION.

WEEK 46

SEEK PEOPLE WHO STRETCH YOU

Take firm hold of instruction, do not let go;
Keep her, for she is your life.
Do not enter the path of the wicked,
And do not walk in the way of evil.
Avoid it, do not travel on it;
Turn away from it and pass on.

PROVERBS 4:13–15

A factor in your personal development comes in the area of your relationships with others. You can tell a lot about which direction your life is heading by looking at the people with whom you've chosen to spend your time and share your ideas. Their values and priorities impact the way you think and act. If they're positive people dedicated to growth, then their values and priorities will encourage you and reinforce your desire to grow.

It's not always comfortable to associate with people who are ahead of you in their growth, but it's always profitable. Try to cultivate relationships with those people who can help you grow, but don't think only in terms of what you can gain. Always bring something to the table yourself. You've got to make the relationship win–win or it won't last.

Your Road Map for Success

Leaders Who Attract Leaders

And men of all nations, from all the kings of the earth who had heard of his wisdom, came to hear the wisdom of Solomon.

1 Kings 4:34

There are two kinds of leaders: those who attract followers and those who attract other leaders. People who team up only with followers will never be able to do anything beyond what they can personally touch or supervise. Look for leaders who attract other leaders.

Leaders Who Attract Followers . . .	**Leaders Who Attract Leaders . . .**
Need to be needed.	Want to be succeeded.
Want recognition.	Want to reproduce themselves.
Focus on others' weaknesses.	Focus on others' strengths.
Spend their time with others.	Invest their time in others.
Experience some success.	Experience incredible success.

To keep attracting better and better leaders, you will have to keep developing your own leadership ability.

Your Road Map for Success

Create room to grow. If you catch a small shark and confine it, it will stay a size proportionate to the aquarium in which it lives, but if you turn it loose in the ocean, it grows to its normal size. The same is true of potential leaders. Be a change agent who facilitates growth.

Developing the Leaders Around You

A Growing Community

They devoted themselves to the apostles' teaching and to the fellowship, to the breaking of bread and to prayer. Everyone was filled with awe, and many wonders and miraculous signs were done by the apostles. All the believers were together and had everything in common. . . . And the Lord added to their number daily those who were being saved.

Acts 2:42–44, 47 (NIV)

Your growth is affected by your environment. If your current circumstances do nothing to help you grow, you're going to have a hard time enlarging yourself to reach your potential. You must create an environment of growth in which . . .

1. Others are ahead of you.
2. You are still challenged.
3. Your focus is forward.
4. The atmosphere is affirming.
5. You are out of your comfort zone.
6. Others are growing.
7. There is a willingness to change.
8. Growth is modeled and expected.

A life of continual growth is never easy, but a good environment makes the swim upstream a little less difficult.

Your Road Map for Success

This Week: List some of the people in your life who stretch you. Do you need more such people? Are you attracting leaders to your team or are you attracting followers? What might you need to change?

GOD'S PROMISE TO LEADERS

Trust in the LORD with all your heart,
And lean not on your own understanding;
In all your ways acknowledge Him,
And He shall direct your paths.

PROVERBS 3:5–6

A LEADER'S PROMISE TO THE TEAM

I'M ENDEAVORING TO BE WISE AND TO HEED WISE COUNSEL AS I LEAD THIS TEAM. I WANT TO HEAR YOUR WISDOM, TOO.

WEEK 47

SEEK WISDOM

The fear of the LORD is the beginning of knowledge,
But fools despise wisdom and instruction.

PROVERBS 1:7

Wisdom can be a leader's best friend, especially in times of decision. Suppose you find yourself in a large committee meeting in which a crucial decision must be made. The committee reaches an impasse and everything stops. Who will become the most influential person in that room? Answer: the one with the wisdom to draw a conclusion that not only works, but which receives the blessing of that committee.

Proverbs 1 describes wisdom as a woman crying out in the streets. What a beautiful picture! Wisdom does not hide herself, but shouts publicly! We must go out and find her and build a friendship with her: What can we learn about decision making from Proverbs?

1. The foundation for every decision is to honor and revere God.

2. We must build off our heritage and conscience: what values are we to embrace?

3. We must avoid the counsel of the ungodly.

4. We must pursue wisdom. What are the facts? What are the options?

5. We must move toward inward peace.

The Maxwell Leadership Bible

The First Principle of Wisdom

Near the beginning of Solomon's reign, Solomon asked for wisdom, and God answered abundantly (1 Kings 3:9). The Bible tells us that Solomon's wisdom exceeded that of any other man. His expansive mind explored the disciplines of botany, zoology, and music, and pondered topics ranging from economics to communication to love. The wisdom of King Solomon helped Israel prosper greatly. Solomon himself became the wealthiest king of his time.

But by the end of his reign, this brilliant king somehow forgot the first principle of wisdom: "The fear of the Lord is the beginning of wisdom" (Psalm 111:10). Only wisdom energized by a vibrant walk with God makes godly leaders.

How are godly leaders to think? Even good wisdom divorced from God can become a snare (Proverbs chapters 2 and 3), but godly leaders think:

Big. They realize God's vision is usually bigger than theirs.
Other people. They always include others in the mix.
Continually. They're not satisfied with today's answers.
Bottom line. They want to see results and fruit.
Continual growth. They want to keep improving.
Without lines. They let God outside of the box.
Victory. They want to see God's rule come to earth.
Intuitively. They have a sense of what will work.
Servanthood. They want to serve and add value to people.
Quickly. They evaluate quickly and see possible answers.

The Maxwell Leadership Bible

LEADERSHIP LESSONS FROM AN ANT

Go to the ant, you sluggard! Consider her ways and be wise, which, having no captain, overseer or ruler, provides her supplies in the summer, and gathers her food in the harvest.

PROVERBS 6:6–8

Do you want to make a difference? Then pay attention to the metaphor of the ant. It's amazing that one of the smallest of God's creatures can become one of His greatest teachers. The lessons the ant teaches us can be summarized this way:

A—Attitude of Initiative

Ants don't need a commander to tell them to get started.

N—Nature of Integrity

Ants work faithfully and need no outside accountability to keep them doing right.

T—Thirst for Industry

Ants work hard and will replace their anthill when it gets ruined.

S—Source of Insight

Ants store provisions in summer.

If we consider and learn from the ways of the ant, we can grow wise.

The Maxwell Leadership Bible

THIS WEEK: List the wise people in your life. How many are your leaders? How many are your followers or peers? Why do you think these people are wise? How wise do others think you are? Do you have a personal plan for growing in wisdom?

GOD'S PROMISE TO LEADERS

A wise man is strong,
Yes, a man of knowledge increases strength;
For by wise counsel you will wage your own war,
And in a multitude of counselors there is safety.

PROVERBS 24:5–6

A LEADER'S PROMISE TO THE TEAM

I WILL FOCUS MY ENERGIES ON OUR STRENGTHS. THIS WILL HELP US GROW FAR MORE THAN IF I POUR RESOURCES INTO BOLSTERING OUR WEAKNESSES.

WEEK 48

SPEND TIME WITH YOUR BEST

Now after six days Jesus took Peter, James, and John,
and led them up on a high mountain apart by themselves.

MARK 9:2

Years ago I learned the Pareto Principle and began applying it to my life. It's a useful tool for determining priorities for any person's life or for any organization.

THE PARETO PRINCIPLE

20 percent of your priorities will give you
80 percent of your production
IF you spend your time, energy, money, and personnel on the top 20 percent of your priorities.

Every leader needs to understand the Pareto Principle in the area of people oversight and leadership. For example, 20 percent of the people in an organization will be responsible for 80 percent of the company's success. The following strategy will enable a leader to increase the productivity of an organization.

1. Determine your top 20 percent producers.
2. Spend 80 percent of your "people time" with the top 20 percent.
3. Spend 80 percent of your personal development dollars on the top 20 percent.
4. Ask the top 20 percent to do on–the–job training for the next 20 percent.

Developing the Leader Within You

Bring Out Their Best

Many organizations today fail to tap into their potential. Why? Because the only reward they give their employees is a paycheck. In successful organizations a worker receives not only his paycheck, but he is also nurtured by the people he works for. This nurturing has the ability to transform people's lives.

I use the "BEST" acronym as a reminder that my people need me to . . .

Believe in them
Encourage them
Share with them
Trust them

Nurturing makes people more productive, and it creates a strong emotional and professional foundation within workers who have leadership potential. Later, using training and development, a leader can be built on that foundation.

Developing the Leaders Around You

As you train others . . . The apostle Paul began a miniature seminary in Ephesus, and he also trained men in the lecture hall of Tyrannus (Acts 19:8–10). As he mentored students, Paul remained committed to the people, to the process, and to the purpose. Consider how we can do the same as we develop others:

Be familiar with your strengths and weaknesses.
Know the people you wish to develop.
Clearly define the goals and assignments.
Allow them to watch you serve and lead.
Hold them accountable for their work.
Give them the freedom to fail.

The Maxwell Leadership Bible

Hope Floats

Therefore my heart is glad, and my glory rejoices;
My flesh also will rest in hope.

Psalm 16:9

How do most people feel when they're around you? Do they feel small and insignificant, or do they believe in themselves and have great hope about what they can become?

The key to how you treat people lies in how you think about them. It's a matter of attitude. What you believe is revealed by how you act. Johann Wolfgang von Goethe said: "Treat a man as he appears to be and you make him worse. But treat a man as if he already were what he potentially could be, and you make him what he should be."

Hope is perhaps the greatest gift you can give another person as the result of nurturing, because even if people fail to see their own significance, they still have a reason to keep trying and striving to reach their potential in the future.

Becoming a Person of Influence

This Week: Consider the potentials of your people. Leaders are meant to help others become the people God created them to be. They are called to discover the hidden, encourage the uncertain, develop the untrained, and empower the powerless. Just as Jesus sees potential in you, if you are a leader, He wants you to find and develop that potential in others.

GOD'S PROMISE TO LEADERS

Blessed are the undefiled in the way,
Who walk in the law of the LORD!
Blessed are those who keep His testimonies,
Who seek Him with the whole heart!
They also do no iniquity;
They walk in His ways.

PSALM 119:1–3

A LEADER'S PROMISE TO THE TEAM

THESE ARE OUR GOALS.
I'VE SUBMITTED THEM TO GOD,
AND I'M COMMITTED
TO KEEPING US ON TARGET.

WEEK 49

STAY THE COURSE

Do not turn from it to the right hand or to the left,
that you may prosper wherever you go.

Joshua 1:7

To be intentional means working with purpose, making every action count. Successful leaders are intentional. They know what they're doing and why they're doing it. To become more intentional, do the following:

1. *Have a purpose worth living for.* Willis R. Whitney, the first director of General Electric's research laboratory, observed, "Some men have thousands of reasons why they cannot do what they want to, when all they need is one reason why they can."

2. *Know your strengths and weaknesses.* Playing to your strengths rekindles your passions and renews your energy.

3. *Prioritize your responsibilities.* Once you know the "why" of your life, it becomes much easier to figure out the "what" and "when."

4. *Learn to say no.* You can't accomplish much without focus. If you try to do every good thing that comes your way, you won't excel at what you were made to do.

5. *Commit yourself to long-term achievement.* Most victories in life are achieved through small incremental wins sustained over time.

The 17 Essential Qualities of a Team Player

Set Good Goals

The number of people today who lack a strong sense of purpose is astounding. Pulitzer–winning writer Katherine Anne Porter observed: "I am appalled at the aimlessness of most people's lives. Fifty percent don't pay any attention to where they are going; forty percent are undecided and will go in any direction. Only ten percent know what they want, and even all of them don't go toward it."

Goals give you something concrete to focus on, and that has a positive impact on your actions. Goals help us focus our attention on our purpose and make it our dominant aspiration. And as philosopher–poet Ralph Waldo Emerson said, "The world makes way for the man who knows where he is going."

Use the following guidelines to keep your goals on target. Goals must be . . .

- Written
- Personal
- Specific
- Achievable
- Measurable
- Time–sensitive

Your Road Map for Success

Effective leaders don't drift. The apostle Paul had a plan to reach the Roman Empire in his lifetime (1 Corinthians 16:5–9). He focused on the metropolitan areas, knowing that well–trained followers would bring God's message to the smaller towns and villages. Leaders can do anything, but they can't do everything. What kind of plan do you have?

The Maxwell Leadership Bible

THE DANGER OF TOO MANY PURSUITS

Whatever my eyes desired I did not keep from them.
I did not withhold my heart from any pleasure,
For my heart rejoiced in all my labor;
And this was my reward from all my labor.
Then I looked on all the works that my hands had done
And on the labor in which I had toiled;
And indeed all was vanity and grasping for the wind.
There was no profit under the sun.

ECCLESIASTES 2:10–11

Solomon fervently pursued several unrelated goals in a vain attempt to satisfy himself. Eventually, he reached a high level of success but still felt empty. The axiom remains true: "If you chase two rabbits, both will escape."

How about you? Do you have a way of determining your focus, based on what really matters or what really counts? When faced with a decision, ask yourself:

Is this consistent with my priorities?
Is this within my area of competence?
Can someone else do it better?
What do my trusted friends say?
Do I have the time?

The Maxwell Leadership Bible

THIS WEEK: Write your top three goals for your business, for your family, and for yourself. Are these goals truly in line with your priorities? Do members of your team understand the goals? Are your goals high enough? Do you have a plan of attack?

GOD'S PROMISE TO LEADERS

Now, therefore, you are no longer strangers and foreigners, but fellow citizens with the saints and members of the household of God, having been built on the foundation of the apostles and prophets, Jesus Christ Himself being the chief cornerstone, in whom the whole building, being fitted together, grows into a holy temple in the Lord, in whom you also are being built together for a dwelling place of God in the Spirit.

EPHESIANS 2:19–22

A LEADER'S PROMISE TO THE TEAM

I WILL REMIND US OF OUR TEAM GOALS, AND I WILL CONSISTENTLY ENCOURAGE AND REWARD TEAM EFFORTS.

WEEK 50

TEAMWORK MAKES THE DREAM WORK

But God composed the body, having given greater honor to that part which lacks it, that there should be no schism in the body, but that the members should have the same care for one another. And if one member suffers, all the members suffer with it; or if one member is honored, all the members rejoice with it.

1 CORINTHIANS 12:24–26

If your team members believe in the goals of the team and begin to develop genuine trust in one another, they will be in a position to demonstrate true teamwork. Notice that I mention the team members will be in a position to demonstrate true teamwork. That does not necessarily mean that they will do it.

For there to be teamwork, several things must happen. First, team members must genuinely believe that the value of the team's success is greater than the value of their own individual interests. Second, personal sacrifice must be encouraged and then rewarded—by the team leader and the other members of the team. As this happens, the people will identify themselves more and more with the team, and they will recognize that individualism wins trophies, but teamwork wins pennants.

Developing the Leaders Around You

Build Relationships to Build the Team

Teams that don't bond, can't build. Why? Because they never become a cohesive unit. Why do wounded soldiers strive to rejoin their buddies on the battlefield? Because after you work and live with people, you soon realize that your survival depends on one another. For a team to be successful, the teammates have to know that they will look out for one another. When a team member cares about no one but himself, the whole team suffers.

I have found that one of the best ways to get members of a team to care about one another is to get them together outside of a work context in order to build relationships. Every year in our organization we plan retreats and other events that put our people together in social settings. And during those times, we also make sure that they spend part of their time with staff members they don't really know very well. That way they're not only building relationships, but they're being prevented from developing cliques.

Developing the Leaders Around You

Teammates must collaborate. Becoming a collaborative team player requires a change in four areas:

1. *Perception.* See teammates as collaborators, not competitors.
2. *Attitude.* Be supportive, not suspicious, of teammates.
3. *Focus.* Concentrate on the team, not yourself.
4. *Results.* Create great victories though multiplication.

The 17 Essential Qualities of a Team Player

Like a Rock

Dependability is important to every team's success. Everyone on the team knows upon whom they can and can't depend. Allow me to give you what I consider to be the essence of dependability:

1. *Pure motives.* If someone on the team continually puts themselves and their agenda ahead of what's best for the team, they have proven themselves to be undependable. When it comes to teamwork, motives matter.

2. *Responsibility.* While motivation addresses why people are dependable, responsibility indicates that they want to be dependable.

3. *Sound thinking.* Dependability means more than just wanting to take responsibility. That desire must also be coupled with good judgment to be of real value to the team.

4. *Consistent contribution.* The final quality of a dependable team player is consistency. If you can't depend on teammates all the time, then you can't really depend on them any of the time. Consistency takes a depth of character that enables people to follow through no matter how tired, distracted, or overwhelmed they are.

The 17 Essential Qualities of a Team Player

This Week: Upon whom do you depend? Do these people know how much confidence you have in them? Do the members of your team know they can depend on you? Where among the team members—including yourself—has dependability been tested and found wanting? Where has dependability held firm? How did your team recover after the slip in dependability?

GOD'S PROMISE TO LEADERS

Those who lead good people to do wrong
will be ruined by their own evil,
but the innocent will be rewarded with good things.

Proverbs 28:10 (NCV)

A LEADER'S PROMISE TO THE TEAM

I WILL USE MY INFLUENCE
TO LEAD US IN THE RIGHT WAY
AND HELP US GROW.

WEEK 51

UNDERSTAND INFLUENCE

*"But only speak a word, and my servant will be healed.
For I also am a man under authority, having soldiers under me.
And I say to this one, 'Go,' and he goes; and to another,
'Come,' and he comes; and to my servant, 'Do this,' and he does it."*

Matthew 8:8–9

A person's ability to make things happen in and through others depends entirely on their ability to lead them.

If your dream is big and will require the teamwork of a lot of people, then any potential leaders you select to go with you on the journey will need to be people of influence. After all, that's what leadership is—influence. And when you think about it, all leaders have two things in common: They're going somewhere, and they're able to persuade others to go with them.

As you look at the people around you, consider the following:

Who influences them?

Whom do they influence?

Is their influence increasing or decreasing?

To be a good judge of potential leaders, don't just see the person—see all the people who that person influences. The greater the influence, the greater the leadership potential and the ability to get others to work with you to accomplish your dream.

Your Road Map for Success

Observe Your Influence

It takes more than talk to keep workers in line;
mere words go in one ear and out the other.

Proverbs 29:19 (Msg)

All of us are leading in some areas, while in other areas we are being led. No one is excluded from being a leader or a follower. Realizing your potential as a leader is your responsibility.

The chief influencer of any group is quite easy to discover. Just observe the people as they gather. If an issue is to be decided, who is the person whose opinion seems most valuable? Who do others watch the most when the issue is being discussed? With whom do people quickly agree? Most importantly, who do the others follow? Answers to these questions will help you discern who the real leader is in a group.

Developing the Leader Within You

Make a good impression. If people perceive that you are positive and trustworthy and have admirable qualities, then they will seek you as an influencer in their lives. When you first meet people, you have no influence with them. If someone they trust makes the introduction, you can temporarily "borrow" some of that person's influence. But quickly you either build or bust that influence by your actions.

Becoming a Person of Influence

Extending Your Influence

One of the greatest lessons I've ever learned is that the people closest to me determine my level of success or failure. On my fortieth birthday I discovered that my influence and productivity were growing only where I had identified potential leaders and developed them. My intention in developing leaders had been to help them improve themselves, but I found that I was also benefiting greatly. Spending time with them had been like investing. They had grown, and at the same time I had reaped incredible dividends. That's when I realized that if I was to make it to the next level, I was going to have to extend myself through others. I would find leaders and pour my life into them, and as they improved, so would I.

Your Road Map for Success

THIS WEEK: Integrity is critical if you want to become an influencer. It is the foundation upon which many other qualities are built, such as respect, dignity, and trust. "Good leaders abhor wrongdoing of all kinds; sound leadership has a moral foundation" (Proverbs 16:12). Are you a person of integrity? Where do you need to strengthen your foundation? Do you surround yourself with people of integrity?

Becoming a Person of Influence

GOD'S PROMISE TO LEADERS

As for God, His way is perfect;
The word of the LORD is proven;
He is a shield to all who trust in Him.

PSALM 18:30

A LEADER'S PROMISE TO FOLLOWERS

WE HAVE A VISION. THIS IS A CHALLENGE WORTHY OF OUR CAPABILITIES AND COMMITMENT. WE CAN DO THIS!

WEEK 52

VISION BRINGS VICTORY

Therefore, King Agrippa, I was not disobedient to the heavenly vision, but declared first to those in Damascus and in Jerusalem, and throughout all the region of Judea, and then to the Gentiles, that they should repent, turn to God, and do works befitting repentance.

ACTS 26:19–20

The apostle Paul's vision on the road to Damascus became the captivating force behind his success as a leader. The apostle teaches us the power of a vision. God was Paul's leader, and His vision for Paul accomplished a number of things.

It stopped him. Vision allows us to see ourselves. We see things not as they are, but as we are.

It sent him. Vision allows us to see others. We feel compelled to act.

It strengthened him. Vision enables us to continue despite struggles and lack of resources.

It stretched him. Vision gives us conviction to stand, confidence to speak, and compassion to share.

It satisfied him. Obedience to this vision motivates us to act. It fulfills us.

The Maxwell Leadership Bible

Checklist for Casting the Vision

As a leader, you carry the responsibility for communicating the team's vision and keeping it before the people continually. That's not necessarily easy. People need to be shown the team's vision clearly, creatively, and continually. Whenever I cast vision with my team, I use the following checklist.

1. *Clarity* brings understanding to the vision.
2. *Connectedness* brings the past, present, and future together.
3. *Purpose* brings direction to the vision.
4. *Goals* bring targets to the vision.
5. *Honesty* brings integrity to the vision and credibility to the vision caster.
6. *Stories* bring relationships to the vision.
7. *Challenge* brings stretching to the vision.
8. *Passion* brings fuel to the vision.
9. *Modeling* brings accountability to the vision.
10. *Strategy* brings process to the vision.

With this checklist, your team will find the vision more accessible and will more readily buy in to it.

We need a good challenge. A truly great vision speaks to what team members can become if they truly live out their values and work according to their highest standards. Without a challenge, many people tend to fall or fade away. If you can see vision for your team, then your team has a reasonably good chance at success. Vision gives team members direction and confidence, two things they cannot do without.

The 17 Indisputable Laws of Teamwork

Without Buy–In, the Vision Perishes

All leaders have vision. But not all people who possess vision are leaders. I've known a lot of would–be leaders who possessed vision but lacked the ability to get people to buy in to them. A compelling vision alone will not make someone a leader. Nor will a great vision automatically be fulfilled simply because it is compelling or valuable. Followers need to buy in to the leader.

Once Gideon possessed the vision to deliver Israel from its enemies, he wasn't done. He still needed to get the people to buy in to his leadership. After time and effort, so many people bought into Gideon's leadership that God had to send a bunch of them home. If you look at the way Gideon progressed from being an obscure member of a minor clan to a leader of the Northern tribes, you can see his influence growing the way ripples do when a pebble is dropped in quiet water.

The 21 Most Powerful Minutes in a Leader's Day

This Week: Put your vision into words. If you can't capture the vision on paper, then you probably haven't defined it well enough. Is your vision appropriate for your current team? How might you need to adapt the vision, the team, or yourself?

CONCLUSION

TAKE ME TO YOUR LEADER

Now I saw heaven opened, and behold, a white horse. And He who sat on him was called Faithful and True, and in righteousness He judges and makes war . . . And the armies in heaven, clothed in fine linen, white and clean, followed Him on white horses . . . And He Himself will rule them with a rod of iron. He Himself treads the winepress of the fierceness and wrath of Almighty God. And He has on His robe and on His thigh a name written: King of Kings and Lord of Lords.

REVELATION 19:11, 14–16

In this passage from the last book of the Bible, John, the writer of Revelation, is describing Jesus Christ, the one who will ultimately rule the world at the end of time. In most of the Bible, Jesus is described as a humble and lowly servant. He healed the sick. He forgave the sinful. He washed the feet of fishermen, tax collectors, and the man who would betray him. And he meekly submitted to torture and gruesome death on the cross.

But make no mistake. Jesus is no weakling! In the book of Revelation, we see another side of His character and leadership. He is a captain of war who can rally huge heavenly armies to defeat a strong and bitter enemy. And He not only wins the day, but all eternity. That is a mark of great leaders. They have the strength to conquer, yet they stoop to help the weak and raise them up to join in the victory.

I believe in leadership. I've dedicated more than thirty years of my life to teaching it. But as Jesus Himself said, "What profit is it to a man if he gains the whole world, and loses his own soul?" (Matthew 16:26). If you do not have a relationship with the King of kings, Jesus Christ, then I want to invite you to enter into one. If you acknowledge that Jesus is the Son of God, repent of your sins, ask for forgiveness, and invite Jesus into your heart, you will be saved, and he will become your Lord of lords. And you will join Him, the ultimate leader, in eternity.

INDEX

ACKNOWLEDGEMENTS

Leadership Promises for Your Work Week is adapted from John C. Maxwell's *Leadership Promises for Every Day* (Nashville: Thomas Nelson, Inc., 2003).

Grateful acknowledgment is made to the following publishers for permission to reprint this copyrighted material. All copyrights are held by the author, John. C. Maxwell.

The Maxwell Leadership Bible (Nashville: Thomas Nelson, Inc, 1982).

Developing the Leader Within You (Nashville: Thomas Nelson, Inc., 2001).

Developing the Leaders Around You (Nashville: Thomas Nelson, Inc., 1995).

The 21 Irrefutable Laws of Leadership (Nashville: Thomas Nelson, Inc., 2002).

The 21 Indispensable Qualities of a Leader (Nashville: Thomas Nelson, Inc., 1999).

Becoming a Person of Influence (Nashville: Thomas Nelson, Inc., 1997).

The 21 Most Powerful Minutes in a Leader's Day (Nashville: Thomas Nelson, Inc., 2000).

Failing Forward (Nashville: Thomas Nelson, Inc., 2000).

The 17 Indisputable Laws of Teamwork (Nashville: Thomas Nelson, Inc., 2001).

The 17 Essential Qualities of a Team Player (Nashville: Thomas Nelson, Inc., 2002).

Your Road Map for Success (Nashville: Thomas Nelson, Inc., 2002).

About the Author

John C. Maxwell is an internationally recognized leadership expert, speaker, and author who has sold over 12 million books. His organizations have trained more than one million leaders worldwide. Dr. Maxwell is the founder of Injoy Stewardship Services and EQUIP. Every year he speaks to Fortune 500 companies, international government leaders, and organizations as diverse as the United States Military Academy at West Point and the National Football League. A *New York Times, Wall Street Journal,* and *Business Week* best-selling author, Maxwell was one of twenty-five authors named to Amazon.com's 10th Anniversary Hall of Fame. Two of his books, *The 21 Irrefutable Laws of Leadership* and *Developing the Leader Within You,* have each sold over a million copies.

Notes

Notes

Notes

Notes

Notes